To Pauline

Eva Maria Chapman

&Sasha
Olga A true tale
of survival

Sasha & Olga

A true tale of survival

Eva Maria Chapman

Lothian
BOOKS

Thomas C. Lothian Pty Ltd
132 Albert Road, South Melbourne, 3205
www.lothian.com.au

National Library of Australia
Cataloguing-in-Publication data:

Chapman, Eva Maria.
  Sasha and Olga.

  ISBN 0 7344 0897 8

  1. Immigrants - Australia - Biography. 2. Ukrainians -
  Australia - Biography. 3. Australia - Emigration and
  immigration. I. Title.

  304.8940477

Cover and text design by Ranya Langenfelds
Internal design and typesetting by Ranya Langenfelds
Printed in Australia by Griffin Press

Images courtesy of Eva Maria Chapman
Front cover: Sasha and Olga's wedding
Back cover: Sasha with his 1954 FJ Holden;
Dr and Frau Hoffmann;
Eva Maria Prosikova, 1950.

This book is dedicated to my parents, Sasha and Olga, and all the other millions made homeless in the 1939–45 World War.

Sasha and Olga on their wedding day, with Eva

Contents

Eva's Family Tree

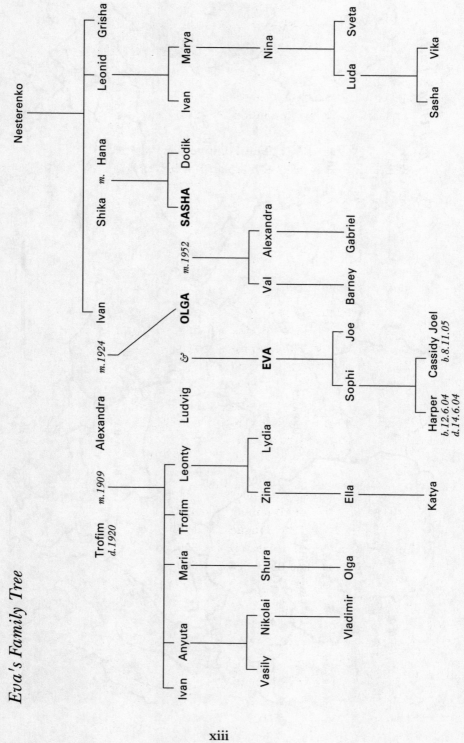

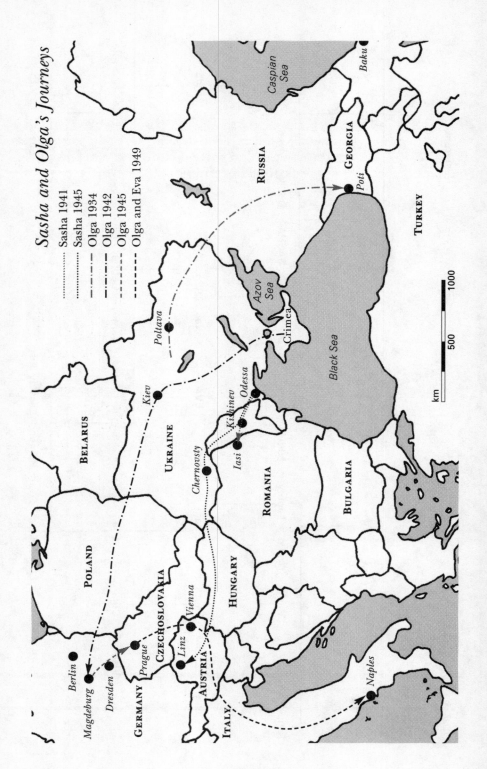

Sasha and Olga's Journeys

- .... Sasha 1941
- ⋯⋯⋯ Sasha 1945
- —··— Olga 1934
- —·—·— Olga 1942
- ——— Olga 1945
- ———— Olga and Eva 1949

xiv

Acknowledgements

To Averill Chase of Lothian Books for her heartfelt response to my story and all her enthusiasm and support in publishing it; to Lilian Bruce for encouragement; to my numerous critical readers for valuable feedback, especially Sophi and Susannah.

To Elena Klimova, my right-hand woman in all matters pertaining to Ukraine; to the International Institute for Energy Conservation for funding my first journey to Ukraine; and to the Ukraine Society for Former Prisoners of Labour in Germany 1941–45, who helped me find Olga's relatives.

To my children, Sophi and Joseph, who value and appreciate the unearthing and rattling of skeletons in the ancestral cupboard. For it is they, plus my nephews Barney and Gabriel, grandson Harper Cassidy and all future unborn children, who make all of Sasha and Olga's trials and tribulations worthwhile.

And to my husband Jake, whose unflagging support and love made this book possible.

Escape

In foreign lands I waste away
And roam without relief;
In longing for my native land
I pine in hopeless grief.
Yakiv Holovatsy

Prologue / Czechoslovakian Border, 1949

'I want Vlada,' I whimper.

'Tchiho!' shushes Mama, yanking me roughly, dragging me deeper into the dark forest. I'm sure I can hear wolves howling. I'm so frightened. Trapped moaning swirls in my belly. I stumble over roots and stumps.

Mama jerks me to a stop. We listen. A low sound rumbles the ground from behind, getting louder and louder. Mama shoves me into a tree hollow with an urgent 'Shhh!' I freeze. The rumble explodes into a deafening roar as arcs of dazzling light pierce the night. I am blinded by zigzag flashes and glints of shiny steel, metal and black, as a band of motorbikes thunders within feet of our trembling forms.

It seems forever before the pounding of light and sound lessens and fades into the distance. But my face goes on shaking; teeth chatter; limbs shudder. And in my head the lights go on leaping. Will they ever stop?

1 / **Break Out**

The fortune teller pulled at Olga's sleeve. 'Oh pretty lady, two hellers for your fortune, one for the flowers!' A glint of gold in the gypsy's mouth caught Olga's attention. She hungered for the promise of a rosier future. She fingered the coins—exactly three— which lay in her pocket. They were meant for a piece of pork that Vlada had asked her to buy at the market. The pull of destiny was stronger than fear of Vlada's wrath, and she handed over the coins. The gypsy, surprised by the sudden capitulation, led Olga to the side of the road where they both sat on a low wall. Having survived the Nazi terror, and no stranger to pain, the old woman was struck by the sadness and longing in Olga's face.

'Ah, that such a young one should have suffered so much,' she murmured, taking the small hands into her own. The gypsy studied the palm of Olga's left hand and felt the rush of anticipation in the beating of the young woman's blood.

'I see there is a little girl.'

'Yes,' said Olga excitedly, 'my daughter Evitchka.'

It was the first time that the gypsy had heard Olga speak and she immediately recognised the foreign accent. Polish? Russian? She wasn't sure, nor was this any particular surprise as the Czech countryside was full of the displaced and the dispossessed, looking for a future in a destroyed world.

'Your journey is far from over and I see you and your daughter on a long voyage to a strange distant land far across the seas.' Glimmers of youthful hope lit up the grey green eyes, and the gypsy could see flashes of the mischievous girl who just happened to be born into Stalin and Hitler's playing fields.

'Oh, I can see a kind man and two more children …' But then her vision was obscured by clouds that came in so fast that the gypsy

3

faltered. She could see no more and she wanted to see no more. She thrust the coins back into Olga's hand.

'You will need these for your journey, and take care of the little girl.'

She wearily raised herself and continued down the road. Olga stared at the flowers that lay tousled on the wall, and drifted through the yellows, pinks and blues to a time of her girlhood when she and her mother would walk to the forest to collect wild-flowers. Singing.

Pashli detki tam gulat, lat, lat
Shtob svitochki tam narvat, vat, vat

Come on children let's go wander, wander, wander
To gather pretty flowers yonder, yonder, yonder

Olga gathered up the flowers carefully. A plan was forming in her mind.

Olga walked into the steaming kitchen where Vlada pounded dough on the floury table. Evitchka, playing with doughy shapes, jumped up excitedly at the entry of her mother. 'Mama, Mama look what I have made for you. And look what Nonda has made.' Nonda was a brown velvet clown with white woolly curls that Evitchka would not let out of her sight.

Olga exchanged the pieces of dough for the flowers. 'Look what I have bought for you from an old gypsy.'

'And where's the pork, may I ask?' Vlada interrupted. 'Oh no, don't tell me you paid three hellers to that good-for-nothing vagabond!'

'Yes, as a matter of fact I did, and she told me my fortune.'

'Oh well, I hope she told you it's piroshki with boring old cab-bage again!' laughed Vlada good-naturedly.

She adored Olga and the little girl and blessed the day their paths had intertwined. She and her husband Kirov were refugees from Bulgaria who had found temporary work in southern Czechoslovakia. One cold night they were woken by knocking on the door. Peering into the dim hall, Vlada made out the weary face of a young woman holding a tiny girl, who in turn hung on to a brown velvet clown. For Vlada it was love at first sight, and with a hasty 'come in, come in', she picked up the child, gasping at how ice cold she was.

The mother and child, who had been walking from Prague for days in the snow, were exhausted and hungry. While Kirov gathered Olga's meagre belongings, Vlada heated up soup. That night Evitchka slept sandwiched between Vlada and Kirov as that was the only way they could find to warm up her tiny frozen frame. Olga snuggled in behind Vlada.

A week later they left together to find more work and larger living quarters. The flotsam and jetsam of war-ravaged Europe were passing on all sides. Exhausted; pinched with hunger—no money, no transport, nowhere to go. Only south. They couldn't go north, east or west. These areas had been ravaged by two of the world's greatest madmen in their crazy game for world domination. The small group toiled on. Kirov found a job as a farm labourer near the border with Austria, and the four of them shared meagre quarters. Evitchka loved Vlada and Kirov. She specially liked curling up on Kirov's lap and playing with his black droopy moustache.

They had been together a few months now and the future looked bleak. The communists, who had taken over in 1948, had extended their iron fist all over Czechoslovakia. The march south was halted, the borders crisscrossed by tall fences of impregnable barbed wire, and manned by soldiers with machine-guns and vicious dogs. The problem of escaping refugees became so acute in 1949 that the newly appointed Chief of Security's orders were to stop them at all costs. He hatched an elaborate, devious plan. Spies were set up along the borders of Czechoslovakia in the guise of 'helpers' who promised to arrange escapes. In places a false border was built to look like the real thing: watchtowers, armed border guards, barbed wire, the lot. The band of escapees were guided through all these checkpoints by the 'helpers'. Just when the hapless refugees thought they had reached freedom, the next bend revealed the real border, the real watchtowers and the real guns. A welcoming committee arrested them on the spot. Most were shot for high treason, but a lucky few were sent off to the frozen wastelands of Siberia. So Vlada, Kirov, Olga and Evitchka stayed put. During the night Vlada would often hear Olga crying. When asked about it next day, she could not bring herself to unburden her soul.

'So, Olya, what did the old gypsy say?' Vlada asked wiping away flour from the table.

'Oh, it's a secret,' answered Olga, guiltily fingering the coins in her pocket. 'By the way, I must go out again tomorrow morning. I'm seeing a woman in town about possible work.'

That evening while Vlada sang Evitchka to sleep, Olga thought about her plan. It was partly true that she wanted to find work; but what she really wanted to do was to escape from Czechoslovakia, so she intended to make discreet enquiries in the nearby town. She knew it was highly dangerous and didn't want to fall victim to the dreaded decoys. She also carried false papers which asserted her surname was Prosikova and that she was from Lvov, Poland. (Her real name was Nesterenko and her place of birth, Poltava, USSR.) This subterfuge had been a necessity after the war to avoid being forcibly returned to the USSR. Stalin expected that all prisoners of the Nazis should have killed themselves and therefore regarded anyone returning alive as a traitor. These unfortunates were stripped of their rights as Soviet citizens, punished with hard labour and, if they survived, re-educated so that Western influence was expunged.

Instead of returning to her family in 1945, Olga made her way to Prague, which was then enjoying a short respite between the regimes of Nazism and communism. Now four years later Olga wanted to escape. And not just from the communists. Stalin had broken her body as a result of starvation and persecution in the 1930s; Hitler had broken her well-being by ripping her from her family's bosom at seventeen years of age and forcing her to be a slave for the Reich. But Prague had broken her heart. She felt that she might recover from the first two onslaughts but did not know if she could survive the third. She and Evitchka had to get away as far as they could. She had heard wonderful things about America, which was where she wanted to go. But she had to do it without Vlada and Kirov as she thought the party of four too large. And she had to act in secret as they would never let her go through with it. She loved them both dearly, but she needed to get herself and her daughter out to freedom, to a new life. The gypsy's foretelling had consolidated the resolve. She was in the hands of destiny.

Next morning after Olga had left for town, Vlada had a visitor. He introduced himself as Ludvig Krakov and said he was Evitchka's father. Vlada thought him a nice well-dressed gentleman, but very sad. Evitchka looked at him with half recognition. Vlada could see the anguish in the little girl's face as she ran to hide behind her skirts and could feel the trembling in her body as she peeked out nervously at the visitor. After a few unsuccessful attempts to coax out the little girl, Ludvig took his leave and said he would return next day.

On hearing the news Olga visibly blanched. She stumbled to a chair and moaned, 'Boszhe moi, Boszhe moi, my God, my God,' clutching her stomach. Evitchka started wailing. Kirov immediately swept up the little girl and cuddled and soothed her. 'Olya, Olya! What is it?' urged Vlada. 'He said he was Evitchka's father. He seemed really nice.' At this Olga started to sob hysterically and got into such a state that Kirov had to get out the precious little bit of vodka he had stashed away. After Olga had calmed down she said she was sorry but couldn't talk about it and needed to go to bed. Vlada lovingly tucked them both in on the mattress in the small room off the kitchen.

Next morning Vlada was making breakfast when Ludvig Krakov called again. She told him Olga and Evitchka were still asleep but invited him to wait and have a cup of tea. Vlada crept into the little room to wake them only to realise with a shock that the bed was empty. Not only that, but all Olga's worldly goods were gone. And so was Nonda the brown velvet clown.

❧

Evitchka couldn't understand why she had to be so quiet that morning and why they were up so early. Olga was tying everything they owned into a sheet which she threw over her shoulder. With her other hand she scooped up the child and quietly moved through the kitchen to the heavy wooden door. Her heart was thumping hard against her ribs but she knew she had to go. She felt desperately sad to leave Vlada and Kirov who had been so good to her and her Evitchka. But life was full of partings. Vlada and Kirov were the latest two in a long line of beloved people she had left behind forever, and who now joined the other painful ghosts in the chambers of her heart.

'What about Vlada!' whispered the child.

'Don't worry we will see her later. Here, carry Nonda, there's a good girl.' They stepped out into the chilly October morning into a totally unknown future.

The early morning mist swirled around them as they walked along a dirt track that wound down into the valley. Olga tried to gather her strength. This had been her plan all along but it was a little sooner than she wanted. She had hoped that she might do some odd jobs in the town so that the number of coins in her pocket would be larger. The thought that Ludvig had visited sent a chill through her body and she walked faster to get away from him. She was positive that he had come for Evitchka. She had to make this strike for freedom now.

Yesterday she had secretly spoken with a man about getting out. But it would not be easy, he had warned. Many people were trying and the authorities were stepping up vigilance. Four Czechs had just been sentenced to death for aiding escapees. Czechoslovakia, the new satellite of the Soviet Empire, was the scene of purges and trials of people who had allegedly collaborated with the decadent West. The borders were being tightened even further. He had told her that her best bet was through a forest about forty miles north of Vienna on the Czech–Austrian border. There were no barbed wire fences there yet, but it was patrolled continually by border guards on motorbikes.

Olga and Evitchka took a bus and then walked the rest of the way. It was nightfall when they reached the edge of forest. Olga had bought some bread, hard boiled eggs and piroshki from a roadside stall with the remainder of her money. Evitchka was hungry and wolfed down an egg and asked when they would be going home. Olga was too frightened to eat and snapped at her daughter to shut up. Evitchka clung to Nonda as they walked through the forest. She was now afraid as it was getting darker and she couldn't understand what was happening. She was also afraid of her mother who was looking pinched and acting crabby.

Suddenly they heard the sounds of motorbikes in the distance. Olga grabbed Evitchka and hid them both in a large tree trunk. Great arcs of light swooped through the forest and created dancing shadows in the canopy overhead. Olga hissed that Evitchka be quiet and not move. Squashed against the tree bark, Evitchka froze. The motorbikes crisscrossed the forest with big powerful headlights, searching for any movement, and came closer and closer to where the mother and child were hiding. Olga could see the black figures of the border guards within feet, and swallowed lumps of cold fear. She could feel tremors of terror in the child she was pressing against the tree. After what seemed an aeon, the roar of the bikes diminished and faded into the distance. Mother and child stayed rooted to the tree for several minutes before they could move.

'Are they bad people?' Evitchka squeaked, through violent trembling.

'Yes,' said Olga. 'If they catch us we will be sent to a very bad place and this is why you must be very quiet. They might come back at any time.'

With that Olga took the little girl by the hand and they continued through the forest. Life had totally changed for the child. She was now in a world that felt evil and unsafe. She desperately wanted to go back to Kirov and Vlada. But if she mentioned it, her mother snapped at her to shut up.

It was now pitch black and they could not see where they were going. Olga started to panic. Her sense of direction had never been very good and she wasn't even sure they weren't going around in circles. She tried to head in the direction of the motorbikes as she figured that the border guards must be patrolling the forest from the Czechoslovakian end towards the Austrian side, so that would be the right way to go. But if this was the case then they would be coming back soon. No sooner had she surmised this than she heard a distant rumble. Evitchka started to whimper. Again arcs of light flashed through the forest. They ran to another large trunk. The whimpers froze in Evitchka's throat as they became one with the tree. This time the bikes passed further away and soon it was mercifully silent again.

The motorbikes passed by again several more times during that long cold night. For hours they kept walking in what Olga thought was the right direction but she really wasn't sure any more. Evitchka was getting more and more sleepy and eventually had to be carried. Olga began to wonder if she was doing the right thing. Here she was in the middle of a black forest, carrying all her worldly belongings and a small child. The child should be sleeping safely tucked up in a bed, and here she was dragging her through danger. She didn't even know how deep the forest was or how far they were from the Austrian border.

As Olga edged her way forward into the darkness, she thought she saw a light. Was she imagining it? It couldn't be the motorbikes, she reasoned, as she could hear no sound. The light got stronger and mesmerised her. It offered welcome relief from the inky blackness that swilled around her. Extreme tiredness flooded over her. She staggered towards the light like a moth to a flame. She started in alarm as the shape of a man materialised before her. Oh no, she thought, perhaps this is one of the 'helpers' planted in the forest to trick would-be escapees. Before she could think what to do, a gruff voice said, 'Ahoy, who's there?' The man shone his light on the mother and child. Olga suddenly felt so weary that she stumbled. The man caught hold of her. Evitchka had woken at the sound of the voice and felt herself being hoisted onto a sturdy pair of shoulders. She wasn't afraid as the voice sounded kind.

The man was a woodcutter and recognised them immediately as refugees. He took up Olga's bundle and said that he would guide them through to the Austrian border. Evitchka felt a welcome safety on his shoulders and settled into the rhythm of his walk. Olga still wasn't sure of him but was grateful to have guidance through the blackness.

It was in the pale light of dawn that the woodcutter finally led them to their destination, an Austrian border point. When Olga heard the German voices she cried with relief. With great gratitude she and Evitchka bade farewell to the woodcutter. It had been like a miracle. God was looking after her and her little girl.

2 / A Strange, Distant Land

'I'm going out to gather shells. You want to come?' Olga looked up at Evitchka, who was sitting on top of a triple bunk bed. Relishing the feeling of being perched up so high, the little girl declined the offer.

'You do know you won't be able to get down on your own after I've gone?'

Evitchka was a bit torn but still decided to stay. She surveyed the huge sea of beds stretching into the distance. They were living in a former hangar, doubling as a displaced person's centre, just out-side Naples. Refugees from all over Eastern Europe gathered here, before being disgorged to different corners of the planet in a fleet of ships.

Olga walked out into the watery sun of a wintry December. The beach was empty and there was a yellow shimmer on the shallow expanse of water that lapped gently against the pale sands. She liked the peace of idly gathering shells and felt she had time to think.

The journey from the Czech–Austrian border to Naples had been long and fraught. After the initial euphoria of having got out of the communist sphere, she had found Austria unfriendly. On many an occasion she had knocked on a farmhouse door to beg milk for Evitchka, only to be turned away or given just water. She had been constantly afraid that her papers would be discovered as fraudulent and that they would both be whisked off to Siberia. She didn't dare speak with Evitchka in her native Russian but spoke German, Czech or Polish. So even though she had got away from countries where secrets and lies were the norm, she felt that she must carry them on since nowhere in Europe felt safe.

She longed to go to America. They had stayed in a displaced person's camp run by Americans whom she found kind and helpful.

The food there had been good and she felt happy seeing Evitchka eat well. Evitchka had always been a thin sickly child and was for-ever suffering from diarrhoea or vomiting. Olga worried obsessively about the girl's health and hated when they were on the road having to depend on strangers to provide them with food. She remembered with burning shame the two men who had taken them in near Graz. At first she thought them kind as they gave them food. But after Evitchka had gone to sleep, they had other things on their minds. She felt dirty like a prostitute. Even now as she walked on the sand, the cool air on her face, it seemed that all the fresh breezes in the world could not purify the dirtiness that she felt inside.

For the sake of Evitchka she pulled herself out of that squalid situation and pressed on. Things had improved as they walked through Yugoslavia and teamed up with other refugees. On several occasions they got lifts in trucks and carts until they reached Italy. Their destination was Naples, from where the big ships sailed.

In a displaced person's camp in northern Italy, people from a country called Australia came and spoke to the refugees. They were told of a land where the sun always shone and where there was plenty of work, food and housing. These people were espe-cially attentive to the blonde, blue-eyed Evitchka and said that she would make a delightful Australian citizen. Olga was very tempted and had a vision of a plump healthy daughter laughing in the sun-shine. They were offered a free passage, in return for which Olga would need to work for two years as a domestic. She hated that idea as she had felt humiliated being a servant in Prague, but she was weary and fed up with trudging with a tiny child for miles each day, not knowing where their next meal would come from. The offer of a free train trip to Naples was tempting. Though she was set on getting to America, she decided to take the train and see what happened when they got to the port.

Now as she bent down to pick up a shell she knew that her dream of going to America was smashed. She had made enquiries and had been told quite firmly that America was not taking any single women with children. She was disappointed, and cursed her shameful predicament. It seemed that Australia was the only country in the world willing to take her and an illegitimate child. She found it hard to imagine this 'strange distant land'. Other refugees spoke enthusiastically about it, though they knew little and until recently had never even heard of it. There was talk of strange animals called 'kangaroos' and that it was overrun by rabbits! The fact that Australia was so distant appealed to Olga and the other hopefuls. They all wanted to get away as far as possible from the terrible times and regimes they had endured. She had heard Australia had wonderful beaches, and as she walked along this stretch of beach, she felt comforted by this as she really loved the sea. And perhaps Australia would be the best place for Evitchka. She wanted her daughter to have a new kind of life, a life of freedom and opportunity. The next ship would be leaving in early 1950. The beginning of the second half of the century, she thought. Perhaps a good omen that the horrors of the first half will be finally left behind.

She was snapped out of her deep thoughts by urgent shouts. 'Olga, Olga, come quickly! There's been an accident!'

Evitchka loved the feeling of height as she surveyed the scene from top of the bunk bed. Below her hundreds of refugees had made their tiered beds their home, and a motley assortment of clothes hung from the tops and sides. She had been in many of these camps now and always liked coming to them. They felt warm and safe.

She hadn't liked the long tiring walks along dusty uneven roads. Her mother had often been very impatient with her and had slapped her hard, told her she was naughty and said that if it wasn't for her they wouldn't be in this mess. Evitchka had been hurt and bewildered by these outbursts. She felt that her mother was cruel at times too, like during the extremely long train journey through Italy. She had been sitting with Nonda on her lap, transfixed by the scenery flashing by and soothed by the rhythm of the train, when suddenly and inexplicably her mother grabbed Nonda and threatened to throw him out of the window. Evitchka was distraught and begged her mother to give Nonda back. Her mother teased her like this for what seemed ages, and only after she was almost sick from sobbing did she give Nonda back. Her mother always seemed better when they were in a transit camp and around other people. Then Evitchka felt like she had her old mother back—a mother who would hug and kiss her and tell her exciting stories about her girlhood in Russia. Czechoslovakia seemed a long way away and her memories of Vlada and Kirov were fading fast.

Now she jumped up and down on the bed, enjoying bouncing higher and higher. After a while she felt bored and wished she had gone gathering shells with her mother. She surveyed the edge of the bunk bed and figured out that if she negotiated herself over the end bit she could slide down the pole to the bed below. She leaned over and started lowering herself gingerly. Oops. A sudden slip and she was hanging by her feet. She screamed for help, feeling her feet slipping further. To no avail. She plummeted towards the concrete floor. Everything went black.

When she came to, she saw her mother's face looking anxiously down at her. Several other people were there too. It reminded her of the time she had fallen down the stairs in the apartment block in Vitkova Street, where she and her mother had lived in Prague. At that time there had been a lot of blood and she had knocked out her front tooth. This time there was also a lot of blood that came from a cut on her forehead. Somebody was mopping it up and applying a bandage. Eventually she was laid down on the bottom bunk bed and her mother crawled in beside her. She showed Evitchka the seashells she had gathered and told her that soon they would go on a big ship and sail all the way to a place called Australia.

'Is it a nice place? Can I take Nonda? And will I have friends?' Her mother laughingly said yes to all her questions, and soon Evitchka was asleep.

*

'I want to play with the children.' Evitchka was excited as she had never seen so many children all together in one place, all screaming and shouting and jumping in and out of the swimming pool. Even louder screaming and shouting came from a large slide at one end of the pool where bigger children climbed to the top and hurtled down into the water amongst wild splashing. It looked terrifying but she was strangely drawn to it. Children pushed her up to the top. She stood there gripping the rail and looked out over the ship.

The *Skaugum* was a Norwegian troop carrier and was one of many similar ships commissioned to carry refugees to Australia. It was utilitarian and lacking in comfort, but from what its passengers

14

learned later, it was one of the better vessels that ferried the trau-matised war-weary and displaced to a new land. It had been built only recently and sported a large state-of-the-art swimming pool that the little child now surveyed from her high perch.

The *Skaugum* was Olga and Evitchka's home for the next few weeks as it made its long journey through the Suez Canal, over the Equator and down to the other side of the world. It had left Naples a few weeks after Evitchka's third birthday. That had been a trying time for the little girl. First there were the horrible series of injections everyone had to have. The worst was smallpox on her birthday! She felt very tiny and brave as she went up to what she felt was an execution. Then there was the spraying. Everyone had to be disinfected from head to foot with a foul-smelling spray, DDT, regarded as a wonderful new chemical that killed all known germs and made sure that all new arrivals in Australia were clean and sanitised.

The journey was supposed to last four weeks, but to Evitchka even the first few days seemed an interminable ordeal. It soon became hot as the ship passed along the Suez Canal and made its way through Egypt. Having just come from a European winter, many people suffered from heat exhaustion. Matters were made worse by the fact that all the women and children were quartered en masse in the large area above the boiler room. To Evitchka's eyes there seemed an endless array of naked breasts and flesh as women, stripped to the waist, tried to cool down their fretful chil-dren. For Evitchka, who had been born in Prague in the middle of the coldest winter for a hundred years and was used to deep snow, this was a real shock to the system.

The swimming pool was very popular with the children, but for Evitchka it presented a real dilemma that she now felt as she stood at the top of the slide. No matter how much she wanted to, she was just too frightened to slide down. So dejectedly she climbed back down the steps. She went and sat where she spent most of her time, on the side of the pool looking miserably at all the laughing chil-dren splashing about and hooting with delight.

The food on board was terrible, and a couple of outbreaks of dysentery among the young and old made Olga even more anxious about Evitchka's intake of food. Hanging around the kitchen hoping for some scraps, Olga befriended a shy young dark-haired man who worked in the ship's kitchens. Sasha was from Odessa and was helping out in the galley in exchange for cigarettes. Occasionally he managed to smuggle out a half tin of peaches for Evitchka which she ate with relish. The little girl and Sasha became friendly and she would often go and sit on his lap when she couldn't stand the strain of the whether-to-go-down-the-slide-or-not dilemma at the swimming pool. She would find Sasha on deck talking about future plans with his friend Kurt Weiss, with whom he had enjoyed a successful black market venture in Austria.

The weather got even hotter as the ship passed through the Red Sea before reaching the busy port of Aden. Here there was lots of shouting, hustle and bustle as merchants in small boats swarmed around the ship. After that they hit the open seas, and Olga began to relax and in fact to rather enjoy herself. Her good looks and curvaceous figure attracted the attention of the sailors and single male migrants. She also became quite excited about this far-off land of Australia. There were English lessons on board, and as she tried to get her tongue around this strange language, she looked forward to a brand new start in life. There was a lot of talk on board about this 'land of milk and honey' they were going to. Films were shown of the new housing that was available against a backdrop of lush greenery and blue skies.

Olga liked Sasha and was grateful for the fact that he spent a lot of time taking care of Evitchka. She knew that Sasha liked her too but he seemed a little too serious. She preferred some of the dashing young sailors she was flirting with. Life had been so dismal for her for so long and now at last she could let her hair down and play a little. Wanda, a fellow passenger who was pregnant, had given her a bathing suit which flattered her slim waist and ample breasts, so she loved to parade herself around the swimming pool.

After a couple of weeks the boat was nearing the Equator and preparations were underway to commemorate passing over it. This celebration, the traditional Neptune Ceremony, consisted of as many people as possible being dunked in the swimming pool and all aboard receiving a 'certificate of crossing'. Blue dye was poured into the pool and over-enthusiastic sailors pursued as many females as possible and carried them shrieking to the edge.

Sasha kept a dignified distance from such shenanigans and sat with Evitchka on deck. Olga came running up to them with telltale blue dye on her hair. She was giggling happily and tried to get them to join in. Sasha shook his head sadly. He felt that there was no way he could compete with the retinue of sailors that continually pursued her. He was shy but also felt disapproving of Olga, carrying on in such a way, especially when she had a three-year-old child to care for. After Olga ran off with several sailors in hot pursuit, Evitchka and Sasha sat quietly. The little girl leaned against Sasha and felt the sadness in the young man's chest. She knew he really liked Olga and also sensed that her elusive young mother was too fun-loving for this serious chap from Odessa. But Evitchka loved sinking into his warmth and lapped up the feeling of safety when she was with him. She knew that she could totally rely on him and that he would never let her down.

The weeks rolled by, and for Evitchka life on board consisted of endless days looking from the blue horizon disappearing behind the boat to even more blue horizon appearing in front. Time stood in hazy stillness and it seemed like she had been on this boat forever. For her mother, life on board was fun and full of new possibilities. She dared to hope that at last she was leaving the bad times behind. She felt attractive and alive. She made several new friends, among them Blanka and Bert Schreiber, a young couple from Prague who had escaped terrible times during the war and further persecution at the hands of the new communist puppet regime in Czechoslovakia. Blanka had a great sense of humour and an ability to put the past behind her and look forward to a totally new existence.

Olga confided to Blanka that Sasha was interested in her, and that she liked him. She especially liked his clothes and possessions, which were of excellent quality, quite unusual for the bulk of migrants aboard. She was struck by the numbers of neatly folded socks she had glimpsed in his suitcase. However, she was worried that he was a Jew. He had told her this in confidence and had said that nobody official must know. He had heard there was restriction on the number of Jews allowed to enter Australia. Like a large proportion of the ship's passengers, he was travelling on false papers—Sasha, who was really Alexander Wenzerul from Odessa, was officially Isaac Levkowicz from Poland.

For Olga, who also was travelling on false papers, this did not present a problem. The real problem was the depth of anti-Semitic prejudice she had been brought up with in rural Ukraine. She felt that she had nothing particularly against Sasha, but was worried that her family would disapprove. Blanka laughed about these concerns and told her to stop being silly. Her own husband was another secret Jew on board the *Skaugum* and she had no qualms whatsoever in being with him. This heartened Olga because she was drawn to the fact that Sasha was so good with her daughter and represented stability and steadiness.

The ship's occupants were sighting land constantly as they skirted the southern edge of Australia. The excitement and tension was palpable as the vessel neared Melbourne. Nobody could even pronounce Melbourne let alone understand where it was. Blanka and Bert were hoping it was near Perth where they had a distant cousin. The constant babbling, in several different languages, reflected the hopes and wishes of people who had seen everything that they had known and loved uprooted, tossed in the air and irrevocably destroyed; had seen futures decimated and promising careers nipped in the bud; had seen all hopes and aspirations crumble into the same cinders as the beautiful ancient cathedrals and countless historic edifices of once proud civilisations. Now they were far away from that seething pit of despair and horror, at the other end of the earth. Here was a country that seemed to be welcoming them.

Most of them were young and energetic, determined to start a new life for themselves. Olga looked over at the glittering lights of Melbourne and took a deep sigh. She was now at last free.

Evitchka sat on a grey blanket that lay folded on the single iron bed that she and her mother shared in the Australian displaced persons camp of Bonegilla. It was raining heavily, and she watched as a big drip fell through the corrugated asbestos roof onto the end of the bed, spraying her slightly with water. But she didn't care as she was licking the most delightfully delicious pink strawberry ice cream. She was in heaven. She didn't care that they were in a small cubicle barely bigger than the single bed she sat on, and that on the other side of a flimsy partition lived a whole other family. She had just been given this ice cream in the large dining hall after her lunch, a revolting affair consisting of some grey piece of tough meat that floated with tasteless vegetables in a brown liquid. Yuk! But then salvation with this pink ice cream. She had taken her cone and very carefully negotiated puddles and slippery concrete slabs to their cubicle, so that she could enjoy this treat in private.

As she was crunching the bottom end of the cone down to which she had pushed the last blob of strawberry paradise, her mother came in and stared in horror at the leak. Olga moved the bed a little so that the drip went on to the floor and told Evitchka that it was time for her afternoon nap. The little girl lay on the bed, contentedly savouring the last taste of pink heaven in her mouth, and allowed the monotony of the drip to lull her to sleep.

Olga made her way to the administration block to complain about the leak. She felt nervous as she didn't know how she was going to explain the problem and hoped that Wanda, who spoke a little English, might be there to help. They had been in Bonegilla a few days and Olga felt far from happy about the situation. The camp was hardly better than the displaced persons camps that they had been stuck in throughout Europe. Bonegilla was a former prisoner of war camp and she felt just like a prisoner of war! Even the trains that had brought them here were little better than the cattle trucks in which she and thousands of other Slavs had been transported to be slaves of the Third Reich. Olga had been disappointed that they had been whisked off the ship and on to the trains so quickly and hadn't even had a chance to see Melbourne. Olga liked bright city lights and was appalled at the bleakness and barrenness of the countryside during the long six-hour train journey that seemed to take them to the middle of nowhere. It was late summer and all the hills and fields were a dull brown colour. Dead trees and an occasional dead cow caught the eye, otherwise starved for something to latch on to.

Bonegilla itself was set in a bare landscape of sun-parched grass with little greenery, save for a couple of large gum trees near a lake. The present downpour of rain brought a little relief. The camp itself was a series of corrugated iron army buildings set in a grid of concrete paths. Each block of buildings had its own mess hall where hundreds of people would stand in queues each day and get a plate of slop that passed for food. Mutton was alien to most of the migrants. For a start few had enjoyed much meat in their war-torn lives, and even if they had it usually was chicken, pork or a Polish-style sausage. But this diet of chewy mutton and what were once vegetables was virtually unpalatable. Some people even cooked their own food in their rooms, like the family on the other side of the partition in Olga and Evitchka's cubicle. The toilet and ablution blocks were a big trek to the other side of the camp. The toilets were deep pit latrines and smelt revolting.

Olga also felt very lonely. Life on board the ship had been entertaining and fun and she missed the attention of the sailors and other young men. Most of the men, including Sasha, had been transported straight to Tasmania where they were to work on a giant hydro-electric scheme. Olga had been with the Schreibers when they had enquired of an immigration official where Perth was. He told them it was not their policy to send people to Perth from Melbourne. However, they could go to Adelaide. Blanka and Bert looked at the map and it seemed to them that Adelaide was close to Perth (only later were they able to comprehend the vastness of Australia). So with tearful farewells they set off for Adelaide. Now, as Olga made her way through the rain and negotiated large puddles of water in between the rows of military style huts, she wondered dejectedly where on the planet she had actually landed.

Evitchka was woken by banging on the roof. Her mother was sitting on a chair in the corner of the cubicle trying to learn the English alphabet. The sounds of this alphabet were so strange to Evitchka. When they were still in Czechoslovakia, her mother had begun to teach her the Russian alphabet which she liked the sound of. But this language was unfamiliar, and she didn't relish the thought of having to learn new alien-sounding letters. She could just about say 'hello', 'please' and 'thank you' but had struggled hard with 'thank you', not being able to say the sound 'th'. It seemed that her mouth, tongue and teeth were unable to produce that sound in any way, so she had to make do with the less than perfect 'sank you'.

Smells were coming from the next cubicle where the family were cooking some kind of soup in a big pot. This intrigued Evitchka, who also knew that the family urinated in the same pot at night. She had seen the mother emptying it in the mornings. She wished that they had a piss pot too so she didn't have to go and pee in the dark outside. The new arrivals had been warned about snakes and she was so terrified of these creatures that she imagined them slithering about in the dark. She was also afraid to go to the smelly latrines as another warning had been issued about poisonous spiders that lurked under the toilet seats.

'Mama, I need to go to the toilet.'

Olga shut the book irritably. 'Oh, you're always wanting something!' she snapped as she yanked the little girl's arm and dragged her out impatiently.

As they hurried down the path towards the latrines, Evitchka thought of Sasha. She really missed him. Where her mother was impatient and often unkind, Sasha had been infinitely patient and always attentive and caring. He also used to slip her pieces of salami from the ship's kitchens. Australia had its compensations, especially ice cream, but she really missed that salami. 'Will we see Sasha again?' she asked.

'You're always asking questions. You drive me crazy! How do I know if we'll see Sasha? I've heard that people can get stuck in Bonegilla for months before finding a place. And especially if I'm lumbered with you! Who's going to give me work when I'm stuck with you? Always asking questions! Never leaving me in peace!' They were in the latrines now and she was waiting for Evitchka to finish. 'And hurry up, I want to get out of this stinking place.'

Olga missed Sasha too. There had been a couple of romantic moments before the ship docked. Sasha had awkwardly kissed her and told her that he wanted to see her again once things were a little clearer. But where would she end up? All she knew was that this place was awful. She hoped that she would get a placement soon. She was bone weary from all the escaping, lying and travelling she had been doing for years. She badly needed to stop and belong somewhere.

At last they got news. Coonong, a station in New South Wales, wanted a maid and didn't mind a small child. Olga was really excited. Had she come finally to the end of her journey? Was the escape finally over?

3 / **Australia, Land of the Free**

Are birds free from the chains of the skyway?
Bob Dylan

I was really excited! I was in a new country and even had a different
name. Not Evitchka, but Eva. And Australian people pronounced it
strangely. Eeeva. And now we were going to a sheep station near
Narrandera. The owners, the McKeckies, were wealthy millionaires
who lived in Sydney. Mama was going to be a kitchen help at their
large country house, which they occasionally visited. Another train
journey. Fortunately this didn't last too long.

But it was horrible when we got out at Narrandera and the
train disappeared into the distance. We were in the middle of
nowhere, me clutching Nonda, and Mama our few belongings. No
other people; no station building; just a wooden platform on
which we stood. Surrounding us as far as the eye could see were
miles of flat wheat fields stretching out to an endless horizon. No
one came to meet us. Just us two, alone under the relentless blue
of the sky.

We waited and waited. Nothing. Just emptiness. Where to go?
We had no option but to follow the dusty track away from the railway line into the limitless Australian plain. We just walked ... and
walked. We didn't know where we were going or what we would
encounter. We couldn't speak the language. At least in Europe
there were others like us on the trail. Here, nothing!

It began to get dark. Fall of night was much more sudden than
we had been used to in northern Europe and no light was to be
seen as darkness enveloped us. We kept to the track with difficulty
and I was just beginning to get scared when we saw lights and heard
the sound of a truck behind us. The truck stopped as two rather

scruffy and bewildered looking Aussies tried to pick out our forms in the headlights.

I can imagine a conversation like the following: 'Gor struth, what's that? Looks like a blonde sheila and a tiny kid. What the hell are they doin' out 'ere at this time o'night?'

'Narrandera! Narrandera! Coonong!' my mother shouted, trying to explain what we were doing in the middle of nowhere. She was putting the wrong inflection on the names and it took quite a bit of miming and exchange of unintelligible words before I was bundled into the front seat of the truck with a rug over my legs, and we were whisked off.

I liked Coonong farmhouse but was lonely. As I was the only child on the premises, everyone liked me and made a great fuss of me. I loved the milkman, and every morning I was up at the crack of dawn with a large glass into which he would pour fresh milk. My mother was very popular with all the local lads, many of whom came a-courting.

Stan the farmhand drove into town each week and offered to take me with him for a ride. It was so exciting bumping along in his truck, and even better when he bought me a beautiful pair of red slippers with bells on the toes. But there was a catch, and it was at an early age that I discovered there's no such thing as a free lunch. On the way home Stan stopped the truck and started to act very strangely. He began rubbing himself up against me and telling me what a lovely little girl I was and that this would be our secret. I didn't fully understand what he was saying and didn't know what was going on. All I knew was I didn't like it. That night I looked down at the slippers on my feet and jiggled the bells. I just loved those slippers.

The next week Stan said he would buy me a dress in Narrandera. I hesitated. 'Go on,' said Mama. 'Go on,' said Grace, the cook. The long day stretched ahead and Stan's smile beckoned. I hopped in the truck. A new dress would be nice.

This time we stopped on the way. My heart sank as he started to do unpleasant things again. This time he was rubbing his strange thing on the place between my legs. My mother called this place my 'buhta', which she said meant 'bay' in Russian. I shied away and said I wanted to go home.

'No, you don't,' he soothed, his large hairy face bearing down on mine. I didn't like his smell. 'This is very good for you, and remember, we'll buy you a pretty dress.'

I doubted very much if what he was doing was good for me. I got the dress, but now I was very uneasy. That night as Mama was bathing me I asked, 'Is it good for me that Stan rubs his thing on my "buhta"?'

I was shocked at her reaction. She just screamed and ran out of the room. That evening there was a lot of urgent whispering and banging of doors. I never saw Stan again but always remembered him as the man with the long red nose. The 'buhta' episode was never mentioned again. I did get to keep the slippers and the dress.

From then on Mama became obsessed with where I was. This, coupled with her obsession with how much I ate, became very oppressive. She would scream and hit me because I wouldn't eat all my food. This force-feeding and beating ritual became such a routine that I thought it was just a normal part of life. Grace, the cook, was to disabuse me of this fact when she interrupted my mother during one of these screaming matches. 'Olga, you shouldn't hit Eva because she won't eat.'

My mother stopped in her tracks and made some feeble attempt at an excuse. 'Of course I should—all children should be hit if they don't eat!'

This interjection on Grace's part only temporarily gave me relief from my mother's relentless onslaught of shoving food down my throat. However, I always remembered and valued it because I instinctively knew Grace was right, and this helped me in the arduous years ahead. I was really pleased that she had stuck up for me. The force-feeding became so bad that I became a chronic vomiter and alarmingly thin.

There were some large pens at Coonong where geese were kept and I was warned not to go near.

I see the baby goslings through the wire mesh. They are so yellow and fluffy. I badly want to hold one. I have my red slippers on and must move gingerly or the bells will ring. I creep up closer and closer and am just about to touch a gosling when a voice barks.

'Ged ouda there! Gedaway, you foreign brat!'

I whip around and see a man pointing a rifle at me. I am so terrified

24

I stumble backwards out of the pen and run for my life, losing one of the slippers. I must get away before he shoots me. I run, run, run and hide quaking in my room for ages.

Later Mama asks where's my other slipper, but I can't tell her.

Occasionally the McKeckies came down from Sydney. There was great bustle every time this happened as the staff frantically got everything shipshape for the boss and his wife. They were kindly people, well into their forties, who seemed to take a great interest in me. I had learnt enough English by now to sound very polite and very cute. The more I smiled and wriggled my fair tresses and said lots of 'pleases' and 'thank yous', the more these strange Australian grown-ups seemed to like me. Especially Mrs McKeckie, who would come out on the veranda that ran along the entire perimeter of the farmhouse and look at me longingly.

One evening, my mother was summoned into their private living room. She was quite nervous about this and wondered what all this was about. The other staff were envious of this unusual privilege. My mother told me many times later what transpired.

'Olga, we want to have a very serious talk with you. We have thought very long and deeply about what we are to tell you. We see you as a young, very attractive woman who has her whole life before her and a great future in this country. We see you have a lot of suitors and it will only be a matter of time before some nice young Australian man will make a proposal of marriage to you. So we have a serious proposition to make to you. As you probably have noticed we are childless. This has been one of the tragedies of our life, but no child has ever come along and now it is too late. We would like to adopt Eva. We believe that this would help you a lot because you are still so young. You don't need to be held back by a small child. And with us she would be in excellent hands. We will send her to the best schools in Sydney. We will give her everything she needs. She will mix with princes and the best that society can offer [the McKeckies were the personal friends of a Bengali prince—Grace had told Mama that he once had come to stay]. Please consider our offer seriously.'

My mother refused. This was a mixed blessing as far as I was concerned. I am pleased that she loved me enough not to let me go, but during the long hard years ahead I sometimes wished she had. I wouldn't have minded an alternative future that promised the best schools in Sydney and hobnobbing with royalty!

✦

Sitting on uncomfortable boards we saw our first movie in a sheep shed, flickering up on the makeshift screen. I was amazed by the giant faces.

Sasha came back into our lives. He saved up enough money from the measly wage he earned in Tasmania to fly to Narrandera for a few days. He arrived all awkward, shy and looking spruce in a stiff new khaki shirt. I was delighted to see him and jumped into his arms. Mama was less enthusiastic. She had been flirting with many young men and was struck again by Sasha's shyness and seriousness. Sasha had landed a job in Adelaide at the large Holden car factory and invited us to join him. He was obviously smitten by Olga, and she was tempted. He went off with a promise that she would seriously consider his offer. Olga was fed up with being in the outback and the promise of city life appealed to her. Bert and Blanka Schreiber were also in Adelaide. After discovering the vast size of Australia and that Perth was another two thousand miles further west, they had stayed put. The real problem was Sasha. She did not love him. However, his offer of an airfare was attractive and meant she could escape the boredom of the outback.

A few weeks later saw us in a little rickety plane flying to Adelaide. I vomited into a paper bag most of the way.

For the first year or two we moved around from place to place depending on where my mother could get a job as a live-in domestic. She continually fell out with people we stayed with. This was partly due to her volatile nature and partly because she couldn't bear being a servant. At one point we lived, together with Sasha, in a huge mansion in Springfield, the abode of a Russian Jewish dentist who had emigrated many years earlier and had made good in Adelaide. Sasha cycled several miles to work each day and Mama helped look after Jennifer, the spoilt two-year-old grand-daughter of the dentist. I ran around and played in the exquisitely manicured gardens and continued to be force-fed. But it was not long before we moved again, this time after Mama fell out with Jennifer's mother after refusing to wash the nursery walls which Jennifer had smeared with excrement.

Speaking of which, I disgraced myself one night by eating a whole packet of Laxettes that Jennifer's older brother had given me. Laxettes were given out like sweets and a popular jingle of the day was 'Boys and girls come out to play/Happy and well the Laxette way'. I hated the stodgy, starchy, unpalatable Australian food and can now see why Laxettes were an essential part of that diet. I ate the Laxettes, which tasted like chocolate.

That night my mother literally disowned me and refused to have anything to do with my 'squits'. 'Always sick—always diarrhoea— you are the cause of all my troubles!' The usual refrain. Sasha, on the other hand, was a hero. Even though he was tired after a double shift at Holden's, he lovingly washed and changed my clothes and sheets throughout that long and horrible night.

We moved again, and from time to time my mother couldn't cope with me. On a couple of occasions she even put me temporarily into a children's home.

The plate of food is shoved before my face. I hate the smell. It is baked beans and green mushy peas. I push the little lumps around the plate, my tears making them salty. I don't know why I am here. Big people keep talking to me in oily tones and I don't understand what they are saying. I'm sent to bed and it is still daylight. I am in a dormitory with lots of other beds and I watch the dust swirling in shafts of evening light, spilling in through the high windows. I miss Mama and Sasha terribly and wish they would come and get me out of here.

As if on cue my wish is granted. There is a commotion at the door. It is Sasha! He comes to the bed, scoops me up and takes me home.

Sasha had saved me again. He told me that he could not bear me being away from home and had come to get me immediately he discovered where I was. I really adored this man from Odessa. But he could also be uncharacteristically cruel. Once when my mother was out, I played with her box of powder and spilt it all over the bedroom. Sasha came in, blew a fuse and hit my bare bottom with a brush until it was raw and bleeding. Mrs Bates, who lived next-door, was horrified and comforted me. She and her husband became lifelong friends. I would often stay with them, which gave me a little breath of normality, and my mother, who was less and less able to cope, some rest.

We all moved to Commercial Road, Unley, another wealthy suburb where my mother looked after a frail elderly lady, Mrs Bressler. I was the only New Australian (as we migrants were then called) in the street and looked longingly at the children who played outside. These were times when children always played in the street as cars were rare. Every day I begged my mother to put me in front of the big fence so I could play. She was reluctant as she had to close the gate from the inside, so when I was out there I could only get back in if she opened the gate.

She finally relented at the sight of my beseeching eyes. 'Okay, but I am very busy so I won't be opening the gate for half an hour!'

I stand there shyly squinting into the afternoon sun, not knowing how to break into their games. Some of them seem to be looking at me and whispering. I have waited so long to play with other children so I just wait and hope. After what seems an eternity, a pretty girl comes up to me and wiggles her yellow ringlets. Oh, how I would like such a girl for my friend! Just a few nights ago some children visited me in the middle of the night. It was so wonderful and I was so happy as they sat on my bed. But when I told Mama, she laughed and said it was just a dream. This girl in front of me looks just like one of those children. And this is no dream. It is broad daylight. Ooh, she's going to talk to me.

'We don't like you. You talk funny, you smell funny, you dress funny.'

The street becomes ominously silent as now all the children are looking at me. I try to merge into the wooden fence. I can hardly breathe. I feel as if I have been kicked.

'In fact we hate you so much we have decided to shoot you.'

I can hardly comprehend what she is saying, and I am just wondering if my slender command of the language is misconstruing what I think she is saying when I see the cowboy. Now there is no doubt. The afternoon, so full of sunny playful promise, has transformed into a nightmare. I am definitely going to be shot. A boy of about seven (to my four-year-old eyes he seems huge), with his cowboy suit, mean eyes and a set of gun-laden holsters, swaggers slowly down the street towards me. The children are deathly quiet as they watch the impending execution. The panic rises like bile in my throat. I try to claw my way over the gate. It is too high. The executioner moves relentlessly closer. I hear a terrible screaming and realise it is coming from my own throat. I scream and scream and pound on the immovable wooden gate.

'Mama! Mama! Help! Help! I'm being murdered.' I continue banging, not daring to look around—expecting any moment to be blown to oblivion.

An eternity later the gate suddenly opens and I fall into my mother's arms sobbing and retching. She instantly appraises the scene and shouts a torrent of Slavic abuse at the children, who all run away.

At the end of January 1952 I went to Unley Primary School. I was the only New Australian in the whole school. My mother made my lunch and when I opened it on the first day, I was mortified. Children visibly moved away at the smell of garlic sausage sandwiches. 'Pooh!' they exclaimed. But worse was to come. As we unpeeled our hard boiled eggs, mine turned out to be not hard and oozed cold yellow all over my garlic sandwiches. 'Ooh yuk!'' they squealed. I hastily threw my lunch in the bin.

'You threw your lunch in the bin, didn't you!' interrogated my mother.

'N-no, I …' I stumbled wondering how in the hell she knew. She always seemed to know everything. My lunch became a huge problem every day—whether to risk ridicule, chuck it or force some of it down and be sick.

School was confusing. Adelaide was a colonial backwater of the British Empire. Every morning we had to sing 'God Save Our King' and then do marching practice. I had no idea who this king was but we had to salute and curtsy to him and save him with heartfelt gusto. After a week of this, Adelaide was suddenly plunged into mourning. This king, despite our exhortations to God, had died. I felt really bad that we couldn't save him. Pictures of George VI, festooned with black ribbons, dominated all the big shop windows. We had to stand interminably at school assemblies while grave adults droned on for hours. The next week we had to sing 'God Save Our Queen'! Australia was a very strange place.

My mother seemed to get on well with Mrs Bressler and her spinster daughter. She was always making them laugh. She continued to be erratic in relation to me. She would be very funny one minute and then be obsessively strict the next. She would regale me with stories about Baba Yaga, a Russian witch who would always be everywhere, watching to see that I behaved myself, see that I went to sleep, see that I ate my lunch.

As well as Baba Yaga there was Bogh. 'Bogh' is 'God' in Russian, and Bogh took up monolithic proportions in my imaginative head. Bogh especially would get very angry with little girls if they did not go to bed early. My mother's obsession with me and sleep was almost as great as her obsession with me and food. She would send me to bed every afternoon and again at six o'clock in the evening. One night she relented when I asked if I could take the milk bottles out with Sasha, which meant staying up till seven o'clock. I held Sasha's hand very tightly as we went outside. But at the gate I suddenly screamed and ran inside straight to bed. I had looked up and seen a big black cloud. It was Bogh coming to get me.

I had a room to myself in Commercial Road and would lie awake for hours as I wasn't sleepy. I would stand at the window and watch the Wells sisters, two elderly spinsters next-door, having their supper and reading and knitting. It was as exciting as watching paint dry.

*

In February 1952 Olga and Sasha were married. It was a happy day, and I was allowed to wear my hair loose in curls instead of the usual tight plaits. I now became Eva Levkowicz, not Eva Prosikova. I would have preferred to be something like Eva Smith. Much easier at school. Mum had dyed her hair platinum blonde and wore an exquisite dress, hat and gloves. Sasha looked dapper in a new suit. His old friend Kurt Weiss and his wife Katherina, newly brought over from Austria, were the witnesses.

Two years of double shifts at Holden's, seven days a week, meant Sasha had saved money to buy a house. Within a few months we moved to 17 Pudney Street, Seaton Park, a western suburb of Adelaide. It backed onto Hendon railway station where thousands of workers spewed forth every morning into the nearby Phillips factory.

We were among the first New Australians in Pudney Street and were awkwardly ensconced between the Mellows and the Pounds, whom Mum unsurprisingly fell out with in a short time. They resented us New Australians with our loud ways and curious habits, like digging up the front lawn and growing potatoes. They especially resented the fact that we started a full-blown chicken farm to supplement our income. Our backyard wasn't large by Australian standards, just an ordinary-sized suburban plot, so the Mellows and the Pounds didn't take too kindly to cocks crowing at dawn and the babble of two hundred chickens all day long.

We sold eggs and ate the chooks. Olga chopped off their heads with an axe and I watched in horrified fascination as they jerked about, bloody fountains spurting from bereft necks. I was even more fascinated by the pageant of eggs in different phases of formation within their disembowelled bodies. Sasha had a hard time learning about diseases that affected poultry because he couldn't read English. Many a time found me trying to translate some chicken owner's handbook while holding tightly on to a very energetic rooster, which protested vigorously as Sasha injected its scrawny feet. Our kitchen was home to a large box of hundreds of small yellow chicks. Olga chopped up hard boiled eggs for these yellow scraps of fur that had only just pecked their way out of an egg themselves.

And, oops, I mustn't call him Sasha any more. Ever since the wedding I had been instructed to call him Tata or Dad. I didn't mind this. I loved him and felt he was like my real Dad. And he worked hard for the family. One Easter a brand new shiny swing appeared on our back lawn. My mother told me that she saw a large white rabbit scrambling over the back fence. For many years I believed that the Easter Bunny had brought the swing and often wondered how a rabbit could carry such a large object.

All through these early years in Adelaide, as I struggled with the new culture and the new language, I felt like an outsider. The prejudice against New Australians was quite vicious at times. In the early 1950s there were relatively few new immigrants compared with later in the decade. For the first three or four years at school I was the only one in the class who had a funny name. It was always mispronounced, and sometimes the teachers would not even call out my name when the roll was called. Were they not able to pronounce it? By the time I was in high school it seemed that half the class had funny names so I didn't feel so different. As I discovered in Commercial Road, children were the cruellest in their rejection of anything new or strange but were only repeating what their parents were saying behind closed doors.

I was acutely embarrassed by my family and their peasant-like New Australian ways. I was especially ashamed of my mother. I'd hate her taking me to my new school, Hendon Primary School. It was even worse when, on a cold day, she would cycle to the school with hot soup on the back of her bicycle and proceed to spoon-feed me lunch. To be subjected to the sheer torture of having a woman with a peasant scarf feeding me soup at the school gate was absolute hell. I would rather have died. But I stood there swallowing gulps of soup and humiliation while all the 'lucky' Australian kids went past with their shilling's worth of fish and chips.

As I got older and my mother suspected that I threw my lunch in the bin, she made me come home for lunch, which I hated. The trouble with going home was the raw garlic she forced me to eat. I can still see it on the side of the plate staring at me ominously, three or four large fat cloves of it. I was so fed up with 'Pooh, you smell' from my Australian classmates. Most of the time I managed to shove the offending cloves into my pocket or keep them whole in my mouth before depositing them down the toilet. Whatever I tried, the smell encircled and permeated my aura wherever I went. Garlic was at that time alien to the Australian food experience. It was inextricably lumped with New Australians and their disgusting foreign habits.

The prejudices went both ways. I thought Australian food was disgusting—the worst form of bland English food imaginable. I was nauseated by the sight of a plate of mushy peas and it took years to get used to lamb.

As I struggled along in my own way trying to integrate into the Australian way of life, things were not great for my mother. She felt the prejudice acutely. She always seemed to be served last in shops. Both she and my father struggled with the language. By the time I was seven I already had an Australian accent and was better at English than my Australian classmates. It put me in a curious position in the family as it gave me a lot of power. I was the one that my parents continually turned to for help, and I always had the job of translating for them in public situations. This often landed me in a right pickle. I once had to explain to a bunch of tetchy security guards in the gardens at Government House that we were trying to have a picnic in what my parents thought were the Botanical Gardens (which actually were about a half a mile away).

My mother also felt that she hadn't really got away from the communists. Australia in the early 1950s had its own form of virulent McCarthyism. Communists were under the beds and infiltrating the borders. All migrants were harangued about the evils of communism and how they especially had to be vigilant. The Red Peril was everywhere.

I told a teacher at school one day that my parents had come from Russia. I happened to mention it to my mother that night at the meal table. She hit the roof and said that I must *never* tell anyone that we were Russian. We must not speak Russian outside the privacy of our house. I didn't really understand at the time why this was such a terrible crime, but after that I was always a lot more circumspect. Even in a free country, my mother had to hide who she was.

Occasionally a Russian ship would dock for a few weeks in Port Adelaide. Mama would take me down to look at it. We tried to get on board but were always barred. Only Australians were permitted inside. Russian refugees were regarded as enemies of the USSR and were therefore not allowed on board. This broke my mother's heart and she would wander, with me in tow, for hours around the docks, looking wistfully at the tall unwelcoming sides of the ship. Hearing strains of Russian music drifting across the waters, Olga would walk and cry and cry. I would hold her hand helplessly as darkness fell. I could feel her desperation and didn't know how to help her.

Her relationship with my father was also not working out too well.

We are in the front room of 17 Pudney Street. I sleep in the corner. My impression of the room is that it is blue because there is a large blue candlewick bedspread on Sasha and Olga's bed. Finally we are in our own house. Each time I call out to Sasha, Mama swoops down at me like a black crow and snaps, 'You must call him Tata.' I love him like a dad and he is much kinder to me than Mama. She shouts and hits me and cries a lot. Why isn't she happy in her new house? She was always nagging Sash—, oops, Tata that she needed her own house.

I'm just falling asleep with all these thoughts when I'm woken up by a terrible screaming I can't escape from. The lights are all on and Mama is pulling the blue bedspread off the bed and hurling herself against Tata and howling like an animal. I am so frightened I can't move. Please, God, make her stop!

They had terrible rows most of the time. School became an escape from home. I dreaded returning as I didn't know what to expect. Often the house would be strewn with broken dishes, which Mama would hurl at Tata when he would come home from the factory. She was a social animal and loved to go out and dance. Tata was terribly shy and too exhausted from working to go out and socialise. One evening she organised a party for our friends, hiring a five-piece band so she could dance. Tata sat morosely the whole time and didn't join in. He didn't hide his dislike for some of her friends, especially the ones who came from Ukraine where she had been born. Next day she screamed at him, 'You drive me mad with your gloomy face that looks like you're going to be hanged tomorrow.'

For his part, he felt she was being extravagant with his hard-earned money. The thing that attracted her to him in the first place, his ability to put food on the table, was backfiring horribly for her. He just wanted to work hard and save all the money. She wanted to spend the money and have a good time. 'What's the point of making money if you don't spend it!' she would scream. Tata would just set his jaw and grimly go about his chores.

Usually Tata would just ride out Mama's taunts and jibes, bury-ing the hurt, rage and humiliation and looking more and more like he *would* be hanged the next day. But occasionally he would explode, with terrible consequences. One day Mama bought me a sumptuous red raincoat with a fur collar. It was expensive and lux-urious. I loved it and couldn't wait to wear it to school and show it off. But when Tata came home from work and saw this raincoat, he flew into a terrifying fury, fell upon the garment and tore it to shreds. He shouted that it was a total waste of his hard-earned money, that my mother was being far too extravagant and that we would all end up on the bottom of society's heap if this kind of thing continued. My mother and I were mortified. I remember gazing at the pile of savagely torn red fabric and fur in speechless incomprehension. A few days later I got a regulation plain navy raincoat, dull and utilitarian, with no hint of frivolity.

The battle slugged on. Olga would take me to the pictures and shows and we would stop in expensive coffee shops and eat deli-cious German tortes before going home in a taxi. To little avail I would beg my mother to take the bus, knowing my father's reaction if we turned up in a taxi. She would scoff at my protestations and say, 'Money is for spending. What use is it going to be when I'm dead?' I would watch the clicking taxi meter in a rising panic as the fare mounted and we got closer and closer to home. Even today I find it difficult to take a taxi. I must force myself not to take notice of the ticking meter. It always feels too extravagant and to carry the threat of dire consequences.

In the summer my mother would take me to the beach. Adelaide is blessed with some of the most beautiful beaches in the world and they would become crowded in those heady, pre-ozone hole days. Gold medallions glinted on the sunburnt chests of Italians as they played ball, in amongst bronzed bodies lying prone on the baking white sand. Summer holidays were spent on the beach.

One late afternoon, on Henley Beach jetty, fate dealt a surprising twist and provided Olga with some much needed succour. She and I were walking up the jetty with our fish and chips when we saw a ghost from the past. A man with a drooping black moustache was coming towards us.

'Kirov!'

'Olga!'

It was a dramatic reunion. Kirov and Olga fell on each other in disbelief. I didn't recognise him at first but felt a strange tingle of familiarity as he enfolded me in his warm, smoky embrace. It transported me back to what seemed another life and another time. A crowd of tearful immigrants gathered around us, all swept along in the drama of people who had last met in one of the old countries.

Kirov took us immediately to see Vlada. They were tomato pickers and lived in a tin shed among glass houses not far from the beach. Vlada was beside herself in frenzied jubilation at the sight of us. 'Olya! Evitchka! At last God has returned you to me!'

The initial euphoria gave way to recriminations as to why Olga had run off as she did. While the adults reminisced and caught up with each other, I was staring open-mouthed at their home. It was literally a tin shed, and their two baby daughters, Elizabeth and Jane, lay in tomato boxes, their faces crawling with flies. I was shocked at the poverty. Kirov and Vlada had come from proud, wealthy families in Sofia and were now reduced to such squalid conditions.

However, it wasn't too long before they moved into a small bungalow on the tomato farm. We visited them many times over the next few years, and it was one of the few places where Olga could go and unburden her soul.

4 / **Coming Apart**

Terror is my daily diet. I wake up each morning with dread and try to claw my way back into my dreams. Even the monsters in my dreams are preferable to the monster that my mother has become. I can at least wake up from a nightmare. I cannot wake up from my mother. She is my jailer, meting out my daily punishment. Scalp traumatised by hair being ripped into two tight plaits—any flinching slapped into stillness—lumpy semolina forced down a gagging throat. Out of the door.

'You be home on the dot or else!' screams the demented one.

Phew, off to school. Over the BIG *road. Ah, the school gates. Fear grips my belly. Will they like me? Please like me. I'll die if you don't like me. Put on my best smile. It's all I have. Plaits, clothes, heavy brown boots—garlic smell. They don't like me. Crestfallen. I'm not one of them. I speak a funny language, have a funny name, smell really funny. I've been to three different schools already and not yet seven. I'm trying so hard. I'm so good at my school lessons. Too good.*

'Shame on you,' says the teacher to the class, 'here's a little New Australian girl and she can spell better than all of you!' They glare at me— all the Beverley Smiths, Cheryl Butlers and Jane Browns—girls with short bobbed hair, pretty sandals, pronounceable names and normal lives.

I'm so good in the afternoon. Please be good, rest of class, so we aren't kept in. I've got to be home straight after school, or else! I visualise the dreaded strap hanging on the back of the door and my thin limbs contract.

But sometimes she isn't so bad. Just like the old Mama. All smiles, kisses and gentle strokes, and lots of gooey delicious chocolate. And my skin is just about to relax into its natural elasticity when she turns into a monster again. I'm late home from school. It's because I couldn't find my raincoat. It is that horrible blue raincoat. I'm still heartbroken for the red raincoat with the fur collar. Out comes the strap. It tears into my flesh. I contort my body, trying to receive the blows on my back. In that way I won't be ashamed

36

of the blue and red weals on my arms and legs when changing for PE class.

I scream at her imploringly. 'I looked everywhere for the raincoat in the locker room!'

She doesn't believe me. The beating goes on interminably. The pain sears through me and my skin shrivels up tightly over my bones.

At last the demented madwoman stops, exhausted, and I'm sent off to bed. Tearstained and trembling I cuddle up to Nonda. He is now a bit the worse for wear. I inexplicably cut off all his lovely white curls after the last beating. I fall into a fitful sleep. I'm cowering in a hole in the playground. All the other kids are standing around me, jeering and laughing and throwing mud at me. I wake up in a cold sweat. I take Nonda and start rubbing him between my legs. It's really nice. I rub him more urgently. Images of a big fat guy hitting a little guy in a slapstick comedy I once saw swirl around with the jeering laughing faces of all the Beverleys, Cheryls and Janes, and the feeling between my legs becomes unbearably pleasurable—I plunge Nonda's face into my buhta—a crescendo—and then it is all over. I lie in the dark, Nonda limp on my stomach.

Olga continued to be volatile. At times she was funny, laughing, gregarious and generous. She loved practical jokes and had a natural ability to make people laugh. She would either be running around the kitchen with a saucepan on her head or dressing up the latest poor kitten in my dolls' clothes. She bought me an array of beautiful ribbons to weave into my plaits and told me of her girlhood when she and her sisters would make paper peonies for their hair. She loved going to the movies and bought all the latest magazines. She became obsessed with American film stars. She continued to dye her dulling hair blonde, wore bright red lipstick and kept up with the fashion of the time. The tight tailored tops and flared skirts suited her curvaceous figure. She badly wanted to emigrate to America because she believed that was where dreams came true. She gorged on a diet of Marilyn Monroe and Debbie Reynolds and lived in a fantasy world of what it would be like to be in star-studded America. She begged Dad to buy her a mink coat and after several arguments ended up with a mink stole.

The rows between her and Dad became more frequent and violent. A few times she packed her bags and stormed out of the house with me in tow. She would tell me she was leaving Sasha. I would feel a mixture of relief and also great insecurity. I loved him and had totally forgotten he was not my real father, but I also knew it was hopeless between him and Olga. However, we would always end up back home after a few days.

When I was seven her moods became more and more unpredictable. One minute she would be plying me with chocolates and calling me 'zolotka' (precious) and the next she would become a screaming demon, violent and merciless, blowing up at the slightest thing. I could do nothing right.

I learn to read my mother's gestures and moods. I try to anticipate what will please or displease her. I am holding my breath, always on guard. I never feel safe. I desperately love her and I dread her too. I dread when she says, 'I'll give you such a beating you will remember it your whole life.'

And there I am again, cowering on the floor, flinching away from the dreaded strap. I try to get away from the searing lashes. She screams and whips, whips and screams—or are they my screams? I try crawling under the bed. She drags me out. Nothing can protect my skinny frame from her demented fury. I shrink to my bony knees and beg and scream for mercy: 'Mercy, Mama, mercy! Why can't you have mercy upon me?' The entreaty is useless and seems to inflame her even more. Exhausted, she finally stops. I lie on the wooden floor like a broken toy, not daring to even whimper as that might set her off again.

She's right. I do remember the beating for the rest of my life—every lash. Each one tears through my being like piercing rain.

There was a period of what felt like years when my body would be covered in weals. I was too embarrassed to do physical education at school because it would mean changing clothes and risk the lash marks and bruises being noticed. I became obsessed with whether this sort of thing happened to other kids and would feel comforted if I heard that they too were getting beaten. Perhaps what was happening at home was normal, I would kid myself.

We hardly saw my father as he buried himself in double time at Holden's. He was largely unaware of the hell I was living through. My mother's favourite piece of torture was to make me kneel in the toilet on a coir mat for hours on end, as punishment. I was not allowed to cry or she would double the time I had to be there or beat me again with the strap, sometimes the buckle end. I knelt on the mat feeling utterly humiliated and wretched. I drew patterns on the walls with the silent tears that flowed down my cheeks. She would scream for the umpteenth time that she wished I had never been born and that I was the cause of all her problems; that I had been a shitty difficult baby and that I was a scourge on her existence. Now I was nothing but trouble, always naughty, never eating my food, never sleeping and driving her crazy. If it wasn't for me she would have been able to do what she wanted to do and wouldn't be stuck in this hellhole.

I feel sad having to write this. It feels a betrayal of her. But I kept the horrible secret inside for too long. I believed what my mother was telling me. Like all children who have such unbearable love for their parents even when they abuse them, I turned it all in on myself. I felt humiliated, degraded and worthless. I never told a soul about the private hell that we were both in. I don't feel bitter or angry, just deeply sad. I look back on that little child and admire her enormously for how she bore her suffering. I remember how she prayed fervently every night and begged God to make Mum and Dad stop fighting and make Mum happy again. Now that I understand that my mother was heading for insanity, I admire that child even more for her fortitude and ability to cope.

For Olga there was little respite. She hated her life. She was continually tortured. She wondered why she had escaped starvation in Ukraine, bombing in Germany and humiliation in Czechoslovakia. She would look at my father and his 'I'm going to be hanged tomorrow' face and then look out at the bleak flat hot landscape of suburban dry Australia and say, 'What am I doing in this God-forsaken hellhole, in this flat desert at the edge of the world a million miles from nowhere? Is this what life is?' Then she would escape into her dreams of America and the film star life.

When I was seven-and-a-half, my sister Valentina was born. I was thrilled. I had somebody to share it all with. More importantly, my mother had someone else to pay attention to. It wasn't all plain sailing though. She found it hard to cope with the new baby and often I was forced to stay home from school and look after little Val. This was a huge quandary for me because, however much I loved my sister, I hated being away from school and was very scared of getting into trouble. We could only stay away if sick, and if we did we had to bring a note. My mother could not write in English. So I would lie that I had been ill and that I had forgotten to bring a note. My whole existence right down to my very surname was a tissue of lies. To avoid beatings, I became an adept liar.

'Oh no!' My mother's white scarf has fallen on the floor and is filthy. I know I am in real trouble. Mum will strap me for sure. I run home and tell her a fantastic story. 'Two boys beat me up on the way home and stomped all over the white scarf.' She is outraged, but I'm saved from a thrashing.

However, next day she marches up to school, baby in tow, and demands to see the headmaster. An urgent assembly is called in the yard. There is a hush over the whole school as the headmaster speaks. I really like Mr Hussey who is always nice to me and a lovely caring headmaster, but I do not relish being brought out in front of the whole school to stand next to him.

'This little girl was set upon last night by two boys and I want to know who they are.'

Silence. No movement. Nobody steps forward. I tremble in my boots. It has gone too far to stop now.

'Right,' says Mr Hussey in careful measured tones. 'Go back to class and Eva and I will visit every classroom until the culprits own up.'

So the whole charade continues. Around we go to each classroom.

'Eva, I want you to look at every boy and if you recognise one I want you to point him out to me.'

I feel terrible anguish as I walk around the aisles. One classroom, two, three and so it goes on. It is like a living nightmare. We are up to about classroom eight when a strange new twist is added to the tale. I am walking around the aisles when a boy called Barry, who is always in trouble, bursts out, 'Please, sir, I saw the whole thing. I saw her being beaten up!'

I can't believe what I'm hearing. I'm beginning to wonder if I really had been set upon. This farce is getting worse by the minute and I am now so deep in shit I can't imagine any way out. We trudge to the next lot of classrooms with Barry in tow.

We are in the last classroom. I must choose somebody. I look at all the boys' faces. They, like all the other boys in the school, look solemn and apprehensive. I see a tiny, spindly boy, the kind of boy who would never hurt a fly. Probably the tiniest, spindliest boy in the whole school. I stop. I point.

'It's him, sir!' The little boy nearly faints with fright and starts blubbering.

'Yes, it's him,' agrees Barry.

'N-n-no, sir. I-I-it wasn't me,' stutters the puny boy.

I am rooted to the spot. I have just accused the smallest, weakest boy in the school. What will happen next?

Mr Hussey has sussed that something is horribly amiss. He soothes the frightened little boy, sends Barry back to the classroom and takes me to my mother waiting in the office.

'I think, Mrs Levkowicz, that Eva has told you a fib.' Neither my mother nor I have heard this word before. She takes me home rather puzzled, but is suitably mollified by the fact that Mr Hussey has taken my accusation seriously. I am saved from a beating.

My mother struggled with learning English. She found the language perplexing, and often her pronunciations and juxtapositions were embarrassing, like 'Christmas Father' and 'centre shopping'. Communications between school and home gave rise to bizarre situations. We children were asked to bring in a saucer and cotton wool in which we were to plant seeds. Both my mother and I figured out that a saucer must be a saucepan. To be on the safe side (and to make matters worse), my mother gave me one of her large saucepans. I toddled off to school with this ungainly object. When the teacher asked us to put out our saucers and I saw the dainty little receptacles emerge from schoolbags, I didn't have the heart to plonk the unwieldy pot on the desk. I kept it on the floor, wishing I could make it disappear. When the teacher asked where my saucer was I felt sick and pointed miserably to the offending pot. I joined in with the ensuing hilarity.

Another time we were asked to bring some felt to school with needle and embroidery thread. I didn't know what felt was, so rather than ask and expose myself as a dumb New Australian, I went home and looked up a dictionary. Under 'felt' it said 'carpet'. So my poor mother put on her coat, caught a bus into town and found a carpet shop. She was a bit worried because it was expensive, but as she wanted me to get on well at school she went ahead and bought a square yard. Again, embarrassment and humiliation suffused my being when everybody else produced a small square of soft felt and I my large square of thick carpet.

For some odd reason that escapes me to this day, the teacher made me cut up the carpet into small pieces. I then had to try to embroider one such piece. I couldn't even get the needle through the thickness of the pile. Every day, it seemed, my mother would ask me about the carpet and I would lie, saying I would bring it home at the end of term. At school I would struggle trying to embroider the ridiculous pieces. As the end of term approached I became more and more panic-stricken. This featured in my prayers every night for weeks. The fateful last day arrived. I walked home with a bag full of carpet pieces and bent needles.

A small miracle saved me. I always walked down a narrow lane between the barbed wire fence of the large Phillips factory and the backyards of the houses on Pudney Street, one of which contained a bulldog farm. Every time I walked past, a bunch of ugly snarling bulldogs would rush at the fence. I had just managed to run the gauntlet of the bulldogs and was worrying about how to explain about the bits of carpet to my mother when a little voice piped up from the hedge, 'Hullo, Joey. Hullo, would you like a cup of tea?' I looked around, and there sitting on a branch was the most delightful little budgerigar that I'd ever seen. Its feathers were a brilliant and subtle mixture of blues. I can still see it sitting there looking at me expectantly. It flew on to my shoulder and accompanied me home. My mother was sufficiently smitten by this small bird and its huge repertoire of amusing sayings that she totally forgot about the carpet. No one ever claimed Joey, and he brought great happiness into our lives before he disappeared again a few months later.

My mother continued to be unable to cope with the baby, so she acquired live-in help. The first lady was an angel. Mrs Myrtle O'Donnell was a widow of seventy and had the most beautiful, kind face, framed by a cloud of white hair. We all crowded into one room so that Mrs O'Donnell could have the front room. I loved Mrs O'Donnell so much that I couldn't bear it when we had to part company at night to go to bed. I would creep into the hallway and watch her through the key hole. She would undress herself, and I saw her white wrinkled bottom as she sat on a chamber pot. I didn't care. I just worshipped the ground she walked on. She protected me against my mother and was incredibly kind. She would read to me and brush my hair, oh, so gently, and tell me how beautiful I was. She had a large trunk in her room full of her treasures which every now and then she would show to me. They were keepsakes, mementoes and photographs of her family and I loved to hear about them. One of her prized possessions was a glossy book of photographs of Queen Elizabeth's visit to Australia in 1954. I had gone with my school to see the Queen ride past in an open car with the Duke. I adored the Queen and really loved poring over this book.

Unfortunately, the idyll of this angel living in our house was short-lived. My mother began to have screaming rows with Mrs O'Donnell. About what I do not know, but the tragic upshot of it was that finally Olga threw Mrs O'Donnell out. I don't know who was more devastated, her or me. The leave-taking was heartbreaking, but she never said an unkind word about my mother. Before she left she gave me the beautiful book of the Queen and other treasures from her trunk. Several years later when my mother was diagnosed as mentally ill, I sought Mrs O'Donnell out. She was frail and died soon afterwards. What I remember most was the depth of compassion she expressed towards my mother.

Olga shouted away a succession of live-in helps and it became more crucial to find people to look after us. There were times when she just couldn't cope and started screaming. It seemed to be worse when she menstruated. I didn't really understand what menstruation was and was often shocked with the sight of blood dripping down her legs. Once it got so bad I had to run to our neighbours, the Tylers, who lived several hundred yards away and ask for help. To do this I had to take the back road past a crowd of commuters waiting for the train. On this particular morning I was barefoot and still in my night-dress. I just ran, the hot shame and humiliation spurring me on past what felt like hundreds of pairs of eyes piercing my vulnerability. When would this nightmare end?

5 / **Glimmer of Hope**

Sasha was steadily becoming more prosperous but the double shifts at Holden's were taking their toll. 'Slave labour' he called it. As an oxy-welder, he worked on a production line of eight men for sixteen hours a day. The management arranged that alternate slots on the line were filled with fast workers to ensure that the slower workers between them kept up the pace. Sasha, being the super hard worker of all time, was always in slot two, four, six or eight. After five years, this unremitting, mind-numbing routine was beginning to destroy him. He wanted out, and he would discuss various business ideas with Kurt Weiss, his old buddy from his wheeler-dealer days in Austria.

Once Kurt brought over his father, who was visiting from Germany. I was fascinated by this dapper old gentleman as I had been sworn to secrecy not to tell a soul that he had been a high-ranking member of the Nazi Party. I knew that Nazis were bad because they had killed off Dad's family. It intrigued me that Dad was so friendly towards someone who had condoned the murder of his parents yet shunned my mother's Ukrainian friends.

Dad and Kurt Weiss wanted to start a business together but any attempts to do so disintegrated into a power struggle, the last one over whether to call their new enterprise 'Weiss and Levkowicz' or 'Levkowicz and Weiss'. Dad also disapproved of Kurt's constant womanising and felt very sorry for Katherina, who had recently given birth to a son. Eventually Dad decided to strike out on his own. He had his eye on a newly built delicatessen about three miles away in the suburb of Woodville Gardens. The snag was that he did not have enough capital to start up the business. Salvation came from a surprising source. My mother had worked occasionally as a domestic for Mrs Fricker, a rich widow who took a great deal of interest in our family. She inspired my love for reading by passing on stacks of books that had belonged to her grandchildren. She loaned my father £300 with which he acquired the delicatessen.

Life changed substantially. Mum and Dad would now regularly disappear off on their bicycles, farming us children out to a succession of neighbours. Val, despite her chaotic mothering, was developing into a delightful child who sang beautifully, was very funny and good company. The excitement of the new shop and the lucrative business it engendered cheered up both my parents, especially my mother. Within three months, Mrs Fricker was surprised to get her money back with interest.

Although the hours were long and the work was hard, it suited Olga as she had another avenue into which to direct her energies. It also appealed to her gregarious nature to chat to and serve the constant stream of people who came into our shop. For me it meant an unprecedented amount of joyous freedom. Our care was divided between a German couple, newly moved in up the road, and the Tylers, a staunchly Methodist family. The German couple were very easy-going, and their son Charlie and I would run wild around the neighbourhood, often until after ten at night.

The Tylers were a different kettle of fish. Mr and Mrs Tyler were an unlikely couple. She, large and stout, dominated the household, with traces of self-righteousness and self-sacrifice lingering wherever she plodded. He, small and frail with huge fogged-up, horn-rimmed spectacles, worked in the meat department at Myer's department store in central Adelaide. Every Saturday, it seemed, he would have a terrible migraine and have to lie in a darkened room. They had had their son, Graham, late in life, and Mrs Tyler always feared for his future in case she or her husband should die. Mrs Tyler's attitude to me and my family was decidedly hostile. She bitterly resented that we New Australians should come over to Australia and do as well as we were doing, while her family struggled on the small wage that cost her husband a weekly migraine. She looked after Val and me adequately but never let us forget what a sacrifice she was making.

I believe that my parents paid her well and my mother was very generous with gifts and extra money. Every Sunday, for example, Graham's cousin would drive over and take the Tylers, including us children, to Mrs Tyler's family for the day. Even though this was only two to three miles away, my mother would give him ten shillings for the petrol, far in excess of what it actually cost. As it was for a journey that the Tylers were making anyway, I minded terribly each time the cousin just took the money. My mother didn't know how much petrol cost, and every time she said, 'I hope this is enough', he would assure her smarmily, 'This should cover it.'

If I feel bitter about anything, it is about people taking advantage of my mother's generosity. She was generous to a fault and believed that if she had fortune she should share it with others. One Easter we were walking around exchanging chocolate eggs with neighbours. We were at the Tyler's back gate after such an exchange when a bunch of small boys came up to us looking longingly at my mother's basket of chocolate eggs. They were from the poor Pearson family whose six boys were always dressed in ragged clothes. Unhesitatingly my mother reached into her basket and gave out some eggs, unwittingly including the Easter present that Graham Tyler had just given me. Mrs Tyler let out a strangled sob and ran weeping into her house. Graham, looking suitably mortified, followed. My mother stood there incredulous, wondering what she had done.

Later, when my mother had gone off to the shop, Mrs Tyler didn't fail to let me know the source of her grievance. 'Graham saved up all month for that Easter egg and your mother just gave it away to those undeserving brats. How insensitive! How could she do that to poor Graham?'

Sundays, bloody Sundays! We had to suffer the Tylers' morbid relatives and Methodist Sunday school. Mrs Tyler's aged father was looked after by the pious Margaret, a fortyish spinster, and her brother Fred, bald, cross-eyed and a bit odd. We had to be terribly quiet in their house because all were devout Methodists and regarded Sunday as the Lord's day of prayer. The old boy insisted that I sat on his lap at every available opportunity, and the whole family would frown every time I giggled and shrieked. What they didn't know was that the giggling was an hysterical cover up on my part to avoid letting on what their pious old father was doing under my dress.

I hate Sunday afternoons. This horrible house with its atmosphere of unpious sanctimony. Oh no, the old man is leering at me and beckoning with his gnarled fingers.

'Hello, Eva, come and sit on my lap, there's a pet.'

'No,' I squirm uncomfortably, 'I'm happy sitting over here.'

'Go on, Eva, keep Grand-dad happy,' commands Mrs Tyler, settling her bulky form into an armchair. I dutifully sit on his lap and then it starts; the tickling! But it's just a cover for the gnarled fingers to make their way underneath my dress and into my underpants. I squeal and squirm and try to unsuccessfully wriggle myself away from the offending, probing, lascivious fingers.

An alternative scenario could have been:

We are all in the starched living room. I can see the old boy leering at me and patting his lap. Reluctantly I go over and sit on that lap. Next minute:

'You filthy old bugger! Get your bony fingers out of my dickie!'

Shock and horror freeze the room into glass. Fred giggles hysterically. Margaret has a stroke. Mrs Tyler implodes and Graham rushes out of the room crying.

Unfortunately in real life this doesn't happen. Anyone who has suffered sexual abuse knows the shame and torture that I was going through when an adult stepped across that sacrosanct line. Why was I protecting the old man? I think that instinctively I knew that such a sordid and shocking truth would tear the whole facade of that family apart and too many ugly worms would crawl out from under the stones, so carefully laid down to present a veneer of staid Methodist respectability. I didn't have to squirm away from the prying fingers for too much longer, though, for the old man died soon afterwards.

Mrs Tyler continually berated me for my appearance. I had very long hair which was braided unfashionably in two plaits. All the other little girls who went to Methodist Sunday school had short bobbed hair, and wore white frilly dresses and short white socks with shiny, patent-leather court shoes. My mother, who was still smarting from the torn raincoat episode, went through a phase of buying me very plain practical dresses which I wore with sensible lace-up boots. To my mind I stood out like a clumsy New Australian, awkward and gauche, and looking like I had just come from working in the fields. I badly wanted to be like the other girls, and thus the comments Mrs Tyler constantly fired at me pained me greatly. I would implore my mother to allow me to cut my hair. She staunchly refused. Keeping my hair in long plaits was one link she could maintain with the old country. Oddly enough, she was totally the opposite with my sister. She kept her hair cropped really short, which made Val miserable because she thought she looked like a boy.

◆

The delicatessen was a financial success and within a year a big surprise arrived in the back drive: a 1954 FJ Holden. My father's pride and joy. It was a real achievement to have such a car in those days; hardly any of our neighbours owned one. In fact, the Pounds next-door only had enough money to build the back half of their house first, a common feature of the poorer suburbs of 1950s Adelaide. The path of making it in a new country was sealed when Sasha, Olga and I became Australian citizens. My father also bought a block of land behind the shop and started to plan the building of our new dream home.

This pleased my mother to a certain extent, but deep down she was not happy. When I was ten she went through a particularly bad patch and gave us all hell. She particularly resented my father and the time he spent in the delicatessen. She was restless, wild even. I often woke at night to her screaming uncontrollably at my father. I found these episodes agonising as I felt so helpless. One night there was blood all over the house and the doctor was called. I didn't know what was going on, but there was a lot of whispering behind closed doors. I eavesdropped and overheard the doctor say, 'Well, I'm afraid you've lost the baby.' Later I saw my father scoop up what appeared to be a large bloody liver off the sofa and put it in the rubbish bin.

Olga would sometimes have strange spells of feeling faint. She worked less and less in the shop. Often she would accuse me of betraying her and the inexplicable beatings would start up all over again. I remember not receiving any birthday presents for my eleventh birthday because of some betrayal that I was supposed to have committed. Dad felt sorry for me and slipped me a couple of books as he knew I loved reading.

Approaching my twelfth birthday, we moved into our brand new house in Essex Street, Woodville Gardens. My mother insisted on all the most expensive fixtures and fittings, furniture and carpets.

My father reluctantly obliged her and no expense was spared in creating a luxurious house. Life was supposed to be better from now on because the shop was only a few minutes away and my father could come home for lunch and spend more time with the family. But the new house was like a mausoleum.

My mother's behaviour became worse. She would often go into my father's shop, open the till and throw the money everywhere. 'What good is all this money?' she would scream. 'It's destroying my soul.' She would then go on a rampage and start throwing cigarettes and bars of chocolate from the neatly stacked shelves. She began to get the reputation among our customers of being 'as mad as a hatter'. My father would just set his jaw and do what he always did when things were tough: eat garlic. Not just one or two cloves but several heads. Stank the shop out!

Mum's rages became worse and worse, and she would regularly throw tantrums and hurl things at Dad. Only once did I see him become violent and strike back. He beat her black and blue. He just suddenly blew and started bashing her and swearing, 'You bloody fuckin' bitch. You are fuckin' ruinink my life. I wish you were fuckin' dead!' Aghast, I stood watching, not knowing what to do. At times like these I would envy Val, who would run to her bed, block her ears and sing loudly to drown it all out. Sometimes it was Chief, our Alsatian dog, who offered the only solace as I buried my head in his furry chest.

At about this time Mum begged Sasha to take a holiday with her. He loved his shop and hated the thought of leaving it. Half a day off on Christmas Day was as much as he could manage, so he refused. But he did pay for her to go on an expensive holiday to Surfer's Paradise. She was very excited about this, and as I helped her pack some beautiful dresses, I was struck by how desperately sad it was that she was going alone.

When she returned she had a strange glint in her eye and looked happier than she had in years. As she unpacked her things in the shiny new bedroom, she called me in saying she had some very serious things to tell me.

'Eva, I want to tell you many things. The first is that I've fallen in love with another man and I'm going to leave Sasha and start a new life. I also want to tell you that Sasha is not your real father. We left your real father behind in Czechoslovakia. His name was

Ludvig Krakov. He was the son of wealthy people who I had been working for as a maid. It was impossible.'

She said all these things very calmly. She was the most lucid and bright I had seen her in years. The fact that Sasha wasn't my real father was a great shock to me. In my mind I had totally forgotten we had met him on the migrant ship. As far as I was concerned he was my real dad, and I was torn apart to hear this news.

My mother went on, 'What I have to say to you, Eva, is very hard for me. I know I have been very terrible to you. I'm very sorry for all the times I have beaten you. I regret it terribly and wish that I hadn't been like that to you.'

I looked into my mother's dear face. I forgave her immediately. I didn't care what had happened in the past. I adored having my mother back. She was really present, very real and glowing with new determination. I loved her so much and was struck by the new strength she seemed to be displaying. I wondered who this man was that she had fallen in love with, but did not dare ask. I felt great changes afoot but was afraid as well as hopeful.

What happened after that is a blur. There were huge rows with my father. Once he emerged from the bedroom with a bleeding forehead where she had struck him. I remember the doctor coming back and forth and overheard snippets of his saying things such as 'But why aren't you happy? You have a good husband, two beautiful children and a wonderful new house!' He prescribed tranquillisers and left. He also prescribed cold baths, which she loathed. Would they really make an unhappy person feel better?

I valiantly tried to adapt to being at my new high school, but as I struggled to cope, I kept having accidents such as breaking my wrist and cutting open my foot. The next thing I knew my mother had had a 'nervous breakdown' and was in a private mental hospital. Val and I were shipped off to the Tylers. I slept in the dining room next to the waxed eggs, stacked neatly in buckets. All the adults around me shook their heads and said they knew all along that it would come to this. Something had always been amiss with that Olga. Not quite right, never had been. I watched it all like a slow motion movie unfolding before my eyes.

I observed that not one of these so-called 'friends' went to visit her or tried to talk to her. I remembered my mother's generous gifts to all of them. Never had she visited any of these people empty-handed. It was always an expensive pair of gloves or a leg of good ham or a delicious cream cake. As I realised later, people stayed away in fear. Nervous disorders were little understood at the time. The human being that my mother was, was ignored. She was drowning in a sea of ignorance and drugs.

I visited her several times in the private hospital, which my father never failed to inform me was so excruciatingly expensive. It seemed a nice place with lots of plush sofas and immaculate nurses in white uniforms, who dispensed pills like sweets to children at a carnival. Our conversations were stilted and sometimes she just cried quietly and swallowed some more pills. The man she had supposedly fallen in love with was never mentioned again.

After a few months my father refused to pay any more private hospital fees and she was put into a state mental hospital. Her dream of a rosier future slipped into a forgotten furrow of time never to be realised by the young woman from Poltava with the laughing, grey-green eyes.

6 / **Falling Down**

'Somebody help me!' she screams to the dark street. Silence. No one, not even God, heeds her heartrending cry into the Australian night. The starry dome above offers no warmth. She stands forlorn at our front gate. I watch helplessly as Dad puts a light hand on her arm and leads her to the car.

It is the usual Sunday evening scenario in our family life: getting Mum back to the loony bin at the end of the weekend. Tonight has been relatively easy. Often she runs down the street screaming and Dad has to get into the car and drive after her, then play cat and mouse with her as she hides in the bushes. The neighbours keep well behind their curtains, pursing their lips. Other times a psychiatric nurse has to come in an ambulance and put a straight jacket on her, or inject her with something that makes her compliant.

But the worst time, the time that will always be etched on my brain, was when I had to accompany her in the back of a police car. That night my mother was acting up worse than usual, screaming and causing such terrible havoc that my father had to call the police. She saw the police car and tried to run up the street again. I caught her and grabbed her arm.

'Come on, Mum, come on, it's time to go.'

I manoeuvred her into the back of the police vehicle and off we drove. The two policemen in the front were smirking and joking about 'this right old loony' in the car, oblivious to the life and death struggle that was developing on the back seat. As we sped through the quiet Sunday night streets of Adelaide, Mum was opening the back door and trying to jump out. I, using every muscle in my body, was trying to drag her back in. She even managed to hang half way out of the car, inches from the spinning road underneath, me grasping her legs. With superhuman strength I pulled her back into the car. While this gargantuan battle was underway behind them, the policemen continued blithely to joke in the front seat, ignoring what was happening.

It all comes back to me vividly as I sit here writing, and I sweat even now as I remember that awful night. I wonder why I struggled so hard to save her life. Wouldn't it have been better to have let her jump out? Wouldn't it have saved her years and years of abject misery as she graduated from drugs to electro-shock therapy to the queen of psychiatric surgery, lobotomy? Wouldn't life have been so much easier for me? While other teenagers lived happy carefree lives (or so I imagined), my teenage years were dominated by visits to the mental hospital during the week and heart-wrenching weekends when Mum came home. Her happiness on arrival soon slipped into deeper and deeper melancholy as Sunday night approached.

The mental hospital she was so intent on not going back to was a daunting Victorian edifice in a leafy part of Adelaide. When I was a child it had a horrendous reputation. Parkside Lunatic Asylum was used continually in jokes. 'Oh, you belong in Parkside!' was a favourite put down. In the 1960s, the twelve-foot-high walls came down, except for those around the maximum security wing at the back. After the facelift it was renamed Glenside Hospital. My mother lived in Paterson House, one of two reception wards at the front of the hospital, modern low-rise brick buildings surrounded by grass and flower beds. Here people passed the time playing cards, yellowing their fingers with incessant smoking, and dutifully imbibing powerful cocktails of what are now called the 'first wave' of psychotropic drugs. Somehow these were supposed to unhinge the delusions that wrapped sinuously around their brains.

The drugs didn't do anything of the sort for my mother. In fact, her delusions got worse. She would have conversations with voices that told her she shouldn't have married a Jew, or that my father was having sex with me, or that she should give all her money to the starving. Were they even delusions? I would often get confused.

Occasionally my mother would be allowed out for a few weeks at a time, especially when she seemed to be behaving herself or was so dosed up with a variety of whatever drugs were in vogue then that she sat around like a large docile cow. Her once slim and attractive figure had ballooned outwards as a result of the drugs and starchy hospital food.

Her mental state continued to disintegrate. She became convinced that 'They' were persecuting her. 'They' came around at night and flashed blinding lights at the window of the spare room in our house where she slept. (Voices had told her she must not sleep with the Jew.) To escape from these lights, she often dragged her bed into the hallway where there were no windows. There was never any question of me bringing friends home because it was impossible to explain why there was a bed in the hallway. (Don't all households have mad mothers who have to sleep in the hallway to get away from persecuting lights?)

Once, when I was about fourteen years old, she was so persistent about this story that she convinced me to go with her to the Adelaide police station to report the persecutors. Off we went by bus to Victoria Square in central Adelaide where the police building, a tall glass structure, loomed over the southern end. As we approached the impersonal reception desk, I knew in my heart that this was a doomed and hopeless expedition.

'Excuse me,' I began, 'we need to talk to someone about people shining lights in at our windows at home.'

The policeman at the reception desk blinked at me. 'I beg ya pardon, love?'

'Oh, um ... well, you see, there's these people that come to our house at night and shine lights in at the window.' I faltered thinking how crazy this sounded already. My mother nodded encouragingly at the police officer. Her command of English was still pretty slender and she always had a touching faith that I could be her mouthpiece in public situations.

The policeman, looking somewhat dubious, rang through to various departments. Eventually we were sent up to the eighth floor to see a detective. I was very nervous, thinking the whole thing utter madness. But the determination on my mother's face flipped me around, and for a fleeting moment I felt hopeful. Perhaps there really were lunatics who persecuted hapless Russian refugees. In the early days we migrants were always being warned about communists under the bed, and there were stories about communists who had pursued escaped Russians half way round the world. Hadn't Stalin's henchmen tracked Trotsky down somewhere in South America and hacked him to death? Perhaps my mother had something to be paranoid about. Perhaps 'They' were really out there; the police would find them, lock them up and my mother would be happy again.

We knocked at the door. 'Come in,' said a cool voice.

I was shocked to discover that the detective was a woman and not at all what I was expecting. She was in her thirties, incredibly glamorous and with a dark, sleek haircut. Her nails were very long, very manicured and very red, just like her lips.

'Yes, and what can I do for you?' she asked crisply, looking at me and then at my mother.

My mother, feeling encouraged that we had got to see a detective, launched into her story in her broken English. I sat and squirmed uncomfortably. After about two minutes, when she had barely got to the important part, the detective lit a cigarette, turned to me and spoke as if Mum was not even in the room.

'You're mother is as nutty as a fruitcake and this is wasting my time. She doesn't need me. She needs a doctor. I've got better things to do.'

I felt sick. 'Look, she thinks people are shining lights at her, and do you think you could possibly just send a patrol car to check? It would really help.' I was desperate.

But the detective was not listening any more. The brightness of the sky through all the glass blinded me. The cold light of day splintered any illusion that there was help anywhere in this impersonal glass jungle. I quickly ushered my bewildered mother out of the room, down the lift and across Victoria Square, humiliation beating at me the whole way.

'What did she say? What are the police going to do?' my mother kept asking.

'They will send a patrol car at night,' I lied.

For a few nights I forced myself to stay awake and watch out. These vigils played havoc with trying to understand French and maths at school, but I was full of resolve that I could convince my mother that she was not being persecuted. I told her next day that I had kept watch and there were no lights. She did not believe me.

I tried a different tactic. I gathered a big pile of pebbles and arranged them in a precise pattern on the concrete path outside the spare room window. I showed her this pattern. Next morning I took her out to see if the stones had been disturbed. They had not. I did this for a few days. I calmly and logically explained to her that here was objective evidence that no one was coming up to the window and shining lights in. She would listen to what I had to say with a glazed expression and look vacantly at the undisturbed stones, but nothing seemed to sink in. I did not know then that rational argument would never work; that she was victim of past nightmares that crashed into her present with terrifying reality; that she believed she could never escape the 1949 border guards with their blinding searchlights.

And so Mum sank further into insanity. Her stays at the hospital became more frequent. One day I went to visit her at Paterson House and she wasn't there. 'She's been transferred,' they said, but no one knew where. With sinking heart I crossed over to the central reception area situated under the massive clock tower that dominated the front of the main building.

'I'm looking for my mother, Olga Levkowicz. She's supposed to be in Paterson House, but I can't find her.' I purposefully kept the panic out of my voice, praying that there had been a mistake and she might still be there. The alternative was too hard to bear. While she was in Paterson House, there was still hope. People were known to leave Paterson House and go back into the world. Although disturbed, people in Paterson House were not regarded as chronic. There were parties at Paterson House—grim parties, a few patients shuffling about to music played badly on the piano in the main lounge, but parties nonetheless. People still wore their own clothes in Paterson House.

As if on cue, I saw two straggly lines of women in nondescript hospital clothes shuffling past, the gloom of early evening closing in. I watched the troupe dully, hoping that this was not to be the fate of my mother, at the same time keeping an anxious eye on the receptionist who was still unable to find out what had happened to Olga Levkowicz. Then I saw her. She was at the back of the line of grey women. I could hardly distinguish her from the others. Despair cracked my soul.

Nooooooooo!

My silent scream shattered the universe. This was the end of the line. We had been through so much, she and I, and now she was gone. Our journey together was broken. She had succumbed to the forces of darkness. Some nameless doctor, or panel of doctors, had decided her fate. The jaws of the hospital had clamped over her. She was now an inmate. And very few of those ever came out.

She suddenly saw me.

'Eva!' She tottered towards me, her face beaming with happiness as she held out her arms, arms swathed in shapeless Salvation Army garb.

'Mum, what are you doing here? You don't belong here. Why aren't you in Paterson House? Where are your own clothes?'

'Ah, Olga Levkowicz,' the receptionist's voice cut in from behind, 'she's been transferred to Ward C.'

'But why?' I whip around. 'Who said?'

The receptionist shrugged and turned away. A psychiatric nurse in charge of the motley band came over and led my mother back to the line.

I stood there and the loneliness and darkness opened up like a chasm before me. The once vivacious Olga, gaiety shining out of her eyes, resumed her place in the line and stumbled away into the darkness. *You're leaving me,* I moaned inwardly. *Don't leave me!* I was bereft. My companion on the long journey we had begun when we had escaped from Czechoslovakia in 1949 was disappearing into the shadows of the mentally insane.

Vivid parts of our journey flashed before my eyes. Sheer terror in a dark forest. Roaring motorbikes. Lights flooding the blackness. An urgent 'Shhh!' as a hand clamped down on me. Where were we? Why were we here? Menacing border guards. Bad men. We might be killed. Endless walking. Safety. Freedom. A long train journey. A sea of triple iron bunks. Falling down. (I fingered the scar on my head where I had hit the concrete.) Endless hot days on a ship. Sweat. Heat. Leaning on Sasha. Australia at last. A tearful goodbye to Sasha. Train. Migrant camp. Waiting. Narrandera. Adelaide.

It had been a long, fraught journey all that way from Prague, and we had been on it together.

These memories flashed through my mind as I watched Olga shuffle off to Ward C. Was this her fate? After Hitler, Stalin and thousands of weary miles tinged with hope, was the end of the line to be a grey, hopeless ward in a grim mental hospital in the south of a vast continent, thousands of miles from anywhere? Our journey together was over. She had entered a world where I could not go. The attractive, enthusiastic young woman who had dazzled all the jackeroos within fifty miles of Narrandera was gone.

I had lost her.

7 / **Descent into Hell**

Terrible it is to die in chains
And in captivity
But worse it is to be free
And forever in oblivion be
Taras Schevchenko

The back wards of Glenside were pretty grim in the early 1960s. Ward C, my mother's first port of call, was decidedly so. To get there, I had to walk right around the left side of the hospital towards the nether regions of the grounds, past what I can only describe as large pens full of demented, lost souls. Old women would run at me as I walked past and claw at me through the chicken wire, trying to snatch a piece of human contact.

Ward C was where they housed old women who weren't dangerous. The most obvious distinguishing feature was an ancient outside staircase that wound around a kind of tower, four storeys high. I didn't really understand why my mother, still in her thirties, was in such an awful place. It smelled disgusting, and hopelessness hung like a pall over every surface. Women with faded grey hair shuffled up and down the staircase despondently. Once when I brought Mum some bananas, a demonic woman rushed up to me, grabbed one and shoved it in her mouth, eating it skin and all.

Often when I visited, Mum had just come out of shock therapy and would be extremely disorientated, dribbling badly and not able to coordinate her limbs. I wasn't quite sure what this electro-convulsive therapy was, but it seemed all the rage in those days and was hailed as a miracle cure. I would hear from nurses and doctors that it was supposed to be doing her good, but I instinctively recoiled from the idea of it. I could only see my once beautiful mother disappearing behind grey twitching skin, a foaming mouth and eyes without lustre.

Somehow, though, her spirit was not yet broken. We were informed one day that she had escaped from Ward C and that the police were looking for her. Everyone was so concerned. How would she cope? What would she eat? But inwardly I was exhilarated. *Good on ya!* I secretly cheered.

Inevitably her freedom was short-lived. She was picked up soon afterwards and was put into Ward K, a high security ward. This was where the dangerous people were incarcerated. Visitors had to go through various checkpoints to make sure we weren't bringing in anything that inmates could use to harm themselves or each other. All the knives were locked away and food was eaten with inoffensive spoons. For a while after her escape, Mum was kept locked in a small cell and the drug dosage and shock treatments were stepped up. When I eventually did see her, she was like a demented wild animal. She grabbed me and implored, 'Eva, you have to get me out of this hell. They're trying to poison me. I'll never get out of here. Help me!' I felt helpless and hopeless. On one level I knew she was right. She was in hell. She was being 'poisoned' with a lethal cocktail of drugs. The doctors and nurses told me she was getting worse. 'She even thinks we are trying to poison her and refuses to take her medication. We have to force it down her or inject her!'

By now my mother had been officially diagnosed as a paranoid schizophrenic. As she sank further into darkness, I sank further into despair. Sometimes when I visited her she would physically attack me and accuse me of being part of 'Them'—those people who were out to destroy her. I realise now she was right. I was conspiring with everybody to keep her there. We were the 'healthy ones'. We 'knew' what we were doing, with our regime of padded cells, straight jackets, capsules, injections and electro-convulsive therapy. But at the time this perspective was not formulated in my mind. I didn't really understand what was happening. I was in awe of the important-looking psychiatrists who seemed to have endless case conferences. I felt crushed and hopeless at the swelling mass of mad humanity that clung to the shiny green walls of the endless echoing corridors. I would watch people who seemed to be prisoners of long lost scenarios in which they had been physically or psychologically defeated endlessly trying to resurrect and resolve them. They would have the same arguments over and over again for years and years, haranguing an invisible audience that had long forgotten their existence.

I would watch nurses bathing the inmates' sallow, lifeless bodies before putting them into their grey, shapeless clothes. I would often come out of Ward K and not want to leave the hospital grounds and go back to 'normal' reality. Something about the place held me in its thrall. I was witnessing so many horrible, crazy scenes that it didn't seem possible to return to normality. On these days I would wander into the bowels of the mental hospital, wondering what lay in store for Olga after she disintegrated further and got too bad for Ward K. I saw cages where old men crawled and twitched in dark corners. I saw large pens where hideously disfigured and mentally retarded vegetable-type people tried to eke out some sort of God-forsaken existence. I would come away dreadfully shaken by what I saw.

I wanted to make sense of it all so started spending a lot of time in various Adelaide libraries, searching through ancient books about mental illness. It made depressing reading: endless dusty tomes about dementia praecox and schizophrenia. These mental illnesses were definitely hereditary according to these books. Offspring had a fifty per cent chance of succumbing and even grandchildren couldn't escape. These books were written in the 1930s, but contemporary ones offered little solace with their mechanistic approach and emphasis on different combinations of drugs, shock treatment and psychosurgery.

I scrutinised myself for signs of mental illness. Was I being paranoid? Were people laughing at me? I tried to hide the twisted pain that swirled in my intestines. I developed twitches around my face. With rising panic I fought to keep my face straight and appear normal. I developed debilitating migraines where half of people's faces would disappear. The middle of the blind spot would unfurl into a zigzagging arc of frenzied light. At its peak I would vomit violently. I worried myself sick that I was on the way to becoming mentally ill and any future children had little chance of escape. No one would marry me because I had a mad mother. It seemed even more imperative that I keep her a deep, dark secret.

However, I did have one friend to whom I could tell everything. Luda's family was equally bizarre. Her parents were highly creative people from the Soviet Union whose talents and careers had been blighted by World War Two. Her mother, Yevgenia, had been an opera singer and her father, Ivan, a talented painter. After being thrown about Europe by events beyond their control, they had ended up in Royal Park, a refugee suburb of Adelaide. Not being able to pursue their chosen careers they both took on labouring jobs—Yevgenia at the Phillips factory which, in conjunction with Holden, employed large chunks of the migrant population.

Life was frustrating and their creative energy became highly destructive. Luda witnessed dreadful rows, and as a seven-year-old was faced with the horrifying spectacle of Ivan trying to chop her mother's head off with an axe. It was only Luda throwing herself between them that stopped a brutal murder. After that her father would do strange things like threaten to hang himself at her birthday parties. Eventually her parents separated, and Ivan moved to a dark little house in Rosewater, another migrant suburb in the north-west of Adelaide.

Luda and I would visit him occasionally. It was a scary experience. All his living room walls were covered in giant oil paintings, each depicting a version of Ivan the Terrible, a mad sixteenth-century Russian Czar, bludgeoning his son to death. We were assailed by these vivid, disturbing canvases, splattered with crazy staring eyes and bright red blood, as we sipped black tea. Ivan himself looked like his namesake Czar in the pictures. What ghastly stuff was in his head, I wondered? Luda told me that he had fought in the Red Army, but when forced to be a spy on his fellow soldiers, he had refused and was thrown into prison. Here he was treated worse than a dog so made a hair-raising escape and defected to the Germans. Now he lived alone, haunted by the past. He had a cachet of guns and was suspicious of everybody. From behind the curtains he would train a rifle on a stranger who might be straying too close to the front fence.

Luda's mother was crazy as well. She was cruel to Luda and her younger brother, Peter. It would be either physical, when she would try to twist Peter's fingers off, or mental, when she would harangue Luda for hours about trivia. Luda felt her mother pulverised her emotionally into mincemeat.

When Luda was about seventeen she got fed up and went to live with her father. This didn't last long. One evening she came running to our place, trembling and terrified. She had tried to open the gate to Ivan's house but noticed it was all chained up, dark and barricaded. She climbed over, but as she neared the house something made her very wary. She called out a couple of times but there was no reply. Then she heard the unmistakable sound of a rifle click. She turned tail and ran.

All this was pretty horrifying, but on the other hand it did give me comfort. I felt I had a true friend who knew what it was like to come from a mad family. Luda and I helped each other to cope and to stay sane. We kept our sanity by laughing a lot, sharing the most bizarre and ludicrous sense of humour. School teachers would be driven to distraction by our classroom giggling. Everything seemed to be enormously funny, and being told off or sent out made it even funnier. Looking back I see it was a very valuable safety valve.

The years rolled on. The diet of drugs and shock therapy rendered my mother a compliant vegetable. As a result, weekends at home became more frequent, and she would meekly return to her prison on a Sunday evening. She was slipping more and more into psychosis. She still fervently believed 'They' (or as she pronounced it, 'dhey') were out to get her. She was Queen of Australia and 'They' had it in for her. She was too rich and above herself and 'They' hated her. She had married a Jew and 'They' had punished her.

One night I woke up and heard her creaking up and down the hallway. On investigation I saw that she was carrying bowls of water and putting one under each leg of her bed. Aghast, I demanded, 'Mum, what for God's sake are you doing?' She went on mechanically doing the task as if she had been programmed. When she had put the last bowl of water under the last bed leg, she said, 'Dhey are tryink to electrocute me and I been told dhis is dhe only way I can save my life.' She then got into bed and prepared for sleep.

I went back to my own bed feeling highly disturbed because it seemed that my mother was well and truly mad and there was nothing I could do about it. When I look back on her behaviour now, however, it makes sense to me. She was really trying to save her life. During shock therapy, she was strapped to a bed and electrocuted. As a new migrant she had been told over and over again, 'Beware of communists under your bed!' The Soviet Union was punishing her by barring us from Russian ships. She would accuse Sasha and me constantly of working for 'Them', often in bizarre ways. She saw me as Debbie Reynolds pretending to be Eva and spying on her in the hope that she could give 'Them' more information. She was right in her world. We were conspiring with the psychiatrists to keep her in her hell.

When I was sixteen my mother became quite emotional. She would just cry and cry and it would break my heart. She put on more weight, which we attributed to the many drugs she was ingesting. Then one day shortly after my seventeenth birthday she began having severe stomach pains. I telephoned the family doctor, who said he would come as soon as possible.

Over the next hour or two the pains became excruciating. My sister Val and I, together with Fanya, an old lady friend who was visiting, were all really worried and wishing the doctor would hurry. We scoffed when nine-year-old Val said it seemed like Mum was having a baby. My father was busy at the delicatessen. Suddenly at seven in the evening Olga screamed, 'A baby, a baby!' We ran into the bedroom and there on the pink linoleum floor, squirming in a pool of blood, was a baby. My mother, blood all over the front of her dress, was staring at the infant in shock. Fanya scooped the child up in a towel and told me to run and tell my father.

I rushed to the shop, which was a couple of hundred yards away, dashed in and blurted, 'Dad, ring an ambulance, quick! Mum's just had a baby!'

'What ... er, what?' He stared at me in total disbelief. The colour drained from his face and it took him quite a while to collect his thoughts and clumsily make the phone call.

I ran back to the house. My new sister looked like a little angel wrapped in a towel. A single tear glistened below one eye. She seemed fine even though she had been catapulted head first onto the shiny linoleum floor as she entered unexpectedly and unannounced into this world.

The doctor and the ambulance arrived at the same time. The doctor was flabbergasted that my mother had been pregnant all this time. Neither he nor any of the doctors at Glenside had noticed anything different about her. The ambulance took mother and child to hospital leaving my father, sister and me too stunned to even begin contemplating the effects of this sudden new addition to our family.

Olga started out breastfeeding the baby but never connected with her. She regarded the child as an alien being. Eventually Olga was transferred to the psychiatric wing of the maternity hospital as she rejected the baby more and more.

My father and I were summoned to a case conference with my mother and several psychiatrists. Olga announced to the doctors that the baby was an immaculate conception and had been implanted by 'Them'. The long, thick, heavy skirt she wore despite the warm weather was, she told the doctors, protection from being implanted again. Darting terrified looks out of the window, she fearfully pulled the skirt more tightly around her.

Having received this bizarre explanation, the doctors now turned to my father. 'Mr Levkowicz, have you, er, had, er, sexual relations with your wife?'

Sasha, beetroot with embarrassment, opened his goldfish mouth a few times but no words emerged. Olga interjected, poking my arm frantically,

'Say to dhem, Eva, say dhat Sasha and I not sleep togeder five year. Tell to dhem—different bedrooms. Say to dhem I not want dhat Jew near me!'

It was now my turn to be embarrassed, if embarrassed is the right word in this crazy situation. I concur that truth is stranger than fiction. I don't think anyone could ever make up such a scene.

'Well,' I piped in a high, nervous voice, turning towards the psychiatrists, 'it's true that Mum and Dad have slept in different rooms for many years and she has been in hospital for most of that time ...' My voice trailed off. Perhaps it was an immaculate conception after all. I stared dumbly at my mother's thick serge skirt.

My father eventually found a shaky voice. 'Eva, remember when you and Val went away for weekend last May, well, your mahder and I ...'

'Is lie!' screamed Olga. 'Eva, you say to dhem! I not been near Sasha! Say to dhem no period for five years! Tell to doctors everytink! You know!' She looked up at the ceiling in fear, clutching her skirt.

The psychiatrists fixed their attention onto me as if I had all the answers to this perplexing problem. My father looked stricken and his imploring eyes sought out mine. He was trying to tell me, as embarrassing as it was for him, that it was true; he and my mother had done the deed, once. Olga, on the other hand, was adamant that she and my father hadn't had sex for years. It was also true that she hadn't menstruated in a long time. The doctors had previously decided that she had had an early menopause brought on by the regime of drugs. Could it be possible that somehow she had produced one egg in five years and that this unlikely event had somehow coincided with the one time they had had sex? An immaculate conception seemed more probable. And here I was, barely seventeen years old, being asked to adjudicate on what was true.

'Well, if you say so, Dad, when Val and I were away ...' My voice felt weaker and thinner as I betrayed my mother and her thick skirt.

Olga was sent back to Glenside. And the baby, what of the baby? She was a few weeks old by now and utterly adorable. She seemed unscathed by the stunned disbelieving reception she had received upon entry into such a strange family. But who was going to look after her? My mother continued to insist she was an alien and wanted nothing to do with her. I had just begun university and teachers' college. My father worked fourteen hours a day in his shop and Val was a child. We put her in a nursing home for young babies, having called her Alexandra after my grandmother, and visited her several times a week. I would often visit Mum at Glenside and then pop down to the city and see little Alex.

She was the happiest baby I have ever known. The nurses at the home adored her and lavished plenty of attention on her. After a few months we couldn't stand leaving her there any longer. Dad decided to sell his shop and to stay home full-time and look after the baby. The day she came home was wonderful. My father gave her a bath nervously. Was he handling her in the right way? She responded by expelling several little turds which floated around the bath. This caused Dad great consternation, and us great mirth at his attempts to catch the offending pieces of flotsam. Sasha was the model parent. He was so gentle, caring and loving with this tiny motherless thing.

She blossomed. Her cot was in Val's and my bedroom. On waking I would see this bright bubbly little being who would be thrilled to pieces that I had woken up at last. She was like an enormous ray of sunshine that shone into our bleak and fraught lives.

But the sunshine failed to light up Olga's life. She still came home occasionally on weekends, but she treated Alexandra with indifference. Olga had well and truly descended into hell. I became the mother figure to my sister. This was fine in one way but terrible in another. It coincided with my own bid for freedom from the nightmare in which I lived.

8 / 'No Boys!'

'Fanya, you know dhat Sasha and Eva have sex when I in hospital!'

My father went white and clenched his jaw. We were sitting around the table one Saturday lunchtime with Fanya, one of the very few of our old friends who still visited this madhouse. I was shocked and felt badly for Val, who was only ten, and for Alexandra sitting in her high chair.

'God, that's such rubbish, Mum, just shut up!'

Of course it wasn't true. My father would nearly die of embarrassment if I inadvertently caught him half naked in the bathroom. But it is said that schizophrenics do pick up strange truths on other levels. And the truth was that sex was very repressed in our household. My father was the typical immigrant father who forbade me, even as an eighteen-year-old, to have anything to do with boys.

These were the years of *Father Knows Best* on TV, where happy, fresh young fourteen-year-old American girls went out on first dates, sipped colas with boys in milk bars and kissed them on the back seats of cars at the drive-in movies. The irony was that I thought it would be my mother who would be the difficult one. She had been terribly suspicious of me before I'd even developed breasts. From the age of eleven onwards she would accuse me of carryings-on with a variety of people. If I was friendly with the postman and chatted to him too long at the gate, she would remark on my return, 'I know what you do wit' postman.' Once I came out of a photography room in the house of some family friends: 'I know what you do in dark room wit' Dimitri.'

If I put on black drainpipe pants, which were the fashion of the day, she would say disapprovingly, 'You bodgie widgie'. Bodgies were the Australian version of Elvis-quiffed rockers. Widgies were their girlfriends. The widgies hung out in the front of our shop with teased up bleached hair, white faces, black eyes and fags hanging out of gum-chewing mouths, pretending not to care that the black-leathered, foul-mouthed owners of the motorbikes they straddled were ignoring them.

'She want to be bodgie widgie,' Olga would say to some customer in our shop, pointing to my stick-like legs on which even drain pipes looked baggy, and then shake her head and mutter, 'Trouble!' She'd accompany these remonstrations with the mime of a big pregnant belly.

Olga would regularly twist the facts to fit me into whatever lewd picture was running inside her head. She came to see me in a school play where I was playing one of the *Macbeth* witches. Caked in green make-up, nose transformed into a hideous papier-mâché monstrosity and long hair frizzed out in a large, sprayed green halo, I met her and seven-year-old Val in the school library during interval. I looked so dreadful that Val ran out screaming. While my mother and I chatted in the library, some of the other cast came in, including David Galliford, who was playing one of Banquo's men. I introduced them all to my mother. When I got home there was a big scene. 'I know what you do in library with dhat boy!' she screeched. 'I catch you out? No? I know you well!'

No matter how much I protested and tried to tell her the facts as I remembered them, it was to no avail. The image of me getting up to hanky panky wearing a giant papier-mâché nose with a boy barely out of short pants (whom I didn't even fancy; I fancied Ray Wride, who played Macbeth) defies any normal imagination. But then 'normal imagination' didn't get much of a look-in during those crazy years. I was secretly glad when my mother's stays in the mental hospital became longer and longer. It meant she would be out of my hair and I could get on with the serious business of 'Boys!'

Unfortunately, I had not counted on the man who admired Stalin. I had regarded Sasha as a mild-mannered, kindly man who was always working, but who, when around, would protect me from the harsh tantrums of my mother. I now assumed him to be a benign presence who would foster my blossoming into young womanhood. It seemed perfectly natural when I was a fourteen-year-old to present him with a dilemma I was facing. I went to Woodville High School, a respectable school in the western suburbs, which was divided down the middle between the boys and the girls, this boundary being strictly upheld by the teachers. The only time we girls, our growing bosoms straining in our blue-striped uniforms, could see these boys was at the opposite counter in the school tuck shop or outside the gates after school. One boy started smiling at me over the meat pies in the tuck shop and loitered outside the school gate when I wheeled out my bike. He put his hand over mine on the bike handle (flutter, flutter, flushes in strange places!) and asked if he could walk me home.

Afire with confusion, flattery, delicious sensations and shock, I mumbled that I was expected home and shot off on my bike. This was true as my parents still insisted that I come home immediately after school. This put paid to any sports, friends or after-school activities. Rehearsals for *Macbeth* had been reluctantly agreed to after a lot of hoohah because I was studying it for my Intermediate Certificate.

The evening of the 'boy flesh on my hand' episode, I broached the subject with my father. Thankfully this event coincided with one of my mother's stays in the mental hospital.

'Dad, I don't know what to do. There's a boy at school, who doesn't have a bike, who wants to walk home with me. What do you think I should do?'

To my surprise, my father visibly blanched and became quite agitated. You would have thought I had announced that I was pregnant. But then probably that is what he *was* hearing, or at least the imminent danger of it. And come on, Eva, was he that far off the mark? The excitement was twingeing in a forbidden place!

'Nah, nah!' he pronounced. 'You come out of ahder gate. You come straight home. Orkai! No good!' he shook his head. 'You come home, look after Val. Work in shop! No boys!'

The disappointment was crushing. I'd just got rid of one into a mental hospital and now I had this one! The bud of sweet desire warmed by the flesh of boy froze and sank into a cold wasteland of despair. There it waited. The warmth of the father's cognisance, the reluctant blessing that all fathers who are entrusted with the care of daughters are called to give, was unforthcoming. What does a girl do in such a case? And there are countless girls like me whose fathers do not have the wisdom, the capacity or the where-withal to give this blessing. What do we do?

I drove my sexuality underground. Any unsightly sprouting of it was churned into the ground by Sasha's jackboots. I secretly put curlers in my hair after I went to bed. One night he came in unexpectedly, saw the protruding plastic devices and ripped them off, pulling out large chunks of hair.

'What's t'is? Tryink to look sexy, huh! I give you sexy! You prostitute, just like your mahder!'

I was allowed to go to the school dance once a year. But there were conditions. No make-up or finery. My hair was tied back severely from my face, which made the pimples on my forehead stand out like forest fires. My mother's ghastly 1950s clodhoppers graced the ends of my stick legs. A babyish dress flattened my bra-less breasts. (I couldn't possibly request a bra from these two inmates from hell who masqueraded as my parents!) And to top it all off, my father would appear early to pick me up, his head bobbing anxiously at the back of the school hall during the last slow dance.

On my sixteenth birthday I was close to crazed. It was a hot January. I was serving in the shop. The Kinks blared out of the transistor radios belonging to the Coke-swilling bodgies out the front, the screeching beat building up to an orgasmic crescendo.

In despair I picked up a broom and danced around with it. I went up to my father and dared, 'It's my birthday. Sweet sixteen and never been kissed. Meet my boyfriend, Dad.' I introduced him to the broom. To the customers it looked like a bit of harmless horseplay. To me it was life and death. The real words were: *Please let me have a boyfriend. A boyfriend who holds my hand and kisses me. Please let me be like other girls. Like Rosemary Leedham (a pretty girl at school who was going steady with the ex-Macbeth). Please let me have a bra. Please let me grow up and be normal!*

The predictable answer? 'Nah, nah, nah, no boys! You got work to do, gel! Sweep the floor! Hot day, plenty customers. Hard work best.'

He fervently believed that hard work was the answer to these silly, frivolous notions that swirled around in my fevered brain. I sank further into despair. Ronny, who worked for Dad, furtively kissed me around the back of the shop. That was pretty vile. Wet and slimy! Roger, another shop help, was different. I really had the hots for him! He invited me around to play cards. 'Nah, nah, no good. You look after Val,' said guess who.

Roger and I burned at each other for over a year as we sliced the Fritz and brushed past each other in the narrow alleyway behind the counter. Once he secretly took me for a drive on his day off. We stopped by the river. I sat close to him on the front seat of his Holden FB. His arm hovered above my shoulders, hand useless in suspended animation. My skin ached for his skin. We watched the black swans float effortlessly past. The silence was deafening, the agony palpable. Nothing happened. We drove home as if in a funeral cortege. Whatever was going on inside Roger, whether it was loyalty to his boss or terror of the inevitable explosion of desire if our skins had touched, I will never know.

My parents' great fears of what might happen propelled me towards potential disaster. I kissed Boris behind the bike shed and orgasmed when he touched my breast. I took long bike rides on a Saturday afternoon. I would bike to Luda's and we would walk alluringly along Tapley's Hill Road. We counted the number of hooting cars and often got into them with piles of boys. Hot petting exploded on back seats with a retinue of strangers. We didn't care. As long as they were male and raring to go. On a couple of occasions we narrowly escaped being raped after being taken to various houses. Shamefully I once left Luda fighting off two drunken men while I made a run for it. She escaped, thankfully, virginity intact.

At seventeen I went to university and met Trevor on the first day. The bombshell of Alexandra's birth had not yet hit our life. Trevor and I went bowling and kissed down by the Torrens River. His lips had the texture of dried apricots, but I was happy. The Beatles reached the top of the Adelaide charts with 'She Was Just Seventeen'. The new-found freedom of university meant I could have a boyfriend during college hours and pretend that I was normal.

Unfortunately this dream was short-lived. A few days later I was walking down Rundle Street in the centre of Adelaide, holding hands with Trevor. I felt great. I loved the normality of having a boyfriend. It was a hot February day and the city of Adelaide was busy, teeming with vehicles and people (Rundle Street was not then the traffic-free mall it is today but a busy thoroughfare for cars). We didn't notice when a great commotion began in the middle of the road, accompanied by shouts and loud honking of horns. Trevor and I barely paid attention and continued to walk on, enjoying the feel of each other's hands. The shouts and blasting of horns grew louder but we were oblivious to the unfolding melodrama. A woman tapped me on the shoulder. 'Excuse me, dear, but I think there is a foreign gentleman in the middle of the road trying to grab your attention.' I froze and dropped Trevor's hand like a hot brick. Time swung into slow motion as I turned to see my father bellowing from the open window of the all-too-familiar FJ Holden, his face purple with rage. He had swerved over to the wrong side of the road and traffic was held up in long queues in both directions. The orderly centre of Adelaide was reduced to chaos as it witnessed the next farcical enactment of the Levkowicz father-and-daughter drama.

'Get in car, you bitch! Get in car, now.'

Trevor, his hand suddenly bereft, rushed gallantly into the middle of the road.

'We've done nothing wrong, sir. It's our lunch hour. We were just holding hands! We were on the way to our next lecture,' he pleaded, apricot lips puckered with worry. Horns blurted impatiently and hot, red-faced motorists emerged exasperatedly from cars. A crowd gathered on the pavements. This must take the prize for the time in my life when I most wished for the ground to open up and swallow me. I stood rooted to the spot.

My father, totally ignoring Trevor, continued to yell in a dangerous range of decibels for me to get in the car. Legs weak with terror, I approached the vehicle. I noticed my mother sitting in the front seat, repetitively smacking her top lip over and under her bottom lip, a bad tic which often possessed her face and became worse under stress. I hated it because it unmistakably branded her a demented loony. She swung a badly coordinated slap at me which missed as I clambered into the back seat.

'Naughty girl. After all we done for you!'

The FJ finally roared down the road with Trevor chasing it. My father continued shouting as he drove me to the college steps. 'Get your tings, get on bus and go home! Wait till I come back from hospital. Do you hear? I deal with you later!' He shouted down any protestations I made and ordered me to do as he bade. Just then Trevor came puffing up, having ran the half mile from Rundle Street. He again started to try and reason with my father, who shouted obscenities at him and drove off, my mother smacking her lips frantically in great agitation.

I was distraught and didn't know what to do. I certainly did not want to go home and wait for that New Australian madman. I told Trevor I was going to see the College Warden, tell her my predicament and see if I could leave home. My teachers' college grant could just cover me if I found cheap accommodation. Trevor, after his initial gallant efforts, turned into a big ninny. He was in his third year and on probation. Any hint of trouble and he would lose his grant and get thrown out of teachers' college. I spelled trouble, so he ran. That was the end of Trevor.

I explained my sorry tale to the warden who, although sympathetic, couldn't help me. 'I'm afraid the problem is that you are only seventeen and don't have a legal ground to stand on. Go home, endure it for another year and then come and talk to me again when you are eighteen and we'll see what we can do.'

The good news—I could escape in a year. The bad news—I was terrified of going home.

I went to the Bateses, the people who had often looked after me since childhood. Mrs Bates still adored me and was very welcoming and sympathetic, but being quite old and frail, couldn't really help me. The phone rang and Dad, sounding even more furious, demanded that I get myself home quick smart. I took the two long bus journeys home with a sinking heart. My father bashed me across the head a couple of times and said that this was the end to my freedom. (What freedom?) From then on I had to show him a timetable of where I would be and what I would be doing every minute of the day. I had to wear plain clothes and a plain hair style. Finally he said, 'You doan' even look at boys until you twenty-one. You hear? And even then we'll see. Got it! NO BOYS!'

I cried myself to sleep that night. I felt wretched and bereft and robbed of my young, pretty years. Robbed of the simple pleasures of a first date, of holding hands, of going steady, putting on lipstick, going out on Saturday nights. I felt hateful and murderous towards my jailer. What kept me going was the possibility of leaving home at eighteen. Two weeks later Alexandra was born, and yet again Fate had intervened with a surprising hand.

For a few months I was distracted by events such as Mum's rejection of little Alex, her further descent into psychosis, the baby's sojourn in a nursing home and her eventual homecoming. But the sexual repression was eating into the bones of my nascent young womanhood. I began to become obsessed with the fact that time was passing me by and that all other girls of my age were going on dates, wearing make-up, getting phone calls—living it up, it seemed, with the blessing of their parents. The pain of missing out hurt. It hurt badly to the point of despair. It gnawed at my insides. I felt like a starved beggar at a banquet overwhelmed by delicious offerings which I was condemned never to taste. I had the fantasy that, if and when I left home, I would go to another country, assume another identity and pretend I was five years younger than I was. I could then relive the years I was missing out on.

My persona at home and my persona at college took on Jekyll and Hyde proportions. At home I wore no make-up (any light brush of mascara or lipstick was ordered to be scrubbed off). I tied back my hair and wore dowdy clothes and long skirts. I would go off to the bus looking like the sexless, studious, proper girl that my father would approve of. On the bus I would sit at the back and take the twenty-one-minute journey into Adelaide to metamorphose into the sex kitten that would emerge at the other end. I would hitch up my skirt to a dangerous height, put on coloured tights (all the rage at the time), lipstick and mascara my face and untie my long fair hair. Donning impossible stiletto shoes, I would venture into lectures, seminars and the refectory on the hunt for good-looking boys. I would talk to and be with as many boys as I could before boarding the bus home at the appointed hour and disposing of this identity into a bag. At night I would recall every event of the day and obsessively count the number of boys who had spoken to me, smiled at me, touched me or even kissed me. The higher the number of such encounters the better. I could somehow delude myself that these scraps were enough for the starving beggar to be able to live for another day. I would sit in the university's Barr Smith Library but not a lot of studying got done. I stalked boys with my eyes. I developed the fine art of being able to orgasm while ostensibly reading a library tome.

Freshers' Week at Adelaide University was great for me. This was a series of day-long parties and drinking bouts during which students got totally blotto at the beginning of each academic year. I was eighteen and got seriously drunk for the first time in my life.

I wound up in a pub and spent the next few hours passionately kissing a succession of delectable boys. I lost count at six. I was saved from more serious consequences by a couple of 'decent' boys who had been watching this rather disturbing spectacle and decided that it was about time they rescued me and sobered me up.

Events like this became more and more frequent. Time at university was BOY time. I joined the drama club, which meant I could stay late for rehearsals. Dad, who had now busied himself with Alexandra, became a little less obsessed with what I was doing at uni. At home I acted like sex never entered my consciousness. Perhaps this dangerous undercurrent of tumultuous repression was what my mother was picking up when she accused me of having sex with my father.

As I approached my final year of university, Dad became increasingly unhappy that I might be sent away to teach in the country. From the age of fourteen I had been signed to the South Australian Education Department, which promised to pay for all my university education in return for my teaching for three years when I finished. All new teachers were sent to the country to places like Ceduna, which was hundreds of miles away. I couldn't wait—the further the better as far as I was concerned. I had abandoned my plan of leaving at eighteen because, as well as Val, there was now a second small motherless girl, and she doted on me. But I had to get out soon, and teaching in Ceduna sounded attractive.

But Dad didn't want this to happen. He wanted me to live with him for the rest of his life. In the Russian tradition, if the mother is ill, the eldest girl stays and looks after the father and family.

Towards the end of my third year at university, there was a period during which Sasha became depressed and glum for weeks. I asked him what was wrong. When it finally spilled out, he said he was really upset because I had joyfully run up the steps to uni after he had dropped me off. He felt that I enjoyed university more than I enjoyed being at home with the family. He was also upset by one of my girlfriends. Leonie's crime was that she wore culottes, but even worse, she smoked! Dad was afraid that he would lose me. This fear was to be realised sooner than we all thought.

9 / **I Finally Get Away**

'I kill you, you whore! I t'rash you till you dead,' shouts Dad, brandishing a broom. He is naked except for a pair of Y-fronts, their whiteness standing out luridly in the dim hall. I swallow terror. I know he means it. I run to the front door. Will I be able to unlatch it in time? Get out before the fiend fells me with his weapon? Everything is in slow motion, just like a dream. I fumble with the catch. I just manage to open the door. Dad is hot on my heels, trying to drag me back. I trip into the black night, my stiletto heels stabbing the front lawn. I don't even have a split second to take the ridiculous things off. Will I get to the wire mesh fence in time? A recurrent childhood nightmare flashes before me.

'Nyet, Mama, nyet!' I scream as I run through the grass of the long backyard. She is crazy and wielding the dreaded strap. Chasing me. I gulp for breath. The fence looms closer. Will I be able to climb over it before she pulls me back?

I get to the fence, drag myself up the splintery wood and jump the enormous drop to the other side. Phew! But relief turns to horror. No! I'm in the same backyard! The madwoman is still behind me. I feel her breath on my neck. The long yard stretches in front of me. Run, run, run towards the same high fence. Run, run. Scramble up over. Jump. Doom. The same backyard! Will I ever be free?

At least the wire mesh fence isn't as tall as the wooden fence of my dreams and I am now fully grown. Mum wielding a strap has metamorphosed into Dad wielding a broom. Can I really get away? I start climbing over the fence with Sasha now half way across the lawn.

'Come here, you bitch. Doan' tink you can get away from what you got comink!'

76

I lose a shoe as I jump over the fence and land on the footpath. I pull off the other shoe as the Y fronted demon starts to scale the fence. I run down the road barefoot in the pitch dark. It is so late that the street lights have been switched off. I am determined to get away from this madman in his underwear.

After a few yards he gives up, runs back and gets into his car to drive after me. By this time I'm down the other end of the street. As I see the car lights blazing towards me, I dive into someone's yard and hide behind a bush. I am running for my life. As I crouch down getting my breath, I remember Olga running down this very road, refusing to get in the car that was to take her back to the mental hospital. She always managed to get to the end of the road but no further as the glaring headlights of the same FJ Holden trapped her like a rabbit and she was dragged screaming back to her prison.

I'm determined I won't be caught. Enough is enough. I am twenty years old. I refuse to be dragged back to prison.

I had just started my final year at Adelaide University and had been invited to a party which I decided to go to straight from campus. This was by design because I didn't want to upset Dad by looking like I might enjoy myself, and I didn't want him to see how glamorous I looked. I went to the hairdressers and had my blonde hair piled sexily on my head. I then ensconced myself in the university changing rooms and put on a long slinky dress and shoes with three-inch heels. The party was not a great success because the boy I liked gave me the cold shoulder (I was a virgin and refused to go the whole way). I ended up a little drunk and feeling sorry for myself in the bathroom. My friend Leonie came and comforted me and, before I knew it, I was bawling my eyes out about how sad I felt that my mother was incarcerated in a mental hospital. I hadn't really told my friends about this before because mental illness was a taboo subject. I wore it like a dark, lonely secret. I was dreadfully ashamed and fearful that Mum was in Glenside, so it was with trepidation that I shared this with Leonie. She was very supportive and probably understood more than most, due to the fact that her father worked in the same psychiatric hospital. A while later I rejoined the party.

At about one o'clock in the morning I got a lift home and crept in the front door, hoping that Dad was asleep. No such luck. He was waiting for me in the hallway, dressed only in underpants and in a decidedly angry mood.

'What kind of time is this to come home!' he bawled. 'Where you been? What you been doink?' He glowered suspiciously at my hairdo, shoes, make-up and dress.

My feeble attempts at explaining where I'd been and the difficulties of getting lifts did nothing to appease his rising fury. Very soon we were shouting and screaming at each other. He hurled accusations at me: 'You prostitute! I bet you not tink of your poor mahder while you dancink round at fancy party! You nuttin' but drunken whore.' It was a bizarre sight, me in stilettos and glamorous hairdo and him in just white Y-fronts, shouting at each other. He built himself up to a crescendo of screaming. 'I fix you! You need good beatnik! I kill you!' With this he raced to the broom cupboard, got out the broom and ran towards me threateningly.

Now I am cowering at the end of Essex Street. Where to go? What to do? I am too afraid to go on the roadway in case Dad finds me or the police pick me up. All I possess is one shoe and a long sleeveless dress. No money, no identification, nothing. Although I am twenty years old, I look about fourteen. I force bus drivers to give me an adult fare. The police will probably take me straight home and that is the last place I want to go. So I decide to head east to Kilburn, a few miles away, where my friend Leonie lives.

The night is very dark now, the time about 2.00 am. I stumble through many backyards, avoiding the main roads. Progress is slow, and I seem to wake up every dog in the neighbourhood as I keep to the back streets. Trudging through what I think are deserted factory yards, I am stopped in my tracks by the sound of voices. Freezing behind a fence, I make out some shadowy figures conferring together near a few cars. Have I stumbled on a secret rendezvous of a bunch of criminals? I creep stealthily around the perimeter of the factory so that they don't see or hear me. I don't care what nefarious dealings may be going on; I have my own drama to contend with. At last the never-ending stretch of factories stops and I find myself on a railway line. I bounce along the wooden sleepers for quite a distance. A strange, wonderful feeling of elation spreads over me. I am running towards freedom. As I pound along rhythmically, I am mesmerised into a reverie of escape. I am fleeing tyranny and hopelessness and running towards liberty and happiness.

A thunderous roaring and shaking shocks me from my trance. Hurtling towards me in the gloom is a monstrous train. I jump off the tracks, landing in something wet, murky and smelly as the train screeches overhead. I lie there thanking God that I haven't been mown down prematurely in my dash toward freedom. A faint light is beginning to appear on the horizon and I realise I have jumped into a sewer. The train track cuts through a giant sewerage farm, the smell of which often assails our nostrils when a hot north wind blows across the flat expanse of Adelaide's north-western suburbs.

I pick my way gingerly across the sewerage plateau. Even though my legs and dress are smeared in some kind of smelly grunge, I still feel euphoric. This quagmire is a small price to pay for the enormous haven of freedom that I am moving towards. I eventually come to the edge of the sewerage farm, and in the emerging greyness of dawn, I discern that I am in suburbia again. It is an upward climb so I figure I must be approaching Enfield, which is the suburb before Kilburn. I don't have too far to go.

In the distance I see a milk float doing its morning rounds and am conscious that people will soon be about and that I look highly suspicious. By now my beautifully coiffured hairdo is hanging in a beleaguered and forlorn fashion over my grimy face and my long evening dress is filthy. I am still clutching my one stiletto shoe. I find a churchyard with an outside tap and proceed to wash off some of the filth. I remove my tights, tie them around my waist and hitch up my long dress to make it look shorter. In a scrap of old towel I wrap up my shoe, which I am really attached to. It is the only possession I have. With this semblance of looking more normal, I make my way through the silent streets, and finally arrive at Leonie's house at seven o'clock in the morning.

I knock on the door, ready to apologise for the early intrusion and to explain my sorry tale. Leonie's mother answers the door with the words, 'Oh Eva, thank God you're safe. The police have been looking for you all night and have already been here.'

She sees the dishevelled, filthy state I'm in and packs me straight into a hot bath. This bath still stands as the best bath of a lifetime. The police arrive. I am interviewed by a policewoman who says my father had reported me as a missing juvenile and that I am to return home immediately. When she discovers that the 'missing juvenile' is twenty years old she is amazed, and wonders what all the fuss has been about. I tell her a bit of the story, and both she and Leonie's parents think it unwise for me to go back right now, especially in light of the circumstances in which I ran away. The police suggest that they accompany me to my house to get some belongings and that I stay with Leonie for a while. I am very pleased with this idea. Going home represents a return to doom, gloom, madness and despair.

However, as I arrive at my house in a police car I am overcome by great sadness that it has to be like this. I am also very frightened and feel relief that the police are with me. I know that my father will not take kindly to this new plan. He doesn't. When the police inform him that they are waiting for me to get some belongings, he goes berserk.

'You bastards! You all the same in this goddamn country. You always on side of young people. You support their loose morals and bad attitude. You not support morality, decency and family loyalty!' This, in a heavy Russian accent, is shouted so that the whole street can hear it.

Trembling, I walk into the house. Fortunately Val and Alex are not there. I couldn't have faced them. My father follows me down the hall, shouting about what the world is coming to. When I have feverishly bundled a few of my clothes into a bag, he comes towards me brandishing pen and paper.

'Write this down,' he yells. 'I, Eva Levkowicz, will never set foot in this house again. I will never see my sisters again. I will not contact them in any way so I doan' contaminate them with my loose morals and depraved way of life.'

Keeping an anxious eye through the window on the police, who are standing at the front gate having been forbidden to enter, I shakily write these words down. I'm too terrified to dispute the contents. I am so desperate for freedom at this point that I'm willing to pay any price. I then sign away my previous twenty years. My father marches up to the police and shouts out what is on the paper and orders them to witness my signature, saying he won't let me go until they do. By this time the police are of the opinion they are dealing with a New Australian lunatic and refuse to sign. They also say I am of an age where I am free to come and go as I please. This stimulates another torrent of abuse on how useless this country and its law enforcement agencies are. He finally makes me sign the paper again. At last I am allowed out of the gate.

My beloved Alsatian dog, Chief, yowls mournfully from the

backyard as I get into the back of the police car with one small suitcase. My father storms inside and stands at the window, parting the venetian blinds. I see his grim, tragic face fixed on the police car, his eyes deep, inchoate pools of misery. A profound sadness sits heavy on my heart as the car pulls away and I leave my childhood behind.

The Iron Curtain

War's memory is carried through time like the genes we inherit.

John Freeman

Prologue / East German Border, 1975

Closer and closer it looms as the bus trundles through the pale dawn.
I peer through the window fogged by the breath of forty passengers.
We arrive at the East German border. My stomach churns as I glimpse
the automatic machine-guns wielded by border guards who man the
parapets on top of the Wall. The Iron Curtain at last, and it looks every
bit as huge, forbidding and impregnable as in my fantasies. My four-
year-old daughter, Sophi, slumbers peacefully on the seat next to me
oblivious to the terror that grips her mother.

'Come on, Eva,' I reason with myself, 'it has been a quarter of a
century since you escaped from the communists through that forest.
Now you are going back behind the Iron Curtain as a grown woman.
What have you to fear? You are safe on a bus going on a holiday to
Poland. Pull yourself together!'

Oh, if only rational argument were enough to quell the demons
of the unconscious.

The bus lurches to a stop. Passengers, exhausted after a thirty-hour
trip from London, wake up to the sound of East German border guards
barking orders. The Polish bus driver announces that we have to hand
in our passports. I scrabble in my bag and pick up something wet and
clammy. Damn! A bottle of water has leaked all over my passport. I dab
it as best as I can and hand it in. I am relieved we don't have to get out
of the bus.

The two guards gather the forty passports, march across the
quadrangle and up the stone steps to the top parapet, to check and
stamp them. The bus driver's 'Won't take long' is reassuring enough
to send some passengers back into a doze. Fifteen minutes elapse and
another fifteen. Drumming of driver's hands on the wheel. We wait.
At last movement from the parapet.

A guard marches down the steps towards the bus but alas, no

84

passports in sight. Instead a stream of guttural invective is hurled at the driver and then at us. I'm really afraid. He sounds mean. The translation, delivered by a very disconcerted driver, renders me a quivering heap:

'We are highly insulted that someone on this bus has handed in a wet passport. We, the Democratic Republic of East Germany, regard this as an insult from the Polish government to our country and will not let this bus pass through our territory until this passport is dry!' With that announcement the guard, whipping his automatic weapon high on his hip for emphasis, marches out of the bus across the quadrangle and up the steps to the watch tower.

A stunned silence envelops the bus. This is unbelievable!

A watery sun splashes feeble rays over the parapet, offering no warmth to the steely grey shadow emitting from the Wall. A wet passport will take hours to dry. But not my mouth. All trace of moisture within it seems to have evaporated as terror shrivels every cell of my body .

'Whose passport is it?' At last a response.

'Yeah, who's handed in a wet passport?' Shifting and looking about.

I open my mouth. Out comes a small squeak.

'Me.'

Forty pairs of accusing eyes find me. I wither under the scrutiny and, to my eternal shame, put the blame on my sleeping child.

'Um ... um ... my little girl was having a drink in the night and spilled water all over it ...' My voice trails away weakly.

'It might help,' offers the bus driver, attempting to quell the hostile mumbling that reverberates around the bus, 'if you go up to the watchtower and apologise.'

Fear wallops me. Arcs of blinding light flash before my eyes. The roar of motorbikes in a dark forest assails my ears. I am three years old. The bad men will shoot me. I am clammy and cold. I force myself back into the present and look miserably out of the window—it seems a long way to walk up those steps to the machine-guns above. I look down at Sophi, who thankfully is still asleep. I take a deep breath and know what I have to do. Circumstance (and my unconscious, it seems) has provided me with a perfect opportunity to face a life-long terror.

I step down from the bus and walk across the quadrangle. It is grey, forbidding, vast and I am ashen, tiny, forlorn. I climb leaden steps to the parapet. Walking to my death. So scared I'm nearly sick. I enter the watchtower, trembling. The two guards, standing by a table on which sits the offending passport, look up in surprise.

I point at the passport and stutter feebly, 'I'm very sorry. It was an accident and not intended to insult the East German government ...' I stumble. It feels like I am acting in some crazy farce.

I am blasted by a torrent of German. The words 'Polski' and 'Deutsch' are punctuated by frenetic gesticulations.

I am suddenly struck by the utter stupidity of all this palaver about Poles insulting the East Germans. My fear evaporates. Emboldened, I shout back, 'Don't you get it? I'm here to apologise for the wet passport. Me (pointing at my chest)! Nothing to do with the Polskis (pointing at the bus). Polskis nein! Polski Deutsch nein!'

More wild gesticulations. More guttural spitting.

After a few more torrents of exchange, with me reiterating 'Polski nein!' and miming my socks off, the guards pick up the passports in exasperation and shove me out of the watchtower. I am marched back to the bus, the passports are thrown at the driver and, after a bit more yelling and spitting, we are waved through the checkpoint. All cheer as the bus starts up. We drive through the Iron Curtain into the glorious rays of the rising sun.

10 / **Ghosts of the Past**

Peter and I drive to Port Adelaide in my two-toned pink and white Holden to buy some fish at the Saturday market. Barefoot, blue-jeaned, short spiky Mia Farrow hair, blackened eyes, I am at last free to live the kind of life I think a young person lives. On my tight, lime-green T-shirt that shows off my bosom, made more ample from taking the Pill, sits a 'Fuck Don't Fight' badge. It is 1968, and Peter my boyfriend has evaded being called up for Vietnam.

Full of jaunty, youthful enthusiasm, we mill about the crowd survey-ing the fish on display. I turn to look behind me and freeze with horror. There stands my father, his back to me. I would recognise that square head anywhere. Without the wherewithal to even say anything to Peter, I sidle away through the crowd and start running like a mad woman towards my car. Sweating in terror, I scramble on to the back seat, rip off the badge and furiously rub the black off my eyes. On no account must my father see me like this. I carefully raise my head to look out the back of the window and, horror of horrors, see my father walking towards the car. I dive to the floor in the narrow place below the back seat. I am so terrified I nearly vomit. After a few agonised seconds I peek up through the window. My father has walked past and got into his car, which is on the other side of the road. I see both my sisters inside, apparently waiting for him. I am even more appalled.

Did they see me running like a mad banshee down the street? Will they tell Dad? I hold my breath. The car drives off. I am saved.

A few minutes later Peter looks in the window and sees my face streaked with black make-up. 'What the hell's going on?'

'Dad,' I choke. 'I nearly bumped into Dad.'

Peter has already witnessed this sudden diving for cover when I have spotted Dad or his car before, and is mystified that anyone could be so frightened of their own father.

87

My father kept to his word. The Iron Curtain between my family and me was rigidly in place. Everything I sent to my sisters, such as birthday cards and Christmas presents, was sent back unopened. He assumed the spectre of a giant ogre in my psyche and accompanied me thus through life. My three marriages would at times become battlegrounds in which the sulky, suppressed adolescent railed against the tyrannical father.

The first holiday job I took between university and teaching was as an usherette at the plush Metro Cinema in Hindley Street in central Adelaide. A year had passed since that fateful night of escape from my father. I was in the process of being shown the special seats for hard of hearing people when, shock! I saw them. My sisters. They were sitting with a Russian woman whom I vaguely knew, waiting for *The Ugly Dachshund* to begin. Much to the puzzlement of the head usherette, I turned and ran out of the cinema. She found me later, quivering in the rest room. After spilling out some of the tragic story, I returned to my station at the back of the cinema while the film was in progress. Alexandra's distinctive childish chuckle would burst out at regular intervals, and my heart ached with the pain of missing her and Val.

During interval I plucked up my courage and sought them out. Alex seemed pleased to see me, Val went white with fear and the Russian woman launched into a condemnatory attack, saying I must apologise to Sasha. And moreover I should do it after the show, when Sasha was coming to pick them up.

'No, no, please,' Val piped up. 'Please don't, it's a really bad idea.' The dread in her eyes was enough for me. I hid in the rest room for the remainder of the afternoon, the usherettes vowing they would stop any raving Russians breaking through.

I regularly visited my mother at Glenside, once narrowly missing my father who had just left. Phew! The nurse on duty, whom I had come to know well, looked at me quizzically and asked, 'What's happening? Your father was just here, and when I asked him how you were, he blew a fuse and started shouting terrible things about you!'

'Yes, I'm afraid we have fallen out.'

'And by the way, I never knew you were his stepdaughter. One of the things he was yelling was "I loved her more than my own flesh and blood and look at the thanks I get!" '

Olga's condition continued to worsen. She was becoming more and more aggressive. A few months after I left home, her doctor invited me to his office to discuss an operation called a lobotomy which, he said, had a small chance of improving her state. Dad had been approached first but had eschewed the responsibility and asked that I be contacted to make the decision. This hung heavily on my twenty-year-old shoulders. The doctor, who was barely older than I was, explained that the chances of success were very small but that hers was a hopeless case and there was little else they could do.

I told him some background to my mother's life and he exclaimed that none of what I was telling him was in the notes: 'She never told anybody any of this!' *Did anyone try to understand her halting English?* I wondered, thinking of the many migrants I had seen drooling against the green walls.

I joined the death squad. I signed the lobotomy paper.

At the next visit, seeing the scar throbbing freshly in the shaved flesh above the heart-shaped hairline, I looked into the endless vacancy of her eyes and wondered what I had done. She certainly stopped being outwardly aggressive. Otherwise there seemed no improvement. She became mute. Was she unable to speak? Or was she refusing to communicate as a final desperate rebellion against the living horror that her life had become? The visits became more of a strain and began to seep into my dreams as the living nightmare they were. I saw her less and less.

The last time I visited Olga was to see her before I left Australia at the age of twenty-four and to show her my daughter Sophi, who was just a few weeks old. She tottered out of her wheelchair towards us, looking wasted and wan, dried food splattered on her faded clothes. She looked at me and looked at Sophi. Very slowly she scooped out a smile of recognition from the wastelands of her soul. The smile became broader and broader as I informed her that she was looking down at her new grand-daughter. No words came out of her mouth; lack of speech had rendered her mouth and throat a corroded mess. But I saw 'her' in her eyes. Whoever Olga was came out just for a small while. She laid a thin hand on her grand-daughter, the smile unwavering, blessing her with her spirit—a spirit that remains intact deep within all people no matter how wounded, blasted or destroyed they may appear.

Twelve thousand miles away I tried to get on with a new life, but always in my heart lay a wounded woman languishing away, lost in limbo. Mental hospital nightmares bedevilled my sleep. Twitches broke out unbidden on my face. Zigzag migraines crippled me. I sought help. The guilt of cutting Olga's brain in half eventually led me to give up teaching and train as a psychotherapist, so I could listen to and help others in crisis.

In 1974 this new profession took me to Vienna, ironically the birthplace of Freud, the man who elucidated the power of the unconscious. This felt a significant journey as it was the closest I had been to the country of my birth and was the first city that my mother and I had reached as refugees after escaping from Czechoslovakia. I was nervous as Vienna was only forty miles from the Iron Curtain. I would come out in cold pustules of fear every time I had to go through passport control or cross a border. This happened even at Heathrow at the start of my journey when, to my consternation, the passport official handed back the passport without stamping it. Wrong passport! I had picked up three-year-old Sophi's by mistake. The plane was leaving soon, and there was no time to get home and get my proper passport. What to do?

'Well, we will let you through here, but I don't know whether they will let you into Austria.'

I decided to take the chance. By the time I reached Vienna I was highly anxious. No, they would not let me through. I pleaded and cried. My way was barred. I had to ring home and ask for my passport to be put on the next plane.

I spent the following twenty-four hours waiting for the correct passport in an unlocked police cell in Vienna airport. But it may as well have been locked as I grappled with my demons—the uncontrolled ones that 'by accident' had picked up the wrong passport. What was I trying to do in travelling with the passport of a three-year-old girl? My Jungian and Freudian colleagues would have had a field day.

'What do you think, Dr Freud? What is this patient doing?'

'Well, she is trying to heal a significant trauma. She is stuck as a three-year-old child and needs to face this trauma before she can move on.'

Whatever I seemed to be 'doing', I tossed and turned all night in the police cell, reliving the knots of terror that had seemed to

90

twist my guts into permanent states of anxiety as I wrestled with ominous border guards who threatened me with death. Was I to be locked forever in the cold dungeons of my fear?

Whereas the police cell afforded me a confined space in which to struggle with the ghouls at leisure, the fiasco at the East German border when I travelled to Poland a little while later enabled me to face my fears more directly. Shouting at the East German border guards provided a real-life psychodrama to discharge buried feelings.

I was beginning to learn a very important lesson—that unresolved issues lie deep within, like big undigested obstructions, and influence everyday life until they are brought up, faced and finally dealt with. How far this particular trauma was on the way to being resolved was still to be tested.

My first trip behind the Iron Curtain, when I took Sophi by bus to Poland, was the closest I had got to my roots. In a market I met a Ukrainian woman selling painted wooden eggs. My heart ached for Olga. I had abandoned her, left her to rot with two drug-sodden halves of a brain sawn apart. While I was in Poland, my second husband, Brian, who was visiting his own mother in Australia, also visited Olga in hospital. She had deteriorated even more and could not rise out of her wheelchair. Brian showed her a current picture of me and Sophi, and told her that we loved her very much. For a long time Brian saw no response in her wasted features until he spied the glistening of just one tear that welled up out of one eye.

Two years later Olga visited me in a dream. She appeared normal and she was smiling. She looked at me lovingly, lay a tender hand on my stomach and kissed me on the brow. I woke up next morning feeling strangely peaceful and told Brian the dream before I went off to work in North London. When Brian picked me up later, he took me home via Hampstead Heath where he very mysteriously led me to sit under a large oak tree sprouting new growth in the May sunshine.

'I am going to give you something to read and then I am going to go and sit under that tree over there. When you feel you need me, just call.' He then gave me an envelope and left.

Intrigued with all this mystery, I opened the envelope. It was a telegram.

'Your mother Olga died peacefully last night in her sleep.'

A yawning chasm opened up before me and I felt excruciatingly bereft. Even though I had really lost her years before, it was only now that I could grieve her departure. I grieved the good mother she tried so valiantly to be but failed to be in such a spectacular fashion. I stayed a long time alone under that tree.

It was a few weeks later that I discovered I was pregnant with my second child, Joe, and that Olga had died shortly after the conception. The visit in the dream was an affirmation of her sane maternal instincts. The mad mother legacy had handicapped me with my first child. Sophi had to share me with the therapy world as I spent years attempting to heal my own inner tortured child. My crippled maternal instinct was healed a little more by my mother's dream visit, so much so that I was able to be a better mother to both my children. I was never a brilliant mother, but I did my best given the circumstances, as did Olga.

A few years later Sophi, Joe and I visited Glenside hospital. It was wonderful to be supported by them as we walked around the hospital grounds and saw the buildings in which Olga had spent the last seventeen years of her life. In the hospital chapel I broke down and sobbed in the arms of my two children.

I saw and heard little of my sisters for years until there was a knock on the door of the house in England that I shared with my third husband, Jake, and the children.

'Does Eva Levkowicz live here?'

The broad Australian accent was unmistakable. There stood Val, tears brimming out of her eyes: an emotional reunion after fifteen years and a pleasure to meet her boyfriend, Denis, and catch up with each other's lives. Val was a successful comedienne and actress in Melbourne—much to Dad's disapproval, she explained ruefully. He regarded such a living as frivolous and superficial. Alex was a bright teenager doing very well at school and a champion rower. Val had had a bad time in that she had been saddled with the family after I left, and that had been a big burden for her twelve-year-old shoulders.

I hoped that Val's visit might lead to a thaw in the Cold War that existed between Dad and me, but no, that was not to be. As far as Dad was concerned I was still persona non gratis.

The new-found connection between Val and me proved too

fragile to maintain. She resented that I had escaped to the other side of the world and had left her with all the responsibility. She retreated behind the Iron Curtain.

The bland face stared impassively through the thick plate glass window, fat fingers shoving my passport back at me. 'No possibility of visa,' the face barked. 'No exit papers, no visa. Next please!'

I was standing at the front of a long queue at the Czechoslovakian Embassy in London, trying to get a visa so I could return to the country of my birth. It was turning out to be as difficult to get back in as it had been to get out. It was 1988, and even though glasnost was spreading throughout the Soviet Union and its satellites, Czechoslovakia was still well and truly communist and did not look too kindly on people who had baled out to the West illegally. When I first reached the large plate glass window with my visa forms, I was asked when I had left the country. I knew that my mother had escaped with me in late 1949, but I also knew I couldn't divulge this information as that was well after the communists had taken over and the borders had been closed. I pleaded ignorance. I had been a baby and wasn't sure.

'Was it before April 1948?'

'I think so, but I was just a baby.'

'So where are your exit papers?'

'I don't know.'

My answers had to be shouted through the plate glass so that the entire queue behind me could hear the exchange.

'If you left legitimately you must have exit papers.'

'I don't have any exit papers.'

'Why did your father and mother want to leave?'

'I don't know about my father. I never knew him. As far as I know he is still in Prague.'

'Why did your mother leave?'

'My mother did not get on with my father and wanted to get away from him.'

'So when did you and your mother leave?'

'I—I don't know—I think it was when I was a very small baby.'

'Where is your mother now. You could ask her?'

'She is dead.'

'Did you ask her before she died?'

'She was mentally ill for a long time and died in a mental hospital.'

I was feeling intimidated by the KGB-style interrogation and squirmed as all the people in the queue were treated to this segment of the Levkowicz family saga.

'Well, we can't let you through. It is our policy not to let anyone into Czechoslovakia who left illegally after April 1948. Next please.'

The queue by now was stretching to the outside and my throat was hoarse from shouting. I couldn't believe what was happening. I could see my mother's tragic face standing at Port Adelaide docks after being refused entry to the Russian ship. I was experiencing a sliver of what she must have felt. It was a ruthless, punishing energy—you are very naughty for having left and now you will not be permitted to come back. I decided then and there I would not budge until I had that visa. I refused to be intimidated and crushed as Olga had been.

'No, I want a visa. I'm not sure when I left, but I am confident it must have been before April 1948, and I really want to go and find my birth certificate.'

'You don't have a birth certificate?'

'No, I've never had a birth certificate. This is why I want to go to Prague, to find it.'

'No, our policy is not to give visas to Czechs who have left the country illegally and do not have any exit papers. Next please.'

This was becoming really ridiculous but I was determined I wasn't going to leave until I had the visa. It was then that I had a brainwave.

'But I don't even have the paper that proves I was born in Prague, for Christ's sake, or proof that I was even there in the first place, and you want an exit paper for something that happened over forty years ago?'

The official looked at me despairingly and went to talk to somebody else behind the partition. I looked around at the people in the queue, who all seemed riveted by my life story that had been shouted out in front of them. 'You stick to your guns,' murmured somebody behind me.

The official came back with a second official. 'Where is your exit paper for leaving Czechoslovakia? If you do not have one we have to assume that you left the country illegally.'

'But we are all assuming that I was in the country in the first place. I have Prague written on my passport but that was only on my mother's say so—I have no proof of that. How can you expect an exit paper when you have no proof that I was even in the country in the first place?'

Both officials looked quite dumbfounded by this time. I don't know if it was my indisputable logic or the manic gleam in my eye (after all, they had just heard that my mother was mentally insane) but the capitulation was dramatic. Perhaps they simply wanted to get rid of me. After a lot of vigorous stamping and tut-tutting, my passport was shoved back. The queue broke into spontaneous applause as I stalked past them, visa in my triumphant grasp.

This was all a piece of cake compared with trying to get my birth certificate. First to get past the Iron Curtain. The train journey was nerve-racking, and it seemed that we had to show our passports several times throughout a long and halting night of stopping at the East German and Czech borders. I was extremely careful that I did nothing stupid like spill water or lose my passport, and was relieved when the train finally pulled into Prague station. It seemed that the showdown at the Czech Embassy in London had been enough to conquer any remaining unconscious demons. I had sailed back easily.

Communist Prague was grim; grey, faded, sad; officialdom hostile, unfriendly, decidedly unhelpful. It took me a few days to find the right department for birth certificates, and with the help of some Czech friends I finally got to speak to a uniformed woman who did not look unlike a Nazi commandant. I was pleased to be speaking to her through an interpreter, my friend Ceslav, as it was he who got the brunt end of her rudeness.

When I had finally got across the date when I was born and my name, the response was blunt. 'Impossible!'

'Why?'

'There were forty districts in Prague then—which district were you born in?'

'I don't know.'

'Well, I am not going to waste my time looking through forty different districts, each with a multitude of entries. She should know which district!'

This was barked at Ceslav, who relayed it to me in a much

kinder tone. Jane, my friend, and Joe, my son, stood helplessly by.

'Ask her to look in District One,' I said. Ceslav relayed my request.

The official shot an angry look in my direction and laboriously got up. She thumped over to a wall of files and took out a large dusty tome for District No. 1, 1947. I held my breath as she looked through the entries for January. With a note of triumph in her voice she announced that there was nothing under Prosikova for January 5. She shut the book with a flourish and took it back to the files. Ceslav looked at me as if to say, *You're out of luck.*

'Tell her to have one more go. Try District 2.'

Ceslav reluctantly passed this on. The official glowered at me thunderously and issued a torrent of words which quite clearly meant 'Not on your nelly!' I took some money out of my purse and shoved it at her. I was quite prepared to resort to bribery, and from the greedy gleam in her eyes, she was quite prepared to be bribed. Out came the 1947 tome for District No. 2. I crossed my fingers and we all held our breath. And there it was, the entry for my birth. Even the official seemed quite excited to have found it after all. I went over and saw my mother's name written in ink: 'Olga Prosikova, rabotnika.'

Just the sight of those words hit me profoundly and I started to sob uncontrollably. Jane and Joe rushed to hug me and I continued to sob. After all these years of not having a formal identity, not having roots, I now had some tangible proof that this was where my mother had been and where I was born. The tears were a mixture of joy—'I exist! Hoorah!'—and great sadness for the young lost woman Olga, a refugee without a home, with a false identity and in a strange city, a humble 'rabotnika' ('worker').

The official, moved by my tears, changed her whole attitude to the task at hand, and set about performing it with great zeal. The official birth certificate would be sent to me later, but she wrote down all the details on another piece of paper so that I could take it away with me.

Listed were the name of the hospital I had been born in, my christening date, the name of the priest, the name of my godmother and my mother's address at the time of my birth. 'Unknown' appeared after 'Father'. I felt overwhelmed by all this information and read it avidly. It was proof that I existed, that I had a recorded starting point. The official was positively beaming by now and we left thanking her profusely for all her trouble. We visited Apollinaire Maternity Hospital, a gothic-style building with a charming statue of a pregnant woman in the foyer. The hospital was next to the botanical gardens where I sat, imagining the young Olga sitting there with a tiny baby all wrapped up against the freezing snows of January 1947, the coldest winter for a century.

Even though it was like a faded fairy princess, I loved Prague. I walked along the street where Olga once lived; felt kinship with the purple and red cobblestones where Olga once walked; was thrilled by the stained glass windows in St Vitus Cathedral that I knew I had seen before. All my life I had loved stained glass but was never satisfied with the windows in the cathedrals I visited. Now I found what I had been searching for and felt fulfilled. Something deep in my soul was nourished by the symphony of glorious blues and reds, greens and golds that shone down.

But the people of the city were sad. A hauntingly beautiful hymn was sung in the cathedral, calling on King Wenceslas, an old hero of Prague, to set the people free. All Czechs I spoke to felt that they would be under the yoke of communism forever.

'But what about Gorbachev and glasnost?' I had forgotten the Czech language but could still speak Russian. They hated this language as they were forced to learn it at school, but at least I could make myself understood.

'No way will Gorbachev ever set us free. He's just putting a fine dusting of pretty powder over the edifice. Look at where 1968 got us. Nowhere. We are screwed!'

On the way out of Prague on the night train to Germany, I had a vivid dream. It had the hallmarks of what I call a true dream. In it Czech children were all joyfully singing, 'We are free, we are free'. When I awoke I knew that it would come true and told my fellow travellers, Joe and Jane. I wrote to my Czech friends that they must keep up their spirits as I was confident that freedom would be theirs. The Prague Velvet Revolution, when half a million Czechs demonstrated and brought down the communist regime, happened within a year.

Even though I was to go back to Prague to look for my birth father years later, I am gratified to have been able to return while the Iron Curtain was still in place. It was a victory against fear, the kind of fear that had blighted my mother's life and extended its pall over me.

Tackling the Iron Curtain between my father and me was another story and required a lot more than standing up to border guards and communist officials.

11 / 'Your Mahder Was No Angel'

'Don't waste your money by coming to Australia. Dad doesn't want to see you.' My sister's words swirled around my head as we rang the doorbell of a beautifully kept house in a leafy and affluent suburb of Adelaide. I was shaking like a leaf. My husband Jake rang the bell again. No answer. My terror of meeting the house's owner changed to a deeper terror of possible rejection.

'He's not there,' I faltered. 'He's decided he can't cope with me seeing him and he's gone away!' A despairing emptiness ravaged me. Had I travelled twelve thousand miles for nothing? Well, my sister had warned me.

Jake went around the back. Still nothing. The house was shuttered up and impregnable. Then, at last, sound and movement. The inner door opened and an old man stood blinking in the light. I was so grateful that he was there that I hugged him. It was like hugging the rock of Gibraltar and there was not even a faint giving of the jaw as I kissed him on the cheek.

'Hullo, Dad. I'm so pleased that you've consented to us visiting you.'

After my sister's unwelcoming letter had arrived about a month before our departure date for Australia, I decided to come anyway because I felt I had a very important mission—to face my father as a grown woman, not as a cowering infant.

It was now 1996, over twenty-nine years after my escape from home. It was another house, bigger and grander than the last, reflecting the accumulation of my father's hard-earned wealth. The front hall was graced by two elegant statues and a grandfather clock. We followed him into his lounge. I knew I had to rid my mind of the internal ogre and start seeing my father for who he really was. Something had changed. Sure, as we found out over the next few hours, he had mellowed a little, but much more significantly it was I who had changed. The change had been wrought very slowly and painfully over the past thirty years and here I was, ready at last to look my father in the eye despite the blighted love, broken dreams, betrayal, madness and death that had contributed to our long estrangement.

I had taken my children, Sophi and Joe, to see him in 1986 but he had ignored me and only spoken to them. My betrayal of the family and my mother's madness had hung like an impenetrable, viscous curtain between us. Sophi had visited again in 1993. She found it hard to listen to Dad's description of me as a combination of Judas and Jezebel incarnate—harbouring genes of betrayal and sexual debauchery. The Judas genes, according to Dad, had been handed down to me from my real father who had horribly betrayed my mother, and the Jezebel genes from my mother who had, it seemed, screwed her way through the dregs of post-war Europe.

My daughter valiantly defended the gene pool and used all the psychological maturity that her twenty-two year old self could muster by reminding him that there were always two sides to a story.

My father's response to this was delicately put. 'Bullshit! There are no points of view in this story, just the facts, and the facts speak for themselves. No honour. Ungrateful, lazy, good-for-nuttin' whore who walked out on her family. End of story!'

My daughter bravely battled on, asserting, 'Certainly there are facts, but equally important there are interpretations of the facts. My mother has tried very hard to see things from your point of view. At least you could try to see things from hers.'

'Rubbish! I sacrifice my life for her, give her food on table, give her education. What she do? Piss on it all!'

Further gallantry on my daughter's part could not shift the deep-seated stalemate. It had been entrenched for nearly three decades.

When Sophi told me this story, I knew it was time for me to go and face my father myself. I couldn't have my daughter fighting my battles for me. She had in fact been far too generous towards me. Certainly I had made some headway on seeing things from my father's point of view, but I still had a long way to go. Standing in the shoes of someone who is utterly opposed to you is supremely difficult. It requires a deep sense of self and at the same time a corresponding sense of selflessness. You have to imagine the world from a point of view that sees you as a fundamentally evil person. And to achieve that you have to accept that that point of view is not a malevolent one, no matter how much every ounce of your being screams that that person has it in for you.

So there I was in my father's lounge, facing the ultimate test. Had I changed enough to really accept his point of view? And did I have enough moral integrity to actually receive it without feeling that I had sacrificed the sense of self that I had fought so hard to develop? I was bolstered by the belief that this quest was part of the evolution of human consciousness—to be able to hold and understand many points of view without falling into defensiveness, blind prejudice, derision or hatred.

The first half hour or so of the visit was filled with discussion of the energy and cooling efficiency of the house. Dad liked the single malt whisky we had brought for him and offered us some of his own, housed in an elegant glass cabinet adorned with a variety of expensive cut crystal glasses. The mirrored surfaces reflected a variety of cocktail equipment. The bottom section revealed expensive single malt whiskies. The lounge was stuffed with antiques: a deep buttoned red Chippendale leather suite, a nineteenth-century French chaise longue and a china cabinet boasting delicate miniature sculptures and French china. The beautiful piano, which my father bought for me when I was thirteen, stood in a corner. On top was a photograph of me playing it, accompanied by a grim-looking Val sawing away at a violin. Phew, at least there was a photo of Jezebel in the house. On the walls were some original paintings. The pièces de résistance were some elegant Art Deco lamps and two intriguing statues.

After a while we moved out to my father's kitchen, which was perfectly preserved from the 1950s, like part of a film set. There was the large refrigerator we bought new when I was little. In the laundry stood the same washing machine with its attached mangle for squeezing the clothes. This and other gadgets and machines from that era were all in mint condition, and my father still used them all. He would still have had our 1954 FJ Holden if it hadn't been involved in an accident. Instead, a slightly newer 1968 Holden stood in the garage in immaculate condition. The large swing I received when I was seven straddled the back lawn.

The table was laid out with cheese biscuits and chunks of Polish sausage, so we sipped the whisky and stuffed down the biscuits to avoid getting too drunk. We were crammed into two benches that flanked the formica table in an alcove of the room.

During the polite pleasantries, I observed my father. He was seventy-two years old and wore a hearing aid—a large 1950s contraption that protruded from the side of his head. 'Buy at auction for fifty cents,' he announced proudly.

He still had the same stubborn jaw and the tight lines around a mouth that was set against life's hardships. The gold tooth, a real stamp of New Australianism, glinted inside his mouth. The tattoos that had saved him from extermination in the Nazi death camps glistened among the greying hairs of his forearms.

I had written to him and said that I wanted to write a book about my mother. I hoped that this would be an easy way to begin discussing an extremely difficult subject. However, every time my mother was mentioned in passing, he looked dejected. He was very interested in Jake and liked the fact that he was an energy efficiency expert, a university professor and a successful businessman. This was very important to me because deep down I wanted my father to be proud of me and approve of whom I had married. So the conversation went fairly easily as he and Jake shared their views on many subjects.

I began to relax and was thinking how swimmingly all this was going when he suddenly accosted Jake, fixing him with a steely stare, and barked, 'You are husband number t'ree. What makes you tink you are the last?'

We were both taken aback by this outburst. Before Jake could respond, my father continued, his voice rising to a shout, 'Husband number two come to visit. Seem orkai chap. What she do? She dump him!' Severe shaking of head.

This was referring to the time when my second husband, Brian, visited years earlier. At the time Brian had told him that I sent my love. My father's response was to bang on the table and shout, 'Bah, she knaow nuttin' about love. I tell you about love. My aunt Sonia—her husband Igor—he killed in war and now fifty years later she still cryink. That what I call love!'

The beady eyes pinpointed Jake. 'Mark my words—when there's husband number four you will be on scrap heap with the ahders! I tell you!'

I interjected at this point and said that this marriage would last; that Jake and I were committed to working through difficulties, especially since this was our third relationship each. His eyes blazed at me and I felt the stuff coming out of my mouth begin to sound like drivel. I couldn't believe how my father had this effect on me. The drivelling went on for a while until light seemed to dawn on Dad's face and he shot out in a loud mocking tone, 'Aah, now I knaow what this is. I knaow in which department you like this husband. I knaow what you like!'

Indignantly I rebuffed his lewd suggestion that I was with Jake because the sex was good. Not in a million years would I admit that this was partly true. I became this pathetic spouter of holier-than-thou reasons why I was with Jake. Dad didn't take a blind bit of notice and was just warming to the subject.

'Remember Kurt! The women couldn't keep away from him. He left his poor wife Kat'erina and little Curty for some blonde tart!' He was shouting now.

I wished I hadn't worn my low cut dress. I felt just like another blonde tart trying to defend my holy, apparently sexless marriage to Jake. Jake came to the rescue by describing the basis of our relationship from his point of view, but Dad was sticking to his Jezebel image of me. I was quite relieved when he eventually stopped talking about Kurt's exploits in the bedroom and started describing his own long, tortuous relationship with this sexual hell-raiser, who by some weird twist of fate had become his best friend in Austria just after the war. As well as taking the heat off me, I was pleased that my father was starting to talk about his life. He had always found it difficult and would rarely speak about it. He, like many other war-torn refugees, had buried the past and just wanted to get on with the day-to-day business of survival.

My father, Jake and I spent a few hours talking in that kitchen As well as telling us stories about the past, he told us news about my sisters, who were both now living in Melbourne. Val had married Denis and had a son, Barnaby, who was now two years old. She had virtually cut herself off from the family. Alex was in a poor mental state, bordering on being schizophrenic, and had threatened suicide several times.

Every now and again Dad would look at Jake and say, 'I tink you from MI6. I knaow. You sure you not spy?' At one stage when I had been crying Jake passed me a tissue. My father pounced. 'I knaow. You hidink tape recorder?'

My father would be the first one to admit that he didn't trust a soul. When we invited him out to a restaurant he vigorously declined. 'Nah, nah, nah. Alexandra persuade me to go to Chinese restaurant one time and I swear to you we were served cat. Mixed up with chicken, but definitely cat. Nah, I only eat what I cook myself. I knaow where it comes from.' End of story. He wouldn't even come to where we were staying for a meal. However, he did invite us back the following Thursday for a roast dinner.

I was pleased with this encounter. It felt like we had talked about real things and that we'd had some good exchanges. However, we had not broached the subject of my mother and the nitty-gritty issue of my leaving home. This was what he had never forgiven me for and I doubted that he ever would. In my last letter I had said that I did not expect forgiveness, that he did not have to change in any way, that I just wanted to see him.

There were a few days until Thursday so I had time to ponder how to proceed. Ideally I wanted us to really understand each other's point of view, to fall into each other's arms and be really close and loving. Many things had led to the alienation between us, one of the big factors being my mother's illness. We had never talked about it all those years ago and it was still difficult now. Perhaps we never could share our grief and despair at watching Olga disappear.

For almost thirty years I had agonised over the guilt I felt for having left home. In my father's eyes I had betrayed my family, left my young sisters without a mother and turned my back on my duty. I defended myself against this damning indictment by thinking that Sasha was a silly old-fashioned fool. If it wasn't for his extreme reaction on that fateful night and subsequently in sending back all my presents and cards, I could have gone on interacting with my sisters. I spent many years self-inspecting, attempting to resolve the huge mess, and had made some progress. But I still blamed my father for suppressing my sexuality, and as I had linked this in with leaving home, I couldn't really look at the issue of failing in my duty to the family.

The next few days I plunged afresh into my psyche. I really wanted to hear my father's point of view, but I knew I could not receive it when I was still blaming him. Blame always covered up unresolved issues. Blame kept things stuck. While my father blamed me and I blamed him we would be locked forever. I couldn't make him stop blaming me for leaving or make him change in any way. The only way forward was to look at myself, at my side of the blame story. I had to revisit the painful world of my teenage sexuality.

Jake helped a lot by putting himself in my father's shoes and role playing what it must have been like for him, suddenly faced with the prospect of a mentally ill wife and three young daughters to bring up. Sasha had had no experience of girls, his only sibling being a younger brother. Now he was living in an alien culture and his oldest daughter was developing into a pretty blonde who looked like her mother. And Sasha knew only too well what her mother had been like. Attractive, flirtatious and pregnant out of wedlock. Alarm bells! Right. The answer? No boys! Whatever else, no boys!

Jake sounded very funny in his attempt at a Russian Jewish Australian accent as he took on Dad's persona. 'No boys!' he shouted, waving a fist at me. Though the reality had been far more painful, it was liberating to step out of being identified with the crushed, squashed one as I laughed at Jake being Dad and faced how I myself was continuing to suppress my sexuality—as I had at Dad's when discussing my marriage. I went to bed lighter and felt a space had been created in which I could look at the issue of guilt about leaving the family.

That night I had a strange dream.

I run through green meadows and to the edge of a large lake, a glorious snow-capped mountain on the other side. Some giant actors perform a mime on the side of the mountain. I know they are acting out my family drama. As I watch and try to understand the meaning, the water level of the lake starts to rise alarmingly quickly—I am up to my knees and start to run for dry land—I panic and feel that the water will engulf me. It is swirling over my head when I wake up.

Next morning I spoke to Val on the phone and nervously asked her if I could visit her in Melbourne. She was frank and said she did not want to see me. She explained that she had closed the door on the family and I was just dragging things up and creating a myth about the past. She felt she had accepted the way things actually were and thought I was making too much out of everything. She confided that she had had a bad time after Barnaby was born, had begged Dad to come over and help her and he had refused.

'Why didn't you phone me? I would have come straight over,' I interjected.

'You know what, Eva, it didn't even occur to me.' Boo-boom. I felt dreadful.

She told me how terrible it was for her to take on the role of mother and wife at the age of twelve. She felt thrown into it by my departure but, unlike me, couldn't leave. At the same time she understood why I had left. Now she felt she was doing the same in order to save herself and that there was no way to heal any of it. She had cut herself off from Alexandra, who was acting more and more irresponsibly, had cut down on her contact with Dad, and wanted to cut off from me. She didn't want me to visit her as she couldn't cope. She said she bore me no malice and wished me well.

The dream of the snow-capped mountain came back to me. There now seemed to be more to my life drama than I knew, and it could submerge me. I felt overwhelmed by the telephone call. The water had risen over my head and I was drowning. My heart hurt terribly and I let go the floodgates and just howled. I howled for the little lost lamb that Val was as a child, as Mum was pretty demented after she was born. And even though I was really hurt by her refusal to see me, I applauded the fact that she had finally stood up for herself and said 'No!' This was what she needed to do to save her life and I felt proud of her.

But it threw me into crisis. Was she right? Was I, as she had said, just swanning in from my cushy life and stirring up sludge that should really just stay at the bottom of the murky pool? Was I willing to take responsibility for what might come to the surface? Did I really want to look after this family that I had walked out on? Could I really cope with my younger sister, who seemed to have fallen off the rails? I couldn't cope before, so why should it be any different now?

It was with a heavy heart that we went to Dad's roast dinner. I was grateful that his interest in energy efficiency dovetailed with Jake's life-long passion and fuelled quite an animated discussion between them. Every time the conversation drifted towards me or the past, Dad became withdrawn and morose.

Still feeling flat, I was surprised when he brought up the topic of my mother first with an unexpected question.

'So why you tink your mahder went mad?'

I launched into my theory that she could never shake off the persecution at the hands of Hitler and Stalin and that this, combined with her guilt at having an illegitimate child and not being able to adjust to an alien way of life in Australia, tipped her into insanity.

After I had finished, he looked at me and said bluntly, 'Bullshit!'

I was rather taken aback by this response to my articulate explanation.

'Your mahder went mad for two reasons. One, she never got over the pain of beink rejected by your real fahder'—he looked at me pointedly when he said this, as if to intimate that I was just like him—'and two, she suffer terrible from premenstrual tension and postnatal depression, 'specially as a result of all abortions she had.'

I was shocked. Even though I knew about my Czechoslovakian father I had never heard Dad mention him. The second reason was a complete surprise. My father, who had always been excruciatingly embarrassed about such topics, now seemed very well-informed and knowledgeable about premenstrual tension and postnatal depression. And I knew nothing of any abortions.

My father went on: 'Every time your mahder talk about what happen in Czechoslovakia, she couldn't stop cryink. She really loved your fahder and he betrayed her. When she became pregnant with you, his parents said, "You must choose. Her or us. If you choose her we will never see you again." He choose his parents!' My father was almost shouting, still angered by this dastardly deed.

I seized my opportunity to ask if my real father's name was Ludvig Krakov. He glared at me and looked suspicious, as if we were part of MI6 again.

'I need to know if I want to write a book about Mum.'

'Maybe, but she doan' say much about him.' That was all I was going to get.

My father continued about my mother. 'Then she suffer terrible from her periods and postnatal depression. The doctors doan' know about t'ese kind of tings in t'ose days so she not treated properly.' He looked at me sharply. 'You suffer from postnatal depression?'

'No,' I stuttered, 'well, not that I'm aware of.'

'I tink it hereditary. I read up on it and I sure t'is was cause of

Mahder's problems. She also had many abortions and miscarriages.'

I flashed back to lots of unexplained blood that seemed to be on my mother's clothes, on the floor and on beds. My father had obviously gathered a good deal of information about all of this, because he went on to explain that the hormones were playing havoc with my mother's body because she had had some abortions illegally and he believed that her system had not had a chance to recover properly. I was intrigued by these abortions and enquired if they had been with him or with others. He looked straight at me.

'It may hurt you what I have to say and she is not here to defend herself, but you should knaow that your mahder was no angel.'

I wasn't hurt. I knew. Olga had yelled at me countless times, 'You ungrateful wretch, after all I've done for you. I had to prostitute myself to feed you.' I imagined this must have happened before we emigrated to Australia. My mother had obviously confided in Sasha about her so-called sullied past. But my father did intimate that some of the abortions and miscarriages were when she was with him. I told him that I remembered she had lost a baby when I was about ten. Had she brought it on herself? My father was unforthcoming about the precise details.

'She really doan' want to be pregnant with Val and had terrible time and was crazy after the birt',' he offered. This made sense to me, because it was around the time when she behaved extremely unreasonably toward me and would beat me viciously on many occasions. My father continued, 'When she pregnant again and lost the baby she really began to be like crazy woman. I sometimes wonder,' he mused, 'if your real fahder pick up that she crazy and that's why he reject her.'

A light dawned in my head. I wondered if my mother had had postnatal depression after I was born.

I am being held in someone's arms. We are at the front gate looking down the street. I see a woman approaching us. She is smiling joyfully at me with arms out. I am in turmoil and don't know what to do. She looks so familiar yet so strange. I cling to the woman who is holding me. The smiling woman beckons. Could this be Mama?

I had told Olga about this vivid memory when I was older. She was surprised that I recalled this event as she said I had only been nine months old. She explained that she had had to go away to hospital for quite a while. I shared this story with Sasha, who didn't know any more details.

He went on, 'Yes, your mahder was no angel, but as far as I knaow she never cheated on me.' I said nothing about the man she said she was in love with when I was twelve years old. 'And that's why I stuck by her right till end. I visit her every week without fail even t'ough she couldn't talk. I owed her that. She didn't cheat on me.' He looked very sad, a hint of tears in his darkened eyes.

'But she was hell to live wit'—enough to put me off women for the rest of my life! How you put up with her?' This last question was directed to Jake, indicating me. Apparently I had been tarred with the same brush. Mother and daughter—promiscuous Jezebels!

'Oh well, Eva has never cheated on me.'

'How you knaow? As teenager she never worked in the shop. Always runnink around with boys!'

Unfair! Screaming silently inside. He was probably referring to the time he caught me in Rundle Street with Trevor. But I shut up. *For God's sake,* I inwardly chided myself, *at least you are in your father's kitchen talking. Don't blow it!*

Instead I took a deep breath and broached the crucial subject of leaving home.

'Look, Dad, I'm really sorry I left you in the lurch, leaving you to bring up Val and Alex on your own.'

Dad stared ruefully at his whisky. 'Yeah, you should have stayed. You used me up and when you doan' have any more use for me you dump me.'

Unfair! Silent screaming. Deep breath.

'That may have been how it felt for you, but that wasn't the way it was for me.'

'It sure as hell was the way it looked!' Sadness hung over the kitchen like soft rain.

That was all. No huge breakthrough, but a little progress nonetheless. A tiny chink in the Iron Curtain. For my father to acknowledge that there might be a difference between the way he saw the past and the way I saw it was progress as far as I was concerned.

He didn't ask me how it was for me, and to tell the truth I wasn't sure any more. The wind had been knocked out of my sails. Was I trying to bite off more than I could chew? Was I full of (as Dad so pithily put it) 'bullshit'? Would I ever be able to really step into the shoes of another person? Who was I kidding? It was a noble quest and I drew strength from other people who had achieved it. But the hope that my own humble odyssey could succeed and inspire others was just a fantasy.

12 / **I Want to Heal My Family**

I wrote dozens of caring, friendly letters to my father and sister for the next few years, trying to capitalise on the small breakthrough. What did I get back? Zilch. I began to wonder if there had been a chink in the Iron Curtain at all. The stony coldness of my family's rejection lay heavily upon me.

In contrast, my life in the UK was eventful and rewarding. Our energy efficiency business was doing well. We had merged with a much larger company in 1996 and our experiment of converting an inherited authoritarian structure to a person-centred one had finally worked. But what hard work! I had been against the merger initially as I could foresee how demanding it would be to achieve our goal. Jake had promised that if I went along with the task for three years, he would then support me in whatever project I wanted to do for the following three years. That time had now arrived.

I thought long and hard about what I wanted to do with my life. It was 1999, I was fifty-two years old, my children had grown up, my marriage was happy and I was materially successful. In taking stock I evaluated my progress by the state of my relationships. A glaring hole was the relationship with my own family. Grim. My father was still not communicating with me, Val was shutting me out and I didn't have a clue what was going on with my younger sister.

The desire to heal my Australian family was the task I finally came up with. I now had the time, money and support to devote myself fully to the challenge. Little did I know what an amazing train of events would be set in motion by that phrase 'I want to heal my family'. It had tripped so lightly off my tongue.

As my relationship with my stepfather had hit a stone wall, I decided to start the task by tracing back to my roots—to search for my real father in Prague and to see if I could find my mother's relatives in the former Soviet Union. Olga had been torn from the bosom of her family in 1942. I wondered if any of her kin were still alive and if anything in the family history could shed light on her tragic fate.

Tracing my real father was a problem as I was not totally sure of his name. Finding my birth certificate in Prague in 1988 just before the Velvet Revolution had given me a few clues, but nothing about him. 'Father Unknown', it said. However, I did have the address given at the time of my birth and the name of my godmother, Marie Krikavova. Did this name have any connection to Krakov, his possible surname? It was now eleven years later and I wanted to have a crack at finding him. Armed with this flimsy information, I went off to Prague, again with my friend Jane.

In the decade since the Velvet Revolution, Prague had been transformed from a faded, bedraggled fairy princess into a magnificent shiny queen, resplendent with newly painted facades and fresh vigour. I was struck by the sense of humour that had sprouted up everywhere, particularly manifest in the art and pottery; a wry, intelligent humour that had lain dormant for so long. With a new spring in our steps, we went hunting for clues to my past. We were accompanied by Ceslav, who had been so instrumental in finding my birth certificate eleven years before.

It seemed sensible to start with the address where my mother lived at the time of my birth. It was in the old part of Prague, 16 Vitkova Street, a tenement building with several floors and a winding staircase up to the top. A strange tingle of familiarity ran through me as I climbed the stairs. I had fallen down these very stairs and knocked out my front tooth on the edge of a rubbish bin. This left me with a gaping hole until a new tooth grew when I was seven. We knocked on a few doors seeking out the oldest inhabitants who may have lived there for over fifty years. It seemed a pretty tall order but worth a try. We did find some very old people, but no one remembered a young 'Ukrainka' with a small baby. I was subsequently to discover that 'Ukrainka' was misleading and that my mother had actually been passing herself off as 'Polski' at the time.

Phoning up all the Marie Krikavovas in the telephone directory was similarly fruitless. With fingers crossed we rang the only Ludvig

Krakov in the phone book. A woman answered, and in response to Ceslav's query that a possible relative was searching for Ludvig, snapped that Ludvig wasn't home and not to bother to ring back. We couldn't fathom the vehemence of the response but decided to abide by her wishes. The British Red Cross in Prague seemed the last hope. The staff took all the details and said they would see what they could do. I returned to England feeling disappointed.

Several weeks later I received a letter from the Red Cross. They had approached Ludvig Krakov with my story, but he had said that he did not want to reply. Although this was an upsetting response, it seemed an indication that this man must be my father because otherwise he would have said, 'I don't know this person. I can't help.' Sasha had explained how terrible the whole Prague episode had been for Olga, so I could understand why my real father would not want to revisit this painful episode in his life. I also wondered if my godmother was actually my father's mother. Krakov and Krikavova were not dissimilar and I knew my mother's habit of pronouncing things strangely. But the mystery of what happened to my mother in Prague remained impenetrable. I turned my attention to Ukraine to see if I could find out anything about my mother's past.

I didn't really have a clue where to start. When I had asked Sasha about any letters or information he might have about my mother's relatives, he had been singularly unhelpful and had told me that Val had the suitcase containing the correspondence my mother had had with her relatives in the early 1960s. But when I approached Val, she said that no such suitcase existed. So all I knew was what Mum had told me, which was that her real maiden name was Nesterenko and that she had been born near Poltava in 1924 (not far from the current border with Russia). I also knew the names of her brothers and sisters and of her father, Ivan, and her mother, Alexandra. I had even less to go on to find my stepfather's relatives in Odessa—just his original name, Wenzerul.

I decided to go to Ukraine and stay there for a month. But I didn't want to go just as a tourist, so signed up to do volunteer work for an international charity with a base in Kiev. I went in my professional capacity as an energy consultant to do some research on energy efficiency progress in Ukraine.

Kiev was challenging. The poverty was upsetting and I found the Ukrainian language hard to understand. The country was enjoying independence at long last and had made Ukrainian the official tongue; to me it was quite different from the Russian my parents and I had spoken when I was a child. I stayed with a couple who knew little English and their three young children in their 'Khrushchevsky' apartment. This was a name given to millions of apartments that had been built in the Khrushchev era throughout the USSR. They were tiny, poorly built and unbelievably energy inefficient. I slept in the one main room, with the rest of the family crammed on the other side of a curtain. Attached was a primitive kitchen and bathroom with ancient plumbing. The apartment was in a block of fifty others six floors high. This block was in turn one of hundreds of identical blocks in a grim outer suburb of Kiev. To get to the city and the charity office, I had to take two trams and one bus. This was a nightmare. When I arrived back, I couldn't distinguish between the blocks of apartments and took a long time with my halting and unpopular Russian to find the right one.

Eventually I found a more convenient place to stay in central Kiev with Olga Kramskaya, who spoke English. Her father was a survivor of Stalingrad and was still alive at eighty-three. I had recently read Anthony Beevor's *Stalingrad* and knew what a major achievement it was to survive that mother of all battles. After a particularly delicious evening meal, Olga told me her father's story. In December 1942 he was badly wounded by enemy snipers in a bloody street battle. In the bitter cold he was ferried back across the Volga under heavy enemy fire to where the Russian field ambulances were stationed. When his boat finally landed, he was the only one left hanging to a thread of life. A score of soldiers who had been thrown in on top of him had not survived the crossing but their ebbing warmth had kept him alive. As Olga told this story, she burst into tears and we both sobbed, remembering the thousands of young lives that had been lost in probably the deadliest and goriest land battle of the twentieth century, egged on to oblivion by two of the maddest leaders in the history of the world.

I visited Kiev Museum, where I was fascinated by a picture of Lenin that was made up entirely from the works of Karl Marx written in tiny Cyrillic script, snaking neatly around each contour and even into the crevices of the great one's nostrils. Lenin also stared down at me from the walls of various dingy offices where I met with petty officials who harangued me with how Ukraine's scarce energy resources were being drained away by an inefficient, wasteful bureaucracy. The soullessness of their offices, painted in a regulation putrid lime green, mirrored countless other such drab offices throughout the former Soviet Union, testament to some cruel joke where the worker as cog in the Capitalist machine had been replaced by a similar cog in the communist machine. However, I was lifted from this bleakness and drabness by the wonder of the Kiev spring. The city was inundated with warmth, sunshine and scented breezes. Clusters of chestnut blooms dripped from trees, drifts of petals wafted in gutters and heavenly lilacs were carried by pretty girls.

Aleksandre, whom I met through the energy efficiency charity, was willing to drive me to Odessa. We stayed in the centre of town with his mother, a teacher who had not been paid for three months but continued to teach because she felt devoted to her pupils. She was one of many thousands of people throughout Ukraine who were not receiving regular wages. The economic situation since the fall of communism was dire as profiteers from the West milked the natural resources and Russian mafia snaffled the rest.

I took many photos of Odessa to send to my father. I could see the city had once been gracious and opulent but now it looked abandoned and sad. I walked in on a concert in one of the more elegant streets and sobbed my heart out as accomplished sopranos and baritones sang sad Russian songs.

Most of the Jews in Odessa had been wiped out by the Nazis, and no one had heard of anyone by the name of Wenzerul.

*

Elena Klimova marched efficiently into the boardroom and sat next to her boss, Mikhail Mezshebovsky. She was the energy efficiency marketing manager of a company in Kharkiv, and she and her boss were meeting the illustrious Dr Eva Chapman, energy expert from the UK. I was getting accustomed to these meetings and enjoyed basking in the Very Important Person limelight. Some of the time! When it came down to it, the meetings were mostly tedious, especially since my interpreter was an insipid, colourless man who didn't believe in being passionate about energy and therefore acted like a damp squib, delivering the interpretations of my impassioned speeches with the dryness of a withered stalk in the Sahara desert. The fact that the recipients themselves were colourless grey men in cheap, shapeless suits didn't actually help matters. But hey, I was Dr Eva Chapman on a mission to save my ancestral country from being squeezed dry by Russia and Turkmenistan, which were charging exorbitant fees for the gas and oil they were selling to cash-strapped, fledgling Ukraine.

Elena Klimova was different. She was stunning to behold—a tall elegant blonde, hair fashionably styled in a bob, feathery bangs wisping alluringly over green eyes. Dressed immaculately in a smart suit, she would have been perfectly businesslike if it hadn't been for two discordant and dramatic features: her exquisitely manicured fingernails, fiendishly long, tapered and painted black; and her neckline, which plunged down to show off an ample bosom. I was transfixed not only by her appearance but by her manner. She was haughty and commanding, and when she spoke she sounded like a cross between a Gestapo interrogator and a Politburo communist, but with a disarmingly deep, sexy voice.

Little did I know then how important she would prove to be in my mission to heal my family.

We started our discussion of what energy efficient measures her company was undertaking with me playing the super-cool UK expert and her the super-cool marketing manager. Mezhebovsky and my interpreter, Vladimir, entered the discussion occasionally but the real action was between Mrs Klimova and Dr Chapman. I felt quite intimidated by her, for as well as being drop-dead gorgeous she was very knowledgeable about technical issues and fearsomely bright. She was equally as passionate about energy efficiency as I, and even though she pleaded inadequacy in the English language, we were soon conversing without the interference of the interpreter. I could understand her Russian, and her English was accomplished as well.

After about an hour discussing the intricacies of the Ukrainian barter system (her company was paid in tractor parts!), Lena's formidable manner softened and something surprising and lovely clicked between us. For the second hour of the meeting, the energy efficiency discussion was a camouflage for deeper soul sharing.

Afterwards we had lunch before Vladimir and I were to catch a bus to our next stop, Poltava. Over a delicious plum and pork casserole, I was feeling sad at leaving my new-found friend when Lena said, 'Eva, I would like to invite you to my parents' dacha [country cottage] just outside Kharkiv. It is a May holiday for the next few days. My family would feel honoured by your presence.'

I found her invitation compelling but felt torn. I had an important meeting with the mayor of Poltava next day. As well as discussing energy efficiency in schools in the Poltava region, I hoped to find my mother's family. Yet I also did not know if I could stomach Vladimir's company and interpreting for another few days. I made a snap decision.

'I'd love to come. I've only known you for two hours but I know it is right for me to come to your dacha. I must go to Poltava first for important business and then I will catch the bus straight back and join you.'

' Eva, you cannot know how happy I am. I am waiting for you at the bus stop tomorrow evening with my father.'

The five-hour bus ride to Poltava was bumpy, and while Vladimir droned on about the ins and outs of portable loos in Ukraine, I gazed out of the window watching the landscape race by. It was punctuated by abandoned collective farms interspersed with quaint wooden cottages. The farms were full of the disused, rusting hulks of machinery that, like the previous communist state, was now defunct and forlorn—a reminder of a glorious worker's revolutionary fantasy that had bitten the dust. The closer to Poltava we trundled, the more emotional I felt. Sadness pricked the back of my eyelids and I felt the heavy weight of my mother on my heart.

After a night in a communist-style hotel we made our way to the offices of the mayor for the next important meeting in the schedule of UK expert Dr Eva Chapman. Again I was at a formal table full of suits. This time the mayor was flanked by four men who looked like they were straight out of the Kremlin. Dogged by Vladimir's tedious interpreting, we spent the first two hours plodding through the usual machinations of how their good intentions to make schools more energy efficient were tied up by government bureaucracy etcetera, etcetera, blah-blah-blah. However, the mayor had started some initiatives, and a few schools were experimenting successfully with saving some energy.

The meeting was drawing to a close when I said, 'I am so pleased to be here, Mr Mayor, and to hear that you are making some progress with energy efficiency in Poltava. This means a lot to me as my mother was born in this ...'

But I couldn't continue for as I said these words, tears welled up unbidden, the heaviness in my heart became too much to bear and I broke into loud sobs. Vladimir, on the edge of interpreting what I was saying, stared stupidly. I looked up through the tears at the assembled Kremlin. To my amazement, tears were welling up in the mayor's eyes. He jumped out of his seat, ran over to me and hugged me, saying, 'Zemlyak! Zemlyak!' The rest of the Kremlin cracked too, and the wooden puppets suddenly changed into human beings who all started crying and echoing the mayor— 'Zemlyak, zemlyak'—and coming over to join in the hug.

I couldn't believe that this stuffy formal meeting had turned into a love-fest. The word 'zemlyak' felt very familiar to me. It meant 'fellow countryman'. The men from Poltava were crying, laughing and welcoming a fellow countryman back to the fold. The room, in stark contrast to five minutes previously, felt warm and alive. Even the cold fish Vladimir was being drawn into the emotion of it all. His interpreting skills were now redundant. We were speaking the language of the heart and that needed no decoding.

The mayor became even more animated and started showering me with gifts. On finding out that I had not yet seen the Poltava sights, he assigned me a chauffeur and limousine for the rest of the day. We visited the perfectly preserved eighteenth-century house of the famous Ukrainian writer Kotlyarevsky and the monument to the Ukrainian poet Taras Schevchenko. I was feted and fed and plied with gifts until my return bus journey to Kharkiv that evening.

I also told the mayor about my quest and he took all the details of my mother's family, photographs and as much of the history as I knew. He was very interested that my mother had been taken prisoner by the Germans in 1942 and said that that fact alone offered the best chance of finding my relatives. The Germans had prided themselves on their efficiency and kept accurate records of all the prisoners they took to work as slaves for the Reich. Poltava had been an important German base during the war and Hitler had come to the city for several crucial meetings with his generals. It was unknown to me at this point that this was to prove a red herring and that Poltava was not where Olga had been taken prisoner.

At the bus station the mayor hugged me warmly and said, 'Leave it with us and we will do the best we can.'

I also left Vladimir there, so I spent the next five hours in the bus blissfully alone, and ecstatic about my good fortune. My mother had always said that her countrymen were a warm, emotional, friendly lot and I felt that I had just experienced this first hand. I didn't know if anything would come of their explorations—it was fifty-seven years since my mother had been put in a cattle truck and carted off to play her part in the German war machine. Was it possible that her relatives were still alive, and if they were, would they remember her? I had a vague recollection that when I was about eight she had sent her cousins near Poltava some photographs and a letter but had never received a reply. She had presumed that they were all dead or gone elsewhere.

13 / Lena's Dacha

'You can't invite her here! She will just curl up and die when she sees our toilet!' Lena's father was horrified when told she had invited a woman from the affluent West to the dacha. I laughed at Lena's woeful face as she showed me the object in question, a wooden affair over a large hole at the back of the garden. I was delighted by it and told Lena my mother's stories of being afraid to walk out to the toilet at night in case she encountered the fabled Russian witch Baba Yaga, and how in the winter she and her five brothers and sisters had only one pair of boots between them and had to wait their turn to trudge through the snow to the toilet. I found that hard to imagine as I breathed in the warm blossom-filled air, and thought of my mother as a laughing young girl enjoying a balmy spring day and being excited by the future.

I had been met the night before by Lena and her father Vitaly in an ancient Muskovitch car. I instantly liked Vitaly, who spoke no English but whose warm greeting rendered words irrelevant. Meeting Lena's husband, Sergei, was a different experience. He regarded me very suspiciously and kept me at arm's length. I gradually ascertained that I was the first Westerner he had ever met, and the picture of such a person he had built up from communist propaganda was not very flattering. Lena's two children, who shared the family's tiny one-bedroom flat, kept gazing at me in awe.

Next day we all drove to the dacha and I met Irena, Lena's mother. As with Vitaly, this was love at first sight. She was a highly respected surgeon and had been given the land for this dacha during communist times for her services to medicine. Vitaly had built the dacha and had looked forward to retiring from his job as a military professor at Kharkiv University. But then communism collapsed and with it the prospect of a comfortable retirement. He

120

lost his job, as did most other people. Lena lost hers as a university teacher and Sergei his as an aeronautical physicist. Only Irena kept up her busy medical work and brought in the grand total of US$50 a month to support the entire family. This also comprised Lena's sister Tanya, her child Vadim, her boyfriend Volodya and Irena's old invalided mother. Lena had been working at the energy efficiency company for a couple of years but had still not been paid in cash. The company owned a quarter of a tractor, but even if it did ever own a full tractor, there were few buyers to purchase it. Both the younger men of the family were unemployed.

Fifty dollars a month was not enough to keep them all, so Vitaly, with everyone's help, tilled the land around the dacha to grow the yearly fruit and vegetables that the ten-strong family needed. In the winter months Vitaly drove his rusty Muskovitch several hundred miles north to Smolensk, where his mother lived. There he cut holes in the ice and caught fish. After drying these on her old wood stove, he drove back and sold the dried fish to Kharkiv pubs.

We arrived at the dacha at lunchtime and immediately Irena served us a wonderful mushroom soup cooked on the wood stove. The mushrooms had been gathered and dried the previous Autumn. Of the array of breads, cold meats and salads on the table, I particularly liked the beetroot and cream salad, which was a delicacy of the region. All this delicious food was washed down with copious amounts of alcohol. There was beer in a barrel, wines, a variety of plum, cherry and apricot brandies and of course vodka by the ton. They had their own home-brewed variety too— samogon—and it was lethal!

We ate for about three hours, and when that was finished out came dinner: chicken, rissoles, something delicious wrapped in cabbage and lots of sweetmeats. For the next three days all we did was eat, drink and talk. I was ecstatic as this was just how my mother had described life was in her homeland. This is what she missed in dry old 1950s Adelaide—people who ate, talked and drank for hours. Warm, happy company, delicious food and loads to drink.

I found that the longer I was there, the more easily I could understand the language, which was closer to what I remembered as a child. It began to flood back, and even by the end of the first evening I could string a few awkward sentences together. With that and Lena's help I found myself in the middle of long animated conversations. Her family wanted to know all about me and I found them sympathetic, attentive listeners as I told them the tragic story of my mother and her life in Australia. They were eager to know all about life in the West and told me they thought it must be wonderful.

'Yes, it is wonderful in lots of ways,' I concurred, 'with all the material comforts imaginable. But you know, many people in the West are lonely, isolated and depressed. Look at my mother! She had a beautiful house, fur stoles, a car and lots of money, but what she really craved was what you have here. Togetherness, family, warmth, a sense of belonging. She hungered painfully for it, and in the end this craving drove her mad. I actually think that she made a mistake. She should have tried harder to come back to Ukraine. She should have returned to the bosom of her family, back to the warmth and generosity that is so typically Russian.'

'No, no, no, not at all!' Vitaly and Irena were adamant. 'She did right to leave. She did right to get you out. She did right to get you a much better life.'

'No,' I countered. 'Her sacrifice was too great. She paid too high a price. She couldn't cope with a strange new language, couldn't cope without the support of a like-minded community. She had suffered too much pain during the 1930s and the war to be able to withstand the coldness of the West.'

I was really warming to my subject now as I just loved the feeling of camaraderie and togetherness. I felt that my soul, like my mother's, hungered for this. I had known these people for less than twenty-four hours, yet I felt like I had come home at last and was finally spending time with my very own people. So what if they drove a badly made, rusty, unglamorous Muskovitch and had to traipse outside to a smelly loo at the bottom of the garden? These were my people who ate raw garlic for breakfast and laughed hard from the bottoms of their bellies.

'The people in the West have unbelievable wealth. Most families have two or three cars; most have houses and two or three television sets. But they don't have this!' I was shouting now and knocking back a samogon or two. Candles that had been lit on the table and mantelpiece intensified the romantic nature of the evening. The dacha had been without electricity for a couple of months as power cuts were the norm in the new Ukraine. This just seemed to add to the point I was making. Material plenty did not lead to happiness.

However, Vitaly and Irena were just as animated.

'Eva, we want you to understand that we think your mother did the right thing. She got you out from this hellhole that we live in. Look at you: you've had freedom all your life, fantastic opportunities. The world has been your oyster. You have the opportunity to live the good life, to know that your children have a future. Your mother's sacrifice was worth it, and I bet if she could speak back from the grave she would agree with us.'

Irena came close to me, took my face in her hands and looked at me with such love that I just melted and tears coursed down my cheeks. I felt that I had come all the way to Ukraine just to hear this. A raw wound in my heart was beginning to heal. I often thought I did not have a right to happiness because my mother had suffered so much and had died such a long, lonely, institutionalised death. I could only imagine the empty horror of all those years, languishing in such desolation, and could not bear that that had happened to my own dear mother. Now this woman was reaching right into me and saying that all that pain had been worth it.

'But how can you be so sure?'

'Do you think this life we live is good? We worry day in, day out for our children's future. Recently our grandchild was very ill and we did not have the money for an expensive operation, and it was only through contacts in a Moscow hospital that we managed to save his life. We have all had top educations. Look at Lena: she has three university degrees and where have they got her? The proud owner of a tractor part that no one will buy! Look at Sergei, Volodya: they can't get jobs anywhere. My frail eighty-five year old mother has to sleep in our freezing front room because the state can't get enough gas to heat our leaky, draughty, badly built apartments. We have been living in the most unbelievable corruption all our lives. You probably think that the communist state provided free education. Sure it did—in theory. But we had to bribe everybody, right from kindergarten teachers to university professors, so that our children could get a decent education. And everybody bribes everybody all the time!'

'It's not that great in the West,' I weakly countered, but even though the conversation continued in this vein well into the night,

I had got the message. My mother's sacrifice had been worth it. I felt that this was the truth. It reinforced a similar message I had received on a meditation retreat the previous summer—that what I owed my mother was to be happy, otherwise all the hardship and sacrifice she had made would be wasted. As I had discovered in Poltava, there was only a very slim chance of finding my mother's relatives, but now I felt that it did not matter too much. I had found the kind of Russian Ukrainian family I had been looking for.

After the children had been washed in a tub by the back door and put to bed, out came the dominoes. What ensued was one of the most hilarious nights of my life. We played dominoes till dawn, but it was really just an excuse to go on talking and drinking in a new context. Over and over again we were reduced to weeping hysterically with laughter because everything was so funny.

Amazingly, the next morning I did not feel even slightly hung over, which just went to illustrate a long-held belief of mine, that if you drank the alcohol that was produced in the region you were in, you would be okay. I had already noticed that if I drank ouzo in Greece I was fine, but if I drank it in London I was violently sick.

After a huge breakfast, Irena, Lena, the children and I went for a walk and lay in the grass looking up at the deep blue of the sky. As we did so Irena started to giggle. 'You know if anyone told me that I would be lying on the grass with a Western woman I would have thought them an idiot. I never believed that such women could ever lie on the grass like this.' I was discovering an interesting fact, that the more I gleaned of the Russian point of view of Anglo-Saxons, the more I could see them as an insipid, correct, formal, colourless lot.

The next day and evening was more of the same. God, did these people know how to party! Again we talked seriously, again we ate, again we drank, again we laughed ourselves sick. They found some of the swear words my mother taught me as a child, and the way I said them, incredibly funny. I just had to say 'sraca' every time I was trounced at dominoes to precipitate a spell of hooting, snorting and howling with mirth. Apparently 'sraca' was a very vulgar village swear word that, roughly translated, meant 'disgusting, shitty, smelly bum'. And for them to hear a proper Western woman utter it was just too much to take.

We went out into the garden to hear the nightingales. It was the most delicious of nights—a bright full moon, wafting scent of apple blossom and a melodious choral symphony of several nightingales. Lena's family were amazed when I told them that this was the first time I had ever heard a nightingale sing and had always wanted to, since I had read Keats' 'Ode to a Nightingale'.

'What, there are no nightingales in London, in Berkeley Square?'

'No, I'm afraid they are long gone—too many bright lights, too much noise and pollution. I don't even hear any in the countryside where I live, more's the pity.'

'God, Eva, you look like a Ukrainian dumpling' was Jake's welcome home remark. What returned from a month in Ukraine was me, plus a good few extra kilos. And there was I thinking that in post-Chernobyl Ukraine I might be lucky if I could scrape together a few scrawny irradiated carrots. The food had been stupendously good everywhere, and had only been outweighed in abundance by the generosity of the people. I had come across some people who used radiation detectors, but for a few years they had pronounced the food clear. The bulk of the Chernobyl fallout had gone north at first and landed on poor Byelorussia.

I sent off a bunch of photos of Odessa to my father. I waited vainly for a response. Similarly I heard nothing from Poltava. I didn't have much hope about finding any relatives and felt blessed to have found Lena and her family. That summer I invited Lena over to the UK as a return gift for what her family had given me. She came as an energy efficiency expert on a business visa, and just couldn't believe what life was like in the UK, where her English improved in leaps and bounds. She was getting fed up being paid in useless tractor parts and thought that she could make more money by teaching English to the rising new class of Ukrainian bourgeoisie. The local swimming pool has never forgotten Lena and her revealing string bikini.

The next stage of my 'healing my family' project was to visit Australia. I wanted to tell my father first-hand all the impressions I had gained of Odessa, seek out my younger sister Alex and reconcile with Val. I also wanted to welcome the new millennium at the Sydney Harbour fireworks with my children Sophi and Joe, who were both working for the Sydney Olympics. I wrote again to my family telling them of my plans and that I was looking forward to seeing them.

*

A strange packet arrived in October. What fell out was a Ukrainian newspaper with a picture of my mother on the front page—and a letter with the heading 'Ukraine Society of Former Prisoners of Labour in Germany 1941–1945'. I deciphered from the very poor English that the mayor of Poltava had passed on my mother's details to this Society and they had placed a picture of her in a local newspaper, announcing that her daughter, Eva Chapman, would like to contact any surviving relatives. This had been put out the previous August, and amazingly the Society had just been contacted by a Mr Babenko, who claimed his wife was a cousin of Olga Nesterenko. I was utterly overjoyed and flabbergasted at the same time.

'I've found some relatives, I've found my relatives!' I whooped and hollered.

This was momentous for a person who, as a child with only a mother and stepfather to my name, would manufacture make-believe uncles from the announcers on local Adelaide radio. I believed that Uncle Bob and Uncle Dick, local Adelaide radio personalities, were my real uncles. I even used to wait for them to come out of the back of the large valve radio that sat in our kitchen.

'I've got some relatives, hoorah!'

Jake regarded me quizzically. 'God, you're trying to gain relatives where I'd be quite happy to get rid of some of mine!'

The Society of Former Prisoners of Labour in Germany—that is, former slaves of the Nazi regime—had been set up after Ukraine's independence in 1991 to fight for the recognition of those victims who had been regarded as non-entities during the time of the Soviets. All people who had returned to the USSR after the war, expecting to be welcomed home after having been brutalised by the Nazis, were sent off instead to be 're-educated' in hard labour camps in Siberia or in the Donetsk coal mines. They were punished like dogs for not committing suicide on the spot and having succumbed to Nazi slavery. This Society worked hard so that these miserable people could be pardoned and have their stigma lifted. This was achieved in 1996, when all who were still alive after fifty years were at last granted a pardon. The Society now took up cases similar to Olga's, tracing lost relatives of 'slaves' who had escaped overseas.

I wrote back to the Society and said I planned to come back to Ukraine next spring after my three-month trip to the Southern Hemisphere. Then we left for Australia.

A letter was waiting for me when we arrived in Sydney in November 1999. It was from my sister Val and it knocked the stuffing out of me.

14 / **The New Millennium**

You are not welcome. That was the main theme of Val's letter. I had mentioned in my own letters that I wanted to do something to heal the rifts in the family and to continue gathering material for a book about my mother. Val's letter got straight to the point. Why did I want to rake up the past? It would just stir up more pain and misery. I'd had nothing to do with their lives for so long, so what was the point of coming back in a hit-and-run fashion and then jetting back to a happy life in the UK? I was informed bluntly that Alex was in an institution for the mentally ill and had a small child who was in the care of the Human Services department: 'some happy tidings to chew over in this healing-the-family charade'.

A dull, sick feeling gripped my stomach. It was impossible. I felt like giving it all up. It seemed that I had not made any headway at all. The news about my other sister and her little child shocked me to the core. I resolved to go to Melbourne and try to find them both.

'Why hadn't anyone told me about this before!' I ranted and railed. 'What a family!'

Fear gripped my belly as I dialled my father's number. It took ages for him to answer, and when he did he shouted a high-pitched 'Helaoih!'

'Hi, Dad, it's Eva,' I gasped, trying to sound like I was really normal and not that I'd prefer to run away to the North Pole and live in an igloo.

'Who?'

'Eva!' I shouted.

'Hang on.' I heard the whining and whirring of what sounded

like a small helicopter but guessed it was him fiddling with his hearing aid.

'Oh, it's you,' he finally answered, sounding distinctly unimpressed.

'I'm in Adelaide and Jake and I would like to come and see you.' I was still quaking in my boots. *How can you be so afraid of someone who wears a small pink helicopter in his ear,* I admonished all the scared little girls quivering in the basement of my being.

'When?' he shouted. Phew, at least it was 'when' and not 'never'.

'When does it suit you?'

'I'm here all the time.'

'How about tomorrow at twelve?'

'Orkai.'

'Bye.'

I hung up the receiver with relief. It had taken all morning to marshal the scared little girls together in order to telephone. I was convinced after that letter he would tell me to go away.

So here we were again at his front door, knocking loudly for what seemed ages. The door opened into brilliant sunlight and a shrunken face blinked out from the darkness within. I was shocked. My father looked like death. We followed him down the long corridor into the kitchen, still all 1950s and neat as a pin. I regarded him during the awkward opening pleasantries. He looked so different: haggard, much thinner and a lot older.

'Is your health all right?' I blurted out. He looked at me obtusely.

'Yeah, not too bad. I got diabetes.'

'Oh,' I say, not too convinced that he could have deteriorated so much as a result of diabetes. But I left the topic as he obviously didn't want to elaborate.

'How's Alex?' I continued. His face twisted with pain. It seemed that there was no safe topic of conversation. So I launched into Ukraine and rattled on about Odessa, Poltava and finding my relatives. This aroused a modicum of interest only to be followed by a diatribe against Ukrainians, basically around the theme of what evil, back-stabbing rats they all were.

I changed the subject. 'Did you get the photos of Odessa?' He did, and I assumed he liked them. A conversation ensued about the wonderful buildings and architecture in Odessa. He warmed to this topic and told us stories of the port in previous, more illustrious times. He seemed sad when I told him how poor the people were and how empty the port now was.

The kitchen table was full of big plates with assorted goodies on them and we ploughed through the Polish sausage and gherkins as we talked. What was missing was the whisky and vodka. After about an hour he offered Jake some whisky and said he wasn't allowed to drink it any more. I leapt on this clue to his obviously fading health and asked why. He didn't answer just looked ahead and belched.

'Is it the diabetes?'

'Yeah,' he said as a way out.

'I got a difficult letter from Val,' I ventured, taking the conversation into danger areas again.

'You gotta understand someting about Val. She a tough cookie. She just like her grandmahder. No compromise. Very forceful. Calls a spade a spade. God, sometimes she give me such earful on phone!'

I was quite envious of Val and her ability to strike fear and get obvious respect. To be compared to his beloved mother was high praise indeed.

'Yeah, well, she said she doesn't want to see me, and as I didn't see her last time I am quite upset.'

'Well, I swear to God I doan' hear her say a bad word about you, but you must understand that she felt badly that you left home and turned your back on her. Jus' like my mahder, she doan' forgive. A tough customer!'

A bit like you too, I thought, but of course I would never have dared say it.

'She says Alex is ill. Do you know anything about that?'

He looked pained and then launched into an angry diatribe. 'You know, I rang up Dr Fitzgerald and said to him, "You looked after Alexandra all her life—why doan' you tell me there is mahder's illness in her? Why you not warn me?" ' His voice has risen several decibels. 'How can he, a doctor, not see that someting is wrong—give her some treatment to help prevent this tragedy.'

'Have you seen her? Is she in a mental hospital?'

'Nah, she in a home in Melbourne.'

'Have you the address? I'd like to go and see her.'

'No, I have phone number. She ring me every week. I 'specially set up reverse charges! Yeah.'

Although saddened in talking about Alex, Dad was proud of the fact that he was so generous in having set up reverse charges so she could ring him. I noticed that throughout this conversation he didn't say anything about a child. Something held me back from mentioning this and it struck me that possibly he didn't even know about it. For my father, a child born out of wedlock would bring huge shame on the family.

We talked on. Dad and Jake discussed energy policy and shares. Even though my father's command of English left something to be desired, his general knowledge was wide and informed. He diligently read his *Time* magazine every week and had done so since 1962. I could see he was ill and there was an even sadder expression in his eyes. I imagined that Alex's mental illness had floored him. Alex had always been his pride and joy, excelling at school and as a state rowing champion. Her trophies sat forlornly on the mantelpiece.

His attitude to me was quite distant but still a lot better than I had expected after my sister's letter. I dropped some invitations for him to tell me more about Alex, but no. Just sadness. We left promising to return the next month when we planned to drive from Sydney to Adelaide via Melbourne.

Afterwards I felt flat. So much had been left unsaid, and my father had been more wary of me than on our last visit. It seemed little progress had been made. I thought there had been some kind of a breakthrough last time and that the relationship should have at least thawed a little and been a bit more normal. But no; just the usual minefield of having to watch what I said and ducking when I inadvertently put my foot in it. Jake tempered my post-visit ruminations: 'By God, it was much better talking to your dad than to some of my relatives. At least he's got a bit of spark to him!'

I also felt guilty about Alex. I remembered the last time I had seen her, on a visit to Adelaide fourteen years previously. She was a sparkling young twenty-two year old and we met for the first time since the *Ugly Dachshund* cinema episode.

She walked into the pub where we had arranged to meet, a perky elf with dark shoulder length hair and huge brown eyes. Out of all of us three girls she looked most like my mother, but with heavy overtones of my father. He was certainly imprinted in Alex's genetics, which put paid to my mother's assertion that Alex was an immaculate conception.

We sat and looked at each other, Alex nervously fingering some wooden beads around her neck that had belonged to our mother. But the first pleasantries had hardly been dispensed with when she suddenly and alarmingly burst into tears. 'You look just like Mum,' she sobbed, and clung to me as if I were her mother. I sort of hugged her back but felt rather uncomfortable.

Later she filled me in on her life as a young adult. She had fallen out with Dad when she decided to go to art school rather than become a teacher or a doctor as he wanted. She had a lot of confidence in her artistic ability and believed that one day she would be famous. When I saw her art later, I didn't doubt her. It was quirky, colourful and original.

As I was getting ready to go, she clung to me again and pleaded to come and stay with me for a while at the house I was temporarily renting in Adelaide. I saw her as a forlorn, motherless girl and consented, against my better judgment. She stayed for a few days, and most of the time it was great getting to know each other again. But there were things that disturbed me—mostly her underwear. It was disgusting, like old worn-out rags. This really bothered me as it took me back to a time when some of my own underwear looked only marginally better. I saw the repulsive-looking clothing as a mark of an uncontrollable, demented beast that lurked beneath the surface of our lives. We couldn't escape our mother's craziness. It haunted us in our dreams and oozed out into the cracks, where the image we presented to the world did not match the unloved, ugly child that hovered underneath.

Jake had been horrified at the glimpse of self-hatred and self-abandonment that this displayed, and from then on always made a point of buying me beautiful silk underwear at Christmases and birthdays. That bit was easy, but to learn to love the ugly little denied dwarf of a girl inside was much harder. Those grey rags that hung in the bathroom when Alex stayed with me chilled me to the bone. They were the incontrovertible evidence that this motherless girl was in deep trouble.

Alex, I realised then, was looking to me to provide the mothering she had missed. I felt guilty enough as it was to have left her at the age of three. I had been the unwilling successor of the mother who had treated Alex as an alien at her birth. I had dipped out then, and I am ashamed to say I dipped out again.

After a few days I asked her to leave. I was as kind as I could be, but after a lot of soul-searching and self-inspection I said, 'I'm sorry, Alex, but I can't handle you being here. This is my problem and is not your fault. It's just that when I see you I feel a great burden descending upon me and I feel that I should be your mother. At the same time I fight against it. It's driving me mad. I feel very bad that I left you when you were three, but I had to get out then. Right now I need to be here on my own. I am more than happy to meet with you every day and go to the beach or go for a coffee.'

She was very gracious and said that she really understood. She left and we did meet up several times during my stay in Adelaide. I felt no malice or resentment from her, for which I was grateful. There was just a little niggle deep within me that while I had been fortunate to be able to learn to look after myself a little, she couldn't or didn't know how. But my own ugly little girl within me took most of my time. I felt I didn't have room for another one.

15 / **Madness Stalks the Family**

It was like rolling back the years when I saw her. She looked just like Mum, shuffling heavily along on the heels of her feet, her hand up in the air with two fingers forward, her gaze fixed in mid-distance, mesmerised by some inner drama that was running that day. Her thick, luscious hair was cut unflatteringly short and her once tawny skin was a mass of eruptions and red blemishes.

'Alex, it's me, Eva! Hello.' She looked at me blankly for a second, her mouth twisting to the side, and then recognition spread happily over her face.

'My favourite sister,' she burbled, grinning widely from ear to ear as she showed me up to her flat.

She was living in a half-way house in northern Melbourne, one of many that had sprung up in all the major cities of the world since the closing of the old-style mental hospitals. It was pleasant and purpose-built, about a dozen flats in all. Alex introduced me to her flatmate, a huge lump of a woman who just sat and chain smoked on the veranda, staring vacantly into space. Other people wandered aimlessly outside and around the stairwells. While it was less depressing than the closed wards of earlier times, the people had the same slugged, defeated look. These residents were being encouraged to eventually go back into the community. Each had a case worker who kept an eye on their progress and reported this to a psychiatrist, who then prescribed the particular concoction of drugs that was supposed to help. Each flat had a kitchen, and Alex and her flatmate were assisted to do the shopping each week and were responsible for their own cooking and washing.

'And this is Twinky. Isn't he adorable?' I peered at the photographs she was showing me and saw a delightful looking baby. 'You know, Eva, all the nurses said I had produced a wonderful baby—

the best baby they had ever seen.' I was filled with a barrage of questions. Where was the baby now? Who was the baby's father? Did Alex look after the child at all?

During the next few days we took Alex out for meals, coffee and drives in the car. In her own haphazard way she started to fill me in on the last few years of her life. I also noticed that the longer she was with us, the more 'normal' she became.

One afternoon over coffee in her flat, she told me she had looked after the baby for a while and then it was taken away to be fostered. I could see she was incapable of looking after a child.

'What about Dad and Val?' I asked

Her face crumpled with dejection. 'Oh, Dad was furious and still is. You know what he's like. He said I had brought shame and disrepute to the family. As for Val, she wrote me a terrible letter.'

'Not you too? I got an awful one as well.'

'Oh, this was really bad. She said some very hurtful things and told me she didn't want to see me.' She stared dejectedly into her coffee.

I fumed inwardly. So Dad knew all along that Alex had a child! Why the hell didn't he tell me? This was the year 2000, for Christ's sake! The stigma of unwedded motherhood had lifted, even in Ireland. What kind of Dark Ages world did my father inhabit?

'What happened to the baby after he was taken from you?'

'Oh, he went to a foster family. Did you know his first name is Gabriel, after the Archangel Gabriel, and his second name is Francis, after Francis of Assisi? And he is like a little saint.' She stared at the photo of him and cooed, 'Little Twinky. Oh, my sweet little Twinky.'

She then pointed to another photo showing a blond, rather dazed-looking bloke with glasses. 'This is John and he was the love of my life.' Her eyes filled with tears. 'My care worker says I'm traumatised by his death. Oh Eva, I wish you had met him. He was wonderful. He and I were made for each other.'

'When did he die?' More questions filled my shocked brain.

'A few months ago.'

'How?'

Her face clouded over at this. She wanted another cigarette, her third in about five minutes. Yellow fingers with rather long ugly nails pulled one from the packet. 'He was a severe epileptic and, like me, knew we had to be looked after for the rest of our lives. So we decided to commit joint suicide. We each took 150 of the pills he used to control his epilepsy. He succeeded. I didn't.' Tears rolled down her face. I stared at her, aghast. 'We should have gone together and now I am devastated. You know, his mother comes and visits me every Friday.' She tried to puff some strength from her cigarette.

I looked at her dejected face and felt terrible. My poor sister, who had a child in care and the father dead. Well, I presumed he was the father. 'Was John Gabriel's father?'

'No, no, that's Greg.' Now I was impressed. For a severely ill person she did not seem to be short of boyfriends!

'So is Gabriel still with the foster family?'

'No. When Twinky was in foster care I hunted Greg down. He's a half Maori, you know. I said to him, "Greg, if your great-grandmothers could speak to you now, what would they expect you to do if they knew that you had brought a child into the world?" Family and ancestors are really important to Maoris, you know. Anyway, now Twinky lives with Greg.'

Now as much as I thought it was laudable that this Greg, who-ever he was, had been whipped into line by the threat of the wrath of his ancestors, I was getting confused and felt I needed to know some facts. I had already had one round in this lifetime of a member of my family living in a fantasy world, and I was a little unsure if everything my sister was telling me was true. Alex intro-duced me to Leo, one of the care workers on duty. Before she went outside to have another cigarette, she proudly pointed out a paint-ing on the wall. One of hers. It was an abstract in a swirl of blues, and rather fine, I thought—and said so out loud. I was delighted that she was still painting.

Leo corroborated Alex's story, including the suicide attempt, and filled in some more facts. Gabriel was now three years old and was indeed being looked after by his father, Greg, at an address nearby. Alex had been tracked by Human Services for a few years, having been thrown out of various places by several angry land-lords, and had been registered as vulnerable when she was preg-nant and had nowhere to live. She became severely depressed after her family rejected her because of her pregnancy, and had been placed in a mental care facility where she had people helping her out. After the baby was born this care continued and she was helped to look after the baby. After a while it became obvious that she couldn't take care of herself, let alone a small baby. Apparently Human Services had contacted Dad and Val to see if they would take the baby, but both refused.

I fumed even more at what I felt was the appalling behaviour of my family. What were they? A bunch of hard-hearted ghouls? And why hadn't anyone told me? I would have taken him.

I became impatient to see Gabriel and made that my next stop. I was so excited that I had a second nephew. I had never seen even my first nephew, Barnaby.

The door of the shabby-looking house opened to a tiny little replica of my father, who smiled up at me and jumped up and down excitedly. 'Aunty Eva's here! Aunty Eva's here! Dad! Dad!' Greg, an amiable looking chap, ushered us into a house which was remarkable for the fact that it had such bare, dirty walls. His liquid, almost coal-black eyes gleamed at us.

'Drink?'

While we sipped our Cokes I feasted on Gabriel. He was utterly adorable and I could understand why my sister fussed over him. As family-starved as I was, I was convinced that I wasn't biased in thinking that this kid was indeed an angel and had the kind of smile that could unlock the heart of Genghis Khan—or even my steely faced father. He ran about showing us all his toys and roped Jake into a ball game. Even though the house was spartan and rough, Gabriel was dressed well and looked healthy and cared for.

In between squeals of delight as Gabriel and Jake charged about the house, I asked Greg his side of the story.

'So how long did you know Alex?'

'Well, I'd known her for quite a while. She was always skittin' from one boyfriend to the next and movin' all over the place. Then out of the blue she asks me to come to Ballarat. So off we go and live in a flat together.'

'Did she show signs of mental illness?'

'Not that I noticed at the time, but funnily enough she started acting strange one evening. We'd been in Ballarat for a couple of months and I thought things were goin' good between us, and one night we went out to this restaurant. She started actin' a bit weird, and when I asked her what was goin' on she just got up and said,

"I can't hack this" and walked out. Just like that! Right out of the restaurant and just disappeared.'

'She wasn't back at the flat?'

'Nah, she just upped and left, leavin' me to pay the rent.'

Greg had still not got over how amazed he was at her behaviour.

'It's only when I see the way she is now that I think she was already actin' funny then. And this wasn't the first time she'd stung me for loot. She was always owin' rent to someone or other.'

'So when did you see her again?'

'Well, not for ages, and I'd given up on ever seein' her again. It was the next Christmas when I got an answerin' machine message out of the blue, sayin' I was a father.'

'What, you didn't even know she was pregnant?'

This story was getting weirder by the minute and this guy was supposedly sane. I was pretty sure he was sane, although I did think he was a little naive. My sister had really given him the run around.

'Yeah, so I was a bit shocked, but then I counted back the months and it seemed to fit. Mind you, she said she was on the Pill. It took me a while to track her down, and by then Gabriel was in the foster home and Alex in some sort of hospital, in love with this guy John.'

'Did Alex give you the spiel about the grandmothers?'

'Yeah, she did, and Human Services contacted me too. Don't get me wrong. I really wanted to look after Gabriel, but there was a problem. You see, I'd been married before and had a kid, but my wife was a heroin addict and cleaned me out of all my money and then left. In fact, she pissed off to your part of the world, Leicester, I think, and took the kid with her. I was so upset that I started to drink heavily and got into big problems with alcohol—you know, couldn't control it when I had a drink. It was fairly under control when I was in Ballarat, but by the time I was back in Melbourne and found out about Gabriel, I was pretty pickled most of the time.'

Phew, this story got worse and worse. My mentally ill sister and an alcoholic get together and produce a child. I almost felt an inkling of sympathy for my father and Val's position.

'Anyway, I'd been so upset about losin' my little girl Tracy that I was determined I wasn't gonna let this kid get away too. So I went to AA and in a few months I'd licked the booze enough to try to claim Gabriel. I took a paternity test—only because Human

Services advised me to, mind. Yeah, it came up trumps. But then I was sent to parentin' classes and began to visit Gabriel so we could get used to each other. He loved my visits and we got on like a house on fire. This all took several months and then finally, when he was eighteen months old, everyone was of the opinion that I was ready to take him home.'

I had great admiration for this guy who had looked after my nephew for the last eighteen months and seemed to be doing a great job.

'Part of the deal is Gabriel has to have regular contact with his mum. So we visit her every week and sometimes she comes and stays for the weekend.'

'And have you heard at all from Alex's family?'

'Nah, not a snotter. I think they don't wanna know. Alex rings up her ol' man from time to time but that's about it.'

I felt compelled to apologise for my family so explained some of the history. 'Oh, if only Dad would meet Gabriel, I'm sure things would change.'

A plan was beginning to take shape in my mind.

16 / **Breakthrough**

We took the glorious Great Ocean Road to Adelaide, spending a couple of weeks camping and exploring the beauty of wild Australia. I had a lot to digest and take in. I was deeply saddened by the state of affairs in my family and felt that it might take a miracle for any healing to take place. The divisions felt so deep and entrenched.

I was reading a novel, *The Sound of One Hand Clapping*, that had many parallels to my own story. It was the fictitious account of Slovenian migrants who had gone to Tasmania, about the same time as Sasha, to work on the hydro-electric scheme. The wife hated it so much she committed suicide, leaving a husband and child to pick up the pieces. The suicide had blighted the father and daughter's relationship irrevocably just as Olga's insanity had ours. The daughter eventually escaped to Hobart to live and became pregnant. This drove the relationship further apart as the father had similar reactions as Dad had to Alex's pregnancy. But this tale has a happy ending. The father had an epiphanous experience, built a cradle for his future grandchild and became reconciled with his daughter.

I fantasised reconciling with my father, crying with him, laughing with him, even us hugging each other. I fantasised him falling in love with Gabriel and forgiving Alex …

I shook myself back to reality. This was just fiction I was reading. Real life was much harsher.

Real life was more like the movie *Shine*, which had been filmed in Adelaide and had come out the year before. This cut even closer to home. The father of the crazy pianist David Helfgott was the Polish equivalent of Sasha. He gave the ultimatum to his son that if he left to pursue his musical genius, he must not darken the door of the family home again. With this came the familiar diatribe of a poor, dispossessed migrant to whom family was everything because most dear ones had died some god-awful death in the war. It was me and David Helfgott, both banished to damnation because we dared leave the family nest, the family that the father had broken his back to keep together safe and sound in this strange new world.

David and his father never resolved their differences. David went spectacularly mad and ended up in a loony bin (the same one in the film as my mother's). *So,* I thought grimly to myself. *This healing-the-family business is pie in the sky. And let's face it, a leopard never changes its spots.*

It was with this gloomy disposition that I made my way back to the leopard's den. I rang several times but there was no reply. We banged on doors back and front. Nothing. I started phoning the major hospitals in Adelaide. 'Well, he did look pretty terrible last time we saw him.'

Then I struck the right hospital. He was recovering from major surgery. We went.

He was still under observation, so we found him in the emergency section surrounded by lots of technical equipment. I saw the back of his head first and he looked like the 1950s cartoon character Mr Magoo, balding egg head sunk into his shoulders and sporting huge dark-rimmed glasses. Ears encased in headphones, he was twiddling with a portable radio. He spotted us and, looking annoyed, took off the earphones and scrabbled for his pink helicopter, grumbling under his breath.

No 'hello' or 'it's nice to see you', but: 'There's someting rotten going on in the world and it's only people on the ball, like me, who knaow what's goin' on.' He vigorously pointed at the radio. 'But you knaow what? I have to be very careful as they doan' want anyone to find out that I knaow.'

He delivered this in a meaningful tone of voice, mingled with sarcasm. I didn't have a clue what he was talking about. I finally gathered that he had been tuning in to his short-wave radio and was interpreting the ensuing garble as secret code-sharing between nefarious groups. He was sure he could hear Russian and Arabic and claimed he had tapped into some kind of plot. I didn't understand what disaster was being cooked up and I didn't care. All I could think of was *Gee, Dad, you've gone totally potty too. What kind of a world do you live in? Am I supposed to stand here and listen to some weird, fantastical conspiracy theory again? I had enough of that from my mother. God spare me!* (Now as I write this post-September 11 I am wondering if Dad was on to something. Perhaps I should have listened!)

Anyway, I'm in this hospital trying to see my father for what he actually is—a very sick cadaver of a man who, while trying to save the world from catastrophe, has just had half his colon removed. 'Cancer,' he pronounces ominously. 'Cancer. Who would think that I would get cancer? I have eaten good food, excellent food.' He pretty well shouts this at us, convinced that escaping to the good life in Australia should have entitled him not to fall prey to cancer.

The sister at the nurses' station directs a concerned eye over at Mr Magoo waving his fists angrily and comes over tut-tutting. 'Now, Mr Levkowicz, take it easy. Isn't it lovely that your daughter has come all the way over from England to see you?' She smiles benevolently at the supposedly harmonious family reunion. I oblige the charade and smile back, covering up the thought, *Hmmph, he's as happy as a sandboy—can't wait for me to leave so he can get back to intercepting some coded conspiracy and saving humanity.*

It is time to empty his colostomy bag so Jake and I leave, promising to return next day. The nurse gives me his doctor's number so I can be brought up to date with what is going on. Dad has indeed had part of his colon removed; the operation was successful and he has come out of it remarkably well. He also recently underwent heart surgery. However, the bad news is that spots detected on his liver mean the cancer has spread. The doctor advises against any further treatments because of Dad's age and thinks he has probably between one and three months to live. A dire prognosis.

I am shocked by this unexpected news. I ring Val, who sounds hassled. She finds it stressful and expensive to fly back and forth to Adelaide from Melbourne, especially when she has Barney to look after and Denis has an acting job in Sydney. To lighten her burden, I tell her I will take as much responsibility as I can off her shoulders. I tell her about Gabriel and what a good job Greg is doing bringing him up. Big mistake. Greg is not her favourite person. She regards him as just another irresponsible bloke in a long line of unsavoury characters that Alex ran around with in Melbourne. She also informs me that within a week of Dad finding out that Alex was pregnant, he had a diabetic collapse. Val believes Alex drove Dad to ill health with her 'gung-ho, fuck-the-consequences' attitude to life.

So Eva, how is the healing of the family going? It seems to be going from bad to worse! Val and Dad are right. It is all a charade.

When I walk into the hospital room next day, Dad is in intimate conversation with a stylishly dressed, attractive, thirtyish woman. He introduces her proudly to me as Lee, and I immediately say something crass like, 'Goodness, aren't you pretty?', genuinely shocked that someone so attractive could be remotely interested in my father. *Ah, so this is the young woman Sophi told me about.* She had visited Dad the previous year, and he had mentioned an Italian woman who had invited him over for Christmas a few times.

Lee and I like each other immediately, and over coffee later she satisfies my curiosity by filling in the details of her friendship with my father. She answered an advert Dad had put in the paper selling furniture. Immediately she walked in the front door she fell in love with the antiques, ornaments and paintings. But this was not their only shared passion. It seemed that they really understood each other. Sitting at the kitchen table, my father had poured out the story of how his wife became mentally ill and eventually died, leaving him with two motherless children (I had been cast out as the ungrateful miscreant who had turned her back on the long-suffering hero). The story had affected Lee deeply and she had sobbed into one of his handkerchiefs. Over the next couple of years she had visited Dad regularly and they had become very close.

'I'm the kind of person who finds it really hard to make friends,' she says. 'I'm a real loner and so is Alexander. He seems to understand me like no one else does. We talk about anything, everything. I am so devastated that he's got cancer.' Her dark eyes fill with tears. I find it hard to believe that Dad is a real human being and is capable of a deeper relationship.

I go back the next day. He still acts tough and distant with me. He can't quite equate the story in his head about me as a degenerate betrayer with me as the devoted daughter visiting him in hospital. But now I become quite useful to him because he can't eat a lot of the food he is being served and I can do something about it.

Amazingly enough, this hospital, one of the many in Western civilisation lauded as advanced and in the forefront of modern medicine, has ignored any connection whatsoever between major abdominal surgery and what the patient is fed. A large proportion of my father's gut has been removed and a crude hole made in his stomach wall. But the food churned out from the hospital kitchens assumes that all recipients have got cast iron guts. My father regards his tough piece of leathery steak, adorned with glutinous gravy and lifeless vegetables, with queasy uncertainty. He is caught in a dilemma. Having paid heftily into his private health scheme, he imagines that this private hospital is the best that money can buy and that he is receiving superior care. He is now intimately acquainted with what comes spurting out of the hole in his stomach, and frankly it does not look good. He also hates the sugary orange cordial that appears in a plastic container on his hospital tray. He actually *knows* this is bad for him as he is a diabetic, but he doesn't dare to confront the nurses since he holds them in such high esteem.

And so I enter the picture. I have no illusions whatsoever about the sanctity of the medical profession and have always loved good food. I firmly believe that a sick, old, de-colonised man who has to watch the contents of his stomach spurting into a kidney dish should not be fed this garbage. My first victory is to get the sugary orange cordial replaced by fresh orange juice. I can see myself going up in my father's estimation. I then ask him what he feels like eating. He thinks for a while and answers 'some kind of potato soup'—but how impossible that would be since lunch is now over and his steak has coldly congealed in its gravy. I go and speak very nicely to the nurses and tell them that I am prepared to go down to the kitchen and cook the potato soup myself if necessary. They understand the depth of my intent and very shortly a bowl of potato soup appears alongside the much-welcomed fresh orange juice.

My father is reappraising this degenerate outcast of a daughter as he contemplates the potato soup. He looks so weak and helpless sitting there in his white gown that I pick up the spoon and start feeding him. He meekly accepts. I am surprised. The archenemy is happy to be spoon-fed. I blow on the soup to cool it and very gently place it in his mouth. He swallows it gratefully, and I can see that this is what his poor battered system needs: easy, gentle nourishment administered with love. Yes, I feel love for him, and tenderness. I love his nearly bald Mr Magoo head. Most of all I love it that he is letting me feed him. This simple action speaks louder than hundreds of words with all of their possibilities for misinterpretation. He finishes his soup, lies back and falls into a contented sleep. With strict instructions to the staff about what he should be given for breakfast, I slip out. I feel strangely at peace. This has been a good day.

Next morning he is distressed. His insulin levels are fluctuating wildly and he is having problems with his lower end. He complains that no one is listening to him. The staff have been promising a drip feed to stabilise his insulin but it has not yet materialised. In steps 'super hero'. Within fifteen minutes a drip feed is wheeled in and hooked up, and Dad is feeling a whole lot better.

I am really pleased that force of circumstance is giving me an important role to play. I am becoming my father's champion and he looks forward to me coming to visit. He seems to have abandoned his earphones and mission to decipher heinous plots to blow up the world, and instead samples small pieces of his favourite food that I bring for him.

One evening I come in and he is sitting in a chair reading the paper by the side of the hospital bed. This has afforded a welcome change from being in bed all day. He is feeling a little stronger and has already begun to talk of going home. He makes to get up from his chair to get back into bed but his strength fails him. I instantly jump up to help but he stops me.

'Nah, nah, nah! I must do this myself. I must build up my strengt'.'

I watch for the next few minutes while he psyches himself up to raise himself. With absolute determination he grips the sides of the chair and lifts. There follows the straining of sinews, the corralling of wasted muscles, the marshalling of inner strength, but all to no avail. Collapse. It all begins again.

After the third abject failure I go to him again to help him up.

'Nah, nah, nah, it will happen.'

I marvel at the persistence of the man. He has had two recent bouts of major surgery and been blasted by a cancer that has now spread to his liver; his body is readjusting to a drastically altered digestive system; his insulin levels are up and down like a yo-yo. Yet he is determined to get up out of that chair, stand up and get into that bed, even if it kills him. After another few minutes of futile attempts, I cannot bear it any more and escape to the rest room. I busy myself for as long as I can, hoping that when I return, the agony will be over and he will have lifted himself out of his chair. I linger on the way back, spying around the corner at what progress has been made. I observe him, gleaming Slavic flat-topped head, open-backed white hospital gown, jaw set, still mustering up deep reserves of Jewish resilience and Russian fortitude to get up out of that damned chair.

He gives me a shake of the head that signifies something like, 'I didn't survive the Nazi extermination of my countrymen to be defeated now by this blasted chair!' I resign myself to watching helplessly again.

After a few more interminable minutes, I snap. I approach. I put a hand gently on his arm.

'Dad, please let me help you. You are really ill. You have had serious surgery for a life-threatening illness. You haven't yet regained your strength. It is no shame if you let me help you.'

I increase the pressure on his arm. I feel the stubbornness through his skin. I grasp his other arm with my hand. A deep love for this man swells inside me. I acutely feel his struggle, and with my touch I try to get across that there is no loss of dignity if he lowers his resistance and allows another being to help him. I realise that for him it is not just an old man's struggle to reach within for the last vestiges of a younger man's strength, not just an obeisance of a resolute iron will that deems he can do whatever he sets out to do, but something else altogether, something unfamiliar and alien: to trust and open up to another person and allow himself to be helped. The fact that this other person is his estranged daughter whom he cast out of his heart thirty-three years before makes the moment even more poignant.

He allows me to lift him to his feet and together we shuffle him to the bed. I help ease him in, bearing the weight of his wasted body as he lets himself lean on me. I am holding my breath at the momentous nature of the act, and not wanting to draw much attention to it, fuss about with blankets, fluff up pillows and scrape chairs unnecessarily.

'T'anks, Eva.' More scrapings and fluffings follow as I disguise the lump in my throat. This is the first time that my father has called me by my name in a third of a century.

I sneak a look at him sideways but he is not gazing at me lovingly. He is in fact making funny movements with his mouth. Then he takes out his false teeth. 'Blasted! I forgot to clean my teet'. It hurts on my gums.' He points the offending dentures towards the washbasin, which is now outside his reach.

'Oh, give them here. I'll clean them for you.'

Dubiously he hands me the teeth, which look pretty disgusting and manky. I turn to the sink and clean them gratefully. Tears mix with the water that swills over them. I feel ludicrously happy to be sluicing and poking out the rotten debris that has attached itself like barnacles to the underside of the dentures.

My father is allowing me back into his life at long last.

He puts his teeth back in and looks at me.

'How's Alexandra?'

I report how I think she is. He keeps shaking his head sadly as I speak.

'Poor ting, jus' like Mahder. I doan' knaow what I did wrong. She was such lovely normal child.' He looks so broken and sad.

I reach out for his hand and he doesn't resist. His hand is gnarled and a large arthritic lump grows like a gargoyle on his forefinger knuckle. I place my hand over it protectively. I look at him and I see him, not only as a frail, sick man attached to a drip, but as an innocent young Jewish boy watching in unbelievable horror as the world turns ugly before his eyes. Underneath all the gruff exterior is a mild-mannered being trying to make sense of a world gone mad—the SS shooting his family; returning orphans from Mengele's experiments; the loss of his teenage brother on the Western Front; being blacklisted by the Stalinist regime for having survived the Nazi terror. I see a simple-hearted man who escapes to Australia under a false name, endures great prejudice and takes on my harassed refugee mother and me, her three-year-old child. Again this simple soul watches helplessly as my traumatised mother cannot survive in this strange new country and lurches from drugs and ECT to lobotomy, convinced that 'They' are out to get her. Then his stepdaughter, whom he took on whole-heartedly and loved dearly, skives off, leaving him to cope with two small, motherless girls, the youngest of whom is now falling fast into the same mental illness as her mother.

I look into the sad eyes and very softly say, 'Dad, it's not your fault that Alex is mentally ill. It's not your fault that Mum was mentally ill. I'm really sorry that I left you to carry the burden on your own. But I had to get out. I had to find happiness.'

I feel that I am entering risky waters here, the very waters where I have been condemned for leaving home instead of sacrificing my life and staying with the family forever, mourning the tragedy that had befallen us. But this simple being just blinks at me and does not withdraw his hand, so I continue.

'I have felt Mum's presence a lot, and in Ukraine I understood very clearly that I owe it to Mum to live a happy life. Otherwise her sacrifice of leaving her beloved homeland forever, and all the consequences of that, will have been in vain. I owe it to her, and to you, to be happy.'

His silence speaks volumes. He is not arguing.

17 / Lifting the Iron Curtain

That night I say goodbye to Dad for a couple of days. Jake and I are off to the Yorke Peninsula, a pleasant undulating leg of land about two hundred miles from Adelaide. I am as high as a kite. I feel a huge breakthrough has happened and that my father and I have opened up to each other. I can't quite describe what has happened, but I feel there has been a definite shift. However, I am apprehensive when I phone him next day from a beach on the Peninsula. Will the shift still be there? Or will old hostilities be resumed?

'Hi Dad.' I am hardly breathing.

'Eva! How's tings?' A good start. A very good start. I can hear the pink helicopter being adjusted.

'Oh, pretty good. The beaches are lovely but the weather is a bit cold. How are you feeling?'

'Oh, you knaow, not too bad.' I love the sound of his voice.

'I really miss you. I wish I was there with you.' It's true I just want to be looking after my dad.

Pause.

'You knaow, Eva, you're orkai!'

I'm choked. This, from my father, is wonderful praise. Yes, the connection is still there. My fears have been unfounded.

'I'll be back tomorrow and I'm really looking forward to seeing you.'

'Me too.'

I hang up and look at Jake. I am shining.

'It's all okay and now I know it's permanent. I was really worried that last night was just a fluke and that today Dad would be back to hating me. I now know that things between us are irrevocably different. Sure, we still have lots of things to talk about and sort through. But he said I'm okay. His attitude to me has totally shifted.'

Jake is really happy for me. He has witnessed the long hard slog that I have made to get to this point.

*

Greeny-brown gunge spurts from the angry red hole in Dad's stomach. He is being taught by the nurse how to change his colostomy bag for when he goes home from hospital. It looks a complicated affair to me; you have to clean the area around the gaping hole carefully before you stick the sides of the bag on to the skin. Unfortunately, peristalsis has a mind of its own and does not conveniently wait until this procedure has finished. Having to trap waste matter like this makes the connection between what you eat and what comes out exceedingly graphic, both in sight and smell. My father soldiers bravely on, attempting to plaster over and hide this offending material as quickly as possible.

He is recovering well from the surgery and is preparing to leave hospital soon. I am definitely still in his good books. When I kiss him or hug him he still does not reciprocate. He has been alone for far too long to be used to physical contact. But he is definitely pleased to see me, and I am delighted to sit with him and help him with his physical tribulations.

I have a desperate urge to save him. I still see the young vulnerable seventeen-year-old that his mother, Hana, last saw in 1941. I feel her presence now. I say to her silently:

'Hana, Sasha has done really well. He has survived terrible horrors in the war. In Australia he has led a comfortable although sad life. He is now seventy-five and has cancer. You gave him something very solid in his early life and that has helped him through. Val looked after him as best she could and now I am here.'

Dad and I talk a lot about my mother and Alexandra. I show him photos of Gabriel. He is reluctant at first even to look at them, but when he does I think he is shocked and secretly pleased how much Gabriel looks like him. He is still scandalised by the fact that Gabriel was conceived and born out of wedlock. This fact weighs very heavily on him and he feels deeply ashamed that this has happened in his family. I extol the virtues of Greg and describe how seriously he is taking the responsibility of bringing up his child.

After a few days I feel he is beginning to soften on the Gabriel issue. I have a plan. I want Dad to see Gabriel before he dies. But I keep this plan to myself. I am just sowing the seeds.

I tell Dad about finding Mum's relatives. He seems quite reserved about this subject. A darkness crosses his brow when I say I will be meeting them soon. I wonder what hidden pockets of memory have been stirred.

The next time I come in, Dad is agitated. 'Nah, I woan' go into nursink home!' he shouts. 'No! I woan' go! I go to my home!' Val has rung saying he should go into a nursing home.

I phone her and say, 'I will talk to the doctors and to Dad and find out the best thing to do. I know that you have been bearing the brunt of looking after Dad and I understand all your concerns, but I am here now and prepared to do anything that is needed to make him comfortable.'

I feel like piggy in the middle. My sister, on the one hand, believes quite reasonably that, with his diabetes, weak heart and cancer, going home is out of the question. Dad, on the other hand, would rather die than go to a nursing home. Such places are anathema to him, especially given the fact that his private insurance does not cover them.

The new-found understanding between us is strengthened even more when Dad looks at me and says, 'I want to go home but will do what you tink is best.' I feel very happy that he trusts me to come up with the best solution.

I spend time speaking to Val, nurses and doctors and looking at all the alternatives. He is free to go home when he wants, but support there will be minimal. Nurses can come in every day, but the rest of the time he must fend for himself. I find a compromise. He can go into a convalescent home for a week and then go home. As well as giving him more time to heal, this has a huge benefit as far as Dad is concerned in that it can be paid for by his private health cover. I also discover that his local council can offer home help.

He is very happy with this solution, trusting my judgment that he needs to recuperate a little while longer before being able to manage at home on his own. I also promise that I will be back as soon as possible.

I manage to convey a future scenario that also mollifies my sister. She is happy to come over for a while to help after his stay in the convalescent home.

*

'Shika, Shika,' my father calls for his cat. But Shika is ensconced in his hiding place in the shed and is very wary of me. I have been feeding him for several days, but he only comes out for the food after I'm gone.

'I knaow how Shika feels. He jus' like me. Doan' trust nobahdy. Here Shika, c'mon Shika.' Shika finally ventures out and purrs against my father's legs.

We are on the way to the convalescent home but have stopped by the house to get some clean clothes and other supplies. Dad surprises me by putting a bundle of furs into my arms.

'For mahder's relatives! You give 'em. Very expensive. Mink, you knaow. Belonged to mahder.'

One of them looks pretty grotesque with its legs and head still attached. But the other two are very beautiful. I remember with sadness my mother wearing them in the days when she saw herself as a rich grand lady. She'd seen the film stars wearing minks and wanted to be like them. Of course my father was outraged, but after yet another episode of her throwing money around the shop and screaming, 'What all zis money for, you miserable bastard!', he succumbed and bought her the furs.

'Yes, I'll take them to Ukraine. I'm sure her relatives will be very happy to have something that belonged to her. Thank you very much.'

Dad is very pleased with the convalescent home as he has a room to himself which also contains a fridge. I go out and buy all the goodies he likes from the Adelaide Market, including Polish sausage, garlic, gherkins and rye bread. He is a bit worried about offending the nurses if he or his room smell too much of garlic. As I am leaving the next day and want him to be as happy as possible, I speak to the head nurse.

She laughs. 'If you could smell some of the odours I have to confront in this place, I assure you garlic would make a most welcome change.'

Dad and I have some cosy chats. We speak of Alexandra and

Gabriel again and he is much more open to the existence of Gabriel. I tell him of the plan I have cooking that when I return to Australia I will bring Alex and Gabriel to see him. He is a bit reluctant, but in the end agrees.

Now that Dad has some of his strength back we talk about his health. He knows he has spots on his liver and the doctor has told him he could have as little as a month to live. I play this down, saying that no one but God knows how long he has got. I tell him I will do a whole lot of research and inform him of his chances. I also find out some local cancer groups in Unley for him to attend. I think I successfully instil in him that his health is a challenge and that he shouldn't just resign himself to a death sentence. We both agree that he must try not to get as stressed as he has done in the past.

I am very sad to be leaving the next day. I feel pleased that he is getting much better and I promise to be back within a couple of months to look after him some more.

*

I CURED MYSELF OF LIVER CANCER IN SIX WEEKS! As soon as I return to the UK, I plunge into the vast array of colon and liver cancer sites on the Internet, ranging from the sober and official to the more zany that promise amazing cures. I am fired by a zeal to heal Dad. I have just started a new love relationship with him and don't want to lose him yet.

I arrange to take my sister Alex and her son to Adelaide. I write to Dad telling him of the plans and send him a lot of information about cancer and some ways he can start helping himself immediately. I phone him every few days. Often this is an ordeal as I have to shout over the whirrings of the pink helicopter. He is back at home now and seems to be coping well.

Dad has a Greek neighbour, Ephrosia, who has lived next-door for over twenty years. I met her when I was feeding the cat and she told me that she had tried to be a good neighbour but Dad was rude and unfriendly. In hospital I confronted him about this, and after listening to a particularly long rant, finally discovered the source of the dislike. When Dad first moved to Northgate Street, Unley Park, it was a very wealthy street and only prosperous families of the well-established Adelaide middle classes lived there. Dad felt like he had made it and was rubbing shoulders with the people who really mattered. When the house next-door came up for sale and Ephrosia and her husband bought it, he was totally incensed and still hadn't got over it. The fact that Ephrosia had emigrated to Australia in the 1930s and came from a well-established, successful Greek family made little difference. 'I move to Nort'gate Street, I am somebahdy! And what happens? Bloody Greeks move in and lower tone of neighbourhood.'

Having thought that I had lost the battle of changing Dad's attitude to Ephrosia, it now transpires that since our conversation Dad has let her help him, and occasionally has accepted her homemade dolmades. I feel more secure in the UK knowing that she is keeping an eye on him.

Val has been over to see him once or twice as she is putting on a play in Adelaide at the end of May 2000. She says that he constantly refers to being on death row and wants to talk about his past. She feels she can't cope with it and thinks he needs a therapist! I, on the other hand, can't wait to get back to Adelaide and listen to everything he has to say. I'm very sad that he feels he is on death row and just want to be with him and hold his hand.

I talk to Dad on the telephone about Gabriel and Alex's visit. I pick up that he is uncomfortable and find out that the planned visit coincides with the time that he will be in hospital having his colostomy operation reversed. We both agree that in light of this Gabriel would be too much to cope with and that I should just bring over Alexandra. At least that will be a good start in the family healing process.

I find a new cancer treatment that places biospheres into the liver which supposedly kill off the cancer cells. I send Dad all the details but he is not keen to travel interstate for the treatment. He is more open to a Chinese herbal treatment I have discovered, and I promise to buy him some in Singapore on the way to Australia. He tells me he has been to the Cancer Care Centre in Unley. This is a huge step forward for such a recluse and I enthuse about it. 'That's great. What happened?'

'Oh, I learn how to do—um, what you call it?'

This routine has been played in our family all of our lives. Either Mum or Dad would not know a word and muggins here would have to guess what it was.

'Visualisation?' I venture trying to second guess on very little available information, only that he had been to the Cancer Centre.

'Nah, nah, nah! It's um—er, what you call it?' Annoyance in the voice because I haven't guessed it straight away. What the hell has he learnt to do there? I scour my brain cells.

'Relaxation?'

'Nah, nah! You knaow what it is!' Getting very annoyed.

'Give me some clues. What do you do?'

'You knaow, Eva. What *you* do!'

'What I do?' I am really puzzled now. What has he learnt to do in the cancer centre that I do?

'You knaow, you sit and—Christ, I can't remember the word!'

'Are you sure it's not visualisation or relaxation?'

'Nah!' Shouts down the phone even more loudly than usual. Highly annoyed now!

I've got to get it. I rack my brains. What I do?

'Meditate?' I venture dubiously. The idea of my father meditating is about as alien as George W Bush becoming a Muslim.

'Yes! Yes! I learn meditation!' Bingo and wow! I almost faint on the carpet.

Not only has my father ceased to be Public Enemy Number One, but he is now meditating! Wonders never cease.

'But that sounds great,' I enthuse. 'That will certainly help reduce your stress levels.'

'Lee also say I should see a naturopath.'

Good old Lee. I feel that my father is beginning to fight for himself and not just sit back in a resigned fashion and believe his death sentence.

'But my doctor say it no good and that nuttin' will work.'

'Bollocks!' I launch into an attack on allopathic medicine and it's emphasis on symptoms, and sing the praises of alternative medicine and it's emphasis on treating the whole person.

'Yeah that's what they say at Cancer Centre. You clever, Eva!'

Now this is more high praise. I lap it up like a starving beggar and let it fall nourishingly into the unhealed time and place within me—the seven-year-old child who had just learned English, coming home with a report card, proudly showing I had got 95 marks out of 100, only to be rebuked, 'Where ahder fife marks?'

I ring Dad's doctor long distance and urge him to be a little more tolerant of Dad trying alternative treatments. He is sceptical and thinks I am fostering false hope.

'So what?' I answer. 'While there is life there always is hope.' This goes down like a lead balloon, but I think the doctor has got the message.

My relationship with my father seems to be leapfrogging forward, and even with our being twelve thousand miles apart and communicating by phone and mail, it is deeply satisfying to both of us. How will it fare when I stay with him for six weeks?

But before I return to Australia I have another family mission in Ukraine.

18 / **Tarasivka**

'Za Babs!' This is the traditional Russian toast to womankind. And a tricky one. The men are standing with their charged vodka glasses balanced precariously on their elbows, a large beer chaser in the other hand. The neophyte Jake attempts to drink the vodka, trying to bring his crooked elbow closer to his mouth. He splutters and fails spectacularly, the vodka and beer splashing all over him. We laugh like idiots for at least half an hour, and any new attempt to complete the toast ends in rivers of spilt beer and vodka and more gales of laughter.

We are at Lena's parents' dacha before heading off to meet my mother's relatives. Jake loves Ukraine partly because he can't read or speak the language. As a professor of a university department and an MD of a business, he is always taking responsibility and using his brain, but here in Ukraine he can just sit back, relax and mime if necessary. Wonderful!

The flight from Kiev to Kharkiv taxed both our miming abilities and my slender command of the language. I had bought the tickets in the UK for the short internal flight with Aerosweet, the national carrier. We arrived at the airport, which looked like a provincial bus station, and handed in our tickets at what looked like a check-in desk. The tickets were thrown back with a torrent of Ukrainian which seemed to suggest that they were faulty in some way. After a lengthy, seemingly hopeless exchange, we could see that our tickets said RVV193K and the flight number up on the board said RUU193K. Everything else—the flight time, embarkation point and destination—was exactly the same. The fact there was only one flight that evening to Kharkiv (one of two flights in the whole week) seemed to be immaterial to the desk clerk. She had the impassive square-jaw look of the bygone communist era and would not budge from her position. 'Nyet!' Our ticket was wrong and we could not board the plane.

The next plane was in four days' time and Lena and her father were waiting for us at Kharkiv airport. What could we do? It was like being in some Kafkaesque farce. We ran around the airport like blue-arsed flies and finally found an official-looking person who spoke a smattering of English. We explained the whole story and then had to repeat it again to someone else. With a lot of gesticulating and flourishing of tickets we were getting the same message: tickets useless! The time for the flight to leave was looming closer and Jake frantically started waving American fifty dollar bills around, shouting, 'We want new tickets!' This seemed to do the trick.

'Wait!' said the official. 'I bring you captain!'

'Ah, things are looking up,' sighed Jake with relief. 'At least the plane can't leave without the captain!'

Expecting to see a neat uniformed person with a captain's hat, we were approached instead by a gorgeous young man who looked like a rock star. His black hair was all spiked and gelled and he was wearing a trendy leather jacket. 'This is captain,' announced the official. After more explanations and gesticulations, the deal was done. We gave the rock star one hundred dollars, which he carefully folded into his black leather pocket.

'Follow me,' he ordered.

Carrying our cases, we followed him out of the building, onto the tarmac, up some steps and onto a battered, very suspect-looking twin propeller plane, neither very sweet nor even 'aero'. After showing us to our seats, the rock star casually strolled to the front of the plane and started the engines.

On telling this story to Lena at the other end she just smiled knowingly and said, 'Welcome to Ukraine!'

Jake has a great time at the dacha. He and Lena's parents get on like long lost buddies, despite the fact they cannot speak a word of each other's language. With Lena doing a sterling job of translating, the conversation flows as freely as the drink while Lena's family acquaint themselves with the first Englishman they have ever met. Once on opposite sides in the Cold War, we exchange stories of life in our respective countries and marvel at the deep levels of similarity between us. There are many toasts, some really raucous and silly like 'Za Babs!', but others that take our breath away and bring tears to our eyes.

'We would like to honour our special guests who bring such wit and wisdom to our table and such joy and love to our hearts. Our home is also your home and you will always be welcome.'

We bask in the warmth of the irrepressible Russian spirit and I am delighted that Jake is getting a taste of what my people are like.

Even though corruption in Ukraine continues to be rife, things have got marginally better since I was here a year ago. Lena is now teaching English full-time and the Muskovitch has been replaced by a new Lada. It is in this car that Lena, her father Vitaly and the 'special guests' set off for Poltava the next day. We will be meeting with a representative of the Society for Nazi Prisoners of War who will then direct us to meet my relatives.

I am feeling excited but also a little apprehensive. My fear is that they will be strange and I won't like them. I am deeply satisfied to have found Lena and her parents. They are my ideal Russian family. My own blood family may not measure up.

At four o'clock we arrive at the prearranged rendezvous point on the main road outside Orzhitsa, a provincial town in the Poltava district. I am now decidedly nervous. I spot a group of people sitting in the back of a green army-type bus, vintage early 1950s. Out steps a man in an ill-fitting, shiny grey suit and a very bad haircut. He comes towards me extending his hand.

'Eva Chapman? Petro Babenko,' he answers to my nod. He then turns to a woman in her fifties, greying hair pulled back in a tight bun, dressed in a drab raincoat.

'My wife Nina and your cousin,' Lena translates. Nina is trembling and has tears in her eyes. I embrace her, feeling amazed that I am actually hugging a *cousin*! Then a whole retinue of people spill out of the back of the green bus. Two are Nina's grown-up daughters, Luda and Sveta. Luda's husband, Vas, and two children, Vika and Alex, are introduced. Then in another ill-fitting suit steps out an elderly man, Ivan Leontivich. I gasp. He has the same green-grey eyes as my mother. He holds my hands and looks at me searchingly. I don't quite understand who he is, but I think he is some sort of uncle.

By Western standards their clothes are unfashionable, but it is obvious that they have all put on their best clothes to meet this relative from the West. I find the meeting overwhelmingly poignant and am delighted that Lena and her father are there to keep the conversation flowing. These people are totally without guile or sophistication and all sorts of emotions clash within me. They look like a bunch of awkward New Australians—the sort of people I was once very ashamed of and with whom I did not want to be associated.

Nina's husband Petro grins at me, flashes of gold glinting in his crooked teeth.

'I am the one who spotted the picture of your mother in the *Poltava News*,' he announces proudly. I am pleased that I understand most of what they are saying and relieved that they are speaking a hybrid of Russian and Ukrainian that is very familiar to me. I am also grateful for Lena's translation.

We follow the green army bus to Luda and Vas's house, a substantial brick building in a very large yard, full of ducks, chickens, dogs, beehives and a cow. When I go to the outside latrine I see a pen containing half a dozen pigs. There is a summer kitchen outside, full of jars of honey and other produce. We are ushered into the inside kitchen where a giant feast is laid out for us. It seems that this family has been preparing for our visit for weeks. All sorts of delicacies are brought in throughout the evening. We drink, eat and talk well into the night.

There is a lot to talk about. The last fifty-seven years for a start!

It was in 1942 that my mother was taken as a slave to work for the Reichstag. I discover that Ivan is my mother's first cousin. He and his sister Marya are her only two cousins; their father, Leonid, is brother to Ivan, my mother's father. The three of them, all similar in age, formed a close unit in childhood. Ivan Leontivich says Olga was more like their sister, as her own brothers and sisters from her mother's first marriage were all a few years older. This is all quite confusing because my mother had a brother Ivan and a sister Maria that she often talked about. This takes a while to get used to. No wonder Russians use the patronymic. So the only way to distinguish this Ivan and Marya is by calling him Ivan Leontivich and her Marya Leontivna.

Ivan Leontivich tells me that his family received a letter from my mother in 1945 informing them that she was on her way home. 'Why did she not return?' he asks me almost accusingly.

I explain to him that she was indeed on her way home but had discovered, on approaching the Soviet border, that horrible things were happening to returning German prisoners of war. On hearing that her fate would probably be to work in the salt mines of Siberia, she had turned around and headed for the newly liberated Czechoslovakia. My new-found uncle scoffs at this. 'That was a bad decision. All that would have happened is she would have been sent to the coal mines of Donetsk for a few years and then would have been allowed home. Anyway, my sister Marya, who you will meet tomorrow, was also taken by the Germans as a slave and escaped twice!'

I am dubious if my mother would have survived better in a coal mine than a salt mine but prefer not to argue the point.

I give them a potted history of my mother's life after 1945 until her death in 1976. They are all sad to hear the story. Ivan informs me they received a letter and photos from my mother in 1956. In fact, one of these photos was similar to the one printed in the newspaper. Petro says it was this photo that led him to recognise the similarity. Ivan continues to recount that the very next day after receiving Olga's letter, he was visited by the KGB demanding to know why he was receiving mail from the decadent West. The whole family was interrogated and ordered not to reply. Communist literature would be sent instead to this morally defective and brainwashed relative in Australia. Ivan said it was with a great deal of regret that he couldn't answer Olga, for he was afraid of losing his job and other ignominies. As a child I had always wondered why we received communist newspapers from the USSR. While McCarthyism in the West was warning of communists underneath the bed, in the USSR the citizens were being warned against malignant influences from the corrupt West!

Luda and Vas put us up for the night in the living room. I am reminded of my childhood at the sight of a number of chicken eggs being warmed artificially in the corner. My relatives are lovely, but I cannot help judging them to be less sophisticated and lively than Lena's family. I am excited also because the next day I will be taken to the village in which my mother was born and lived as a girl. It is in this village, Tarisivka, that I will meet Marya, Ivan Leontivich's sister, the one who somehow managed to escape the Nazis twice, apparently walking all the way back from Germany on one occasion. What a feat! I lie in the dark listening to the hum of the egg warmer and feeling secure in the knowledge that I am discovering my roots.

Tarasivka, a small village a couple of miles from Orzhitsa, straddles the banks of a large river, the Sula. We pull up to a pretty whitewashed cottage surrounded by a huge garden. As we walk past the green shoots of garlic, growing rapidly after the recently melted snows, I see a picture of rural tranquillity. A pale brown cow is tethered in front of a barn and munches hay from an old-fashioned haystack. Chickens and ducks run and scratch between several fruit trees.

This has been the home of Marya for over sixty years. Her husband was killed in World War Two and she was left pregnant with Nina. Since Nina left to be married, her mother has lived here alone, milking her cow, growing all her food and baking bread for the whole family. Sveta tells me that her grandmother has been fretting for weeks about my impending arrival, worrying whether her home is good enough for such important visitors.

Sveta calls out to her grandmother that we have arrived, and ushers us through a porch into the main living room. As I walk in I am confronted by a tiny old lady with a white scarf tied around her head, holding forth a round loaf of bread and a container of salt on a wooden tray. She looks up at me, her hands trembling and tears coursing down her cheeks. I am deeply moved. This woman radiates a humility and purity that I have rarely seen in the West. Tears spill from my eyes, and as I turn to Lena and Jake I see they are crying too.

'This is the traditional Ukrainian welcome,' Lena whispers in my ear. 'You as the guest must break off some bread, dip it in the salt and eat it.'

I perform this task while the tiny woman looks at me with a mixture of love and shyness. It is like taking holy communion. Far from her home not being good enough to receive me, I feel I am not good enough for her home. I feel dirty and sullied, world-weary and not so wise. I drink in deeply the simplicity and goodness that is pouring out of the faded blue eyes into mine. We all partake of the bread and salt.

Then Marya hugs me, holds me, kisses me, uttering all the while, 'Boszhe moi, Boszhe moi, Evitchka, Olychka (little Olga), Boszhe moi. Ay-yai-yai-yai!' The language soothes my very soul. It is my language.

Marya won't leave my side and we sit together on a bench that runs along the side of her front room. She beams up at me every few minutes and kisses my cheek with a resounding smack. I am dumb-founded to see a photograph of me up on her whitewashed wall. I am about eight, plaits swinging and playing tennis. My mother sent this photograph in 1956 before the KGB truncated the fledgling communication. I find it simply astounding that all this time, while I have been flouncing from Southern Hemisphere to Northern Hemisphere and back again, rootless and homeless, a photo of me has been smiling down from this wall. For the last forty-five years!

I just can't believe that all this is happening. But it gets better. The old lady shows me how she gets bread out of her oven. This oven is a magnificent affair. It is literally the belly of the house. A large piece of it bulges out into the living room and another dom-inates the kitchen. This bit has a couple of beds above it where people sleep in the dead of winter. I climb up into this inviting alcove and Mum's stories of her childhood come flooding back. I can see her here, snug and cosy, sleeping above the warm heart of the house, wrapping her feather-filled coverlet more tightly around her as she hears the howling of the wolves in the distance.

I speak silently to her ghost. 'Oh Mum, I'm so happy to be seeing all this. I am intimately sharing a part of your life that had been lost to you forever when you told it to me. And you know what, Mum? It is as wonderful as you painted it, and I rejoice in it.'

I give Marya Olga's furs. She drapes one around her vulnerable little shoulders; a ghastly-looking mink's face and a few forlorn toes hang desultorily down her arm. I think I discern that she is a little less than happy with this keepsake of my mother's, but doesn't let it spoil the magnitude of the occasion.

We all go for a walk around the village. There are several old men in caps and women in headscarves loitering around the front gate. They want to see the English people who have come to their neighbour's house. This is quite a big occasion in the village as we are the first English specimens that have graced this part of the world. We smile and bow to them, trying to live up to their expectations of what English people are like. I think the fact that Jake does not wear a bowler hat and is not carrying an umbrella has already shocked their preconceptions.

We go past a gargantuan, deserted collective farm, ugly with twisted rusting machinery.

'They destroyed some beautiful old houses, an apple orchard and an ancient wood to build that kolkhoz. The end of Tarisivka, that,' grumbles Ivan Leontivich furtively, not yet entirely sure if informers are still lurking about, waiting for any ammunition for the next wave of denouncements. I wonder if the ancient wood was the very same one in which Olga gathered mushrooms and wildflowers.

A few snippets of the song she used to sing to me come back and I sing them to Marya.

Pashli detki tam gulat, lat, lat
Shtob svitochki tam narvat, vat, vat

Come on, children, let's go wander, wander, wander
To gather pretty flowers yonder, yonder, yonder

She is delighted that I know this song and sings it along with me, clutching my arm tightly as we walk. She points out a row of large houses.

'This was the posh end of town where Olychka lived. Her mother felt herself above all of us when she snaffled our uncle and took up with him. Thought herself the queen of the village, with all her fancy uppity ways. From kulak aristocracy she came.' Marya's tone emanates disapproval. I was to discover later the tortuous history behind that phrase 'kulak aristocracy' and the rivalries in the family. 'Oh, there's a house similar to where your mother was born. The original has been destroyed.'

This is a very handsome house indeed—larger than my aunt's and with an impressive frontage and red-tiled roof, a step up from tin or thatch. I can see Olga playing in the streets and by the river. I can also see the seeds sown for her future break with reality. Was it that she couldn't cope with the tension and discomfort of living in a place that her own mother felt was beneath her? Wasn't it my mother who often thought she was the Queen of Australia?

We walk through the fields by the river. After the recent melting of the winter snows, they are all a sepia colour blending in with the brownish tinge of the hurtling river. I see Olga in these fields, a sepia 1930s-type image, long plaits and ribbons, brown flowery dress; running and singing, eyes shining in the new spring moon as afternoon gradually turns into evening. I see her watching the swirling river, wondering where her future lies. The family show me where her old school used to be and I can see her walking there every morning, feeling as if she is starving during the time she called 'The Hungry Years'. 'I would have a headache I was so hungry,' she would tell me.

After making a long loop of the village and the river bank, we return to Marya's house. I ask her what she remembers about my mother.

'Olychka? Krasivaya, visokaya i hudinkaya,' she says.

I don't need Lena's translation. I understand. 'Little Olga was pretty, tall and thin.' 'Hudinkaya', the word for 'thin', is a word that I had forgotten, and I find its sound and meaning unbearably poignant.

Thanks to Marya's words I am again back in time, struck once more that it was here that my mother actually lived and existed. All her descriptions of her beloved homeland were of a real time and place and I am right here, right now, breathing it all in. And tasting it! We are given some milk from the cow, unbelievably good—not pasteurised, skimmed, boiled or treated in any way; just good old-fashioned milk. I explain to my relatives that it is virtually impossible to buy milk like this in the West. I also taste preserved fruits, sugared black currants and dill cucumbers. I even have a fantasy of coming and living in this village, growing food in the rich earth and having a simple, uncomplicated life.

It is almost as if Marya senses this and says, 'Evitchka, you are welcome here any time—this is your home.'

She gathers me closer to her and, somewhat conspiratorially, she and her brother beckon Lena to come and translate something of great importance. Jake is outside inspecting the garden.

'Now, Eva, we have to discuss something very important with you. We are a little concerned about you because you have married a foreigner.'

I suppress a laugh at this as I can see they are very serious. I have thought a lot of different things about Jake in the twenty or so years we have been together, but 'foreigner' has never been one of them.

'Well, you have to be careful if you have married a foreigner,' they went on, 'so we want to know if you will be in receipt of a pension—you know, if something should befall you.'

'Befall me? How do you mean?'

'Well, for example, if your husband was to run off with another woman, we want to know if you will have a pension to fall back on.'

I stare incredulously at Lena. Is she making a correct translation? Oh yes, she reassures me, and reiterates how important it is to these people that I, a member of their family, must be safe in my old age. It is even more a worry to them as they do not trust foreigners, especially if they are English (English men apparently have a reputation for running off with younger women). 'And besides,' continues Lena, 'they want to know how much pension you will be entitled to.'

'But Lena, my pension will be about £12,000 a year. I have been paying into a pension fund. You can't tell them that when they are only getting $100 a year!'

'No, not at all,' counters Lena. 'They will be delighted that it will be so much!'

She tells them the good news but they come back worriedly. 'But will this pension be paid to you?'

The problem in Ukraine is that even though pensioners are entitled to the pittance of $100 per year, it is often at best late and sometimes never paid. I reassure them that things are stable in England and I will get this money. After a few more animated exchanges where Lena explains that money matters are much more secure in the West, my relatives begin to look satisfied at last. I feel very touched by their concern—touched that these people who have so little should want to take care of someone like me who has so much, materially at least.

It is soon time to go, and Marya keeps plying me with gifts: a jar of the most wonderful-tasting preserved apricots from one of her trees; a jar of ogurki (cucumbers) from her garden. Yum! She also gives me a beautifully embroidered wedding towel which she made for her own wedding. This towel is a long piece of lavishly worked cotton that has an important place in a Ukrainian wedding ceremony. It is placed on the floor in front of the bride and groom at the altar. Whoever steps on to the towel first is the one who will be the boss in that relationship.

This has been such a rich day for me, and just when I think I cannot possibly shed any more tears or be moved more deeply, Marya gives me a parting gift—a little hand-sewn muslin bag with a drawstring at the top. She presses it into my hand. 'This is a piece of Ukrainian earth to put on your mother's grave.' Again we are all awash with tears as we hug and say goodbye to this remarkable and wonderful old lady.

We return to Orzhitsa for our final meal with the rest of the family. After being plied with even more delicious produce, Lena, Jake 'the foreigner', Vitaly and I drive off towards Kiev.

I am quite overwhelmed by the visit and have developed a resounding cough and streaming eyes. It feels like some profound issues have been stirred deep within, and my soul appears to be weeping. I feel very happy but also churned up, and my body is exploding. By the time we get to Vitaly's friends' place in Kiev, I am ill and have developed a fever. Lyuda, whom we are staying with, and Lena get to work to heal me, Russian-style. First they make a mustard poultice which they put on my back. Then they boil and mash some potatoes and put them on my chest. I must admit that I begin to feel better quite quickly—in fact, well enough to partake of another lavish feast that Lyuda and Anatoly have prepared for us.

It is our last evening in Ukraine and the feast, toasts, vodka and convivial company surpass all the previous similar occasions. I proceed to get uproariously drunk, and as the evening wears on I gradually lose the plot. I have vague memories of dancing on various surfaces and playing bad guitar. Somewhere in this drunken haze, I succumb to a terrible coughing fit and find myself lying on my bed with Lena and Lyuda doing weird things to my back. They are rubbing a jelly-like substance into my skin, saying things like, 'It's okay, Eva, we will cure this cough of yours in no time.' I can feel a strange feeling as if the skin on my back is being sucked up. I am too drunk to resist and find myself swimming back to the past. I am six years old, and Olga is lying naked on the bed with Sasha attaching a number of drinking glasses to her back. He then moves a flame around the glasses, and I watch with fascination as my mother's flesh fills up each glass. Apparently the illness is supposed to be leached out as the flesh rises and forms a glass-shaped hump on the back.

I lurch back to the present. This is what Lena and Lyuda are doing to me! Then, as now, I think this is some kind of crazy Russian ritual smacking of witchcraft, but I am too drunk to care. Even my thinking is slurred: *Wha' the hell, I'm in my homelan' and thas wha' they do 'ere.*

Lyuda and Lena have successfully finished their task. I now have eight glasses on my back and my flesh has risen obediently to fill each glass.

'Just lie there and rest,' orders Lena as she and Lyuda return to the dinner table in the next room. My head swirling, feeling like a fleshy porcupine and listening to the hoots of laughter coming from the other room, I obediently do as I'm told. Suddenly I feel like vomiting, but I don't want to vomit all over the bed. The toilet, quick! As I get up, the glasses fall off the raised lumps. I lurch out into the hall, breasts dangling, eight large lumps protruding from my back. In full view of the revellers, I don't make it to the toilet and vomit all over the hall.

Aware of lots of activity as people rush about with water and mops, I am put back to bed. I don't become fully aware of the horrendous implications of my behaviour until next morning when I groan awake and memories of the night before make their unwelcome impression on my consciousness. 'Oh no,' I mutter to Jake, 'I think I disgraced myself last night. I feel so terrible. But phew, at least I didn't sing!'

'I hate to tell you, darling, but I'm afraid you did sing and you also played the guitar.'

'Oh no!' I am horrified as a vague uneasy recollection comes creeping in of me singing and playing Russian songs extremely badly. 'God, was it really awful?'

Now one of the things I really appreciate about Jake is that he always tells the truth. I think that this is an occasion when I hoped he might lie, but no such luck.

'I'm afraid it was pretty bad. I wouldn't actually call it singing. More like caterwauling.'

Very gingerly and apologetically I creep into the kitchen, where Lena and Lyuda are preparing food. They burst out laughing when they see me.

'I'm so sorry. What must you think of me? I disgraced myself last night. What a terrible spectacle I must have made!'

'You were wonderful!' they both laugh. 'We haven't seen anything so funny in a long time.' And at that they laugh a whole lot more. Anatoly and Vitaly think it all hilarious too, and when I apologise about the singing and playing they won't hear of it. 'You know, Eva, in this country singing together is something we really treasure, and we just loved you playing the guitar and singing from your heart.'

I feel somewhat mollified. Having thought I might be ostracised for my outlandish behaviour, I find that I am loved even more. 'But what about prancing about naked with humps all over my back and vomiting all over your floor?' I attempt.

That apparently was unanimously voted the pièce de résistance. They felt that any vestige of Anglicisation that I might have acquired in the last fifty years was totally blown away by that display, and that in being so totally myself in all my outrageous glory, I was truly one of their countrymen and they were proud of me.

19 / **Mink's Claws**

No sleep all the way to Singapore. Must buy anti-cancer herbal remedies in Changi airport. Desperate to sleep on next leg as will be arriving in Melbourne at 4.30 am, hiring a car, picking up sister and driving like a maniac to Adelaide to catch Dad before his colostomy operation. But sleep is my cross to bear in life. When stressed or excited, I can't sleep and this sets up a vicious cycle. The years of being beaten because I am not asleep, the lying awake hearing Mum screaming or engaging in her odd, nightly manoeuvres to keep 'Them' at bay, have taken their toll. After just an hour or two of fitful sleep, I arrive shattered at Melbourne airport. Have trouble importing Ukrainian earth. Must be taken away and irradiated! Finally get through. Fortunately my son Joe is there to meet me, and will accompany me to Adelaide.

We collect Alexandra, her clothes and a large plastic dispenser full of her medication for the week. She is very excited as she hasn't seen Dad for several years and this is a holiday for her. I start driving along the Great Ocean Road to Adelaide, a journey of about a thousand kilometres, when all I really want to do is find somewhere flat and go to sleep for a couple of days. Instead I switch on my 'I can cope' personality, plaster on my 'friendly' smile and get on with the job of eating up as many miles as possible before stopping for the night. A luxurious three-bedroom apartment with jacuzzi overlooking the southern ocean is just what I need to relax and unwind, after putting Alex to bed with her nightly dose of tranquillisers. Both Joe and I are very unhappy with all these drugs and would ideally like to chuck them in the sea. I have noticed that my sister is slurring her words and that she totters when she walks. I am determined to find out what the drugs actually are and their side effects.

Feeling slightly refreshed next morning, I am anxious to set off reasonably early. But can we budge my sister? She is like a big lump and just will not get out of bed. Is it the drugs? Is it her illness? Or is she just being bloody-minded? I find myself asking these questions many times over the next few days. I fall woefully short of being Mother Teresa and get impatient and cross with Alex easily. Having Joe with me is a godsend and he takes over getting her in and out of the car, in and out of restaurants and up and down the various tourist attractions. I blame my lack of patience partly on the jet lag, but I also know that I am being triggered into an emotional substratum that I don't want to face. Alex's actions, facial expressions, bodily tics and behaviours, uncannily resemble those of my mother to an alarming degree.

As we get closer to Adelaide I phone Dad a few times and tell him we will be arriving about seven o'clock in the evening. He sounds reasonably happy that we are coming.

Joe, Alex and I stand expectantly on Dad's front doorstep. I had fantasised that the front lights would be on and Dad would be waiting with open arms. As I stand shivering in the dark and knocking loudly on back and front doors, I think, *Who are you kidding, Eva? This family that you come from is dysfunctional. This man didn't speak to you for over thirty years. Stop jumping to a storybook ending!* Joe stumbles in the darkness around to the back and knocks there. Nothing. I notice a thin sliver of light in a side window. I bang loudly on that. No answer. I finally walk up the road to a telephone box and ring him.

'Where are you?' he shouts.

'We're at the front door,' I shout back, holding back what I really want to say: *You deaf old git! I told you we would be here at seven. Where the hell are you?*

I get back to see Dad opening the various locks on the front door, wielding a torch.

For God's sake why don't you switch on a light? I scream inwardly. He ushers us into the dark, freezing cold front room. He is dressed for the arctic with a bobble hat, scarf and thick jumpers. We follow him by torchlight down the long hall into the kitchen. There at last he switches on a light and we can say our proper hellos.

He seems quite withdrawn and reticent, with little sign of the warmth I experienced over the telephone. I put it down to the fact that he finds seeing my sister a shock. The initial exchange between them is awkward and hesitant—a difficult time for both of them. A lot of very unpleasant water has passed under this particular bridge. Dad is much more effusive with Joe and seems genuinely pleased to see him.

We crowd into the narrow benches either side of the kitchen table and I make tea. Joe and I carry most of the conversation, pretending this is a happy, normal family. I give my sister her drugs and put her to bed up in her old bedroom. There are no other beds as Dad has sold them to Lee. I take Joe off to stay with Wendy Bruce (my first husband's sister), where I also hope to borrow a mattress. At Wendy's I explode. 'God, my dad's such a miser. He's a bloody millionaire and won't even switch on an outside light to welcome us! And then we have to creep around that freezing mausoleum by torch light, for Christ's sake!' A few more blasphemies and expletives plus half a bottle of wine later, I have calmed down a bit. Wendy has a few stories of her own father's miserliness, so we have a good laugh. I envy Joe staying in this bright, warm, sane house as I, lugging a spare mattress and a dose of normality, make my way back to the madhouse.

A daunting list of do's and don'ts awaits me next morning. Dad has lived in this house for twenty-eight years and everything must be just so: the red kettle must not move off its spot; there must be no droplets of water left in the sink; the blinds and windows must be raised to a certain exact point every day; Shika the cat's elaborate diet and routine must be adhered to precisely.

We leave Joe with the sleeping lump upstairs while I transport my father to hospital for his reverse colostomy. Once we're alone he becomes much more friendly towards me. I am correct about his reticence. He is desperately sad to see my sister in the state she is in. He could never cope with my mother being like that and like me, is shocked how similar to Mum Alex is. He can't bear even to look at her. We were both under the illusion that once in a lifetime, if at all, is enough for anyone to witness the agony of seeing a loved one descend into craziness. Here it is again unfolding before our very eyes. I am relieved to make a loving connection with my father again, and I settle him into his hospital bed. Although the last couple of days have been fraught, it is working out for the best as Dad would not have been able to cope with seeing a lot of my sister. It is much better that I bring her in for short visits before driving her back to Melbourne.

Over the next few days this is exactly what happens, and surprisingly it all goes much better than I expect. Wendy and the Bruce family make Alex feel welcome and Joe goes out of his way to engage her in conversation and various activities. As she feels more loved, she begins to blossom.

She and Dad have some productive exchanges and they talk openly about Gabriel. I am pleased that the big freeze is beginning to melt and good feelings are flowing again between them. Alex tells Dad the story of finding Greg and confronting him with the grandmothers' story. *Greg is getting good press here,* I think, hoping that this will alleviate the demonisation that Greg has been subjected to over the last few years.

I also see my father alone a few times. These times are essential as Dad can communicate how terrible he feels when he sees Alex and how many painful memories this brings up for him. When my mother was ill we never talked about it. We would go to hospital and see her separately, then feel shattered afterwards but for some reason be unable to communicate that fact to each other. Even though it is tragic to see Alex exhibiting similar symptoms to my mother, it gives Dad and me an opportunity to share the numbing horror of watching a loved one slip into a half world that we know nothing about, and to also share the helplessness of knowing that she might be lost to us forever.

A few days elapse and I drive my sister and Joe back to Melbourne. Alex's care worker informs me that olanzapine is the psychotropic drug that Alex is taking, and I express my concerns about her deteriorating motor skills. My sister clings to me tearfully as, with a heavy heart and a measure of relief, I say goodbye and drive back to Adelaide.

*

'Did you give Mahder's relatives the furs?' my father wants to know from his hospital bed. I reply in the affirmative and proceed to tell him about the visit to Tarasivka. The more I talk, the more uncomfortable he gets. He suddenly bursts out, 'I bet she liked the furs! Bloody Ukrainians, I doan' trust em.'

Somewhat taken aback I defend my relatives, saying they are

nice people. Dad is having none of it. 'Yeah, maybe on surface nice, but deep down treacherous. Out for own ends. All the same. They hate your mahder because she marry a Jew!'

'No, they don't. That is ridiculous. They were very sorry to hear that you are ill.'

But all my assurances on what worthy people my mother's relatives are make little difference, especially not today with the mood he is in. I become quite upset.

'But Dad, I felt you were generous with the furs and that it was a genuine gift of yours to them. I enjoyed giving it to them from you.'

What he says next shocks me. 'Bah, what you take me for? Do you tink I would give decent gift to a Ukrainian? I only gave furs away because I get no money for them. I had them valued, yeah, and they are wort' nuttin'! I paid over $2000 for those furs!' He's shouting now. 'Mink, you knaow! Bloody anti-fur lobby! Now market kaput for good furs!'

I am speechless with this diatribe. What the hell is going on? Am I a stooge that takes poison gifts to my new-found relatives? Is this a trick form of revenge from an embittered old man?

'I am really unhappy that you are saying all this about a bunch of very nice people. You haven't even met them and are willing to tar them with the same brush as Ukrainians you knew in the past.'

'Hmmph—you knaow nuttin'!'

Our argument stays stuck in this vein and I can't see any way through, so I just leave for the day. I toss and turn during the night, pondering the exchange. I do understand the source of my father's deep mistrust of the Ukrainians; there is plenty of evidence historically that many of them were deeply anti-Semitic. But I found no evidence of it in my recent forays to the Ukraine.

When I return next day, my father surprises me by apologising for upsetting me.

'But there's some tings you should knaow about Ukrainians. When I was on the run from Nazis, I stayed with a Ukrainian family who I knaow for years. The wife, she not happy to see me—she let me in, but say I must go by night as her husband would turn me over to Nazis if he find me there. Fooie!' He spits in disgust. 'You knaow, Eva, on surface they might be friendly to Jews, but when it come to crunch, they will betray you. I was eighteen years old and I must slink away from that house—of my FRIENDS—like hunted animal. I was safe NAOWHERE because these so-called friends turn treacherous!' All these last words should be in capitals because he is roaring now. It seems each betrayal has punctured a hole in his heart, and he can hardly breathe because he is so angry.

'And your mahder's sister, she hate me. She write when mahder ill, and angry letters after Olga die!'

I reel between shock at this piece of new information and sudden realisation.

'But I saw my mother's *cousin* Marya, not her sister Maria.'

This seems to make no difference to my father, who is stuck in the picture of all Olga's relatives hating him. I think to myself, *My mother's cousin got off lightly with just a dead mink with claws!*

*

I take Dad home next day and expect to look after him. But he recovers quickly and not one to lie about, starts doing everything for himself. Soon he is back to normal.

I am determined that he should eat organic fresh vegetables so take him to the Adelaide market. This is the most wonderful market in the world. I came here often as a little girl—a blissful place to all us New Australians who thought that mushy peas, baked beans, wafer thin slices of plastic pink ham and white, taste-less bread was our fantasy of food hell. The Adelaide market started off as a few stalls set up by migrants for migrants. We bought such delicacies as rye bread, dill cucumbers, quark (curd cheese), olives, peppers in oil and a splendid array of different sausages. My favourite was, and still is, Polish sausage. My mother would buy a couple of fresh rings and the vendor would give me a great big piece to munch as we continued shopping. Food heaven!

Walking around with my father now is an instructive experi-ence. Everyone seems to know him: 'Hi, Alec, haven't seen you for a while!' He is reasonably friendly back but is muttering under his breath, 'Hmmph, why doan' they mind their own business?'

'Alec, hi, it's so good to see you again,' calls out another vendor.

He barks back, 'You only tink it good to see me because you want to sell me some of your rotten vegetables!' I smile apologeti-cally and pull my father away.

We go to a stall where he always buys chicken necks for his cat. While waiting, I notice Dad looking darkly at the Chinese vendor on the next stall. Just as I am beginning to feel uncomfortable with the intensity of his glare, he breaks out, 'Bloody Chinese! You come over and ruin this country with all your wheelin' and dealin'. Huh, why you lookin' at me like that? You know very well what I am sayink. You—.'

But I grab the chicken necks and my father and pull him away before we have the Australian equivalent of the Triads after us, knifing us in some alley. I am struck again how Dad seems to need to have an archenemy at any given opportunity.

We buy rye bread, Polish sausage and cheese and then look at the vegetables. I have a huge problem convincing Dad to buy organic. I have already given him a lecture about how vulnerable his system is and that he mustn't overload it with pesticides and chemicals. So we find an organic vegetable stall. My father becomes immediately apoplectic: 'Look how much they cost—double, no, *triple* the price. Nah, nah, no good!' This is the man who waits until Tuesday at four o'clock when the market vendors slash their prices and give away squashed or inferior produce. This is the man who parks his car half a mile away because he won't pay the parking fee near the market. This is the man who had a heart attack a few months earlier because he was staggering to his car in the hot sun under the weight of two huge bags of bashed, cheap fruit and vegetables. This is the man who boiled boots to survive when on the run from the Nazis! Was he going to pay three dollars a kilo for organic carrots when he could probably bargain for a whole sack for two dollars? Absolutely not!

'Dad, you've got cancer and loads of money,' I protest. 'You can afford to eat food without pesticides.' But no amount of reasoning will do.

He fights a little when I say I will pay but in the end gives in, with a lot of sighing and shaking of the head. I buy a good supply of organic fruit and vegetables; lots of beetroot, broccoli and fresh turmeric. These are supposed to gobble up free radicals and eat the cancer. This is what I tell my father anyway. I am determined to have a good crack at beating or at least delaying the growth of the spots in his liver. He catches my enthusiasm and we go home all fired up.

I take him to a naturopath, an acupuncturist and a Chinese herbalist. Yes, I even persuade him to overcome his prejudice against the Chinese (I pay, of course!). These alternative therapists are gentle and caring, and my father does see the point of being treated as a whole person. They are all appalled that he has under-gone major heart surgery at his age. They say that the surgery was probably unnecessary and has weakened his system. Having the colon cancer and further operations has weakened it further. So armed with diets, pills, powders and potions, we go home, roll up our sleeves and begin the new regime with fervency and optimism.

As we grate beetroot, carrot and turmeric, I launch into a lecture on how he must reduce stress in his life. He agrees that stress is a killer and recounts how Val persuaded him to get a managing agent for one of his flats for this very reason. Unfortunately, just mention-ing this gets the stress levels up, and soon he is in mid-rant about how the managing agent is charging a fortune and the tenant is still troubling him. He is thumping the table and swearing.

I interrupt. 'Dad, this is stress! Just calm down. I will go and see the managing agent and sort it all out.'

He calms down somewhat but this is short-lived because the dog next-door starts yapping. This incites another rant about its owners. Their crime? Well, there are several, not the least of which is that she is the daughter of Russian migrants and he is an undertaker from Gawler. 'From Gawler, do you believe it? Made his money on the grief of ahders and that buys him right to move to Unley Park!' Gawler is a pleasant provincial town just north of Adelaide, but to my father's mind it is the inbreeding ground of country yokels. 'And she with her hoity-toity ways—"My grandmahder was from Moscow, you knaow",' he says with wheedling mimicry. 'And they dare come here and live in Nort'gate Street! This country is goin' to the dogs!' He is not using some irrelevant cliché here. 'How dare they leave that silly, stupid dog locked in their backyard all day and drive me mad? This once was quiet, respectable neighbourhood.'

All my entreaties for him to relax and be less stressed are drowned out by outbreaks of fresh yapping which signal more rants. 'Dad, just turn your hearing aid off,' I suggest, but that's obviously not the point.

Next day I make the mistake of chatting to the neighbours who own the dog. I am struck by what friendly neighbours Dad has, the Greeks on one side and these people on the other. They say they have invited Dad over for afternoon tea but he refused. I then make the even bigger mistake of telling Dad about this conversation.

He is livid, and I am convinced he is about to throw me out of his house. I have committed a capital crime. Any entreaty about his stress levels is blasted away.

'But Dad, they are nice people.'

'Nice people? I give you nice people. You knaow what they did? Those bloody nice people! You knaow nuttin'!'

I wait for elucidation of the next dastardly crime these people have committed.

'You knaow what they did?' He fixes me with glassy eyes. 'They put their rubbish in my bin!' I find it really hard not to burst into laughter. Only certain knowledge that he would probably kill me if I do stops me. I am reminded of Alexander Pope's 'Rape of the Lock', an epic satire on the trivialities of seventeenth-century court life in which a courtier cuts off the lock of a young woman's hair. But I know that my father is not being satirical.

'They tink I doan' knaow what they been doink. But I checked the bin and I saw some schoolwork with their children's name on it! I wasn't born yesterday. I knaow what they are up to. Puttin' their rubbish in my bin!' I ponder the seriousness of this crime but can't seem to muster up the sense of outrage that Dad expects of me. Dad again adopts his mimicry of the Russian woman next-door. ' "Oh Mr Levkowicz, we'd like to invite you over for afternoon tea." Of course I refuse! I am a diabetic. I doan' want her to knaow my business. Aristocrat from Moscow. Bullshit! And then that under-taker let all the ivy graow on my side of the fence! I go out there and trim the ivy and they let it graow again. Twice already this year I have trimmed that ivy. Disrespect! That's what it is. No respect for my privacy!'

I resignedly wait for this outburst to run its course. Any advice on reducing stress in Dad's life is like trying to convince Ulysses to give up sailing.

🍃

'Have you still got the letters from my mother's sister Maria?' I venture one afternoon as we are sorting out the house. I haven't forgotten our conversation in the hospital about the furs and how my father thought I had visited Mum's sister rather than her cousin. I have also been careful not to stir up Dad's anti-Ukrainian sub-terrain.

'Somewhere in a suitcase in attic,' he barks.

At the next opportunity I rifle through the attic like an excited sleuth. Olga talked a lot about her older sister Maria, and I do remember a series of letters from her which delighted my mother. There were also photos of Shura, Maria's daughter. I am intrigued that Maria continued to write to my father after my mother was ill. I find an old suitcase and pounce on what I am looking for—letters from a Maria Sakhno. I can't believe that I am now on the track of finding my mother's siblings. With my rudimentary knowledge of the Russian alphabet I gasp as I decipher part of the address: Kharkov (its Soviet name before being changed to Kharkiv after 1991). This is where I visited the previous year as an energy expert and stayed at Lena's dacha. I had been so close!

Just as I am wondering what to do next with the discovery of the letters and how to get them translated, fate deals its hand in a surprising way. Lena emails me from Ukraine.

'You must come at once! I have made an amazing discovery! Lilia, who has been my manicurist for years, is a relative of yours. Her name is Nesterenko. Moreover, she says that the uncle you recently met in Orzhitsa has something to hide!'

As Val is coming to Adelaide to prepare for her play and is therefore able keep an eye on Dad, I decide to take the opportunity to fly back to Ukraine while my visa is still valid. I can speak to Lilia and check out Maria Sakhno's address, as well as have the letters translated.

The Kulak Princess

*Who thought up the word 'kulak'?
What torture was meted out to
them? In order to massacre them
it was necessary to proclaim
kulaks are not human beings
just as the Germans proclaim
the Jews are not human beings;
thus did Lenin and Stalin proclaim
kulaks are not human beings.*

Vasily Grossman

Prologue / USSR, 1950s

Maria hesitates outside the gypsy caravan. She is visiting Grushinka,
a fortune-teller who has the reputation of uncanny accuracy about the
future. Maria has had a vivid dream about her younger sister, Olga, and
needs the special skill of the gypsy to help her interpret it and see its
portent for the future.

She told her husband she was going mushrooming as he would
disapprove of her assignation. Such a coarse man. She really resents
her mother for forcing her to marry him in order to take on the name
'Sakhno', so hiding her kulak roots. 'Oh, he's so wonderful,' her mother
wheedled. 'So handsome, so charming.' *Well, why don't you marry
him yourself,* she thought—but never dared to say.

So thanks to her mother she has been saddled with this great brute
of a man. They have a daughter, Shura, and live in a small flat in
Kharkov. Maria, now in her forties, has an ethereal beauty that drives
her husband mad.

One of six children, she was heartbroken when her younger brother
Trofim died of starvation in 1933, and distraught when her older brother
Ivan was caught by the CHEKA secret police for trying to steal food for
him. The fact that they had once been wealthy kulaks didn't help and
Ivan was deported and thrown into jail. Maria has never seen her
brother again but still continues to hope that one day he will return.
Of her two sisters, Olga was swallowed by the war in 1942 and Anyuta
lives in the Poltava province. Her youngest brother, Leonid, lives far
away in Seitler—no, Nizhnygorsk, she corrects herself. Stalin in his
infinite wisdom renamed all the old Tatar towns in the Crimea following
the war—after forcibly repatriating Tatars to Siberia.

Olga, who was so cruelly taken away by the Nazis from Seitler
when it was still Seitler, was the subject of her dream a few nights ago.
She had heard that Olga was alive at the end of the war and was on her

182

way home, but then nothing. It seemed she disappeared off the face of the earth. Maria loved her little sister with a passion. Olga, born in 1924 when she was twelve years old, was her special pet. Maria had brought her up while their mother Alexandra was busy building up the farm that had been destroyed in the Russian Civil War. She has pretty well given up on Olga being alive, but this dream has made her wonder.

She knocks on the caravan door. Grushinka is old and wizened with darting eyes. Maria enjoys the warm grip of her hand.

'I've had a dream …' Maria begins uncertainly.

'Ah, a true dream. I can see how it has changed your soul. Tell me, my pretty one.'

Encouraged, Maria continues, 'Well, I saw a young girl sitting in a train. She was wearing plaits like my little sister Olga. Her mother is with her and they are on a journey in a very far-off land. Both the mother and daughter look like Olga. The mother is in trouble and calling out to me. It is so vivid, Grushinka. I feel that Olga is alive and calling me.'

Grushinka takes Maria's hand.

'Absolutely. Your sister is calling out to you. She is in a far-off land and has a daughter. Do not worry. This dream is a message that she is alive and trying to contact you. Very shortly you will receive a sign.'

Maria takes out an old photo and shows it to the gypsy. The photo has Ivan on one side looking handsome and dashing, and Olga next to him, a shy smile in the heart-shaped face. The gypsy looks at the apparition of Ivan and her face clouds. 'I'm sorry, Maria, but I'm afraid that Ivan is no more of this world. His soul departed many years ago. But Olga—yes, definitely she is alive and she needs you.'

'Have you some scissors?' Maria asks calmly.

Grushinka gives her a pair and watches as the younger woman cuts the photo in half. Ivan flutters to the floor.

'In that case the living and the dead should not inhabit the same photograph. Thank you, Grushinka. You have helped me enormously. I now know what I have always felt in my bones. Ivan is dead but Olga is alive. I will now go home and wait for a sign.'

20 / **Hidden Relatives**

I'm on the night train to Kharkiv. A commandant-style station guard with an impassive bucket of a face has handed out regulation grey blankets and sheets at an extra charge. It is like being in a prison as I try and make myself comfortable on the rock-hard bunk surrounded by snoring Russians.

I have left Dad happily ensconced in his home in Adelaide and am looking forward to meeting Lilia Nesterenko and having the letters translated by Lena. But sleep eludes me. While my feverish brain and the snoring symphony don't help, my bladder is the real culprit. Ever since I heard that the toilet doors are automatically locked half an hour either side of a station on this long journey, my bladder has gone into panic overdrive. I am forced to lurch down the corridor in my nightdress, hoping fervently that the toilet doors will be open.

They are shut. I don't know whether we are coming or going between stations. Do I have a few minutes or an hour? Must get sleep. What to do?

I step between the carriages and sway dangerously as the wind howls up from the whirling of tracks below. Precariously straddling the couplings, I pull up my nightie. A blast of icy air freezes my bottom as I attempt to empty my bladder. I am not afraid of being whipped off, sucked under or splattered all over the tracks below. I am far more afraid of being caught red-bottomed by Bucket Face, who regularly patrols the corridors. How would I, Dr Eva Chapman from the civilised West, explain this ungainly position? Is this another ignominy I am prepared to endure in order to heal my family?

I do manage to stumble back, undiscovered, to my bunk. The night is long and horrible. I swallow a sleeping pill. Big mistake.

I wake up feeling suicidal. I think of poor Olga, who was dispensed sleeping pills as if they were sweets. I am convinced that something in my family's genetic make-up reacts badly to barbiturates. But I am luckier than Olga because I am met in Kharkiv by Lena's mother, Irena. She looks into my wrecked, wrinkled, sleep-deprived face with such love that all my angst melts away and I feel whole again. Ready for the next adventure.

The first task is to follow up the address of Maria Sakhno in Kharkiv. The excitement turns to disappointment as we draw blanks. It seems that no Maria Sakhno nor any of her descendants live at this address.

Next up are the numerous letters that I found in my father's attic. Exciting! It is like uncovering an obscure mystery puzzle. Most of the letters are from Maria Sakhno and a couple from her brother Leonid (or 'Leonty', as he was known). My mother often mentioned Maria and Leonty, and it was obvious that she loved them a lot and missed them terribly. I remember how excited she was when she found them at last, and with what care and attention she assembled elaborate parcels to send to them. The letters from Maria are the most illuminating. She wrote regularly until Olga became too ill to reply, and then continued writing to my father, exhorting him to explain what was happening. When she discovered Mum was ill, she told Sasha she wanted to come over and look after her. This was in 1974. Sasha offered to pay her fare, but Maria became ill—and then it was too late. I am so sad about this and touched that somebody in the world cared.

After Olga's death, Maria's letters kept coming. She wanted to know about us girls. She knew I was in England and requested my address. Sasha never told her and never let me know that my aunt was looking for me. The letters from Maria became angry in tone and then dwindled away. I am struck by the raw simplicity of Maria's writing and the passionate love for Olga that sparks from the pages. I am determined to find this branch of my mother's family. But when I worked out roughly how old Maria and Leonty would be if still alive—in their eighties—I sadly came to the conclusion they are probably both dead. I look at the photos they sent of their families and despair of finding any of them. Dejectedly I await a manicure.

Lilia Nesterenko is a pleasant, plump woman in her early fifties who by an amazing coincidence is related to me by marriage. Ivan Leontivich Nesterenko, whom I met in Orzhitsa, is her father-in-law. While spreading a layer of pink pearl on my nails, she tells me that Ivan had let slip that there was another relative he didn't want me to know about and was hiding from me. My imagination goes wild. Is this literally the skeleton in the family cupboard? A demented aunt or uncle incarcerated in an attic? Why is he hiding relatives from me? Lilia shrugs that she doesn't really know, but she suspects it traces back to old animosities between rich and poor peasant. I remember Marya Leontivna in Tarasivka and her intimations of trouble between the families of my grandparents. It seems imperative we speak with Ivan.

Next day Lena, her father and I head for Orzhitsa by car. We stay again with Ivan's niece Luda. After going to meet Ivan, I ask him for any knowledge of my grandmother's family. He doesn't know, he shrugs, looking sad and old. 'Left the district a long time ago. Don't know where.'

Lena pushes him further, remembering what Lilia has said about hidden relatives. It is a tense, delicate moment, but a few gulps of vodka seem to oil some rusty cogs in Ivan's brain. Reluctantly he mutters something vague about some people in a nearby village who might know something about my grandmother.

Lena grabs the moment. 'Let's go now! Papa, please drive us!'

I am dubious and convinced that this is just a wild goose chase, but Lena is adamant. She pushes me into her father's car and off we go, taking Ivan with us.

About fifteen kilometres from Orzhitsa, near a village signposted 'Staryi Irzhavets', Ivan asks us to stop at a thatched, white-washed house to ask directions. We see people here who look like real peasants: grimy, hardened. I have a pang of fear, hoping that any relatives we find are not going to look like this. A woman in her fifties with a weathered face beneath a dirty white headscarf and wearing a tattered blue dress points us to the next house along. Out of this house comes a rough but not unpleasant looking man about sixty, appearing a little unsteady on his legs.

'He's drunk,' whispers Lena. 'It's Victory Day tomorrow and everyone gets drunk.'

He comes up to us jovially in his dirty, dishevelled clothes and Ivan greets him as Nikolai. Nikolai's leathery face is quizzical at the unexpected number of visitors at this time of evening. He apologises immediately for his attire, saying he has just come in from the fields.

'We're looking for descendants of this woman's grandmother.' Lena points at me. 'Her mother Olga went to Australia over fifty years ago.'

'Australia! Why the hell did she go there when it's so wonderful here?' quips Nikolai, whom I like immediately. 'But I don't really know much. You should talk to my older brother Vasily.' With that he points us to the house we have just left. So back we traipse.

By now I am feeling distinctly uncomfortable and shy, and I just want to go home. I think we are interrupting these people's lives unnecessarily.

We are led around to the back of the house to a frail-looking man sitting on a bench, propped up on a stick. He seems in another world, gazing forlornly into the distance. I sit next to him awash with awkwardness. His wife, Olya, the woman in the dirty white headscarf, alerts him to our presence. Again Lena launches into the history of who I am and who we are searching for. I squirm with embarrassment as yet again the story of Olga and her grand-mother is foisted on another bunch of people.

But before the old man can speak, Olya starts babbling excitedly.

'Yes, yes, we know of Alexandra Mikhailovna. She is Nikolai and Vasily's grandmother. Vasily nursed her in the last year of her life and she died in his arms right here at the end of the war, when he was thirteen years old.' She points to the man sitting next to me. He seems agitated by what his wife is saying and huge tears fall from his seemingly lifeless eyes onto his faded grey trousers. I put my hand on his back and he begins to sob. Nikolai has by now walked from the other house and, with excitement in his eyes, sits on the other side of me. He apologises again for being in his dirty working clothes and hugs me warmly. Despite what Lena has said, I cannot smell any alcohol—a bit of sweat and dirt perhaps, but that is all.

'Maya sestra,' he says simply. The word 'sestra' means sister but is also used to mean 'cousin'.

The sun is setting, turning the late May sky blood-red, giving a surreal quality to the whole scene. Here I am sitting between my two first cousins, one of whom is sobbing for our dead grandmother—*my* grandmother, who died on this spot! I can hardly believe it.

Olya starts fussing around Vasily, explaining that he has recently suffered a stroke and should not get too upset. This explains the vacant stare when I first saw him. Nikolai apologises for his brother's tears, but I relish every drop falling on his poor, wasted knees.

More people emerge from the red sky: Nikolai's rather plump but jolly-looking wife Nina; Vasily's son, his wife and their two children. The smallest, a girl, clings to her mother's skirt and the other, a boy, runs about snatching curious glances at this strange foreign lady who is making his grandfather cry.

Olya is now in full flow and, amazingly, knows all about my mother and me. Vasily and Nikolai's mother was Anyuta, my mother's oldest sister, who died in the 1970s.

Everybody is very excited now and insists we stay for a meal, but we explain that food is waiting for us back at Luda's place. We exchange addresses and make for the car. Vasily hobbles out on his stick to see us off. I look into his eyes, which glisten out at me, and I feel a profound connection as I hug him goodbye. I hug and kiss them all, prompting Olya to giggle, 'Ooh, I've never touched or kissed a foreign lady before.'

I feel shell-shocked as we drive away, the full force of it all not quite sinking in. But it isn't over yet. We are not back at Luda's house in Orzhitsa for five minutes before the phone rings.

This time it is a Shura ringing from Kharkiv. She is the daughter of Maria Sakhno. My heart leaps. Lena takes the call and discovers that Shura and her daughter Olga were phoned by Nikolai shortly after we left him. Shura is beside herself and quite hysterical. In between sobs she tells Lena that her mother was looking for me for the last thirty years and died only recently. They are so overjoyed to have found us that Shura and Olga are planning to take an overnight bus to visit us next day. I am overwhelmed that they are dropping everything just to see me. But as Lena says, it is too good an opportunity to miss.

That evening Lena, her father, Jake and I have dinner with Luda, Vas and their two children, Vika and Alex. We have noticed that Luda and Vas look very careworn, so with some gentle probing we get down to what is bothering them. Vika, a beautiful and bright seventeen-year-old, has just finished secondary school with brilliant marks, the best in the Poltava region. However, there is a snag. She will be unable to go to university as there is just not enough money. The US$500 a year it will cost is way beyond her parents' means, even though they both have good jobs—Luda as a teacher and Vas as a computer programmer. They work hard and grow all their own food, but still cannot make ends meet. It seems that the only way people can get on in the new Ukraine is to operate in the black market, but Luda and Vas are not like this—they are honest and hardworking. I can see the lines furrowed on Vas's brow as he worries about his bright daughter's future.

Jake and I, in a private discussion during the evening, discover we have the same idea. Two-and-a-half thousand American dollars for five years of education does not seem a lot to us. We have so much and they have so little, and who better to share our good fortune with than my relatives? We make the proposition to Luda and Vas after the young ones have gone to bed. The reaction is heartbreaking as they both begin to sob in disbelief. It actually takes quite a lot to convince them that it is right to accept our gift as they are proud people and do not want handouts. Next morning, the look on Vika's face when she finds out that she can go to university after all is worth a lifetime of sunrises.

The overnight bus arrives from Kharkiv and I am reunited with my cousin Shura and her daughter Olga, an attractive twenty-six year old. The stalwart Lena is at hand to translate. Shura is in floods of tears and cannot take her eyes off me.

'Boszhe moi, Boszhe moi,' she sobs. 'Eva Maria. Boszhe moi. Eva Maria. Boszhe moi! Oh Eva, I can't believe I am finally looking at you. My mother was searching for you her whole life. She loved your mother very much and pined for her for so long, not knowing whether she was dead or alive. My daughter is named after her. Mama was ecstatic when she finally received a letter from Olga, even though most of it had been blackened out by the censors.'

Shura produces photographs of their family. I am struck by the haunting beauty of Maria. The more I hear about her, the more I feel she was our guardian angel from afar who worried constantly about Olga and her three daughters. 'Boszhe moi, Boszhe moi, if only Mama had met you before she died,' Shura laments. 'She would have then died in peace.' When she discovers that I was in

Kharkiv while her mother was still alive, she wails even more. 'Oh, if only that rascal Ivan had let us know straight away you could have met my mother.'

'Ivan knew of your whereabouts?' I exclaim.

'Of course he knows us. I even stayed with him as a child.'

I am flabbergasted by this information. 'Are you sure that Ivan isn't just getting old and his memory has failed him?'

'Pah, of course not. He was just keeping you to himself. Old grievances! Oh, why is it that my mother didn't see you before she died? It was her dearest wish. Why oh why?' More wailing.

Then many questions. 'What illness did Olga have? Why did she stop writing? What was your father hiding from us?'

I explain some of the facts as best I can and in return Shura tells me some amazing family history that stretches back to the Russian Civil War. We have so much to talk about. And an excellent piece of news. My Uncle Leonty, incredibly enough, is still alive. He lives in the Crimea, half blind and frail, the only sibling of my mother's five brothers and sisters left. I am so delighted by this news, and so afraid to miss out on seeing him, that then and there I decide to extend my stay in Ukraine and meet him. Shura is overcome with joy and says she will come too.

21 / **Tarasivka, 1920**

Who are you, comrades, that zealously and blindly
attempt to strangle Russia?
God has said to us that all men are brothers
and has commanded us to love all men.
White Army song, 1918–1920

Maria trembles as she hides in the cornfield. She pats the top of
her baby brother's head to keep him quiet. Her mother, her sister
and her other brothers watch in horror as the Bolsheviks ransack
their house and begin to set fire to the haystacks. All the hard work
of the previous summer gone to waste. Maria recalls the intense
blue of the sky as the whole family trooped to the fields outside
Tarasivka to harvest the hay. Her Aunt Sonia had a fearsome reputation with a scythe and was said to be able to cut down a field of
hay quicker than any man. And it seemed that her older sister,
Anyuta, was following in her aunt's footsteps. Maria felt herself to
be more dainty and worldly, like her mother, whom she adored.
Maria's job was to carry pots of borscht to the fields, quite heavy for
her eight-year-old arms. She then spread out an embroidered
tablecloth and ladled out the borscht into bowls. These the hungry
workers would pounce on and wolf down with rye bread, freshly
baked by her grandmother. But now that life seems to be in ruins.

The night before a gang of men, drunk on samogon, had
banged on the door of their pretty farmhouse with its red-tiled roof
and demanded the whereabouts of her father, Trofim Ivanovich.
'That kulak bastard!' they had called him. Her mother had ordered
her four older children to bed in the alcove above the oven, while
she, holding baby Leonty in her arms, tried to reason with the
angry gang, explaining she had no idea where her husband was.

191

This was partly true. He had been fighting in the White Army on and off during the previous year because the Whites had promised to help him keep his land and quash the Red Army, who were intent on taking it away. In several heated arguments Alexandra had begged him not to join the Whites, and in fact begged him not to fight at all.

'You must stay out of it. They will kill you, just like they have killed Stefan and the others.'

Stefan, another wealthy kulak in the village, and had been murdered a few weeks before. Other peasant farmers had been deported to Siberia. Their crime? To resist the forcible requisition of their grain, stores and livestock. The word 'kulak' had become synonymous with any peasant who was living off land he owned. He was expected to surrender it to the New Revolution.

Maria, watching from her vantage point above the stove where she and her brothers and sister slept, was frightened when her father's face contorted with rage at her mother's suggestion that he should stay neutral. 'What do you mean "neutral"? I can't stand here and just watch as they come and destroy my livelihood and hound me from the land my father worked so hard for so we could have a better life!'

'Please don't go. What will I do with five children if you are dead?'

But however much Alexandra begged she knew her husband had too much fire in his blood to sit and do nothing. She sank to her knees and implored God to watch over him as he strode off to join the White Army.

In truth, Trofim did not particularly like the White Army. They stood for the Czarist regime with its serfdom. However, it was the Czar's Prime Minister, Stolypin, who had in 1906 introduced reforms that allowed some peasants to leave the huge wealthy estates and have their own pieces of fenced-off land. Trofim was proud of his father, a smart peasant who managed to acquire a good ten hectares of excellent land and handed down to him a sizeable inheritance with horses, several bulls, cows and pigs, and one of the smartest houses in the village of Tarasivka. Trofim had married Alexandra, a proud, handsome girl from the nearby village of Goroshino, and she had borne him four children before the 1917 Revolution. At first Trofim had welcomed it as it seemed that Ukrainians would have more freedom and he would be able to

tend his land in peace. In fact, there had been jubilation throughout the country when the Ukrainian government declared itself to
be independent in 1918. Trofim was delighted when his wife
became pregnant with their fifth child. However, this euphoria did
not last, and in the bloodthirsty Civil War which followed, the
fledgling republic was brutally crushed by the Bolsheviks. The Red
Army was openly hostile to Ukrainians and their search for self-
determination, and those heard speaking Ukrainian, 'a kulak
tongue', were often rounded up as counter-revolutionaries and
shot or deported.

Ukraine remained in turbulent limbo as Red Army fought White
Army. For a while Trofim joined Makhno's home-grown Black
Army, which championed Ukraine's interests, but when that movement seemed to capitulate and join the Red Army, he didn't know
where to turn. All he knew was that he hated the Bolsheviks, particularly that evil Jew, Trotsky. He began to hear of a new White Army
general who spoke sense. Wrangel called for an end to civil war and
for the right of peasants to keep private property. Trofim was
inspired by his call for volunteers: 'Our brothers in the red
butcher's dungeons put their faith in you. Rise up and defend the
glory of Mother Russia and her Holy Church. She depends on you!'

Trofim felt his soul at ease when he went to church and heard
the beautifully sung Orthodox prayers. He didn't want a future
where all that he knew would be stamped out. It had been heartbreaking when the local church was smashed up and the precious
icons pillaged by the 'red butchers'. He volunteered for Wrangel's
White Army. As he was clever and a good organiser, he rose to the
rank of officer quickly, a meteoric rise for a former peasant. Maria
gasped when she saw her father in his smart uniform with shiny
buttons, riding off on his horse.

But now she is hiding in the cornfield, hoping against hope that
her father does not return. Early that morning her mother had
ordered her four older children to put on as many clothes as they
could, carry as many bundles as possible and come to the cornfields
to hide. Their two aunts, Trofim's sisters Sonia and Luba, came too.
They hid on the banks of the Sula River near the bridge that led into
the village. Sure enough, about midday a group of Red Army soldiers rode over the bridge up to their house. They kicked down the
front door, shouting, 'Ivanovich, you white scum, where are you?'

Maria now trembles as she hears breaking glass inside the house. The men are smashing up the contents as they stomp over her life. Some come out and feed their horses with food from the store. A cacophony of squealing and gunshots assails their ears. 'They're shooting the pigs!' gasps Maria's brother Ivan. In the absence of his father, he feels he is the head of the family and must defend it. He starts to run out of the cornfield but is grabbed by his frantic mother.

'Sumashechni!' she cries as she pulls him back roughly. 'You crazy idiot! Stay here!'

As the family helplessly watch the flames licking up through the haystacks, they hear a different sound—the hooves of a horse on the road leading up to the bridge. It is Trofim, his buttons catching the sun as he rides out from the shade of the trees. Alexandra throws the baby to Maria and runs to the road, blocking her husband's path. 'Don't go any further. Come hide. The Bolsheviks are waiting for you. They want to kill you! Please!' She is beseeching him, but to no avail.

'I'll kill the bastards with my bare hands!' he cries furiously, raising his horse to a gallop, storming towards his ransacked house. He flies off the horse and rushes to the door a demented madman, cursing wildly.

Maria hands her baby brother back to her quivering, distraught mother and standing by the little bridge starts to sing. It is the only way she can cope with the horror around her. She sings as she glimpses the flash of metal from an upstairs window and hears the crack of the gunshot that wounds her father. She sings as she watches her father stagger to the door and grapple valiantly with some men who have run out of the house. She sings as they push him over and kick him belly up. She sings as she sees one of them plunge a bayonet through the middle of the row of shiny buttons. She sings as she sees him lying dying, the red blood soaking slowly over the yellow ground. She sings as she hears her mother's stifled cries. She sings as the men shout, pointing to her father's figure, 'This is an example to you all—bloody kulaks—bloody Ukrainians who have kept bread from our workers. Long live Lenin! Long live the revolution!'

She sings as the flames from the haystacks leap into the sky.

The men's bloodlust has been whetted and they start to march towards the hiding family. 'Where are the rest of them? Where are the snivelling kulak vermin who'll grow up tainted with his name? Let's kill them now!'

Maria stops singing and dives into the undergrowth under the bridge, as do her brothers and sister. Baby Leonty starts whimpering, and Maria watches in horror as her mother extinguishes his cries by plunging his head into the river, willing to sacrifice her last born to save the rest of her family. Aunt Sonia jumps into a nearby cabbage barrel and Aunt Luba sinks into a marsh bog. Maria peers through the reeds, fascinated that all she can see of her aunt are a few bubbles on the surface.

It is dusk before Alexandra dares move. She leaves her children by the bridge and runs to her husband. She knows it is no use. He has been lying there motionless for hours. The windows of the house are smashed and everything is ransacked. It has not been burnt down like some of the other rich houses in the village, but she cannot bear to step inside. Her whole life has been torn apart. She looks at her husband, her brave strong handsome husband, lying like a disembowelled dog in the dirt. A terrible pain grips her stomach and she drops to the ground, howling in agony.

Maria rocks little Leonty, who fortunately survived the drowning attempt, and sings him a lullaby.

22 / **Leonty**

More than eighty years have passed since that fateful day in 1920 when a little girl sang forlornly to her baby brother, and I am meeting the eyes of my Uncle Leonty for the first time. One of them is slightly opaque with cataracts, but the other feasts on me with obvious pleasure.

'But you don't look like Olga—well, perhaps a little, around the mouth ...'

Leonty is a little frail now but was obviously once strong and wiry. He still grows all his own vegetables and also cherry and peach trees, which he sells for a small profit. The fruit from these makes a delicious schnapps for which the Crimea is famous. The small trees are selling well since Gorbachev ordered the destruction of all the beautiful old peach and cherry orchards in the Crimea in 1985, a misguided attempt to cure Russians of their love for alcohol. This foolish policy means that Gorbachev continues to be reviled despite being the architect of perestroika and possibly the saviour of the Russian peoples.

I love spending the next couple of days with Leonty, and it seems the feeling is mutual as he takes every opportunity to hug me or sit as close to me as possible. He is the most charming uncle that any uncle-starved person could wish for. He has been driven up from Nizhnygorsk in the northern Crimea by his eldest daughter Lydia to spend a few days with the daughter of his long lost sister Olga, whom he last saw in 1941 before he was forced to dig trenches in a futile attempt to stop the German advance. I gaze into his tear-filled blue eyes, very similar to my own and those of my children, thinking, *You snuggled in the same womb as did my own dear mother.* I have to keep pinching myself—this person played with my mother when they were children. This is like a miracle to me. I am at last in the larger womb of my family, a family like any other, full of different personalities, jealousies and rivalries, but my very own family. And they all seem delighted that I am back in the fold. Lena is also with me, having taken more time off from her busy life, and has travelled with my cousins, Shura and Nikolai, to help translate the next stage of this unfolding adventure.

Leonty has the kind of gentleness that wouldn't hurt a fly and reminds me very much of my son Joe. He is forever making sure that everyone else in the family has a seat or food before he can settle down. Every now and then he points out some similarity between me and the young Olga. Apparently one of my front teeth sticks out in exactly the way hers did. I am so pleased that I never had my teeth straightened; I have a new appreciation for this quirky tooth that occasionally juts out like a small fang.

Over the two days Leonty, with the help of Shura and Nikolai, fills in more of the family story. A lot of it is difficult for him to utter. At one point I nearly blow it when I explain I want to write a book. He becomes extremely distressed, saying to his daughters, 'I'm so afraid something will happen to you. I am now old so I don't matter, but what about you and your families?' He looks furtively around the room as if a spy is sitting in the corner and I am struck how deep the fear of censure is. All his life, he has been severely traumatised by the fact that his murdered father was a rich kulak, as well as suffering all the other usual terrors of the Stalinist regime and the Nazi occupation.

After a lot of reassurance, he recovers his former composure and resumes the story.

Alexandra cannot bear to continue to live in the rich house in Tarasivka, so she and her five children move to Goroshino where her parents live. Civil war rages all around. Frenzied mobs, whetted by the smell of blood, attack each other in an orgy of fratricidal blood-letting that continues unabated. Kiev suffers particularly badly, enduring several changes of regime and the inevitable denouncements and executions that follow as Whites and Reds slaughter each other in their thousands.

In the countryside the Ukrainian peasants refuse to be cowed by the 'red butchers'. Demand for grain from peasant farmers continues. To make matters worse there is a drought in the winter of 1921 to 1922, and this, added to eight years of war and forcible requisition, leads to a severe famine. Possibly a million Ukrainians die of hunger. Leonty feels most sorry for the children who have been orphaned by war. At least he and his siblings have a mother, who since the death of their father has become a tigress, determined her brood will survive. Four hundred children found on a train in January 1922 in Poltava are not so lucky. These 'bezprytulni', or orphans, had been riding on freight trains in search of food and were found frozen to death.

The Bolsheviks win the Civil War and Lenin takes over in Moscow. Wrangel and Makhno both escape into exile. Lenin introduces a bit of sanity by bringing in a New Economic Policy that stops forcible requisitioning and allows Ukrainian peasants to go back to their land. Although sporadic attacks continue against the winning Bolshevik regime, most people in Ukraine are so fed up with senseless killing, starvation and misery that they crave a return to some semblance of normality.

Alexandra moves with her children back into her red-tiled house. She, like everyone else, wants to make up for lost time and get on her feet again. She enlists the help of a handsome young man, Ivan Nesterenko, one of three brothers from the poorer end of the village. He is invaluable in getting the farm running again and is like an older brother to the five children. Tongues wag at the smouldering looks he lavishes on his new mistress. Not only is Ivan much younger than Alexandra but much poorer. Tarasivka is scandalised in the summer of 1924 when Alexandra is very obviously with child. Gossip is rife and only quelled after a hasty wedding. Olga Nesterenko is born in October 1924.

Despite their differences, Alexandra and Ivan have a few happy years building up the farm and watching Olga running around with her older siblings. Little Olga, or Olychka, is a delightful child and a born comedienne. She is always standing up on a box and telling funny stories or singing. Her older brothers and sisters adore her and treat her like a princess as she brings sunshine into their lives. She also plays with her poorer cousins, Ivan and Marya, the children of her father's brother, who are her age. Prosperity returns to the family as the black soil becomes productive again and the livestock is built up. The Nesterenko family are the proud owners of several bulls, cows, pigs and horses and a flock of sheep. They even manage to acquire the latest agricultural equipment to make hay and bring in the grain.

But the good times are not to last. Any fond hope that life would ever return to normal is just fantasy. Ties to the past have been smashed by the Bolshevik revolution. The Orthodox Church lies in tatters, reviled as a sign of backwardness. Olga's grandmother hides her small precious icon under her mattress, kissing it furtively in the dark before going to sleep. After Lenin's death in 1924, the shadowy Stalin successfully isolates political rivals and emerges as the grim face of the Soviet Union. His steely gaze and 'cockroach eyes'* search out the very minutiae of existence of the Nesterenko family.

Leonty visibly blanches as he talks about Stalin, as if his spectre still stalks the land.

Stalin's plans to industrialise the Soviet Union are to deal an even more devastating blow to the inhabitants of the red-tiled house in Tarasivka. He has a low opinion of Ukrainian peasants, regarding their push for nationalism and their continued embrace of religion as evidence of backwardness in the face of the revolutionary change that he wants to sweep through the entire Soviet Union. The Nesterenkos, like millions of others, are hurtled along by the new wave of idealism. The unfolding of history, they are told, is inevitable and predetermined. They must be guided by the supreme leader Stalin, who grandly sees himself as an 'engineer of souls' and purports to know where this tide of history is flowing, how to control it and how to lead them all to greater glory. Any questioning or hesitation is ridiculed as old-fashioned, backward and revisionist. A new breed of unpleasant people begin to infiltrate every corner of Soviet society. They are representatives of the Extraordinary Commission for Combating Speculation and Counter-revolution—the full name for the secret police force CHEKA, precursor of the NKVD (People's Commissariat for Internal Affairs) and the KGB.

In the late 1920s Stalin's push for industrial expansion involves the state purchasing cheap grain from the peasants to sell abroad

---

* From a poem by Russian poet Osip Mandelstam on Stalin, 'The Kremlin Crag-dweller', for which he was liquidated.

for profit. Olga's parents are offered such ludicrously low prices that they and thousands of others in the Ukraine refuse to sell. The CHEKA set out to inflame class animosities between kulaks and poor peasants in the villages, encouraging the latter to rise up against the landed peasantry. Tarasivka is in turmoil.

Stalin is livid with what he sees as kulak pigheadedness and, as a response to what he calls 'sabotage', orders an all-out drive for liquidation of private ownership. Leonty vividly remembers the night in 1930 when the Bolsheviks burst into their home and took all the livestock, food, stored grain and even private belongings. My mother told me stories of when as a six-year-old she was terrified by angry men on big black horses who tore apart their lives.

The beautiful old orchards where the children played and picnicked in the summer are hacked down and the Tarasivkans are forced to build an ugly, giant collective farm. The compulsory collectivisation is carried out with merciless brutality. The CHEKA hunt down and denounce anybody who refuses to obey. Those who resist are shot or deported to forced labour camps in the Arctic and Siberia.

Alexandra, with practised fortitude, again takes the family to Goroshino. But they are hounded there, too, so return to the red-tiled house. The CHEKA are everywhere. The 'stain' of the kulak is impossible to erase. Although everyone is at the mercy of the CHEKA, those 'with something in their past' are watched more than usual.

In order to preserve her family, Alexandra takes some radical steps to lift the kulak curse. She pushes the twenty-year-old Anyuta into marriage so that she can hide under a new surname, and orders eighteen-year-old Maria to work on the collective farm against her will so that the family can be seen to be toeing the new Party line.

The terrible time of ten years earlier seems to be repeating itself—persecution, drought in 1931 and then another famine. But this time it is far worse. Whereas the earlier famine claimed a million lives, this next one is to swallow several million. The toll on the Nesterenko family is heavy. The food in Tarasivka and Goroshino runs out. Olga's grandmother's chickens, ducks and livestock have been dispatched to the collective farm and then out of Ukraine. Even the fish in the Sula River are regarded as belonging to the state. The CHEKA search all the houses fortnightly and even peas, beetroot and potatoes are taken. Utensils and clothes are looted by officials. An eerie silence hangs over the village as dogs, cats, mice and birds are devoured. The people begin to starve. As thousands die, the word 'holod' (hunger) is decreed counter-revolutionary. Leonty and Olga collect bark and cherry leaves which their mother cooks into a type of stew.

'Holod!' dares Leonty out loud, and looks around furtively as if the walls have ears. I remember Olga's stories of the 'hungry years', as she called them—walking to school with no breakfast, walking home from school with a bad headache because she was so hungry, particularly in the winter of 1932 to 1933 when the famine was at its worst.

Small children are kept indoors as hunting parties of crazed people are reputed to capture and cook them. The Nesterenko family starve. Trofim, Olga's middle brother, looks skeletal and becomes very ill in the harsh midwinter of January 1933. In desperation, Olga's eldest brother, Ivan, steals grain from the collective farm to feed his ailing brother. He is caught red-handed and deported hundreds of miles east to prison in Baku, Azerbaijan. Trofim wastes away further and dies before the end of winter. Anyuta, now the mother of two small children, attempts to steal grain to feed them. But the CHEKA and peasant informers who still have grudges against the previously wealthy Nesterenko family are on their toes, and she is also thrown into prison. Her babies, Petro and Vasily, become two more mouths to feed in the beleaguered Nesterenko family.

A short while later Anyuta returns home. Her once jolly, wholesome face is hard and sallow. As the months go by she tries to hide her swelling belly. It transpires that she had sex with a guard in order to gain her freedom. Her husband and family never forgive her, and the daughter she bears is always regarded as a bastard and shunned for the rest of her life.

Anyuta isn't the only young mother who suffers appallingly. In a nearby village, a mother with three young children, whose husband had been arrested, is shot when caught digging up potatoes on the collective farm in the middle of the night. Her children starve to death.

Maria works in the collective farm and is given a pair of red shoes by the boss. He secretly admires her because she is the daughter of a rich kulak. The shoes are immediately bartered for food.

*

I am horrified by what happened to my family during this terrible time and am deeply disturbed by what I read about that period in the present. Stalin deliberately starved Ukraine into submission. He knew that nothing lowers the will to resist, better than hunger. The famine was largely restricted to the Ukraine; the borders were sealed, food was forbidden to be shipped in and no one was allowed out.

But the final death toll will forever be difficult for historians to determine. Bolshevik official history suppressed it totally. As the death rate climbed alarmingly, Stalin forbade the publication of death statistics. Even Ukrainian doctors were forbidden to certify cause of death as starvation. If all this wasn't mad enough already, census takers in Ukraine a few years later were shot for revealing shockingly high mortality rates. It seems that this may have been one of the worst genocides in history.

The writer Arthur Koestler, who was passing through Ukraine at the time, described seeing starving children who 'looked like embryos out of alcohol bottles ... the stations were lined with begging peasants with swollen hands and feet, the women holding up to the carriage windows horrible infants with enormous wobbling heads, stick-like limbs and swollen, pointed bellies'.

*

Alexandra is distraught at the deportation of Ivan and the death of Trofim. She is determined that Leonty will survive. She farms him off to various friends, hoping that this will lessen the stigma of being the son of a kulak. But the CHEKA are everywhere and, still afraid for his future, she eventually sends him to distant relatives in the Crimea, which is several hundred miles away to the south. Maria is forced to marry Mikhail Sakhno.

Alexandra cannot bear to return from Goroshino to Tarasivka, where her dreams for a better life have been totally shattered. She frets for her beloved son Ivan, who has not yet returned from Baku and about whom she can find no information, so in 1934, with her husband and Olga, she makes the long trek eastwards hoping to find him. After several hundred miles the weary travellers stop in Poti, a Georgian port on the Black Sea. It is tough to get into Azerbaijan where they know that Ivan has been sent. So although Baku is still another four hundred miles away, Alexandra decides to settle for a while for Olga's sake. Maria and her new husband join them in Poti.

Life in Poti, although hard, is a little better as this region has not suffered famine and is the homeland of the beloved leader Stalin. Alexandra and Maria sew clothes. Ten-year-old Olga is sent to school. Shura is born in Poti and Olga looks after her while Maria sews. My grandfather Ivan and Maria's husband Mikhail do odd jobs for local farmers, and together they scrape a meagre living.

Alexandra makes several more searches for her son, but to no avail. She now misses her youngest son, Leonty, terribly and becomes fretful for his safety. At the age of fifteen, Olga is uprooted again as her parents make their way back across the vast Steppes to join Leonty in the Crimea, leaving Maria and her family in Poti. Olga clings tearfully to Maria, to whom she has become very close, and is heartbroken to leave her little niece Shura. Alexandra also thinks they will be safer from Soviet persecution in the Crimea as in Poti the family is black-stamped not only for having been kulaks, but also for having spawned criminals who are enemies of the revolution. Their heinous crime? Trying to save their family from starving to death.

Little does Alexandra know that they would be much safer staying in Poti as events unfolding in the west, beyond the German border, will change their lives forever.

In 1939 the Crimea is quite prosperous and Olga and her parents move in with Leonty, who has established himself in Seitler, a former strong Tatar town in northern Crimea. Stalin is pursuing a policy of moving the Tatars away from their traditional strongholds in order to weaken nationalist sympathies. Olga's father joins Leonty to work in the cherry and peach orchards. Leonty is sweet on Katya, a local girl. Olga attends secondary school in Seitler, doing well at her lessons even though her education has been severely disrupted by all the moving around.

In June 1941 the Nesterenko family hear rumours that the Germans may invade. Olga has mixed feelings about this news. Her family have been so hounded by the Soviets that she thinks

German occupation might bring a welcome change. However, she also feels loyalty to Mother Russia. At school she is excelling at German and has dreamed of going to Germany. Anything to escape from the constant bickering of her parents. Sometimes this bickering boils over and Ivan beats Alexandra in a drunken rage.

Calm comes to the family when Ivan is called up to the Front to fight the Germans. Oddly, Ivan, who is over forty, is conscripted but not twenty-two year old Leonty, whom the authorities refuse to take into the army as he is the son of a liquidated kulak. For Alexandra this is the first positive result from the murder of her beloved first husband, especially since Leonty is a sweet, gentle young man. She still has heard nothing of his brother Ivan and is haunted by the memory of holding Trofim's dying body in her arms. Katya is also pleased that Leonty is not conscripted. She is pregnant with his child and they have hastily been married that summer. But Leonty, forever tainted by the kulak stamp, cannot escape, and is press-ganged into digging trenches in south-west Crimea. Alexandra, Olga and Katya cling together as their men are marched off.

Katya gives birth to Lydia in August 1941. Alexandra gazes at the newborn child uttering, 'Boszhe moi, what kind of a world have you been born into?'

23 / **The Crimea under Occupation**

'That bastard Ivan Leontivich!' Nikolai is shouting as he tucks into blood sausage made from his own pigs during the third banquet of the day. The eyes glint fiercely in his weathered, handsome face as he tips back his next nip of samogon. My family—what a treasure to be able to say 'my family'—are arguing passionately about whether or not Ivan Leontivich should have kept the knowledge of my whereabouts to himself. Shura constantly bewails the fact that if Ivan Leontivich had let them know sooner, her mother Maria would have laid her eyes on me while she was still alive. 'Oh Eva, you don't know how much she wanted to see you before she died. She had such a terrible life. Why, Evitchka, why could she not have her wish?' She grasps my hand, the tears spilling down her sad face. I don't know what to answer.

Lydia's flat is airy and light and Lena and I share a room. Leonty and I sit on the bed, swapping tales. He tells me of the wonderful parcels that Olga sent to his family in the early 1960s. 'Such beautiful, expensive materials—blue velvet for Katya, top quality suit cloth for me, and such wonderful toys for the children!'

I remember Mum shopping in the most expensive Adelaide shops and risking Dad's wrath. She wanted nothing short of the best for her beloved family.

Leonty continues the saga of the Nesterenkos in Seitler.

*

While still at school, Olga's life is turned upside down in October 1941 when the Nazis finally occupy Seitler. Olga's headmaster rushes into their classroom announcing that the school is now a German field hospital. All the girls are to put away their schoolbooks immediately and look after wounded German soldiers.

205

Olga has just turned seventeen and is barely out of childhood. Earlier that summer she was shocked to discover blood on her underwear. Not wanting to bother her hassled mother, she washed it secretly. The drying underwear was discovered by the side of the oven. Olga was tersely informed that she was now a woman and this was one of the sufferings of womanhood.

Now she watches her girlhood disappear forever as the desks in her classroom are moved out and makeshift beds set up. Straw is spread and stretchers brought in. There is not much chance to ruminate on the abrupt change from her status as pupil to that of medical orderly, for soon the classroom is filled with bleeding and groaning men, brought in by the wagonload from the front. She is assigned to a German medical officer, Dr Hoffmann. She likes him immediately even though he is the enemy. A kindly, balding man with thick brown-rimmed glasses, Dr Hoffmann is pleased with how well Olga speaks German, and teaches her how to bandage shattered limbs, give tetanus injections and assist him in operations, most of which involve sawing off gangrenous limbs or sewing up gaping holes. This becomes her life for the next few months. She is a hard worker, and soon she and the doctor are on friendly terms. In a rare lull of incoming wounded, Dr Hoffmann shows her pictures of his wife and children who live in Magdeburg, and secretly confides how he hates this war, thinks Hitler a madman and just wishes he could be back with his family.

Life under occupation is miserable. Menacing German soldiers patrol the streets, operating severe curfews on pain of death. What shocks the Nesterenkos is the way they are treated by the Germans. 'Untermenschen' is a word they hear over and over. 'It means subhuman,' Olga explains. 'Dr Hoffmann tells me that the Nazis want to make us their slaves, for they are the Master Race.'

'They can't treat us like Jews or gypsies! I won't be a slave to anybody,' broods Alexandra. She is disappointed as she had high hopes that the German invasion might mean freedom from the Bolshevik persecution of kulaks that her family has suffered so long. Olga loves her proud, handsome mother and has witnessed her toughness on many occasions. Although she often doesn't agree with her, Olga wishes she had more of that tough streak. She herself feels soft and malleable, and can't help feeling optimistic about the future.

Bitter fighting rocks southern Crimea. The elegant port of Sevastopol is suffering a terrible siege and being bombed to smithereens by the Luftwaffe. This is where Olga's father, Ivan, has been sent. Winter is setting in, and he and other Soviet soldiers are shockingly ill-equipped. Not only do they not have proper clothing; they have no guns. Ivan is expected to fight the Germans with a stick. Any Russian who does not fancy losing his feet to frostbite, or being mown down by a machine-gun as he runs towards the well-equipped German army with something as laughable as a stick, is shot on the spot as a traitor.

Even though Sevastopol holds out for several more gruelling months, Ivan is taken prisoner in early 1942. Freezing cold and starving, he and other bedraggled captives are forced to march to a Nazi concentration camp in northern Crimea. This involves a humiliating parade through the middle of Seitler. Women line the streets, hoping for a fleeting glimpse of their loved ones. Olga is among them and briefly spots her father as he shuffles past. She thinks she discerns the slightest hint of a sad smile as she sees him for the last time. Katya, holding baby Lydia, looks vainly for Leonty, but he seems to have disappeared off the face of the earth.

The war rages on around them. Fighting is hard and bitter throughout the Crimea. Kerch, where Leonty has been sent, changes hands several times in 1942, with the Soviets wresting it from the Germans only to be routed soon after. Leonty digs trenches around the quarries outside Kerch, which Soviet soldiers have been defending for months.

More and more wounded pour into the makeshift hospital where Olga works. Still only seventeen, she feels a good deal older with all she has witnessed. The wounded, mostly German and Romanians, have terrible injuries and die in droves. Often she and the other medical orderlies cannot find enough sheets to cover the dead. Usually wounded Soviet soldiers are left to die out in the open. On one occasion a Ukrainian soldier is brought in, but Dr Hoffmann does not turn him away. Olga always remembers what this soldier, who is barely older than she, tells her: 'Stay alive, young pretty one, and bear lots of children. God knows, this country will need them.'

The worst cases for Olga are the men who come in with broken spines. All she can do is remove the excrement from beneath them as gently as possible so that they are more comfortable. The dreadful silence of the nights, when life is snuffed from young manhood, appals her. Why is all this happening? However, she is grateful that she can work as a medical orderly and still regularly return to her family. She loves being with Katya and dotes on baby Lydia as she did on Maria's baby, Shura, in Poti. Most of her friends have been despatched to Germany as workers, and she dreads the thought of being taken away from her family. She has heard that conditions for workers in Germany are terrible and that Ukrainians are indeed treated as slaves by the Third Reich.

The inevitable finally happens. Dr Hoffmann, looking anxious and hassled, takes her aside one night and sombrely announces, 'Olga, I have to warn you that the Germans have now taken most of the Crimea except for Sevastopol and tomorrow I'm being moved closer to that port.'

'But can't I come with you?' Olga pleads.

'I'm sorry, but that is impossible.'

'But perhaps I can stay here and continue this work.'

'I'm afraid that this field hospital will be disbanded immediately and the wounded taken elsewhere.'

'But what will happen to me?'

'That's what I want to talk to you about. I have been charged with sending you and the other helpers here to work in Germany. I'm sorry.' He watches the young girl's face fall. 'But fortunately I have some influence over where you are to go. So I will have you sent to the Krupp armament factory in Magdeburg.'

'But Magdeburg's where you are from!'

'Yes, that's the whole point. When I get the chance I will return and use my influence to try to get you out of the factory. I'm sorry, but that's the best I can do. If anyone found out I was helping you at all I would be in deep trouble.'

Olga looks into Dr Hoffmann's kindly but troubled eyes and knows he is doing the best he can for her.

'Have I time to warn my family and say goodbye?'

'Yes, you go home now and do that and be here by twelve noon tomorrow.'

Alexandra is devastated and clings to her youngest born. Olga tries to reassure her: 'Don't worry, Mama, Dr Hoffmann will look after me and I will return as soon as this terrible war is over.' But

Alexandra doesn't have the same faith in the German doctor as Olga. She has been speaking to a neighbour whose daughter was sent to Germany a few months back. She hasn't heard any news in a long time, and fears the worst. Alexandra packs some things for Olga, including lots of food for the long train journey that lies ahead.

At the train station the next afternoon, under the watchful eye of German guards, Dr Hoffmann whispers to Olga not to lose hope and to await his help. Alexandra and Katya are there to see her being loaded onto the train. Alexandra feels uneasy as she watches her little Olychka being herded into the cattle truck, crammed in with about fifty other girls. She tries to go forward, as do several other anxious mothers, but they are all pushed back by the German guards. Alexandra doesn't want to think the inevitable, but she feels in her bones that she is seeing her youngest child for the last time.

*

Shura and Lydia are making stuffed peppers in the kitchen. My mind is thrown back to similar sights and delicious smells in Pudney Street, Adelaide, where Olga shoved meat, garlic and rice into shiny green peppers. I tell my cousins how life was for the immigrant Olga.

I notice that in our conversation men get short shrift. I attempt to give an unbiased picture of Sasha but Shura is gunning for him. Her mother, Maria, was furious with him for 'hiding information about Olga and the children from her'. Sasha is relegated to a long line of male no-hopers that includes her husband, who was murdered a couple of years ago. Not by Shura (though I did wonder).

My cousin Nikolai has a wicked sense of humour. One evening, while he has been ranting about the state of Ukraine, Shura pipes up, 'You know, Nikolai, I had my eyes shut for a few minutes and you sounded just like your brother Vasily.' Nikolai, who is highly competitive with his older brother, answers, 'Well, Shurochka, in future do me a favour. Keep your eyes open!'

The lively, happy atmosphere of being with my family is in sharp contrast to the continuing grim story of their life under Nazi occupation.

*

Leonty has a terrible time digging trenches outside Kerch. The battle lines throughout the Crimea continue to wave back and forth. The winter of '41 to '42 is harsh, compounding the misery of those involved in the deadly fighting on both sides—all of whom would much rather be at home with their families for Christmas. Leonty thinks about Katya and the baby he has not yet seen, and longs to be with them and take care of them.

In early 1942 a Soviet commander comes up to the trench where Leonty is digging and announces that the battle for Kerch is lost, that the Soviet army is pulling out and all trench diggers must fend for themselves. The Germans will have overrun the trenches by morning, and if they don't want to be killed or captured, they had better get out now. Abruptly the commander turns and leaves. Leonty and his fellow diggers let their shovels fall and stare around in bewilderment. Where can they go? It is a long walk home and the area is surrounded by Germans. They feel like animals in a trap. At least they are in civilian clothes, so the best first step is to scramble away and lose themselves in the countryside.

Leonty joins up with others from Seitler and together they trudge north, avoiding the roads as much as they can. It is early spring when he limps into his apartment in Seitler, tired, bedraggled, thin as a beanstalk, but alive. Katya and Alexandra are overjoyed. The bad news is that Olga has been transported to the West with thousands of others. At least Katya has been spared because of her baby.

Life ticks on as they lie low and scrape a little food together under the next two years of German occupation. Alexandra has her own secret. The stomach pains she has suffered since the murder of her first husband are slowly getting worse and the constant hunger of the war years isn't helping. She feels in her bones that there is something deeply wrong and that she may not have much time left.

She longs to return to her village one more time. Her daughter Anyuta lives in Staryi Irzhavets, near Tarasivka, and has recently given birth to another child, Nikolai. In early 1944, Alexandra announces that she is going to Tarasivka for a short visit. Only she knows she will not return.

Leonty and Katya are really worried for her. Although the German army is by now being routed, the countryside is chaotic and it is dangerous to travel. But Alexandra is determined and finds herself a passage on a goods train. Leonty takes her to the train station.

🍂

'You know, Eva, I can see her now, in her boots and coat with its fur collar. She kissed and hugged us all, then kissed little Lydia one more time and walked down the platform. I waited for her to turn back and wave and ...' Here Leonty begins to cry, remembering the last time he saw his mother. 'And she never turned around, not even once.'

He sobbed some more, shaking his head at the fact that she didn't turn and wave.

'Perhaps she was crying,' I venture. 'Especially if she knew it was the last time.'

'Perhaps,' Leonty says sadly. Then he brightens up as he adds, 'But at least she sent plenty of letters!'

🍂

When Alexandra arrives at her house with the red-tiled roof, she finds it occupied by some young orphans and an old woman. Undaunted, she pulls up her sleeves and makes the house into a kindergarten, taking in more children whose parents have disappeared or been killed. She revives the farm and soon has a flock of hens and some cows. Her grandson, Vasily, comes to help.

Katya writes to her mother-in-law and begs her to return to Seitler. Alexandra refuses, saying she must stay to milk the cows.

Eventually her stomach pains become so bad that she cannot look after the kindergarten anymore. Reluctantly she hands over the red-tiled house to others and goes with Vasily to die at Anyuta's house. The pain is now agonising. Cancer is eating away at her abdominal organs. The war has left the country in shambles and there is no medical help to be had. She resorts to the poor man's remedy for pain, which is to drink kerosene. Vasily is devoted to her and tries to alleviate her suffering as much as he can.

She writes what will be her final letter to Leonty in which she still does not say she is dying even though she makes clear to Leonty her last request. 'When my darling Olychka returns from Germany, please let Katya be her sister and look after her.'

I hold my uncle's hand as he is overwhelmed by tears again. 'You know, Eva, I knew by that sentence, "Let Katya be her sister", that my mother was dying.'

Leonty suffers more trauma. He is caught by the Nazis in 1944 and taken to a concentration camp in north Ukraine. The conditions are dreadful; prisoners die like flies. But by a sheer stroke of luck he manages to escape. A female Ukrainian camp commandant who knew him from school helps him.

'You certainly had luck on your side,' I interject. 'You survived a near-drowning as a baby, a famine in 1921, another in 1933, persecution by the Soviets, digging trenches on the Front and a Nazi concentration camp!'

'Yes,' he answers, 'I have been told that if you survive drowning, that casts a lucky spell over you for the rest of your life. My Aunt Luba, who survived in the boggy marsh by breathing through a piece of straw, also lived to a ripe old age.'

'And what happened to my grandfather?' I ask.

'Ivan survived the war and came back at the end of 1944. He lived with Katya and me for a while. But the stuffing had been knocked out of him in the Nazi prisoner-of-war camp, where Russians were treated abysmally. He was also lost without Alexandra. Even though he mistreated her, he loved her in his own strange way. A leg wound from the war caused him a lot of pain and he drank heavily.

'Then he moved in with a Tatar woman,' Leonty goes on in a disapproving tone, 'and we hardly saw him again. I did make the effort of finding him a few years later and visited, but he was distant and seemed to have erased the life that we had once so intimately shared.' Leonty looks very sad. 'I had no hard feelings towards him. He had always been good to me. Then Olychka wrote to us in 1959 and we were overjoyed to hear from her. She wanted to know if Ivan was still alive. I spent some time hunting him down again, but all I could find out was that he had run off somewhere with that Tatar woman.'

I am intrigued as to what was wrong with my grandfather 'running off with a Tatar woman'. All the family are united in their disdain for Tatar people. I have seen Tatar villages full of dark-skinned, dark-eyed people—very romantic looking, especially the women, who wear bright gypsy clothing in blues and reds. 'What's the matter with them?' I want to know.

'They are uneducated and uncivilised. They steal unashamedly. Look at the hovels they live in.' Their houses look quite solid and adequate to me.

It is time to say goodbye to my Uncle Leonty. He is very sad and holds me close before murmuring goodbye. According to Lena, the goodbye he says means 'farewell forever', signifying that he doesn't expect to see me again.

I fly back to Adelaide shell-shocked. Finding my grandfather's family was amazing enough, but now I have found my grandmother's family. The background of a vast, previously empty canvas is being filled in by many bright colours.

I am now looking forward to developing my new-found relationship with Dad and hearing about his past. And also to seeing my sister's play in Adelaide.

24 / **Resolution**

Well, I'll be darned! Val's play is about our family. When I mentioned to her a while back that I wanted to write a book about Olga, she was scathing—why did I want to drag up the past? Now she has gazumped me, and the play, *Svetlana in Slingbacks*, is to have its premiere in Adelaide.

Val arranges to visit us at Dad's house. Things have thawed out between us since I said I will take care of Dad as much as possible because it is my turn now. She is relieved as she finds it hard to cope with him, especially when he talks about the past. It will be at least fifteen years since I have seen her and I am looking forward to it.

Dad as usual is busy, and carries on washing and mopping floors, as is his wont, while Val and I sit in the back garden. Although things are not ideal between us, the chat is friendly enough. I tell her about finding our relatives but she surprises me with her disinterest. Her attention is on the play and she feels nervous.

She describes it as a black comedy that deals with the heavy issues of our mother's descent into madness. She gives me a couple of complimentary tickets and a warning that her character (Svetana, aged twelve) and mine (Sonia, aged 19) are both a mixture of how we were at those ages.

After Val leaves I enthuse to Dad, 'You should be proud of Val. She won an Arts Council grant to write the play, which is on for three weeks in Adelaide . That's quite an achievement.'

'Well, I can't go and see it.'

'Why not?'

'I can't sit in theatre for two hours with my bowels beink the way they are!'

I commiserate with him. Since his operations, Dad's bowels

have not fully recovered and he has been prone to smelly accidents, much to his distress.

I go to Theatre 62 with Elizabeth and Wendy, my first husband Peter's two sisters. I am pleased that they have come along to give me moral support because the play is harrowing. Elizabeth walks out halfway through as she finds it upsetting and does not like to see a subject like mental illness being treated this way. I find it an astounding experience—to sit and watch my own family drama unfolding in front of me on stage. It is like having an audience in one's own house, coughing and laughing and watching intimacies and events that are raw and private. At the same time I think the play is excellent. The actors are extremely good and the story is riveting.

Most extraordinary of all is that I am seeing my family dynamic from my sister's point of view. The slice of life that we see is when Val was twelve and I was nineteen. It deals with my mother's illness, her subsequent lobotomy and me leaving home. It shows Svetlana doing things that I used to do, like putting stones in a certain formation outside Mum's bedroom window to prove to her next day that 'They' were not shining lights at her. I am portrayed as a stroppy teenager who was much closer to Val's character at that age. My mother's preoccupation with menstruation and blood is graphically demonstrated. There are some surprises. Val depicts our family as far more intelligent than I remember them. I come across as more confident, witty and erudite than I ever saw myself, and Dad is portrayed as more sympathetic than he was. However, Sonia says things to him I never said, such as 'You're not my real father!' I feel hurt by it even though I know it is for dramatic effect.

Val's depiction of my mother's descent into insanity is heartbreaking. Having freshly heard the story of her early life from her brother Leonty, I find it even more poignant that the laughing kulak princess she once was should have had such a sad ending. While watching the play I realise that my understanding of my mother's illness has deepened since finding out more of her history in Ukraine. There was such a sharp juxtaposition between being admired and looked up to for being a kulak and then being persecuted and smashed down for being a kulak. This was mirrored in her inconsistent treatment of me as a child—loved and adored one minute, demeaned and beaten the next.

The most profound message I pick up from the play is how terrible it was for my sister when I left home. Svetlana is so lonely when Sonia leaves. She is left behind to look after her father, Boris. There is a scene at the end where Boris is lecturing Svetlana on how to cook the porridge. Having had the same lecture a few times in the last couple of weeks, I laugh uproariously. What is poignant for me is that Svetlana sometimes tries on the slingback shoes that Sonia left behind.

When the play is over I am stunned. I am reminded of the overwhelming dream I had of giant people acting out my family's story on a mountainside. Was that prophetic?

Wendy is deeply affected too. 'You know, Eva, even though you have described some of what went on in your family, I didn't realise how terrible it was. This has really brought it home.'

My father is waiting up for me when I get back, eager to hear all about it. I enthusiastically describe the play and tell him my impressions. Especially Val's impressive comedic talent—a wonderful legacy of the spirit of Olga.

'By the way, Dad, did I ever shout at you, "You're not my real father"?'

'Nah, you never did.'

'Well, I'm pleased about that as I have always felt you were my proper, real dad and in fact believed you were for several years.'

I also tell Dad how good the play is and that he should be even more proud of Val. I describe the porridge scene and have a gentle jibe at him. He is incredulous that people would find such a mundane domestic scene interesting. I go to bed feeling closer to my dad and sister. Next day I phone Val and congratulate her and also say I understood how lonely she was when I left and how sorry I was to leave her on her own.

In the years to come, her play goes on to be a major success interstate.

My father continues to imbibe his daily quota of shark's cartilage, herbs, raw salads, immune strengtheners and linseed oil. He is beginning to look stronger and healthier. I suspect that this change isn't only due to his fancy oral intake but also to the contact and companionship we are enjoying. Since Val and Alex left, he has been alone. Now he has me, and despite his irascibility and outbreaks of total daftness, I love being here with him. My fingers are permanently purple and orange from grating beetroot and turmeric, but I enjoy the task as I feel I am putting healthy nutrients into Dad's emaciated body.

Mealtimes are my favourite, especially breakfast. He always gets up before me, sets the table and puts on the porridge. He then shaves and performs his diabetic routine. He is proud of the skills associated with this—he takes a blood sample, measures his insulin level, records it neatly in a notebook and then injects himself. When I come in, he pours tea and pops the bread into the toaster. This is a silver monstrosity from the 1950s, same vintage as the refrigerator. Like the latter it has its quirks, which must be handled in a certain way. The toaster only works if the bread is thrown from a certain height at a precise velocity.

I make several attempts but the bread just won't go down. Dad commandeers it patiently and just chucks it with a flick of his wrist. Down slides the bread and converts smoothly to a perfect piece of toast. 'You have to knaow how to treat these machines. You treat them well and they will perform for you.' He is reprimanding me not just for the failure with the toaster but also because I can't open the fridge door gently enough without disabling the closing mechanism.

However, these trifling examples of my ineptitude vanish into insignificance as Dad and I talk. We continue to discuss Alexandra and her predicament.

'She was such a bright little ting. Always laughink and with many friends. I did everyting for that girl. But poor ting she had no mahder. And when you left—'

I immediately feel guilty, so interrupt, 'Yeah, Dad, I'm really sorry I left you alone with two little girls to bring up.'

My leaving home is still a sore point, and although I have apologised for it before, I still feel the weight of the thirty-three year estrangement in which it resulted. Although I know that I needed to leave for my own sanity, I also feel bad about not being around for my wounded family. Now I wait for the 'Yeah, you should have stayed' conversation.

But to my surprise Dad unexpectedly takes the wind out of my sails.

'You knaow what, Eva, I been tinkin'. I been tinkin' a lot in the last few munts. I'm glad you left.'

I can't believe what I'm hearing. This is not what I was expecting.

'Look at you! You've made someting of your life! If you had stayed you would never do all the tings that you done, never achieved what you achieved.'

This is a real turnaround for the books! In one fell swoop he seems to be both acknowledging me for doing well in my life and giving up the tragic story of how I betrayed him, walked out on him and left him to bring up my sisters on his own. I stare dumbfounded into my teacup.

'I should've kicked Alex out. But no, I wait on her hand and foot. She sleep till noon. Did nuttin' round the house. I say, get job! After a while she get job in hotel. I relieved. But she ring me up later and say she got sack. I rush round in car, pick her up and say, "Doan' worry, Alex, it will be orkai." I should leave her there! Say, "Doan' come home till you have job." But no, I go and buy her flat! And where she now? And look at you. Nice house, nice car, good job. You somebahdy!'

Before I glow too much with this rare acknowledgement, I say, 'But Dad, you have always said how much you felt betrayed by me leaving, how you felt badly let down by me.'

'Yeah, I knaow. You knaow why I felt bad about you? I felt unappreciated by you. I felt I made much sacrifice for you but you not willink to do same for me. I must tell you, Eva, that I really wanted to leave your mahder. She was very unhappy and now I realise she was sick. Your fahder and his family—bastards!" He wags a finger at me. "They drive her crazy! I saw that I could not make her happy. So I was goink to leave her. But you knaow what made me not go? It was you.' Boo-boom! I stare harder into my teacup. 'I want protect you. Your mahder, as I have said before, was no angel. She had many men before me and I afraid of what would happen to you. I doan' knaow what she could do, so I was very worried about you and what sort of life you end up with. So that is what stopped me from goink. You.'

He looks at me with burning eyes. I find it hard to take in. I am totally gobsmacked.

Dad has never said anything like this before. Sure, he has ranted and raved about all the sacrifices he has made for me, but I have always thought he meant working hard to clothe and feed me, blah-blah-blah. I haven't realised before how seriously he considered leaving my mother. I certainly have never appreciated the extent to which he considered me in this decision-making process.

The effect that this new information has on me is very humbling. I now understand something for the first time. He could have been free of that crazy woman who made his life hell, but he felt honour-bound to her small daughter. I remember that time when Olga stormed out of the house, me in tow, declaring, 'We are leaving Sasha.' We caught a train to Adelaide. I felt strangely exhilarated. It seemed the right thing to do, but at the same time I was sad to leave Sasha behind. He may have been too quiet and boring, but at least he was stable and reliable. They were both trying to leave each other, but being in a strange new country and without support networks, it was very difficult for either of them to break free. I suddenly recall Maria's dream where she saw Olga on a train with a small girl in plaits and realised that Olga was calling out to her. I get goose bumps.

I am brought back to the present by Dad.

'And then she get pregnant with Val and I knaow then I cannot leave her. So there it is. Ayayayayay.'

I look at my father. His eyes are full and soft. A huge metamorphosis has occurred in him. He is no longer hanging on to the tragic story that has sustained him for so long. He sees that he made the choice to stay with my mother largely because of me, but at last he has separated that from expecting me to make the same sort of sacrifice in return. I see for the first time the care in his over-protectiveness of me, and that helps me let go of any resentment about feeling suppressed by him. I feel humbled and inspired by my father. He has realised that his choice to sacrifice his life for me was not contingent on me sacrificing my life for him. He has managed to let that one go. Any vestiges of the Iron Curtain that has kept us apart have for so long finally come down.

Something new and fresh opens up between us, and now we are ready for the task ahead—to journey back to Sasha's past. This previously reticent man is bursting to talk about his life and is flattered that I want to put it into a book. I sit riveted as I am transported back to another time and place.

The Fugitive

Facts pale after a certain passage of time, and blood shed in the past loses its red hue.

Nadezhda Mandelstam

There is no strength left to cry; steady and continued weeping leads finally to silence. At first there is screaming; then wailing; and at last a bottomless sigh that does not leave even an echo.

Chaim Kaplan

Prologue / Romanian Border, 1941

The unmistakable aroma of cooked rabbit draws Sasha towards the flickering flame. It is dark and cold. He gathers his father's coat around his thin frame. All the food his mother packed that tear-stained evening a few nights before has been eaten. After surviving a close shave at a Nazi checkpoint, he is getting nearer to his destination, close to the Romanian border. He now needs food and somewhere to sleep. The gypsy camp in the forest beckons him. He has always had a soft spot for gypsies. As well as being outsiders like himself, they represent romance and freedom in his boyish imagination.

He is ushered into the circle and offered some very welcome rabbit. Although these people are Romanian gypsies, they speak a mixture of Russian and Ukrainian so conversation is easy. Like himself they are fugitives—expelled from Romania by the new Nazi puppet government under Antonescu—and are on the run. Several of their party have been caught and shot. Despite the terrible stories they have to tell, there is still a fire in their eyes that Sasha finds inspiring.

A middle-aged woman with greying flecks in her wild dark hair takes his hand and asks, 'What brings a sweet young boy out here on such a cold night?'

After Sasha has told her some of his story, she looks deep into his eyes and places her hands on either side of his cheeks. She seems to go into some sort of a trance, but Sasha feels curiously comforted as he feels himself falling under her spell.

After several moments she speaks.

'I see a hard road ahead with difficult choices for you to make. But a good strong heart beats inside you and resonates with deep truth that has been instilled within you. Your life will be hard, but it will be long and productive and you will travel very far. You will be tested to the utmost, but you will not be destroyed.'

She is silent for a long time but still holds his face in her hands.

Sasha doesn't fully understand all her words, but they make a deep impression on him and he carries them in his heart always.

25 / **Horse Scalps**

Dad expertly and lightly pops the bread in the toaster and down it glides. Not all is dark or sepia-coloured in his childhood. His eyes light up with the memories of his homeland.

Summers in Odessa are long and hot and full of bright colours. The scent of the Steppes mingles with the tang of the sea. Sasha is eight years old. He and his brother, Dodik, play in the fields on the outskirts of the city with their small cousins. The sea glistens in the distance and wild flowers swathe the undulating hills as the little ones insist that the two older boys piggyback them one more time. Soon the children are splashing about in the river, laughing, shrieking and pummelling each other mercilessly.

Exhausted, Sasha flops down in the long grass and gazes up at the rich blue of the endless sky. His eye is caught by the intricate orange and yellow patterns of a butterfly as it alights on a nearby grass stem and he inspects it with fascination.

The summer holiday will soon draw to a close and usher in the humdrum routine of chores and school. The glory of the summer day is suddenly clouded by the thought of his beloved father Shika, languishing in jail. He has been there for over a year now, and Sasha and his brother watch helplessly as their mother wrings her hands and cries silently, waiting for his release. They have been forced to move out of their cottage and to live in a tiny room in a relative's house. Shika was arrested after men in Bolshevik uniforms burst into their home, looking for the gold that was supposed to be hidden there. None was found, but they continued to harass the family. When Shika refused to spy on his neighbours, he was thrown into jail.

'Come on, we know you Jews hide your gold. Just last week we found gold hidden in an old piano down the street!'

Only when the gold was found would Shika and hundreds of others like him be released.

Sasha scrutinises the intricate markings on the butterfly as if he might find the answer to the enormous puzzle and uncertainty that seems to flicker over his life. He is very confused. At school he is continually told how glorious this revolution is. Comrade Lenin has risen from the tyranny of Czarism and has saved the Russian people. *All* the Russian people—the communist vision includes the Jews, proclaiming equal rights for them. Sasha remembers his parents' exhilaration as the new idealism first swept the land. The Wenzeruls and their forebears have lived in Odessa for several generations, having arrived from the other side of the Black Sea in the early eighteenth century. Now they are proud of this glorious revolution that will sweep the world, and they, Russian Jews, are a part of the new comradeship.

Shika Wenzerul fought the Germans in Word War One and was saved from death in the trenches by his friend, Igor Gotman. Igor dragged him back half-dead to Odessa, where he was nursed back to health by Igor's sister Hana. Only permanent injury from the hellhole of the trenches prevented Shika from fighting in the Russian Civil War. He married Hana, and although poor they were happy—and even happier when Sasha was born in1924 and Dodik eighteen months later. Meanwhile, Igor married Sonia Gorbman. This marriage now connects Sasha, through his uncle, to the elite echelons of the Bolshevik Party. Sonia Gorbman's sister Golda is married to a Bolshevik hero of the revolution, Kliment Voroshilov. Sasha's mother's family are all proud of their connection to Voroshilov, especially since he has risen to great stature and is now a high ranking People's Commissar in the Bolshevik Army. Stalin himself has eaten with the Gorbmans and has praised Sonia's cooking highly.

Shika is a horse whisperer. He thinks horses are gods and reveres the tracks they make upon the rich earth. He can smell the measure of an animal as it softly whinnies its breath against his face. His gentle father, Moishe, instilled in him this love of horses. The same gentle father, along with his soft mother, were hacked to death in the 1906 pogroms. On a cold, moonlit winter's night, hordes of Ukrainian backwoodsmen attacked and killed hundreds of Odessan Jews with pickaxes. As they angrily dismembered young

225

Shika's life and reduced him to shocked orphanhood, they shouted horrendous obscenities that imprinted scars in his brain. 'You Jews are unsightly vermin and parasites who devour the Ukrainian soul and must be scourged from the black earth!'

Sasha watches as the butterfly flitters away and thinks of the grandparents he has never known, save for a grainy, ghostlike image in an old family photograph. He also thinks of what they are saying at school. Trotsky is a Jew and a hero. It seems that the Bolsheviks are champions of the Jews. The Wenzerul family have embraced the tenets of the new communist revolution enthusiastically and Shika discourages Hana from teaching his sons Jewish prayers. Sasha too prides himself in being a young communist, and believes passionately in the sacrifices that must be made for this revolution. He embraces Stalin's resolve to pull Greater Russia out of the Middle Ages and is fervently behind his grand plan to build an economic and military power that will outshine Germany, Britain and America. Sasha accepts that industrialisation in Russia must be carried out at the expense of the peasantry and the working class. Although he is deeply unhappy that his father is in jail, he accepts it. He knows that there are many people, not only Jews, who have hidden gold and jewels and believes they should surrender it to the state for its future glory. So he waits patiently, trusting that soon his father will be vindicated and released, and that at last his mother will stop crying.

❧

I pour more tea. Although touched by my father's youthful idealism, I am outraged.

'But Dad, the communists threw your father in jail with absolutely no evidence. They reduced your family to destitution.'

'Nah, nah, nah.' He looks at me as if I was born yesterday. 'You knaow nuttin'! Eva, it was a glorious thing that they tried. I felt I was part of a brave new world. I was willink to do anyting for the communist state. Yes, even accept that my father was in jail. That was part of the sacrifice.' He thumps the table. 'You must understand. It was our religion, our passion. I trusted totally that this New Order would succeed.'

His face darkens. I can see the shadows gathering as memory stirs uncomfortably at the gradual betrayal of that trust. It would be a long, hard and painful road to the point where, with deep regret, he finally had to give it up.

$$\mathscr{o}$$

Shika is let out of jail soon afterwards. There is no apology. With characteristic fortitude, he and his family struggle to reassemble the broken pieces of their lives. There is little work, but Soviet citizens are inundated by stories of a worldwide depression, from which they take heart that the evil capitalist order is beginning to break down. It will be up to the Soviet workers to keep their noses to the grindstone and eventually lead the floundering world into a splendid new future.

Shika looks after the horses on a nearby farm and reluctantly takes another job in a factory where products, including combs, are made from dead horses. Hana cooks up baskets of food and sells them to passengers on passing trains. The family manages to rent two rooms attached to the factory and Sasha and Dodik plant potatoes in an adjoining scrap of land. The sacrifices become bigger and bigger. Sasha watches and waits. Stalin's Five Year Plans are lauded at school as masterpiece blueprints for the future, but the reality is hard to watch. The farm where Shika works is forcibly closed down and its kulak owner disappears. Other farms are also shut down. Grain from the massive new collective farms is shipped away. The Wenzeruls become poorer and hungrier. People begin dying of hunger; first just a few, then hundreds, then thousands, then millions.

Shika's work in the factory is not enough to live on, but the Wenzerul family just manage to scrape through the terrible famine that grips Ukraine. Shika brings home horse scalps from the factory that have been used to manufacture combs. Occasionally pieces of flesh are attached to the scalps, and Hana boils them up. The family drinks the resulting broth with its meagre scrapings of life-saving protein.

$$\mathscr{o}$$

'God, Dad, didn't you hate Stalin by now with millions starving to death?' I am still stuffing toast and jam down my throat, unable to imagine what this slow starvation must have been like.

'Nah, nah. I knaow what a hard job the Soviets had with those

227

bastard Ukrainians. They had to be tough to keep that lot in line.'

I think of the poor Nesterenkos being forced to give up their hard-earned grain further east in Tarasivka, but keep quiet.

Even though this is heavy fare at breakfast, I am delighted that my father is letting me into his world. For one thing, it is helping me to understand why he is so careful with his money. Actually, that is putting it kindly. He is in fact a real miser, as I find out when we go shopping at the local supermarket. Dad pounces on a bag of mouldy grapes that are a quarter of the normal price. I find him a litre of low calorie Woodroofe's Lemonade because I know he likes it. He says, 'See how much the two-litre bottle costs.' I walk all the way back. 'But you can't fit that into your fridge,' I remonstrate. I should have known better. In the end we have to buy the two-litre bottle because he will save ten cents.

Now anyone would think that my father is a poor man. No way. He has at least $2 million in property and I don't know what else. But no, we join all the bargain hunters at the cheap goods section. The trouble with all this is that my father's miserliness has rubbed off on me. I have spent my whole life being unable to spend money on myself. I frequent second-hand shops, much to the dismay of my husband. My children call me 'mouldy Mum' because my fridge is full of food past its used-by dates.

After the debacle of our first-night arrival at my father's dark house and following him in by torch, I now have my own special torch, which he insists I use in the evenings when I am walking from room to room. I can't believe that I am in a beautiful house in one of the most affluent suburbs in Adelaide and am walking around with a torch. It is also freezing, so like Dad I wear a bobble hat. *Come on, Eva,* I berate myself. *You're fifty-three years old! A PhD, for Christ's sake! Why are you walking around with a torch and a bobble hat?* So I take a deep breath one night and challenge him. He is offended and says the torch is for convenience, not to save money.

But now I've started I won't be put off. 'You could sell one of your units and use the money to buy yourself some nice things. You don't know how much time you have left! Enjoy yourself!'

Dad scratches under his bobble hat, looking genuinely puzzled. 'I doan' knaow what I would spend the money on.'

'A brand new little automatic car for starters. It would make your life so much easier.' He has owned his 1968 HK Holden since new. It is so large that he has to squeeze past it in the garage, and so heavy that he has to use all of his waning muscle power to turn the wheel. He has shrunk so much he can barely see over the bonnet and the hand shift gears are ponderous. The car has no heating or cooling and the driver's door has to be opened from the outside.

'Why should life be easy? I love that car. It's been with me for over t'irty years. You doan' knaow how happy I am just to sit in that car!'

'A new hearing aid?' I ask. I look at the big ugly 1950s pink helicopter protruding from his ear. It has disgusting little plastic pipes coming out of it which are yellow with age and who knows what else. He is forever feeding this pink monster with batteries that never seem to work properly and make high whining noises at inopportune moments.

'There's nuttin' wrong with this hearink aid. It works perfectly well. Only fifty cents in auction,' he proudly reminds me again.

'A new pair of glasses?' I say, looking at his big scratched horn-rimmed glasses (yes, you guessed it: another 1950s auction acquisition).

'Well, I'll tell you someting about these glasses. When I have to go and fix the toilets of my tenants, often these glasses fall off. I have to pull them out of some pretty bad places, I tell you. And they are solid and can stand rough treatment. T'ese glasses are my friends.' He bangs the table. 'They been with me for years. I can't t'row away my friends!'

Still undaunted, I persevere. 'A new television?' His television is probably one of the first colour sets produced. The picture quality is so bad that only Channel 2 has clearly defined images. 'You could watch any channel you want and you could have remote control.'

'Why?' he shouts, throwing his hands up in horror, 'I doan' need it! I only watch Channel 2. I doan' want to watch those rubbish adverts on the ahder channels. Everyting I want to see is on that channel.'

'A new washing machine?' I venture weakly. His laundry contains the 1950s washing machine that my mother used when I was young, complete with wringer, copper and old cement troughs with their collections of old soaps. He still boils his sheets, puts them in the agitator, and then rinses them before squeezing them through the wringer. 'You could buy a nice little automatic washing machine that would save you so much time and effort.'

'Who needs more time?' he shouts. 'These new machines doan' wash clothes as clean. They rubbish!' He now glares at me, almost apoplectic with rage.

As I don't want him to be stressed because of the cancer, I decide that trying to persuade him to buy a few nice things so that his life is easier and more luxurious is like persuading anyone else to sleep on a bed of nails.

26 / **The Bullock**

Another breakfast—porridge, toast and tea. Dad is really in full swing in talking about his past and is happy that I am keen to know everything.

Now we are under a starry sky. It is 1938 and fourteen-year-old Sasha is looking after his family's cows. The grand arena of twinkling stars beats a fire in the boy's soul as he gazes up at them. His family has survived the famine years and has gradually become a little more prosperous. Shika still works at the factory but has now moved his family into a small house in the suburb of Peresyp on the northern outskirts of Odessa. They rent land nearby where they keep a few cows, chickens and rabbits and cultivate vegetables. Hana milks the cows and carries churns of milk to sell to passengers on the train that stops in Peresyp on the way to and from Odessa. Sasha is doing exceptionally well at school even though he has to do many chores for the family.

'That's how it was, Eva. Dodik and I did everyting! Children worked hard for the family. Not like today—lounge about watchink TV—never raise a finger—no respect.' If I ever got anywhere near a sulk as a teenager, one favourite refrain was 'Go out and dig potatoes—that will fix you up. You doan' knaow you alive.'

I am transported back to the idyllic scene of the young shepherd looking out over the giant fertile Steppe and tending his cows. Sasha also has a difficult specific task, and that is to keep an eye on one particular bullock. This animal always tries to escape and lead the rest of the herd into the nearby cornfields. If let loose there the animals will cause destruction. As he has to go to school next morning, Sasha has devised a method whereby he can have a little sleep as well as protect the cornfields from the ravages of frisky bullocks. His strategy is to gently lie the bullock down and

231

then rest his head on the hefty animal's chest. This is no mean feat, for if he drifts off to sleep and the beast rolls over, he will be crushed. So Sasha finds a way to balance himself on the animal so that he will be woken if the bullock tries to move.

'He try to outwit me many times, but he always failed.' Dad smiles proudly at the memory of quelling the bullock.

'Just as well,' I comment, 'or you'd have been in big trouble.'

'You knaow what, I can still smell his smell and feel the warmt' of his blood. Wonderful, those nights. I would watch moon and stars cross sky. Magic.'

Sasha has developed a keen interest in astronomy as a result of these nightly vigils. He often thinks about school as well. His favourite subject is mathematics and he is becoming quite proficient at German. He also ponders the events of the day. At the moment the news is dominated by the trials of the traitors. He is shocked that so many of the past heroes of the revolution, who are high-ranking Party members, have been exposed as spies. Sasha's head rings with the rhetoric he hears at school and on the radio:

'We must not rest on our laurels. We must persevere under the banner of glorious world communism to rid ourselves of the enemy within. We who have overthrown capitalism and completed the foundations of socialism must not rest for a split second, for these successes do not cancel the ever-present danger of capitalist encirclement. While there is capitalist encirclement there will be sabotage, terrorism, diversions and spies infiltrating behind Soviet lines. We must be vigilant as this treachery is going on in all levels of society.'

Sasha has witnessed denunciations at school. One of his history teachers has been removed, accused of 'seditious perversion of facts' and of being an intellectual. Sasha is very confused about it all as he really liked his history teacher, who made the subject very interesting. His father tells Sasha to just keep his head down and concentrate on his studies. But he can't help thinking of the high-ranking Politburo member Bukharin, who has recently been denounced. Lenin called him 'the theorist of the revolution'. How could he be a traitor? Such a wonderful eloquent man; a hero, one of his heroes. But then he had also felt that way about Trotsky. Trotsky had been his idol, especially since he was a Jew and had lived in Odessa as a boy. Look what became of him! He apparently did some terrible things. Sasha doesn't dare mention that he once liked Trotsky. Anyone who does is accused of 'left deviation', arrested and sent off for rehabilitation. Sasha cannot fathom that these comrades had turned against the revolution.

Sasha's thoughts go to Kliment Voroshilov, his uncle by marriage, who has risen even higher and is now People's Commissar for War. Sasha finds comfort in the thought that Voroshilov looked after bullocks when he was a boy. And now he is a leading light in Stalin's Politburo. Sasha reveres Stalin. He is the heroic, unflinching, determined champion of the life-and-death struggle for the salvation of the grand communist experiment. Sasha believes fervently in the new social system that has been created to protect and provide dignity for the workers, and to eliminate greed and capitalist oppression.

But deep within the boy lurk feelings of doubt that he doesn't want to come to the surface. In the 1920s the Bolshevik Party preached equality for all, which included the Jews. But since then Sasha has experienced an erosion of that equality. For a while he and his family felt protected by the Bolsheviks against centuries-old Ukrainian anti-Semitism, but in recent years they have become increasingly uncomfortable. Rabbis have been persecuted and synagogues closed down. Zinoviev, Kamenev, Radek and other high-ranking Jewish Bolsheviks have been executed. His aunt who married Voroshilov has changed her Jewish name, Golda, to Ekaterina. Why? Just five years ago, the Party introduced an internal passport that identified them as Jews. This made the Wenzerul family uncomfortable, for up to that point they had not been officially classed as Jews. Even though Hana still lit candles every Friday night and prayed, Shika and the boys had pretty well forgotten they were Jews. It became largely irrelevant when they took on board the new religion of communism. Now Sasha has also been hearing rumours that Hitler is actively discriminating against German Jews.

Sasha soon falls asleep on the bullock's neck, feeling comforted by the slow swooshing of the animal's blood against his ear, and dreams of a bright happy future. The next day is very busy as always, and its cycle of household chores and lessons quell Sasha's niggling inner doubts.

*

Dad's attachment to routine and daily tasks, as well as his love of animals, has endured all his life. Shika the cat is a case in point. Dad adores his cat, which he named after his father. For breakfast the cat always has a little porridge with milk, and for supper it is chicken necks.

'I always make sure Shika gets food before me,' he says.

The feeding of chicken necks to Shika borders on obsession. When we return from the market with about fifty chicken necks, Dad shows me the ritual. The necks are divided into groups of three and each group is wrapped in a piece of plastic. And not just any plastic—the *Advertiser* newspaper is thrown daily on to the front lawn, sealed in plastic, and Dad carefully cuts this off and places it in a neat pile in the pantry. Each plastic sheet envelops a trio of chicken necks, which are placed in the freezer. When needed the frozen necks are put into a dedicated bowl. Water is boiled in the dedicated red kettle and poured over the necks. After a few minutes they are removed from the water and placed back on the plastic sheeting. This is put outside by the back door and gobbled up greedily by Shika. This procedure must be followed to the letter each day.

After dinner Dad always settles himself in front of his one-channel television set. Invariably, at about nine o'clock I find him asleep with Shika purring on his lap. I bring a cup of hot Milo and Dad smiles sleepily with toothless gums. It seems that this is the time when he can relax at last, renew his flagging energies and slow down the cancer that is eating its way into his liver.

'Bloody bastards!' My father is cursing the next-door neighbours as usual, having hacked down swathes of ivy that have grown over his side of the fence. I have tried to persuade him to sit down and put his feet up, 'to help the healing process, Dad', but 'too much work to do!' has won out.

At last I get him to sit down and distract him with a drawing. One of the things I did while in England was go to see a medium. I don't usually do this sort of thing because I am quite sceptical. But I had heard through a friend that this woman could heal cancer at a distance, so I thought I might as well try all avenues. She asked me to draw my father's house and the street in which he lived. She then spent some time re-routing the negative energy that supposedly flowed through his house, claiming she could neutralise it and get it flowing in a more harmonious way.

I show the drawing to Dad even though I think he will be even more sceptical than me. He surprises me. He is delighted that I had this done. 'I knaow that there was evil eye on this house. It was that Jew, Federman. He saw how nice my house was and came round here wantink to borrow money. "Come on, Sasha, you rich— you can spare me a few t'ousand dollars?" I say no. Why should I? The man's a thief! Now I knaow he curse this house. The bastard!'

Dad looks at the drawing with great interest. 'You knaow, I can breat'e now. When I was a boy we had to watch that nobahdy put evil eye on our cows. People see you work hard, make some money. They can't stand it! So they put evil eye on you. Not just Federman! Lots of money-grubbers! They can't stand it that I work my way up from Holden's and become somebahdy! And doan' you go tellink people about the bank or we will have more evil eyes cominck on us.'

Oh yes, the bank. My father's pride and joy. He has banked at the ANZ branch on Unley Road for over thirty years. In 1993 the ANZ, like many other banks in Australia, decided to sell off its buildings and lease them instead. The branch on Unley Road came up for auction. Up until this point Dad had bought and sold mostly residential land, houses and flats in exclusive parts of Adelaide and was landlord to many tenants. The commercial sector was a new departure. But he loved the idea of owning his bank so he duly trotted off to the auction. There were several investors interested as the property was a handsome heritage building on a prime site close to central Adelaide. The price went up to over $1 million. Then $1.2 million. My father held his nerve and kept bidding. $1.3 million. All attention was on this little foreign man with steely brown eyes who kept raising his hand. Gradually the opposing bids fell away and Dad secured the bank building for $1.35 million. This at the time was the record for a commercial property of this sort. Dad said that although he was a little worried by what he had taken on, he felt exhilarated. I am so proud of him. It took guts to sit amongst the experienced commercial property elite of Adelaide and keep raising his hand.

However, there is a downside. Every Saturday morning we drive to the bank with a boot full of cleaning equipment. And very soon we are sweeping, dusting and polishing windows. Dad wants the bank to look immaculate but doesn't trust the cleaners. By the front entrance is a cash machine, and while normal people withdraw cash, Muggins here is sweeping and mopping like a 1950s immigrant. But even though I'm embarrassed and think Dad crazy, I know I am doing this because I love him and want to please him. This bank means so much to him. He is always treated like royalty here, as I discover when I am introduced to the bank manager and shown around. Dad is the landlord, after all! Every time he drives past he gazes at the bank proudly. For him it symbolises that he has made it in his adopted new country.

It is time for me to leave. I must return to my life in England. I try to persuade Dad to come with me, but he is happy in his house with his cat. I have arranged for a nurse to see him every day, and various local council bodies know about him and will look in on him. He seems in good health and optimistic that he can live on in a reasonable way for a little longer. I am hoping that his new dietary regime, herbal remedies and naturopathic treatment are strengthening his immune system and keeping the cancer at bay. I promise to be back soon. We have an important date with the continuing saga of his past.

27 / **Storm Clouds**

'You knaow, Eva, I am so lonely in this house that I cry out to the walls,' Dad tells me in one of our many long distance telephone conversations. He touches me with his rawness and simplicity. And the sentiment is totally without strings. He is not trying to persuade me to return. He is just telling me how it is for him. And I am grateful to be able to receive it. He may feel lonely in his house, but at least he does not feel alone in the world because he has me to share his innermost feelings.

On my way back to see Dad two months later, I stop off in Sydney to catch the last few days of the Sydney 2000 Olympic Games. I will also see my children: Sophi, who is in charge of organising media coverage at all thirty-five venues, and Joe, who is helping her. As well as my relationship with my father, another important transformation is occurring for me—my attitude to Australia.

Up to now I have always felt that I emigrated to a second-rate country. To me, the Adelaide of my 1950s childhood felt like the worst dregs of British culture. I couldn't believe how awful the food was, how dull the people were. There was nothing Australian to celebrate. I never saw Aboriginal Australians or knew anything about them or their history. Instead we sang 'God Save the Queen' every morning at school and promised to obey her laws. Even British children didn't curtsy and bow to the English flag every day as we colonial kids did. We studied English history and even English geography. And then we were assaulted by the worst of American culture—Coca-Cola, Mickey Mouse and Burger King. Australia felt to me like a gloomy backwater, experiencing unpleasant whiffs of the fading British Empire and being infiltrated by the emerging United States empire.

But the Sydney Olympics change all that for me. As I left

Australia for the United Kingdom in 1971, I have missed out on the last thirty years during which Australia has emerged as a country in its own right, with a pure new voice in the world. I watch the Opening Ceremony on television and am impressed. Wow! What has emerged from Down Under? An incredible piece of magic that is shaking the world. Stupendous! Aerial shots metamorphose the arena into either beautiful Aboriginal Dreamtime paintings or primeval deserts bursting into a wonderland of Australian desert flowers. I am determined to go to the Closing Ceremony and as many other events as I can.

In Sydney I am struck by the wonderful ambience, and I experience firsthand the helpful courtesy of an army of volunteers from all over Australia, enthusiastically helping visitors or marshalling thousands to their destinations. The atmosphere is electric and hilarious at times. It is wonderful to see your average Aunty Flo's really being themselves and letting their hair down, celebrating humanity in the true spirit of the Olympics.

After the basketball on the final Friday afternoon, I am on my way home feeling peeved that I do not have a ticket to the athletics that evening. Sold out months ago. But somewhere there is a God and I am sent a miracle. The woman I have been chatting to on the bus says, 'I have a ticket for tonight's athletics you can have. I've been trying to find someone to give it to for a couple of days.'

That evening I am in heaven, sitting halfway up the eastern stadium watching a spectacular sunset, and experiencing the magic of medal ceremonies, shot-put, long jump and track events. I sob as people give the physical performances of their lives and receive their various medals with such pride and glory. I love it so much that I want to go to the last athletics event the next evening. Determination, a ticket tout, a fat wad of cash and I am lapping up the electric atmosphere again. By the night of the Closing Ceremony I am a bubbling emotional lunatic—in seventh heaven with my torch and mirrored ball, given to all audience members to help create special effects for the cameras. When Slim Dusty, a familiar hero from my childhood, leads all 110,000 people in 'Waltzing Matilda', I sing with gusto, tears pouring down my face. I feel an overwhelming sense of belonging. I cry for Olga as I know she would have loved to be here. She would have felt that she was welcome and that she had arrived home at last. Here I am in a new century. The murky depths to which we human beings plummeted in the last century are, for me, being partially redeemed in these wonderful moments in the Sydney stadium.

As I watch the spectacular fireworks, I contemplate how my mother sacrificed her life and happiness to get me out of Eastern Europe, to get me to a place to live where I could experience the freedom to say and do as I please, and to be able to celebrate my humanity. Charged with a new vigour and national pride, I head off to support my father and uncover the next instalment of his past.

Two days later we are ensconced in our favourite position, my father expertly throwing the sliced bread into the ancient gleaming toaster, me poised over my notebook. Dad seems in good health and spirits, and visits to the naturopath and acupuncturist have indicated that he is getting stronger. He has, however, been experiencing pain in his legs and I make an appointment for him to see a specialist. He religiously eats his linseed oil, turmeric and shark's fin supplement every day. Whether or not they make a contribution to battling his cancer, at least he feels he is doing something to help himself. In fact, for a man who nine months ago was given up to three months to live, he is in remarkably good shape.

He tells me he has been looking forward to telling me the rest of his story as he can see the importance of passing on what he has witnessed and experienced. 'You knaow, Eva, those poor buggers, all rottink in the ground and nobahdy to knaow what happened.'

We both roll up our sleeves. This eating breakfast and bearing witness is important business.

*

The 1930s draw to a close and Sasha continues to be successful at school. He is destined for university. Dodik is a strong young boy, daring and brave. Hana and Shika are immensely proud of them both. But again storm clouds are looming on the horizon. The Wenzuruls have survived the excesses of the Stalinist regime and the famine that claimed so many million Ukrainian lives, including that of my Uncle Trofim. How will they fare in the next dark chapter of twentieth-century history?

Anti-Semitic antipathies in Ukraine are being stirred up by what is happening in neighbouring Germany. Jews there are being stripped of their rights. Few in Odessa know the extent to which

Hitler is planning to liquidate and eliminate all Jews. Few know that he also regards Ukrainians as 'Untermenschen', and the rich black earth they live on as the future 'Lebensraum', the living space for the new Master Race. Official Soviet propaganda is keeping quiet about the danger that is creeping like an invisible black plague across Europe and hovering at the edge of the Steppes.

The Wenzeruls continue to put faith in the Soviets to protect them. The young Sasha, busily studying his textbooks, is oblivious to the dangers ahead and dreams of becoming a teacher. But it is not long before the rise of Nazi Germany begins to impact on the Wenzerul family. As Hitler's seemingly invincible war machine overruns Czechoslovakia and then Poland, the people in Odessa are made increasingly uneasy by the rumours flying about. Many Jews whom Sasha knows are even converting to Catholicism or Russian Orthodoxy, believing that this might save them in the event of German occupation. Shika and Hana are contemptuous and refuse to believe the gossip. Shika, always willing to see the good in people, says, 'I remember the Germans from the war. They weren't so bad.'

Hana summons her boys and tells them that they should be proud of their Jewish ancestry, and not to succumb to the fear that is flooding in around them. A defiant, strong woman, she commands her sons that they should never deny that they are Jews.

❧

'Oh yes, Eva,' Dad says, spreading a mixture of cottage cheese and linseed oil on his toast. 'My mahder was tough old bird. Strong and proud. You knaow who takes after her? Val. Same tough. Not afraid to say her mind. Tough all right.'

I am curious to know what she looked like, so I take the opportunity to ask Dad to describe her and his father and brother as there are no photographic records. He wracks his memory and provides these snapshots.

Hana Wenzerul: Affectionate. Light olive skin with straight, brown-black hair pulled back in a bun. A strong, pretty face with large eyes and even, white teeth. Fairly tall with a good figure. Usually wore a dark skirt and white blouse with black lace-up boots. Serious and clever, with a witty humour.

Shika Wenzerul: Strong and tall, with dark curly hair and a gold tooth in a mouth of good teeth. Usually wore a corduroy jacket with dark trousers and boots. Light-hearted with a gentle nature.

Dodik Wenzerul: Strong, tall and handsome with dark curly hair. Outgoing and happy; loved sport especially ice skating.

Hitler declares war on the Soviet Union on June 22, 1941. The invasion, code-named Operation Barbarossa by the Wehrmacht, takes the Soviets by surprise. Only a few bombs fall on Odessa, and its excellent defences see the invaders off quick smart. But forces in the rest of western Ukraine, ill-prepared and badly organised, fall like skittles in the wake of the massive invasion by the Germans and their Romanian allies.

Many Ukrainians, having been oppressed, starved and purged by Stalin, embrace the Germans as liberators. Some even greet them with flowers. The Germans further exploit the anti-Soviet feelings of ordinary Ukrainians by lumping Ukrainian Jews together with the Bolshevik regime and lauding themselves as the saviours of the world from what they call Jewish-Bolshevism. This feeds into old antipathies that many Ukrainians hold for the very large Jewish population that has settled in Ukraine over several hundred years. While most Ukrainians are peasants and uneducated, the Jewish population lives in the towns and is highly educated.

Refugees from the occupied areas arrive in Odessa. A Bessarabian Jew tells terrible stories of Jews being slaughtered and buried naked in ditches and describes the agony of dying children and old people. No one believes him and he is pronounced demented. People avoid looking into his eyes, afraid of glimpsing a future too dreadful to envisage.

Thousands of skilled workers, scientists and Party bureaucrats, including some of the more wealthy and better connected members of Sasha's family, hastily evacuate to the east.

'They had money. That's what saved them. But we had none,' Dad says ruefully, putting on a kettle for more tea. To this day Dad is stockpiling his money in the event of another catastrophe. When I try to reassure him, 'Oh, you'll be safe in Australia, Dad,' he says, 'Look at Philippines! You never knaow. You never can tell!' There

241

has been a recent breakdown of law and order in this region and Dad is afraid that somehow this will lead to upheaval in Australia. Here is another reason why he won't buy himself an expensive hearing aid. He fervently believes that having money can get his family out of danger, just as it did for his relatives in 1941. 'Never again will that happen to me,' he mutters.

※

A couple of weeks after the invasion, having got over his disbelief that the Germans would invade, Stalin gives an emotive speech on the radio urging all to defend the motherland. Thousands of men volunteer to fight, including Hana's adored younger brother Jacob, who leaves behind his beautiful wife Riva and her two young sons. Hana is unhappy that Jacob is gone but relieved that Sasha is just too young. Dodik at fifteen is itching to go and fight the Nazis but gets a cuff around the ears for being so foolhardy.

'Sumashechni! Stupid fool!' admonishes Hana. 'Go do something useful and find some tomatoes so we have something to eat.'

Everyone in Odessa is busy hoarding food as the Nazi march eastwards is virtually cutting off the southern port city from the rest of Ukraine and food supplies. Dodik and Sasha, armed with sacks, head north out of the city looking for tomatoes. For a while they walk with a group of university students who are being evacuated to the nearest big town, Nikolaev. Sasha chats with them about the courses they have been doing. He has just finished his final year of high school and his excellent grades ensure him a place at university in the autumn. He is gentle by nature and hopes to work as a maths teacher. Dodik, on the other hand, is tougher and part of a teenage gang which has been raiding tea and sugar supplies from local warehouses at night. Hana has admonished him severely but is secretly pleased to see her cellar becoming well stocked.

The boys leave the group of students and branch out into the fields to hunt for tomatoes. It is hot, and the azure sky seems to extend forever upwards. They horse about, enjoying the fresh breeze on their young brown bodies. Egged on by the impulsive Dodik, they walk further and further, ignoring Hana's entreaties not to go too far. While stuffing their bags and faces with tomatoes, a strange whining noise impinges on their carefree foraging. Looking up, they see several planes that seem to be coming straight towards them. The brothers dive for cover, clinging to each other in terror. The gull-winged aircraft screech overhead, strafing the countryside with bullets.

'Stukas!' hisses Sasha. He has heard of these new German planes that swoop down on their targets with machine-gun fire. They provide backup to the divisions of Panzer tanks that are obliterating the poorly equipped Soviet army as they roll towards Kiev and Moscow.

It is nightfall before the two brothers manage to return home, shaken to the core by their experience, tomatoes long forgotten. Hana is hysterical, believing the boys had been killed. She batters them with her fists and screams reproaches at them for being so late. Sasha and Dodik wonder at their usually calm and demure mother. It is Shika who must tell them that a band of university students walking to Nikolaev were all mown down by the Stuka bullets. 'But we spoke to them!' gasps Sasha, remembering their fresh young faces.

Hana is inconsolable for a long time. What she can't bring herself to also tell her boys is that a next-door neighbour has heard that the Nazis have sent in special mobile extermination squads, the SS-Einsatzgruppen, whose specific task is to kill Jews. Rumours have it that thousands of Jews have been shot already by these squads. Not only that, but some Ukrainians are aiding them in their deadly task.

The Stuka attack that narrowly missed Sasha and Dodik is followed up daily by more and more raids. The Romanian Fourth Army is hovering just to the north of the city. The Soviet army dithers. Should they abandon Odessa and bail out by sea to Sevastopol? Or should they stay and defend this strategically important port? More and more people flee the city. Those who can, leave on the increasingly beleaguered boats and trains. The Germans have captured railway junctions to the north and Hana, when selling food to passing trains, notices that many are not getting past Peresyp station. Hana and Shika consider fleeing, but they could only afford to do so in a horse and cart and know that would bring them into the arms of the waiting Romanians and, worse still, the Einsatzgruppen.

The Soviet army decides to stay and defend the port, and on August 22 Odessa is declared to be in a state of siege. The Party committee sounds the alarm: 'The enemy is at the gates! Every house must become a fortress! Every means necessary must be used against the enemy!'

An order is issued for mobilisation of all males aged seventeen to fifty to join the Soviet army. Hana refuses to let Sasha go, and because he looks young for his age (smaller than his strapping younger brother), he gets away with it. There have been Soviet Army deserters trickling back from the Front, and their stories are horrendous. Ill-equipped youths are easily slaughtered by well-trained Wehrmacht soldiers, and any who hesitate are shot by the NKVD for being defeatists and cowards. Hundreds of thousands of soldiers have been taken captive. Riva has not heard anything about Jacob and weeps silently into her boys' hair as they sleep.

A major task for the Odessans is to construct fortifications around the besieged city. Shika joins a construction brigade to erect barricades. Hana and fellow passengers are hauled off a street car to lug sandbags. A ration card system is introduced with the daily allowance of 400 grams of bread per person. Meats, fats and sugar are also rationed, and Dodik is decidedly smug about the sugar he pilfers. Yet while there are many shortages, at least there is no famine. In fact, in some ways the Wenzeruls are better off than they were during the 1930s.

The slogan continually blasting from the radio and newspapers, 'Odessa was and will remain Soviet', is a comfort to the family. Hana grabs on to it like a blanket around their fragile existence, and firmly dismisses the rumour that Einsatzgruppen squads have now murdered fifty thousand Jews. She also ignores leaflets dropped by German planes exhorting the Odessans to help Nazis get rid of the Jewish-Bolsheviks, deliberate propaganda to incite anti-Semitism among ordinary Ukrainians. Meanwhile, the NKVD continues its favourite occupation of 'spy hunting'. It is rumoured that enemy agents have infiltrated the city and ordinary citizens are told to be on the hunt for them. This often results in ridiculous arrests—for example, a couple of old beggars and a man who just happened to be wearing a Bavarian hat.

Water has always been a big problem in Odessa as the reservoir is fifteen miles from the city and has often run out in summer. A week into the siege, the Romanian army seizes the supply. The daily quota of water becomes a meagre quarter pail a day per person.

Sasha and Dodik join a systematic drive to dig artesian wells. In no time at all some fifty wells are dug. The water ration climbs up to one pail of water per person. A feeling of comradeship and unity inspires the Odessans to use their wits and strength to keep the enemy at bay. In September Odessa is awarded Supreme Soviet accolades for great bravery. Leaflets distributed in the city further boost morale: 'The sacred task of every citizen is to give all his strength and life for the motherland and our native city. Odessa was, is and will be the impregnable fortress of Bolshevism on the Black Sea.'

The Wenzeruls lap up this Soviet propaganda and cling to hope, despite the continuous bombing raids, military ineptitude and mass surrenders in other parts of Ukraine. There are even rumours that the British have landed in the Balkans and are heading towards Odessa to join the defenders. The Wenzeruls fear the inevitable when they hear that Kiev has fallen and that the Germans are threatening the Crimea. To the north of Odessa, a big battle rages between the Soviets and the Romanians in the first week of October. To the south the Germans occupy northern Crimea, and Olga Nesterenko's days as a schoolgirl are abruptly terminated.

Sasha and Shika become suspicious when they see nightly transports of troops, goods and artillery leaving the harbour. Unbeknown to them and to the enemy, a high-level decision has been made to abandon Odessa by the middle of October and send reinforcements to defend Sevastopol (where Olga's father has been sent). Shika is distressed to see horses shot and piled on top of equipment already dumped in the harbour to avoid their being used by the enemy. A dam near Peresyp is blown up and the streets are flooded. On the night of October 15, the last headline of the daily paper is ODESSA WAS AND WILL BE SOVIET. What irony. Next morning at dawn the last of the Soviet troops leave by boat.

An eerie quiet envelops the city. The Wenzeruls look at the fortifications that they have worked so hard to build, now useless, and watch with dread as the Romanians march through easily and take over the city. The inevitable has happened. After seventy-three days of siege, Odessa has fallen and become occupied territory.

'And you knaow, Eva,' says Dad, 'the silly ting is the Romanians were exhausted and on point of givink up! Aaeh!' He shakes his head at the vagaries of this world.

❦

Dad and I take a break from the events of 1941 and attend to more mundane things, like sorting out problems with his tenants. One is complaining about her gas boiler. I go with Dad's plumber friend, Roy, to check it out. The boiler is on its last legs.

Dad wants it to be fixed, but Roy says it is old and useless and belongs to the Dark Ages. And yes, I guess right, it was a bargain at an auction. Dad insists that it must be replaced with another auction acquisition he has stored in his attic, but I am not amused any more. 'Dad, you're not in a state of siege! These boilers are old and decrepit and I am ashamed of them and refuse to be part of putting in another. Buy a new one, for God's sake!'

I am surprised when my father easily capitulates. At the local gas showroom I am amazed when he orders a brand new boiler for $1000 without blinking an eye. While we are sitting in the showroom with sunlight streaming in, Dad suddenly looks closely at my illuminated face and says with some surprise, 'You got moustache! You gettink old!'

I will remember them always and everywhere,
I will never forget them no matter what comes,
Even if they gag my exhausted mouth
Through which a hundred million scream.
Anna Akhamatova

The tired and demoralised Romanians take over a tired and demoralised populace. While the Odessans don't like the Romanians,
they don't fear them as much as they do the few Germans who
come with them. A 'new order' is set up immediately, to be dis-
obeyed on pain of death. Odessans must turn in weapons and
observe a curfew. They are forbidden to gather in public.

The task of the new authority is complicated by lawlessness on
both sides. Looting is rife for the first few days and Hana has to
keep an eye on Dodik, who keeps slipping out and coming back
with all sorts of booty. After a few days the pillaging subsides and a
kind of calm takes over the city.

Hana goes to the market to buy fish. 'What does all this mean?'
she asks the vendors. 'What will happen to us?' She had been
alarmed the day before when a couple of Romanian soldiers
knocked on her door, saying they were looking for weapons. One
spied a jar of sugar on the table and put it in his pocket before
scuttling off. The vendors tell Hana that this has happened to a lot
of people. It seems the Romanians can easily be bribed or
deflected from their duties. Hana goes home feeling slightly easier,
hoping against hope that the Romanians will not discriminate
against the Jews.

But her relief is short-lived. On October 19 the Romanians
start to take action against the Jews. They must report to central

command and wear yellow stars. They are then ordered to clear rubble and repair roads.

'It's beginning,' despairs Hana. 'I knew it.' She is slightly mollified when Shika is spared from rubble clearing and assigned to look after the horses of Romanian officers, billeted in the centre of town. Sasha and Dodik are to help him. There are few people left who know how to care for horses.

On the fateful day of October 22, Shika and the boys are returning home from work when they hear a massive explosion. The former headquarters of the NKVD, where the new regime is now set up, has been blown up. General Glogojeano, the Romanian military commander, and scores of Romanian and German officers and soldiers have been killed. Dodik and Sasha whoop inwardly with delight. Dodik knows of partisans hiding in the catacombs under Odessa and is convinced they are behind it, hoping that a successful counteroffensive is beginning.

But their euphoria is cut short. Retaliation is immediate and cruel. A black cloud of evil descends upon Odessa. Orders are issued from Antonescu, the Romanian dictator, to execute 'Bolshevik Jews' at varying ratios, two hundred for every officer and one hundred for every soldier killed. One member from each Jewish family is to be taken hostage. The very next day five thousand people, most of them Jews, are either shot or hanged by the roadsides and in public squares. The facades of the beautiful buildings are blighted by row upon row of hanging corpses. Next morning thousands more, again mostly Jews, are rounded up and herded into a square near the port. They are shot, doused with gasoline and burnt alive.

Through all this the Wenzeruls remain miraculously alive. Dad is convinced it is because their knowledge about horses is too valuable. However, Shika is given another grim job—to bury the dead.

*

I find hearing about this catastrophic descent into hell horrendous. I sit at the kitchen table gulping down air because I can't breathe. I have read *The White Hotel*, a vivid and gruelling description of the murder in September 1941 of thousands of Jews by the Einsatzgruppen at Babi Yar, a ravine in Kiev, and it shocked me profoundly. But to hear that the same thing happened in

Odessa, under the very eyes of my own dear father, is too ghastly to contemplate.

But it gets worse.

❧

That afternoon thousands more people, mostly Jews, are rounded up and crammed into the town jail. The Wenzeruls quake in their house as large processions of downcast people, guarded by soldiers, shuffle past under the lifeless eyes of the cadavers still hanging and creaking eerily from their makeshift gibbets. Next day several thousand of the incarcerated are marched to nearby Dalnik. As the first few hundred arrive they are bound together and thrown into anti-tank ditches and shot dead. This macabre procedure is repeated throughout the day.

When this method of killing proves too slow, the rest of the prisoners are pressed into four large warehouses which have holes in the walls. Machine-gun nozzles are put into the holes and fired. Three of the warehouses, filled mostly with women and children, are doused with gasoline and set on fire. One is dynamited. As the flames engulf the structures, many of the victims who have managed to avoid the gunfire try to scramble out through windows and holes in the roof. The soldiers on the outside are ordered to kill them with hand grenades and machine-guns. The ghastly spectacle carries on all afternoon and well into the night. Still the relentless slaughter continues. Heartrending cries of people being burnt alive ring through the air: 'Save us! Don't kill us! Don't burn us!' Women, desperate not to be incinerated alive, stand at the windows and point at their hearts, imploring the soldiers to shoot. Many are left naked as they rip off their burning clothes. Other women are so frantic that they throw their children out of the windows. A friend of the Wenzeruls who witnesses this hell on earth sees one of these children, a boy of about five, wandering aimlessly among the corpses, the soldiers unable to bring themselves to shoot. Local residents are forced to dig huge pits into which the soldiers dump the charred bodies.

The reprisals for the headquarters' explosion mount to over twenty-five thousand dead. This brutal, heart-chilling reality puts paid to any harboured hope that the Romanians are more humane than their German allies. The city and its inhabitants are stunned by the ferocious barbarity and the indiscriminate retaliation against innocent civilians. Hana and other surviving women in her street are so appalled by seeing their own neighbours hanging from gallows in Prokhorovsy Square that they are unable to walk through it without trembling violently.

*

I look at my father's rigid jaw and recall my mother screaming at him, 'Sasha I can't stand your face. You look like you're going to be hanged tomorrow.' If only she knew how close to the truth that was.

*

A grey gloomy sickness hangs over the city which even the watery October sun cannot penetrate. Soviet life had accustomed the population to violence and terror, but a secret murder in a NKVD jail had been accepted far more readily than this brazen display of public hanging, shooting and burning. When Shika was in jail ten years earlier, Sasha had felt there was some tortuous rationale for Soviet terror; but for that of these new barbaric masters there is none at all.

The terror continues. Before the end of October another five thousand are arrested. My father's knowledge of German and Shika's skill with horses save the family many times as others are rounded up and marched off. The Wenzeruls cling together and don't know whom to trust. Old anti-Semitic hatreds flare up and many Ukrainians who were once my father's friends turn hostile. To make matters worse, rewards are offered for turning in hiding Jews. The penalty for anyone who does not report a Jew or who helps a Jew in any way is death.

*

I can't bear any more, so I take Dad for a drive to the sea. We sit and have fish and chips at Grange Beach, something we did a lot when I was a girl.

As we watch the sun sink over the water, Dad says, 'Oh, this reminds me of Cherno More (the Black Sea). I love coming here. Eva, I want my ashes to be scattered at sea.'

'Of course,' I say. 'Would you like it to be the Black Sea at Odessa?'

'Yes,' he says quietly.

*

During the first few weeks of occupation, the Germans have had a low profile in Odessa, but that is about to change. Sasha is out in the fields with Shika one afternoon when they see what looks like a squad of German soldiers marching in the distance. A group of people run towards Sasha and Shika, hissing, 'The SS! Einsatzgruppen! Quick, quick! Where can we hide? They are rounding up Jews and shooting them.'

Shika leads the people over a hill to a nearby silo. This, like many silos dotted around Odessa, stores grain. Sasha helps a woman and her baby to scramble inside. All manage to clamber in before the storm-troopers march up over the brow of the hill.

They crouch in trepidation as they hear the Nazis drawing murderously closer, searching the fields around. The baby starts to whimper. Sasha holds his breath, thinking that at any moment they will be discovered. By some miracle the mother manages to calm the child and the killing squad marches by.

*

I, like probably everyone in that silo, take a huge breath of relief. Dad is trembling quite violently now. 'I remember it like it was yesterday. I couldn't believe that the birds could still be flyink overhead while we humans were beink hunted like animals.'

I put my hand on his. 'I can't even imagine what that must have been like, Dad. I live such a privileged life. I'm so sorry that that happened to you. It is so terrible! Do you want to stop?'

'No,' he says hoarsely. 'There's something else I must tell you.'

*

The life of the Wenzerul family hangs by a single thread. Hana and Shika continue to hold their heads high and refuse to be cowed by the terror that is stalking them, even though all they believe to be good and true has long evaporated from the face of the earth. Evil has cloaked the land and there is no escape. Room for manoeuvre has fizzled out. The family watch helplessly as most Jews they know are shot or disappear. Those who remain, like Shika, are forced to perform the ghastly duty of burying their friends who have been murdered by the Einsatzgruppen.

Shika comes home one evening as white as death, but he won't talk about what he has seen. Hana implores him to spill it out. With great difficulty he chokes out that he has found the bodies of her sister-in-law Riva and her two sons. Sasha is devastated as Riva was his favourite aunt and he adored her little boys. Shika found the three of them clinging to each other. He dug a grave wide enough to put them in as they were, covering them with dirt and tears.

I am crying into my cold tea. I feel anguish for Riva and her children. I feel anguish for Shika and Hana. I feel anguish for the countless others who met the same fate. I also feel honoured to receive the story of this nightmare from my father's lips. To help him bear witness.

The kitchen feels as quiet as a church. My father's jaw is set hard. I always remember that about him on the many occasions when my mother was screaming or creating havoc. His jaw would visibly clench as if he was using every ounce of strength to shut down his reactions. He is doing that now and I am in awe of his ability to survive.

29 / **Tattoos**

There is no Ukraine. We must remember we are the Master Race.
Erich Koch, Nazi Commander, 1941

The blue outline of the flying bird stands out luridly on the pale, shrivelled flesh. The tattoo on my father's leg looks incongruous as he undresses in the specialist's office where the pain in his legs is being investigated. There are other tattoos on his body, another further down his leg and two on his forearms. I've always liked them as they are at odds with his austere personality and suggest a wild youth. The doctor makes a joke about the tattoos and Dad seems embarrassed and changes the subject.

The prognosis on one of his legs is not good. Apparently some of the blood vessels have seized up and therefore are not pumping the blood around properly. When I ask what can be done, the response is nothing short of another operation. I am getting a bit fed up with all the doctors my father sees. They seem happy to order batteries of expensive tests which they charge to his private health insurance, and are always wanting to operate on this frail old man.

'Surely massage and hot baths will help,' I offer.

The doctor is sceptical. 'Perhaps.'

Appalled, I take my father out. I feel like screaming at the doctor, 'If you knew what this man has been through in his life, you would treat him better. This is a person, not a slab of meat for you to cut open and poke about in. He needs soft, loving care!'

I'm not the only one annoyed at the doctor. 'Bastard,' says my father when we come out. 'How dare he make jokes about my tattoos! What does he knaow about anyting? He knaows nuttin'. These tattoos saved my life.'

253

That afternoon I massage my father's leg and he continues his story.

*

The new horror of the death of Riva and her children sinks deep into the increasingly isolated and endangered Wenzerul family. Shika and Hana have often racked their brains on how to escape from Odessa, but they have no money or transport. Stalin's 'scorched earth' policy decrees that the Soviet army destroy everything as they retreat from the Nazis: homes, livestock, all forms of transport and bridges.

Ukraine lies devastated and bleeding. Winter is drawing in and the biting cold adds even more misery. Hitler's armies have advanced terrifyingly quickly and are now occupying vast swathes of the Soviet Union. Russia is on her knees, and the Wenzerul family is well and truly stuck.

*

'It was like God was spittink on us,' mutters Dad as I rub more oil into his leg.

*

In November 1941 all male Jews from eighteen to fifty are ordered to the city jail. Hana breathes a sigh of relief. Sasha is seventeen, Dodik fifteen and Shika fifty-one. A close call.

A few days later comes an order to establish ghettos and concentration camps in Transnistria. This is the Nazi name given to the area between the Rivers Dniester and the Bug and includes Odessa in the south. Transnistria has been granted to the Romanian governor, Alexianu, to administer for the Reich. The Jews in each community are forbidden to leave without permission, on pain of being shot.

These developments underscore a new and sinister change in policy towards the Jews. The Reich is cooking up more efficient ways to annihilate the remaining Jewish population. As witnessed in Odessa and Dalnik the previous month, it took a long time for thousands of Jews to be hanged, shot and burnt. The chilling words 'the final solution' are being uttered. New ways to kill people ruthlessly and efficiently are being devised. Shika has noticed mysterious vans appearing on the roads outside Odessa that coincide with the disappearance of more Jews, without shots being fired. These gas vans are forerunners of the gas ovens that are being built all over Eastern Europe.

One small mercy is that the Wenzeruls, respected for their knowledge of horses, are allowed to stay in their house. Other Jews are sent to ghettos and concentration camps north of the city. Several cannot bear the horror any more and either go insane or commit suicide.

Hana and Shika summon the boys for a serious talk. Hana starts off by saying that she is proud they are Jewish but has decided that the boys must from now on deny they are Jews. With great sadness she absolves them of her former entreaty that they should always uphold their heritage. If it ever becomes a matter of life or death, she says, the boys have her full permission to hide the fact that they are Jews.

*

I hold my father's leg tenderly as he shakes his head, sadly remembering his mother's calm determination even though this pronouncement cost her a lot.

*

Hana and Shika have hatched a plan where Sasha and Dodik must change their identities and papers and leave Odessa. The boys refuse point-blank to even consider such an idea, insisting they will stay and defend their parents to the last. Hana, her face wet with tears, begs them, implores them to do as she asks. Shika holds his wife's shaking shoulders.

*

Dad remembers their faces with pride and love. 'Such good people, Eva. Whatever you write, please tell the world what good people they were.'

*

Shika backs up his wife by saying it is now even more dangerous to be a Jew in Odessa. He has heard rumours that the capital of Transnistria is to be transferred to Odessa in December and that

255

the orders of the Reich are that Odessa must be Judenrein (free of Jews) by the new year. Time is running out for any remaining Jews. Even Sasha's German and Shika's knowledge of horses will not be able to save them now.

'Our beloved sons. We are old. It does not matter what happens to us. But it would break our hearts if anything happened to you, our dear boys. You must escape. You must flee. You must start a new life somewhere else. You must do this for us. It will be your greatest gift to us.'

Shika has arranged with some friends to prepare false documents for his sons. These friends are Karaims—Tatars by race who follow the Jewish religion, but who, by some strange quirk of fate, are not discriminated against and can move about freely. Wintry cold is setting in as Sasha and Dodik say goodbye to their parents for the last time. Hana has prepared a pack of food for each of them. Shika gives Sasha his old coat and gold watch. The parents hold their sons close for several minutes.

'May God watch over you wherever you go, our precious ones. And don't worry about us. You being free is all we want. You achieve that and our job on this earth is done.'

With tears streaming down his face and armed with a new identity, Sasha, his arm protectively around his brother, walks away from his parents into the frosty unknown.

Clutching their small hemp bags containing a few belongings and the lovingly cooked piroshki, the two boys head for Kishinev in the north-west toward Romania, planning to meet up with one of Shika's Karaim friends, Rastov. But that is at least several days walk away. Sasha knows a Ukrainian couple on the outskirts of town, so they head there, hoping they will put them up. On the way they run into some of Dodik's partisan buddies, who are heading east. Dodik wants to join them for a while and tells Sasha that he will meet him at Kishinev later on. Sasha is reluctant to let his younger brother go but is quite confident that Dodik can take care of himself.

Sasha strikes out alone for the Ukrainian farmhouse. He arrives there mid-morning next day and sees Viktor, the owner, coming out of his gate. Instinctively he hides, then creeps around the side to where Viktor's wife, Tanya, is in the kitchen.

Her face goes deathly pale when she sees Sasha. 'You can't stay here,' she hisses. 'Viktor will turn you in to the authorities.'

Sasha, exhausted after picking his way through fields full of frozen stubble, is disheartened by this welcome. Tanya was once such a good friend to their family. She sees the disappointment in his eyes and relents.

'Come in, Sasha, and have some tea, but you must leave before Viktor returns. You can sleep in the barn.' Her voice is shaking in great fear. If she is caught hiding a Jew she will be arrested and executed. Sasha is grateful to be able to sleep for a few hours, and slips away before Victor's return.

*

'Bastards!' spits Dad. 'Ukrainian filt'! That Victor, he would have turned me in for a bottle of brandy. That's what ahder Ukrainian scum got paid for a Jew.'

'But Dad, what about the Romanians? They were far worse. They killed twenty-five thousand Jews in retaliation for the headquarters explosion. Why do you hate the Ukrainians so much and not them?'

'You knaow nuttin'! The Romanians only did it to show off to the Germans how tough they were. It was not personal. But Tanya and Viktor, after everyting my parents did for them—they would let me die before raisink a finger. She would have turned me away if I hadn't begged. Scum!'

He is almost purple with indignation. I am struck again by how deep my father's prejudice is against Ukrainians.

*

Sasha now strikes north, and it is like walking into a minefield. There are Nazi and Romanian checkpoints everywhere and the dreaded Einsatzgruppen are still performing their deadly duties. He sleeps that night in a silo sheltered from the freezing wind that is blowing in over the Steppes. His feet ache from having to negotiate stubble, and he sinks his teeth gratefully into one of his mother's piroshkis and the last salted cucumber.

Next day, tired of stumbling over the frozen fields, Sasha decides to risk walking along a minor road. He rounds a bend and his heart jumps into his throat as he sees a checkpoint ahead. It is too late to turn back. Dread suffuses him as he recognises the Nazi helmets of the soldiers. The Nazis order him into a small room and demand to see his papers. Hoping the soldiers don't notice his trembling legs, he shows his documents and assumes the identity of a Volodya Kamirov, a Ukrainian student from Odessa on his way to relatives in Kishinev. As calmly as he can he speaks to them in German, which seems to impress his interrogators. However, they are still suspicious. They are alert to the fact that many Jews are travelling on false papers.

'Are you a Jew?' they ask point-blank. Sasha, quaking in his boots, remembers his mother's directive that he survive at all costs.

'No, of course not,' he says as casually as possible, trying not to let his emotions show on his face.

The Nazis turn to the Ukrainian secretary who sits at her desk lazily filing her nails. 'What do you think, Masha?' one asks. 'Is this boy a Jew or not?'

Sasha can feel specks of sweat burst up like guilty pustules on his clammy brow and he is feeling decidedly hot all over. He pulls up his sleeves.

Masha looks up in a bored fashion. Like many a spectator in gladiatorial Rome, she relishes the feeling of power that she has over life or death. She casts a glance at Sasha and notices the tattoos on his forearms. These nondescript tattoos, one a pair of intertwined hearts and the other the word 'mother' in Cyrillic script, are about to save his life.

'Oh, no way is he a Jew! Any Jew would be far too lily-livered to endure the pain of a tattoo,' she drawls contemptuously.

My father walks out of the checkpoint, his knees still trembling. Ironically her anti-Semitism has got him through.

I stroke the bird on my father's thigh as I finish the massage. I persuade him to have a hot bath. He rarely has a bath as he feels it uses up too much hot water, and does so only when he can use the bath water to wash the floor. But this time he protests only lightly when I start to run the bath and throw in lashings of Radox so he can have a good soak.

'By the way, Dad, when did you get those tattoos?' I'd always imagined that he had had them done in his teens in a flush of youthful exuberance. He thinks for a long time, and just as I am beginning to wonder if he's lost in some time warp, he answers at last.

'I was nine.'

'Nine!' I exclaim, shocked. 'What, all of them?'

'No, only these two.' He points at his forearms.

'When did you get the others?'

Again he thinks for a long time. Surely now he will tell me he was in his teens. My curiosity is about to reach bursting point, when he finally pronounces, 'Ten.'

I am appalled. 'Ten! Why the hell did you have tattoos at such a young age?'

'There were street gangs in Odessa where I lived and all of us had to have t'ese tattoos.'

'What, as part of an initiation rite or something?'

'Yeah, that's it, initiation.'

I am quite horrified. 'How was it done?'

'Oh, with a burnink needle in the street.' Offhand.

'God, that must have been agony.'

'Yeah, it hurt a lot, but we had to prove we were tough.'

I leave my father to his bath. I shake my head at how this man and what has happened to him never cease to amaze me.

I ruminate on how his toughness has served him well, especially the time when a gang of bodgies started letting off firecrackers under his new FJ Holden outside his delicatessen. Furious, Dad stormed out of the shop in his white apron and demanded they stop at once. The bodgies, looking menacing with their slicked-back hair, leather jackets and studded belts, just jeered and swore at him, mimicking his funny accent as they prepared to light the next cracker. Not flinching for a second, Dad marched right up to the ringleader and punched him to the ground. Just like that. The gang stared, stupefied, their leather jackets suddenly looking rather limp. The leader staggered to his feet clutching his swollen eye in disbelief, got on his motorbike and roared away. His mates quickly followed suit. From that day on, Dad got nothing but respect (and excellent custom) from all the bodgies in the north-west suburbs of Adelaide.

30 / **On the Run**

'She has those shifty Ukrainian eyes. I doan' trust her.'

I heave an exasperated sigh. I had rather thought that Anna Lulka's visit had been a success. I had asked her to tea in an attempt to heal Dad's prejudice against Ukrainians. Anna is an active contributor to the Ukrainian Adelaide radio station. I feel a strong link with her as her past is similar to mine. She came to Australia as a three-year-old, lived in the same area and went to the same school. The visit seemed to go well and Dad and she conversed about a number of topics, including her research into the artificial famine foisted on Ukrainians by Stalin. But now she has left, Dad is up to his old tricks again, indulging in one of his pet themes: hating Ukrainians.

I have on several occasions tried to persuade Dad to come to Odessa with me to see for himself that prejudice against Jews in current Ukraine is a thing of the past. I pass on to him that Lena and her family would be very happy to look after us and drive us around. 'Her boss Meszebovsky's a Jew, you know—a great friend of the family.'

But no. 'You doan' knaow, Eva. Mark my words. Ukrainians will always hate the Jews.'

I think to myself, *Then why the hell did you marry Mum if you hated Ukrainians so much!*

After his close shave at the Nazi checkpoint, Sasha continues his trek north. Devastated countryside. Villages in ruins. Everything burnt by the retreating Soviet army or pillaged by the invaders. The road is littered with abandoned Soviet trucks and military hardware. Behind a broken picket fence, Sasha relishes the last taste of home as he eats the remainder of the piroshki. He now has to find food, which in such a devastated landscape is not easy. Winter is advancing rapidly and he pulls his father's overcoat around his shivering shoulders.

*

'Ah, what it was to be a fugitive. Not knaowin' where to sleep at night. Not knaowin' where your next meal is comink from. And the dreadful loneliness. Missink the family.' I remembered my father's favourite television program in the 1960s: *The Fugitive*.

'Is this when you met the gypsy who told you your future?'

'Yes, and she was right. I have lived a long hard life!'

*

After Sasha leaves the gypsy camp, nourished and fortified in spirit, he meets other travellers who share their meagre food supplies with him. They say that the Soviets are still holding out against the Germans to the west of Moscow. The Russian winter is now beginning to wreak its revenge against the invader. The German transport systems, supposedly well-equipped for all terrains, have been severely tested by the rasputitsa, the season of rain and mud, which has done its best to swallow and bog motorcycles, cars and lorries. Much-needed rations have only slowly reached German soldiers at the front and they are ill-equipped for the snow and ice that follows the rasputitsa. Sasha hopes that the Russian winter will vanquish the Germans as it did the French in the previous century.

It takes several days to walk the hundred kilometres to Kishinev. As Sasha draws closer he meets convoys of carts guarded by Romanian soldiers, going east. They are full of people clutching bundles. His stomach sinks to the floor when he sees the yellow stars on their armbands. He stops by the side of the road near a group of Ukrainian peasants, hoping to glean some information. 'Bloody Jidani,' says one who looks like a tramp, eyeing the bundles greedily. 'Those bundles are full o' gold. Smugglin' them out of the Chisinau ghetto, they are.'

'Wait till night fall,' says another. 'When they stop to rest, we can grab 'em. Miroslav reckons he got a couple o' watches and a ring the other night.'

Sasha nervously feels his father's watch deep in his pocket and tries to ignore the peasants' blatant anti-Semitism. He hurries on. 'Jidani' is a pejorative word for Jew, 'Chisinau' is the Romanian name for Kishinev and the word 'ghetto' freezes his blood. He sees many such convoys of wagons and tries not to catch the eye of the occupants or to wonder if they will be robbed on the way. He won't even dare to imagine where they are being taken.

Kishinev, the capital of Bessarabia, is largely in ruins. The Soviets burned the city systematically before its occupation by the Germans. Street signs are missing or hanging in tatters, so Sasha has great difficulty tracking down his Karaim contact. Romanian and occasionally German soldiers are everywhere, so he tries to make himself as inconspicuous as possible. By a series of lucky coincidences he finds Rastov, who takes him to a sympathetic Bessarabian household in the centre of town. He is so grateful to have a proper bed again with a heavenly duck-down duvet. He stays here for a few weeks waiting for Dodik.

Kishinev has been a largely Jewish metropolis for almost a century and was flooded by ten thousand more Jews in 1940 when the fascist Antonescu government came to power in neighbouring Romania. At that time Stalin occupied Bessarabia as part of his denationalisation drive. Many of the inhabitants, regarded by the Soviets as 'potential enemies of the people', were arrested and forcibly moved east in a major operation during the night of June 13, 1941, only two weeks before the German invasion. The Nazis herded the remaining Jews into the ghetto. This, in the old part of the city surrounded by a tall wall with several guarded gates, is not far from Sasha's lodgings.

Romanian rule in Kishinev is even more disorganised than in Odessa. Smuggling, bribery and shady dealings are the order of the day. In order to survive, Sasha has to learn about cheating, lying and deceit. Jews in the ghetto engage in illegal trade, and bribe the Romanian guards to ensure that they can get enough to eat and survive. Rastov is part of a chain of black market traders who buy goods from the Jews and sell them on. Almost all work under a cloak of anonymity or false identity.

Sasha isn't the only one who is carrying false papers. There is a whole underground traffic in false documents. Jews avoid deportation from the ghetto by buying false identity papers which allow them to stay put. There are too many horror stories of what happens to people when they are deported. In such a chaotic atmosphere, the scope for abuse is great.

🍂

'So, Eva, I learnt to become a wheeler-dealer. I sold my father's watch for 2000 lei and bought three watches and other jewellery and then sold them. So I could live!'

Now I know why Dad is so good at auctions. He has had plenty of practice.

He slams his hand on the table and looks at me with burning eyes. 'But on my mahder's soul, I swear I never took advantage of those poor bastards in the ghetto.'

🍂

Sasha gets to know a few Romanians who are highly critical of the Romanian dictator and can't stomach the Germans. 'Bastard Antonescu! He sold us down the river. Sold us to the Nazis,' proclaims Dinu, who becomes a close buddy.

One night in early December, the Romanians drag the shy Sasha out drinking. 'We have something to celebrate, but we must be quiet about it. We've heard on the radio that the Japanese have bombed Pearl Harbour and now the Americans have joined the war.' Sasha feels inward joy at this news and joins in the clinking of glasses and mumbles good luck with the rest: 'Noroc! Noroc!' He has heard great things about the Americans and feels that with them on side, the war may soon be over and he can return to his family and resume his normal life.

Dinu is part of a group who are trying to get back to the Romanian town of Iasi just on the other side of the border. He invites Sasha to go with them. Dinu knows about Sasha's real identity. 'You can easily get lost in Iasi and you will be a lot safer there than here. There have been a few too many Germans coming here to Kishinev. It's time we got out. We want to get to Iasi by Christmas.'

Sasha is torn about whether to wait for Dodik, but having seen the chaos on the roads, he is not surprised that he has not turned up yet. He has a feeling in his bones that Dodik is okay. He is also attracted to Romania since their former king, Carol II, has a Jewish mistress whom he abdicated to be with. He finds this information comforting and feels that Romania may be a little safer for him.

*

We take a break from World War Two and go for a drive to the Adelaide Hills. I ask Dad how he feels now, speaking about the past. He says he is relieved to talk about it all, even the painful experiences, and is pleased I am recording it.

Dad has always hated my first husband, Peter Bruce, and all his family, even though he never met them. It was Peter with whom I lived soon after leaving home, ensuring him a place on Dad's hate-list. Lilian and Cliff Bruce, Peter's parents, live in the Adelaide Hills and invite my father and me to tea. Dad must be really mellowing because he accepts. He even takes time and trouble to get dressed nicely.

'Well, Mr Bruce was big headmaster. I have to look presentable.'

We arrive at the Bruce's country house overlooking a valley full of native Australian trees. My father looks really spruce in his best hat. Lilian is very charming and makes Dad feel immediately welcome.

'Cliff's at the bottom of the garden. He will be here soon. Would you like some tea?'

I am quite nervous as this is another rift that I want to be healed. The Bruces have been like a second set of parents to me, even after I divorced their son. My daughter Sophi is their granddaughter. Cliff comes in wearing his very old, very dilapidated gardening clothes. So much for Dad wanting to impress this former Super Head of South Australian schools. Despite the disparity in attire, Dad and Cliff get on well, and I notice that Dad puts on a more refined way of speaking and is incredibly polite. My fears of him mouthing off about how the Bruces stole and corrupted his daughter are fortunately unfounded.

Even after we leave there is none of the usual post-visit demolition job. In fact, Dad thinks Lilian is wonderful. 'Such a refined gracious lady.'

That afternoon I put Dad's bad leg in a bucket of hot water and gently massage it. The fugitive saga resumes.

*

The journey to Iasi is hazardous. Soldiers and dogs patrol the Romanian border. Any Jews trying to return are shot on the spot.

Dinu warns Sasha that as well as hiding his Jewishness, he must not display any inkling of communist sympathies. In Romania the main rationale for killing Jews is the belief that they may side with the Soviet Union and become spies. This hysteria is further fuelled by the Nazi propaganda that 'Every Jew is a Bolshevik'. This, says Dinu, is because some Soviet parachutists were supposed to have landed in Iasi a few months earlier and hidden in Jewish homes. This led to a vicious pogrom where hundreds of Jews were massacred.

With this news, Sasha's thin hope that his Jewishness may be more acceptable here is dashed. But he has come too far to turn back.

'So, Sasha,' explains Dinu, 'even though you hardly look like a spy, the fact that you are from the Soviet Union will count against you. The Romanians hate the Russians since Stalin recently annexed their former territories of Bessarabia and Bukovina. You've got to say something like you despise what the Bolsheviks have done to your religion and that you are coming to Romania to get away from communist persecution.'

Sadly and with great reluctance, Sasha burns photographs and papers that may in any way compromise him. With help from his resourceful companions, he now becomes Sasha Cherevko, a Ukrainian Catholic from Odessa and a farmhand by profession. The fact that he is among a band of Romanians who are willing to vouch for him and offer him a place to stay eases him through the checkpoints.

The band reaches Iasi by Christmas 1941. Sasha has never celebrated Christmas before, but now that he is supposed to be a Christian, he attends church with Dinu and his family and is awed by the ritual. During Mass on Christmas Eve, he has a terrible gnawing pain in his stomach. As well as hating living a lie, he is convinced that something bad is happening to his parents. He is horrified that Jews everywhere are suffering the same fate as the Odessan Jews. Iasi was one of the great centres of Jewish learning, but now the Jews, confined to one area with severe curfews, are forced to wear yellow stars. Any former Jewish pride lies trampled in the ruins of the synagogues and desecrated graveyards. Sasha misses his parents terribly, fearing that he will never see them again. He now does not even have a photograph of their faces that he can draw strength from.

As Olga is boarding a cattle truck in the Crimea and saying goodbye to her homeland forever, Sasha clings to the memory of his parents' pronouncement that he must survive the madness that has gripped the world for their sake.

*

In November I say a tearful farewell to Dad as I go back to the Northern Hemisphere. I have arranged for Alex, Greg and Gabriel to come and spend Christmas with Dad in Adelaide. As he cannot handle them staying with him, I have set it up for them to stay with Luda, my childhood friend. They can then visit Dad when he feels strong enough to see them.

As I hug Dad goodbye, I can feel a real softening, even though he still doesn't really reciprocate. This latest time with him has been very healing, and especially today we have become even closer. He shared with me that several years earlier, when Val and Alex had still been at home, he had become very friendly with a woman he thought to marry. 'But then I saw Val and Alex standink in the doorway, lookin' like two little lost lambs, and I couldn't do it.'

'So you sacrificed your personal happiness again, just as you did when you wouldn't leave my mother because of me.'

'Yes, Eva, I come from very good people who always put ahders first.'

I am humbled. 'Well, I really appreciate you very profoundly.'

'Yes, I knaow. I feel it.'

31 / **Maggots**

My best Christmas present is to hear that Dad is totally besotted with Gabriel. I regret I wasn't there to see it. Photographs show him beaming at his grandson proudly. Gabriel looks back at him, his face shiny and innocent. Greg informs me that they visited Dad a few times and he seemed in good shape and very welcoming. It is a huge step forward that Dad has accepted Greg into his own home and adores Gabriel.

My daughter Sophi is to be married in the spring and I am busy with wedding preparations, which include making her wedding dress. I offer to send Dad a ticket so he can come to the wedding, but he says he can't leave his cat. His doctors are pleased with his progress and give him another six to twelve months. However, just before the wedding, he goes into hospital to have his colostomy reinstated as his bowels have stopped working properly.

While crystallising violets and primroses for the wedding cake, I reflect on how much healing has taken place within my beleaguered Australian family and wish they were all here for the wedding. It is a real fairytale occasion, with Sophi looking resplendent in her silk dress (despite one or two crises in its creation). She is given away by her three fathers, much to the bemusement of the vicar and local inhabitants. Jake drives her to the local church and hands her to Brian, who in turn takes her half way down the aisle and gives her to Peter, who finally escorts her to Paul, her future husband. The Ukrainian-embroidered wedding towel given to me by Olga's cousin Marya lies before the altar.

Three days after the festivities, I am back in Adelaide, picking Dad up from hospital and bringing him home. On the first evening, he panics when the dressing around his colostomy bag ruptures. I become very intimate with the contents of his intestines

267

as I struggle to attach another bag onto the slimy surface around the pulsating hole; no easy accomplishment. However, we manage to get some sort of makeshift bag in place until the nurse arrives next morning. The funny thing is I really don't mind. I am so happy to be back with Dad and sharing the ups and downs. He is delighted to see me too.

There are a number of practicalities to sort out, and Dad's temper hasn't become any better despite all my exhortations for him to relax and take it easy.

'Bloody Italian bastard! Tryink to rob me. Nobahdy robs me. Nobahdy!'

The victim in question this time is the local panel beater, who won't fix a dent on the side of Dad's 1968 Holden. As Dad has to manoeuvre this tank-like car backwards up his narrow drive without power steering, the car has suffered several minor dents.

The panel beater explains to me that Dad is trying to fiddle his insurance to cover dents that happened at different times. He has already obliged a couple of times but won't risk it any more. Dad has an apoplectic fit. 'Bloody insurance company. They rip off all taxpayers of millions!' Attributing this to his paranoia, I tell him to calm down. But this is like a red rag to a bull. After several more rants, I discover that the insurance company in question is causing a national scandal because of irregularities. 'Look at that bastard director. He owns several fancy homes and cars and woan' even fix a few dents on my car!' I finally manage to calm him down and strike a compromise with the panel beater, who agrees to fix the dents cheaply. Peace reigns again.

Dad pays me a rare compliment: 'A few brains *and* a real looker.' This comment goes a long way to mollify my injured vanity after his previous reference in the gas showroom that I was getting a moustache and looking old.

We slot back into our breakfast routine easily. Dad is eager to tell the rest of his story.

Sasha stays in Iasi until 1944. He turns his hand to many things, including looking after horses.

His most vivid memories are of when he lives with a Jewish family on the outskirts of the city. They, like all other Jewish families, have been torn apart by the Nazi terror. The head of the family, Elezer, was murdered in one of the infamous death trains in June 1941, in reprisal for an alleged communist Jewish plot. These death trains were a series of cattle trucks into which hundreds of Jews were pushed with bayonets and rifle butts and suffocated. Guards nailed slats over the ventilation shutters and daubed the outsides of the trucks with 'Communists! Jews! Killers of Romanian and German soldiers.' His widow, Leiba, battled on with her children, surviving on scraps from a bakery in which she worked long hours. The family were able to stay in their own home but had to wear yellow stars every time they went out, enduring derisory remarks from Romanian and German soldiers who occupied a nearby army barracks.

Leiba is very grateful when Sasha arrives in 1943 and can help out with the children and chores. Sasha is happy to be useful. Food is meagre, but they survive on 'mamalagia', a cornmeal porridge. This is very similar to the 'kasha' that his own family ate in Odessa. He can't help thinking about them, fretting over their whereabouts. He has heard nothing about them or Dodik, and is anxious to get back to Odessa to see what is happening.

The fortunes of Romania have swung violently during this war. Ion Antonescu, who came to power in 1940, backed the Germans in a dangerous diplomatic game to try and retrieve Bessarabia and Bukovina from the Soviet Union. Sasha discovers that Odessa was a pawn in this game—an intermediary sop to the Romanians from the Germans to keep them sweet and to ensure a supply of Romanian battle fodder. The Romanian army has suffered terrible losses, especially at Stalingrad where they lost eighteen divisions of men. Now the Romanian government is becoming increasingly uneasy with its alliance with Hitler, especially since America began supplying the Soviets with mass injections of cash and equipment.

Later in this ever-shifting war, Antonescu will be toppled and the new leadership under King Michael will switch allegiance to the Allies. King Michael's mother, Queen Elena, has continually intervened on behalf of the Jews during the war, even persuading Antonescu to stop deportations of Jews in 1942. Sasha thinks highly of Queen Elena and finds her presence in Romania helps him feel safer there.

A strong clandestine Jewish group has been operating in Bucharest and has a lot of influence in the international community.

Surprisingly, it manages to achieve the liberation of some Romanian Jews from concentration camps. In early 1944 these Jews begin to filter back into Iasi. Leiba's house is near an orphanage, and Sasha sees scores of bedraggled orphans arriving. They are a pitiful sight, emaciated, exhausted and covered in open sores. Leiba takes in three teenagers whose parents, former neighbours of hers, died in the camps.

*

'You should have seen those kids. It was terrible.' Dad's eyes are like hollow pits as he remembers. 'The boys ...' He chokes, not able to speak for a while. 'Those poor boys—experimented on by that bastard Mengele ...'

I wait, aghast, wondering what new horror my father will divulge.

'They had been castrated! They were sixteen and eighteen and could never grow into men. I tinkin' of Dodik—same age. Eva, never in your life could you imagine it.'

Nevertheless I try. I feel it is my duty to take on this suffering and to share the burden of it with my father. These are fellow human beings who endured unimaginable horrors.

'A while after beink back, they grow white and flabby and become like large maggots trapped in child's bahdy. Talk only in high squeaky voices. S'terrible.' Dad rocks back and forth, his hand over his mouth.

We are silent for a while.

'And their sister. She had been the Nazi's plaything. Totally destroyed as woman.'

He clenches his fists as he remembers.

I am catapulted back to a memory too. My father used to hide a book under his bed. It was called *The House of Dolls,* a harrowing true story by Jewish camp survivor Karl Cetinsky. When Dad was out, I would sneak a look at it. It was about a Nazi concentration camp where attractive young Jewish girls were forced to pleasure German soldiers. They occupied barracks called the 'Joy Division'. I was horrified at what I read. Horrified particularly that these poor girls were sterilised beforehand by having a red hot poker thrust into their tender wombs.

Now I understand why my father had this book.

We are silent again for a very long time.

I am cleaning the kitchen like a maniac. I want to do it immaculately to please my father. He is a perfectionist. Just the other day he showed me all his baking trays. They were gleaming and shining, except for one miserable one blackened at the bottom.

'Your madher,' he pointed ominously. 'This was your madher's tray.'

I am not sure what I was supposed to glean from this bizarre demonstration, but here I am cleaning like a mad woman. Or is it that I don't want to be compared to a mad woman?

I finish cleaning, having done it just as Dad likes it. There is not one drop of water anywhere on the sink surfaces and the tiles are blisteringly white. Dad peruses my handiwork with a critical eye. He opens the cupboard below the sink, roots behind the S-bend pipe and triumphantly, it seems, pulls out a small plastic yoghurt pot.

'You missed this!'

My world comes tumbling down. I think of the blackened baking tray skulking accusingly in the cupboard. I think of all the times in my life when I have just not been good enough for my father. His standards have always been high. He is so ordered, which is quite commendable in one way, but stifling in another. It is *his* orderedness—everything in its exact place, everything done how he wants it—and there is no room for me or anyone else in it.

I want to scream. I think of the blackened tray and I can see how he drove my mother nuts. Something tornado-like whirls in my head.

'You know what, Dad,' I snap, 'in my whole life you have never praised anything I have done. I worked hard in the shop for years and all you can remember is that I sat down sometimes. With Mum all you've got to show is a baking tray she didn't clean properly. You forget all the years she helped you in the shop. It's just like now. You don't see all the hard work I've put into cleaning this kitchen. All you see is a small plastic yoghurt container that I missed.'

I take a breath. I am afraid. The victim child is confronting the tyrant parent.

The tyrant takes in what I have said, turns steadily to look at me and, after a pause, pronounces in slow, measured tones, 'May God strike me *dead* if I have ever done anyting to you out of malice.'

271

He claps his hand to his heart dramatically to emphasise the word 'dead'. He is in shock and I realise that it is true. He never *has* done anything to me, my sisters or my mother with the conscious intention to hurt, put down or control (although it sure looked like it sometimes).

'You must understand this about me, Eva.'

I am thrown by the sincerity of his response and impressed by its simple eloquence. I stand humbly before him.

'I tell you someting. You would not like beink one of my builders. I had this German builder once, buildink me a wall. It was an outside wall of my last house. I had two types of bricks. The rough bricks for the inside and the expensive beautiful bricks for the outside. I say to him, "No shoddy bricks on the outside wall." Next day I come and he proudly shows me the finished wall. I see a shoddy brick low down near the ground. He tinks I woan' notice it. I say, "Hey, what's that?' Ah, he pretend he not knaow what I talkin' about. And you knaow what I say? "Pull down the wall and do it again and change that brick to proper brick." Oh yes, Eva, that's what you must understand about me. I can't see the rest of the wall. I only see that one shoddy brick.'

I am enthralled by this story. 'What did the German say?'

'He refused, arguink that nobahdy would notice and that it was too difficult to pull down the wall and that all these other bricks would be wasted. So I say, "Nah, nah, you pull down wall and you do it again." He get very angry and t'reatens me with shovel. But I doan' care if he kills me. This wall must come down. I say, "You doan' pull down this wall, you doan' get paid!" Ah yes, Eva, I am a tough cookie!'

I chuckle at the image of Dad and the irate builder. The symbolism of him, a Jew, lording it over a German doesn't escape me either, but I keep quiet.

The air has cleared. I feel there is a deeper understanding between us. I wash the yoghurt cup in the laundry so as not to mess up the kitchen sink, and the job is complete.

32 / **Return to Odessa**

I longed to return
And like a terrified eagle,
No longer found the nest
And tumbled into the abyss.
Osip Mandelstam

Dad has administered his insulin injections and made the porridge. The toast glides smoothly into the toaster. I am now becoming quite an expert myself at dropping the bread in just so. I sit with my notebook and wait for the next riveting instalment of Dad, the fugitive.

In early 1944 the Soviet army has the Germans on the run, and Sasha hopes that he may soon return to Odessa and seek out his loved ones. The retreating German armies leave havoc in their wake as they get closer to Romania. There are rumours that thousands of Jews have been murdered in nearby Tirasipol. Fearful, Leiba and her family decide to head towards the Romanian port of Constanta to board a boat carrying illegal immigrants to Palestine. She begs Sasha to come too. He is attracted to the idea of Palestine but feels his future lies in Odessa with his family. At the end of April 1944 he is delighted to hear that Odessa has been liberated by the Russian army.

The Soviets continue to drive the beleaguered remnants of the German army further west. By May they are forty kilometres east of Iasi, the sky filling with the whinings and explosions of dogfights. In August the Soviets launch a huge offensive just outside Iasi, encircling the German Eighth Army. Sasha trembles as he hears the pulverising of the guns in a mighty battle that draws nearer and nearer. The German Eighth is destroyed and all

273

remaining Romanian divisions disintegrate as their troops desert the Front in droves.

Sasha finds himself caught up in the melee. He is forced one afternoon to jump into an abandoned tank as Germans and Russians fire at each other in the street. When the shooting dies down, out come the looters, ducking from snipers. Sasha doesn't know who is winning and whose bullets he is dodging when he tries to slip out at dusk. He is held up at gunpoint by a Romanian who accuses him of looting. When he sees Sasha is empty-handed, he lets him go.

On August 23 the new Romanian government under King Michael declares war on Germany and a week later the Russians march into Bucharest.

There is nothing to hold Sasha in Iasi any longer, and with an equal amount of rising excitement and fear, he makes the tortuous trip back home, hitching rides with trucks, horses and carts, or just walking. He finally boards a train that is going to Odessa. It is full of returning refugees like him, who have been hiding out until the German foe has been routed. He makes friends with another returning Jew, Iosif.

He approaches Odessa with confidence. Sasha Wenzerul, a young communist Jew who has survived the German occupation, is going back to the city of his birth. But a shock awaits him at Odessa Station. He is met with suspicion and hostility. 'Why did you leave your native Russia?' he is asked. 'Why did you live in a foreign country?' Answers like 'I escaped so that I could survive' and 'To stay in Odessa would have meant certain death' don't seem to cut any ice.

With growing horror, Sasha realises that all the people he has travelled with are being treated the same. Most are being loaded into trucks and taken off to what are euphemistically called 're-education' camps, including the companion he has just befriended.

'Iosif, what is happening? Where are they taking you? How can this be?'

'They say we are being taken to the Donetsk mines. Sasha, your only chance is if you have any relatives who are Communist Party members and can vouch for you.' Sasha grasps Iosif's hand, fearing he is another in a long line of people he will never see again.

Sasha is permitted to telephone his Aunt Sonia who is fortunately at home, having recently returned from evacuation in Moscow. She comes immediately and persuades the authorities that she will take responsibility for him. With important connections such as Sonia's own sister being married to Voroshilov, now in command of the Western Front, Sasha is set free, but not before he is issued with new identity papers. An ominous-looking stamp dominates the first page. It is a large number thirteen and underneath is printed: 'Has been in foreign territory and under foreign influence during war years.' This stamp is to be a source of great difficulty in the future.

Outside Odessa Station, considerably shaken, Sasha falls into his aunt's arms and dissolves into tears. It is a few seconds before he can ask the dreaded question.

'Where are my parents? Dodik?'

Sonia weeps and cannot look at him.

His parents are missing, feared dead, having been marched out of Odessa in December 1941. Sasha remembers that first Christmas without his family and the gnawing pain that wouldn't leave him. He shudders. He puts a hand around his aunt's shoulder as she weeps for her husband, Igor. Both he and Jacob, Hana's only siblings, have been killed at the Front. Thank God Jacob never found out the fate of Riva and their children.

'But some good news,' she continues. 'Dodik returned in April after the Germans were driven out.'

Joy! 'Where is he?'

'He found out Hana and Shika had been taken away and were feared dead, and he immediately enlisted, saying he wanted to kill as many Germans as possible. You know what he is like! He is now fighting on the Western Front and has already received great honours. Not bad for a boy who is barely eighteen!'

Sasha is in turn proud of his impetuous brother and fearful for him. He has missed him by four months and wishes he had returned sooner to stop him from enlisting. Sasha discovers that his former home is occupied by Ukrainians so stays with his aunt.

As he walks around Odessa, he is saddened by the destruction of parts of the city—especially the burning down of the famous Stolarsky music school by the retreating Germans. It had been a charming, elegant building whose walls once rang with beautiful music. Now remnants of priceless grand pianos lie in strewn heaps between shards of broken colonnades that once graced the front of the building.

*

Dad crushes a piece of toast with his gnarled hand. 'Oh yes, Eva, Odessa was called the Pearl of the Orient—but now ...' His voice trails away.

*

Sasha walks to Prokhorovsky Square. This is where Hana and Shika gathered with hundreds of other Jews on Christmas Day 1941, before they were herded off north. He stands quietly in communion with the thousands of lost souls who must have stood shivering, both from fear and the icy December winds. He tries to imagine his parents' faces and wishes that he had been with them to offer his youthful support.

Even though he has a sinking feeling that he may never see them again, he is determined to find out what happened to them. This is not an easy task as the former Transnistria was full of concentration camps. As well as being filled with Odessan Jews, Ukrainian partisans and other undesirables, they have also been the dumping ground for Romanian Jews, gypsies and political prisoners. Sasha recalls the gypsies with whom he shared rabbit and warm camaraderie, and the weary faces of the Kishinev Jews as they trundled to their fates.

He heads towards Berezovka, a known camp to the north. He looks for anybody who may know anything. Hollow-eyed peasants look fearful and refuse to speak. The same happens in Domanevka further north, where he learns a large contingent of Odessan Jews were sent. He also hears about Vikova in the south, where thousands of Jews have been buried under giant mounds. Sasha shudders miserably. The world is like a giant graveyard. Gloomily he walks back to Odessa.

He must now start to build a life for himself. To get money he becomes involved in the black market, selling flour. It is now January 1945. The Germans are being pushed back further and further west. He starts to look into tertiary education so he can continue where he left off before having his life blown apart. He would still like to teach mathematics. But he is now to receive another shock in the long line of shocks.

In 1941 he finished high school with top marks and was about to study at one of Odessa's best universities, so this is where he now heads. The university officials pay scant regard to his school diploma and ask to see his identity papers. They stare at the number thirteen and write down the details in a ledger. Then:

'I'm sorry, there are no places left.'

'But why?'

'Because you are not eligible.'

'But why? I was accepted in 1941.'

'Things have changed. You are not eligible. Next!'

Sasha backs away from the registrar's desk dumbfounded. He stumbles into the cafeteria to buy some cigarettes to steady his nerves.

A discussion at a nearby table captures his attention.

'You know what? Krein's been dismissed!'

Sasha pricks up his ears. Mark Krein is a brilliant mathematician under whom Sasha hoped to study. He goes over to the table and introduces himself, saying he couldn't help but overhear what the speaker had been saying.

'Moshe's the name. I was Krein's student. Krein was evacuated to the east like all of us academics in 1941. He's now returned to find himself dismissed from his post.'

'But why? What's going on? I've just been told I can't study here.'

Moshe looks nervously about him and draws Sasha closer.

'Are you a Jew?'

A high-pitched whirring is starting in Sasha's brain. He has just escaped the most dreadful persecution imaginable and survived three years on the run. What kept him going was the utter faith that he could come back to the communist system and continue his education.

'Yes, I am a Jew, but what's that got to do with anything? I thought I wasn't allowed to study here because I'd been in enemy territory.'

'That's partly it,' whispers Moshe, 'but in Krein's case that doesn't apply. He hasn't been under German occupation. No, it's because he's a Jew and has been accused of Jewish nationalism.'

The whirring starts up again. Sasha feels the weight of the persecution that has bedevilled his ancestors. It's almost as if there is a kink in his DNA that dooms him forever.

'I'm in for the chop too,' continues Moshe. 'Apparently—just listen to this—I've been told, and I quote, "Your studies are deemed not to be suited to represent Ukrainian culture".'

'But that's crazy!' Sasha spits out the Russian word for crazy, 'sumashechnaya'.

'Yeah, I know. It's all bullshit really. But I've heard rumours that some Jew tried to take a pot shot at Stalin and now Jews are at the top of his hit-list. Stalin's also unnerved by the strengthening of the Zionist movement and sees it as threatening. And—' Moshe lowers his voice even further, '—Stalin is shrewd; he knows he can disperse any discontent that may be around by blaming it on the Jews. Age-old trick.'

Sasha goes back to Sonia and divulges the bad news. Her son, a high-ranking Communist Party member, is sceptical. 'It's all rubbish. My job's okay. I think you've been hearing vicious lies. Look at my aunt, Voroshilov's wife. She goes on holiday with Stalin. I tell you what, you're so good with horses, why don't you try veterinary college?'

But even with his cousin's recommendation Sasha is refused here too. In desperation he tries several more educational establishments, but it is always the same story. He is now ineligible. Number thirteen in his passport is damning him and also, he fears, the fact he is a Jew. The last registrar gets his blood boiling with the suggestion that he should be enlisting and fighting for the motherland, not prancing about getting a fancy education. This really hurts because a central tenet of communism has been that education is a priority above military service for bright students.

Again Sasha thinks of his parents marching to their doom from Prokhorovsky Square, imagines their dear pale faces and wishes he had gone with them.

*

'It was terrible, Eva. Fait' in communism was my life. And now, after all those years of sacrifice and hardship for the glorious revolution, I felt betrayed. I now felt I was beink stabbed in the guts!'

Dad slaps his guts with vehemence as he says the word, and I think of the cancer that has eaten away part of his bowel.

*

In February, with the liberation of concentration camps, lists of the few survivors are posted. Sasha scans them eagerly, but no Hana or Shika Wenzerul. Then he hears the news he's been dreading. Dodik has been killed in action on the Western Front, near Warsaw.

*

Dad pales as he remembers. I know this is particularly painful for him. I remember the only time I have ever seen him cry was when he ran from the living room strangulating a shrieking sob that rose unbidden while watching a Russian film about World War Two in which a man buried his brother.

Dodik was awarded a posthumous hero's medal. 'Of course he was a hero! He was a Jew. What Jew would want to be captured by the Germans?' Dad bangs the table angrily. The toaster and various utensils rattle. His jaw is tightening and loosening in its characteristic manner.

I know the anger is masking huge grief.

*

Even though Sasha has been expecting this bad news, he has also been clinging to the hope that his fearless young brother would somehow cheat death and not leave him to face the future alone. Dejectedly Sasha walks the streets of Odessa. Decayed Romanian signs hang and bang in the breeze like tatters of a forgotten time— the time when Odessa was capital of a now mythical kingdom, Transnistria. Sasha watches one such sign attached by a single twist of wire, swinging like a gibbet, ready to fall off any minute—to fall like Transnistria into the forgotten dustbins of history. A bit like him, he thinks ruefully.

*

'Who has ever heard of Transnistria now?' Dad observes. 'Ah yes, Eva, my life was hangink by a t'read. Where could I go, what could I do?'

*

Just as Sasha is swimming in the bottomless pit of hopelessness, his mate Iosif turns up out of the blue. He has managed to escape from the Donetsk mines.

'It was terrible, Sasha. They were working us like dogs and we were dying like flies. And you know the worst thing? As we walked into the camp, people were calling us filthy Jews! To think we escaped Nazi scum to face worse scum in our own country.'

Sasha is lifted by Iosif's arrival. He doesn't feel so alone.

'Come with me, Sasha. There's nothing left for us here. I've heard of a secret Zionist group. They are smuggling Jews to Palestine. It is risky as the British send back any illegal immigrants they discover. We have to get to Chernovsty on the Romanian border to join this group.'

Sasha reluctantly thinks that this is probably the right thing to do. Be a fugitive again.

*

'It was hard, Eva, to turn my back on the Soviets. I still loved Stalin—I felt that he was my fahder and protector. But I also knew someting was rotten—I could *smell* it! I felt no safety anywhere. At least these Zionist organisations were offerink me someting—a Jewish homeland where I could be safe.'

*

'But my parents,' Sasha pleads.

'Sasha, forget it,' Iosif responds. 'They will be long gone, like my own parents. I heard at Donetsk that all the remaining Jews in Odessa were marched out Christmas 1941, to several different camps. Most died of a typhus epidemic that winter. And if typhus didn't get them or the hunger and cold, the Sonderkommando did.'

'The Sonderkommando?'

'Special units of ethnic Germans, Romanians and Ukrainians set up to kill Jews and other undesirables.' Iosif spits out the words.

Sasha cracks his knuckles in fury.

'Sasha, you must let them go,' Iosif says softly.

With the money he has managed to scrape together selling flour, Sasha bids a tearful farewell to his Aunt Sonia. She helps him again by writing a letter saying she is sending Sasha to stay with relatives in Chernovsty. Sasha will always be grateful to Sonia for helping him during a difficult time. As the train chugs out of Odessa, he takes one last look at the city of his parents, grandparents and their parents before them.

As sadness envelops him, he remembers the words of the gypsy: 'Your life will be hard, but it will be long and productive and you will travel very far.' He is seized with a new determination. *My parents, my brother, they can't have died in vain. I have to forge a new life for myself and for them—they were such good and wonderful people.*

*

'Eva, Eva, come downstairs quickly!' I run down thinking something is wrong with Dad. He is waving a copy of *Time* magazine at me, exclaiming, 'There's hope for me yet. They find cure for cancer!'

He lands the magazine in front of me and, sure enough, emblazoned on the front are the words CURE FOR CANCER DISCOVERED. But on closer reading I find that it is for one very specific form of leukaemia that a breakthrough has been made. Dad is a little disappointed, but he cheers up when I give him the usual lecture about keeping his spirits up, eating well and not getting stressed. He is definitely getting weaker, and I arrange for Unley Council to send volunteers to come and help out, in addition to the usual daily nursing visit.

The storytelling goes both ways. I find myself telling Dad a lot about myself. I realise that there was much he didn't know, especially when he used to work double shifts at Holden's. I tell him about how erratic Mum was with me when he was working, how she beat me savagely, made me kneel in front of the toilet for hours and made my life hell. I tell him how I would really look forward to him coming home from work to protect me. 'I would wait in the old Hendon railway shed by the old Back Road, looking out for your bike.'

'I'm sorry I not there more often. She made my life hell too. Ay-yay-yay-yay-yay.' Dad shakes his head sadly.

I also tell him about the pain of my broken marriages. Dad is particularly moved by this and says, 'You know, it really helps to know that you have suffered too. I feel you understand me more.'

This brings Dad to the painful topic of Alex. 'Why Eva? Why is she like this? Your mahder I can understand. She had terrible time in the war and Prague, but Alex—she had lovely life.'

'But Dad, it's got to come out somewhere. All that pain and agony of World War Two. You can't just sweep it under the carpet. Look at Luda. Her life is a struggle. Look at Anna Lulka. She found it difficult to hold down a job. Look at Val. She gets stressed easily. Look at me! Two broken marriages and I've had to do years and years of therapy to get on top of my demons.'

Dad ruminates on this. For him a good dose of hard work and a half a dozen cloves of garlic are all that's needed to overcome any depression. But he sees the point.

While making notes on Dad's story, I am also researching relevant background on the Internet. Dad is amazed by the wonders of the new technology when I manage to track down a photo of the *Skaugum*, the ship that brought us to Australia. I also find out what had happened to Voroshilov, Aunt Sonia's brother-in-law. Dad knew he became supreme commander of the Western Front and was one of the few of Stalin's men who survived him. This was pretty extraordinary in itself, as Stalin favoured the word 'liquidation' and kept continually and ruthlessly exterminating his Politburo. How did Voroshilov survive?

He giggles when I tell him about a row witnessed by Khrushchev, when Stalin admonished Voroshilov for his disastrous handling of the early stages of the war. Voroshilov picked up a tray carrying a whole roasted suckling pig and smashed it down on the table. But what is of greater interest to Dad is the story of how Dad's Jewish aunt came between Voroshilov and Stalin at the end.

The active discrimination against Jews that Dad painfully discovered at the Odessa university became more and more a reality after the war. Countless Jews all over the Soviet Union were expelled from the Party machine, diplomatic service and military positions. Stalin's paranoia about the emerging state of Israel and the 'Zionist imperialist plots' that were supposedly undermining and subverting the Soviet Union reached hysterical proportions in the late 1940s. He launched a full-scale attack against Soviet Jewry. The infamous 'Doctors' Plot' in the early 1950s saw a number of Jewish doctors arrested for anti-Soviet Zionist propaganda and even for conspiring to kill Stalin by injurious medical treatment. Shortly before Stalin's death, in a meeting where Voroshilov was present, Stalin suggested that all Jews be deported. This provoked defiance from a number of Politburo members who had Jewish wives. The long loyalty of Voroshilov had already been tested when he had chased government agents away with a gun for trying to arrest his Jewish wife a few days earlier. Now he threw down his Party card in disgust and resolutely stated he did not want to be part of the Communist Party ever again. Enraged, Stalin bellowed that only he had the power to determine who remained in the Party and who did not. According to at least one source, Stalin's rage resulted in the massive stroke that eventually killed him.

Dad loves this story. I temper his enthusiasm by saying that this is just one version of many of how Stalin died, but Dad doesn't care. This one has captured his imagination and satisfies a deep sense of poetic justice that it should be Voroshilov's loyalty to his Odessan Jewish wife that caused Stalin's death.

'Ay-yay-yay-yay-yay! Good old Voroshilov!' Deep sigh.

It seems to help Dad heal the profound sense of betrayal he felt at the hands of Stalin and to assuage the guilt he felt for turning his back on the Soviet leader and the great communist experiment. It helps to vindicate his subsequent flight.

33 / **Beriha**

When Sasha and Iosif arrive in Chernovsty, they find themselves amongst fellow fugitives—Polish, Hungarian and Romanian Jews, all looking for salvation in Palestine. All have terrible stories and most have lost entire families. Sasha is particularly interested in one Romanian's story of his experiences in a camp called Vapniarca. He arrived there in the summer of 1942 in yet another wave of mass deportations from Romania. At the camp he found the remainder of a Ukrainian religious sect. They told him the story of a thousand or so Odessan Jews who had been sent there at the end of 1941. Many died of typhus that winter and those who survived were shot. 'Did they say any names? Did they know anyone called Wenzerul?' Desperate questions. Of course, Sasha knows it is foolish to ask. But everyone understands as they are all in the same boat, hoping against hope that one of their loved ones may have survived, or that someone might have a crumb of information to provide a little solace.

Sasha's interest is aroused again when he hears of another Romanian Jew who had been to Domanevka just to the north of Berezovka, where Odessan Jews had been sent.

'You don't want to know,' the man answers wearily to the inevitable question. 'It was too dreadful for words.'

'But nothing is more dreadful than not knowing,' says Sasha and pumps him for more information.

'When we got there most of the Odessan Jews had already died of illness or starvation, and the ones left were hardly recognisable as human beings—dried out and skinny, living off blades of grass. They were housed in filthy conditions with Ukrainian police guards treating them abominably. Do you want me to go on?'

Sasha's face is white with pain and fury. 'No,' he finally manages to say, 'You're right. I don't want to know any more.'

Before the group leaves to make their tortuous way overland to freedom, Sasha has to get new identity papers. There is now another menace that he must pay attention to. He must hide the fact that he is Russian. At the Yalta conference in February 1945, Stalin demanded that all Soviet citizens who were in the Allied zone return to the Soviet Union. This was duly agreed to in a secret pact by Churchill and Roosevelt. As a result, thousands of Soviet prisoners of war and slave labourers were sent back to the Soviet Union regardless of their wishes, and regardless of what might happen to them. Sasha and Iosif know all to well what is in store for these hapless individuals—fodder for Stalin's grim gulag empire.

*

'So, Eva, there was no place on earth where I was safe. Your mahder was the same. She had to pretend she was Polish.' I ponder this in the light of the conversation we had about Alexandra and how unsafe and threatened she always feels. How much of her parents' trauma has been passed on? As a child I never felt safe, and even now in my dreams, feelings of terror engulf me.

*

So Alexander Wenzerul, born in Odessa, becomes Isaac Levkowicz, born in Lublin, Poland. This is the name he still officially has. He could never make the name Isaac stick, though, so has always called himself Alexander or Alec. Sasha is the Russian diminutive of Alexander.

Sasha, Iosif and their group are to be escorted by a young Zionist via a convoluted route through Romania, Hungary, and then into Austria. Their escape is part of an organised clandestine movement called 'Beriha' ('flight' in Hebrew) to enable thousands of Jews to eventually make their way to Palestine.

The journey is very dangerous, and the group has to trek through some high mountain passes in Hungary, way off the beaten track, in order not to arouse any suspicions. But even though it is difficult, Sasha is full of a sense of adventure and opti-mism for the future. He is walking to freedom. 'The feelink I had when we finally came down the mountains into Austria was absolutely indescribable. I still remember it clearly. Beautiful spring day. Orchards full of blossom.' Dad slips into a reverie as he recalls his sense of exhilaration. Unbeknown to the group, they have just missed VE day, but celebrations of the end of the war are still in evidence and they bask in the blissful recognition that Hitler has finally been vanquished.

The small group arrives safely at a large transit camp near Linz, which is filling quickly with refugee Jews from all over Europe. It is exceedingly difficult to go from here to Palestine; some groups have tried, failed and returned. Bindermichl Camp becomes Sasha's temporary home. He attempts to join other Jews in worship but feels woefully inadequate with his lack of experience. He gets upset when others question whether he is a Jew because he doesn't know the prayers. One even implies that Sasha is only masquerading as a Jew so he can stay in the camp. This really hurts him. For years he has been hiding that he is a Jew, and now he can't even prove that he is one.

🍂

'Eva, I became really desperate about it.'

I am surprised by the look of anguish in Dad's eyes. I didn't know how much his Jewishness meant to him. I had noticed a menorah with unlit candles on the mantelpiece in the dining room but thought it was just another auction acquisition.

'I was so desperate that I go to see an old Rabbi and tell him some people not believe I am a Jew.'

Dad starts to shake at the memory. I touch the gnarled arthritic lump on his hand.

'The old Rabbi was so kind. He sat me down, stroked my arm and said, "I believe you, my son," and—'

Dad can't finish his sentence as great sobs begin to rise in his chest and tears stream down his face. Tears gush down my face as well as I watch the almighty dam burst. Several times he tries to finish the sentence but this brings on a new wave of sobbing. It is a momentous explosion of emotion, and the kitchen alcove we are sitting in feels oppressively small.

Finally, interspersed with more wracking sobs, it all comes out. 'The old Rabbi believed me and said that he would teach me to pray. So he did—he teach me Jewish prayers. Ay-yay-yay.' More sobbing and tears from both sides. More sodden tissues and handkerchiefs.

After this torrent subsides, I look at my father's face. A great weight has gone from it and he looks much lighter, much softer. I am amazed that in all the telling of the dreadful times he has suffered, of the ghastly carnage he has witnessed and the painful annihilation of his family he has so stoically borne, he has managed to hang on and not break down. But now the remembrance of the kindness of an old Rabbi, and a deep connection to his Jewishness in the face of denial, have been the trigger to finally unleash all that pain. Hana's candles in Odessa, unlit for sixty years, glow again.

I am profoundly moved.

*

We visit Mrs Schreiber for afternoon tea. She and her husband, Bert, were the Czechs we befriended on the *Skaugum* and who had moved to Adelaide because they thought it was near Perth. Mum and I visited them often in the 1950s.

This visit is important for Dad as he always felt that Olga presented a negative picture of him to her friends. At least in this case Dad doesn't think it was because he was Jewish. Bert, who lost all his family to the Nazis, had been another secret Jew on board the migrant ship. Since her husband's death many years earlier, Blanka Schreiber has officially adopted the Jewish faith. The hug between her and Dad when we arrive feels especially poignant since Dad's breakthrough and deeper acceptance of his own Jewishness.

Blanka has a dry wit. 'Ah, Sasha, we meet again because we are not dead yet!'

Blanka finds solace in her grandchildren. She is sad because her two children don't speak to each other and haven't for years. *A bit like the thirty-three year rift between Dad and me,* I think.

'Why?' Blanka asks, shaking her balding head sadly. 'I just don't understand it. They are bitter about something. I don't believe in being bitter.'

I ask Blanka what she knows about Olga during the war. She tells me some things but is quite reluctant. She is sceptical about the book I am writing. 'What's the point of dragging up the past? Sometimes in the middle of the night dreadful memories come up about Prague under German occupation, but I don't let myself think about it. I turn on the radio and listen to stories and music to drown out the memories.'

I am disappointed as I had hoped to ask her about her experiences in Prague, but any gentle probings in that area are met with a resolute 'Don't go there!' sign.

But can't you see, an inner voice screams out, *the past must be dealt with. Perhaps it has some bearing on why your two children are fighting.* But I also understand Blanka is one of millions who are not ready and who need to keep the door firmly shut. The pain is too great.

❦

Dad and I sit by the beach eating fish and chips. 'Ah Blanka, she look so beautiful,' comments Dad.

I am a bit puzzled as I had been struck by her growing baldness. 'Well, yes,' I say slowly, 'but she is nearly bald.'

'Really? I not even notice.'

I am slightly miffed—he had noticed my moustache, after all! But I also feel humbled. Unlike me, Dad has responded to her inner beauty.

That evening we are in the kitchen alcove drinking tea and we are back in Bindermichl.

'Yes, tings got better after I learn some prayers and I was put on a list for the next boat to Palestine. I was friends with a young couple, Dora Clinger and her husband. They had lost everybahdy and had recently married in the camp and were lookin' forward to settlink in Palestine. Nice couple. Then I got the good news—I had a place on the next boat to Palestine. But the Clingers had just missed out. There was only one more place left and they were a couple. So, Eva, I gave up my place so they could go.'

'Didn't you have another chance?'

'It was very difficult, very strict quotas. But by the time it became easier to go, a couple of years later, I had decided to try Australia.'

We both think about the very different life he could be living if he had gone to Israel.

'Do you knaow what? Dora Clinger still writes to me. She say she has such close bond with me—' At this Dad bursts into tears again. Fatal. I start sobbing too. I offer him tissues but he takes his trusted handkerchief from his pocket, '—and that she wishes I could come to Israel so we can all be togeder.' More sobbing.

I look at my father with all the tears still wet on his cheeks and think what a softy he has become. The set on his jaw has gone. His face moves freely again. Something deeper is settled in his soul. He has finally reconnected to a set of principles more profound and enduring than the set of communist ideals with which he had been indoctrinated. The Bindermichl Rabbi was a true man of God. He represented a far older order, one to which Hana had lit her candles every Friday evening, an order based on the divine principle of love. He had demonstrated this love towards the despairing, lost young man from Odessa in such a way that it could now blossom, over fifty years later.

I lead Dad to the menorah in the dining room. We light the candles. It is Friday evening.

Bindermichl, one of the better refugee camps in Austria, becomes the receiving ground to nearly one million displaced persons— people like Sasha whose lives have been ravaged by war, their former homes now empty graveyards. The logistics of housing and feeding these people are a nightmare. Sasha is made a temporary policeman as some semblance of law and order is put into operation. (Dad is proud of this fact and shows me his special pass. In the attached photo I see a young man with just the trace of what he has been through hovering on his lips.)

Food is in short supply to start with; Sasha has a ration card which entitles him to half a loaf of bread and fifty grams of fat and peas per week. But this improves considerably as international relief organisations become more efficient. Sasha and his fellow refugees are really grateful that they are alive, and after all the deprivation of the war years, just having some food coming in is a godsend.

Sasha decides to give up on Palestine for the time being and settles into life in the camp, carrying out his police duties and training to become a locksmith. As more food and supplies flood in, trading on the black market becomes rife. Sasha often goes into nearby Linz to buy and sell. Here he meets Kurt Weiss, who is fleeing Germany because his father was high up in the Nazi Party. Remarkably they become the best of buddies. They set up a black market business together, trading in anything from furs and watches to foodstuffs and cigarettes. Kurt meets Katherina, a girl from Vienna.

Katherina, who eventually came to Adelaide to join Kurt, was a close friend of my mother and is now a good friend of mine. Dad's relationship with Katherina is fraught. Olga visited her many times when she was having difficulty with Sasha, so Katherina sided with my mother against my father.

'She didn't like me from the start because I was a Jew. I could see it in her face,' says Dad.

Thinking my father paranoid as usual, I decide to ask Katherina about this on a visit. First of all she hotly denies any prejudice. But after quite a bit of talking, she confides in me there is something in what my father senses. She cannot rid herself of a very deep prejudice against Jews.

'I was brought up in Vienna and at that time it seemed the Jews owned the city—all the businesses, shops, offices,' she explains. 'I was forced to work in a bakery at thirteen because my parents were paid such lousy wages by their Jewish employers. I had to work sixteen-hour shifts with no breaks for a mere pittance, just so I could help my family put food on the table.' Katherina's nostrils flare angrily as she remembers.

'I've never told a living soul this before, but it is the truth, and my whole life I've had to cover it up, to pretend that this prejudice doesn't exist. I hate what Hitler did to the Jews in the concentration camps, and I know that a lot of Jews are very nice people. But many of the Jews I was brought up with were mean and miserly and uncharitable to us Gentiles. In Vienna *we* were the ones who were persecuted. They held Vienna in their vice-like grip and there was nowhere we could escape to. I don't mind telling you, Eva, I was glad when Hitler wanted to get rid of their stranglehold over Vienna. I was glad. There, I've said it.'

She looks relieved that she has at last been able to talk about her prejudice openly. I am grateful too because it is her truth. And paradoxically I feel she will now be a little bit less ruled by it. (In fact, when I approached her to check that it was okay for me to include this in the book, she consented because talking to me had helped her to unearth and own this very deep prejudice and move beyond it.)

'But Sasha—such an awkward, shy young man,' she continues.

'He always hung around Kurt and me like a big gooseberry. I'd say, "Sasha, go and find yourself a girlfriend!" but he would blush and look highly embarrassed. I was really surprised when I first met Olga: such a pretty woman with a figure to die for. How could Sasha have landed one such as her? Eva, she was so unhappy with Sasha and would come around and cry and cry. I think he was mean to her—work, work, work all the time. She was a young, attractive, fun-loving woman. But Sasha—always with his long face!'

Dad has a different version of the story. 'Katherina resented me because I persuaded Kurt to bring her over to Australia. She blames me for the fact that she left her beloved Austria. Then, when Kurt ran off with a younger woman and left her with little Curty, I was very good to her and gave her support.'

'Yes,' agrees Katherina. 'Sasha did give me help. We were so poor, and Kurt gave us nothing. But I always thought it was because Sasha felt guilty about getting me to Australia.'

So the wrangle goes on.

As we have been discussing Kurt and Katherina, I suggest to Dad that we go and visit her. This is partly because she is the person left alive who has known Dad the longest, and partly because I am curious to test my father's new emotional openness. He is not over the moon about the idea, but also not vehemently opposed. He is not quite ready to visit her yet but the idea is planted.

Operating between Linz and Bindermichl, Sasha becomes a black market wheeler-dealer and manages to save a lot of money. He and Kurt want to go somewhere in the world where they can start up a business. Australia beckons. Several ships are sailing from Naples, so after a tearful farewell to Katherina, they take the train to the next stage of their journey. Little does Sasha know what destiny has in store for him on that fateful journey on the *Skaugum*.

Dad is suggesting that Jake and I move to Adelaide. I love the idea and especially the fact that Dad wants me to live nearby. We visit the doctor and Dad hopefully tells him about the new cure he has read about. The doctor is pessimistic as usual, and tells me privately that Dad has another three to six months. I don't really know what to believe as this is the same doctor who told Dad that he had one to three months left a year-and-a-half previously.

I take Dad to visit Wendy Bruce and her twin daughters, Ilyia and Anna. The visit is a great success. Dad has them enthralled as he tells the story of his father Shika in the World War One trenches and how he was brought back by Igor Gotman, whose sister he married. Wendy promises to look after Shika the cat if it comes to it. Dad is enormously relieved about this, and is about to launch into explaining the chicken neck ritual when I gently interrupt and say I will let Wendy know everything about Shika and how he needs to be looked after.

I am torn between staying with Dad and returning to England. He is definitely getting weaker but can still pretty well take care of himself. In fact, the previous day I found him up a ladder in the bathroom fixing the leaky cistern. I decide to leave and return soon with Jake. The plan is that we will both look after Dad so he doesn't have to go into a nursing home.

A favourite of mine, Mozart's *Requiem*, is being performed at the Adelaide Town Hall the night before I leave. Anna Lulka picks me up and Dad is surprisingly friendly towards her. I cry all the way through the performance, thinking about Dad. I so desperately want to save him. I feel we have just forged a precious new relationship and I want it to continue as long as possible.

Next day I am terribly sad to leave. Dad stands at the gate looking sweet and vulnerable in his bobble hat. I kiss and hug him and say, 'I will be back soon.'

'That's nice of you.'

'Well, you looked after me when I was little and I will look after you when you are old.'

'That's nice,' he says again simply.

He is such a lovely soul, although he can be a rude ratbag too.

As we fly out of Adelaide north over the Australian desert, the pilot takes us low over the Olgas, a beautiful range of red mountains. I cry for my mother, and my father too.

34 / **The Hospice**

'He needs to be put in a home,' Val insists over the phone. 'You never know what's going to happen to him. Christ, he could drop dead and no one would know.'

'Val, he hates the idea of a home. I am coming soon and will look after him. And surely, isn't it better that he drop dead in his own kitchen than linger for months like some ghost in a nursing home full of lost souls?'

She finally agrees with me, and is further reassured when I say I will persuade him to buy a personal alarm that is hooked up to a next-door neighbour.

But a week later Val informs me that Dad is in hospital with an insulin collapse. Jake and I are soon to go on holiday in Sardinia, so I am torn, but decide to forgo the vacation and fly back to Adelaide. By the time I arrive Dad's insulin levels have steadied but he is still attached to a drip.

He seems to be in perky spirits and is wearing a new white jade pendant around his neck. 'Lee gave it to me,' he says proudly, 'She say it will protect me.'

I look closely at the pendant and am amazed to discover it is an exquisite carving of Quan Yin, my own favourite goddess, whom I pray to occasionally. I feel it is an appropriate time to give him a book about dying by Elizabeth Kübler-Ross. He grabs it and starts reading it right away. He is hungry for spiritual food.

Next day he is moved to Daws Road Hospice so that the doctors can continue to keep an eye on him until they decide what to do next. This hospice is in a beautiful old colonial house and Dad is put into a spacious room of his own. The best part about it, as far as Dad is concerned, is that it is free. It is part of a state hospital network so he doesn't have to pay through his private health insurance. He is overjoyed about this, and is happy I am looking after the house and the cat.

I have brought him a bottle of Johnny Walker Blue Label whisky, the most expensive whisky I could find in the airport. He is in awe of the bottle and treats it like a shrine, looking at it and reading the label over and over again with his big Mr Magoo glasses. We open it reverentially and have a toast. He savours the taste as if it were nectar of the gods. He proudly offers the doctor some. I am pleased as at last Dad is letting himself have something that is really good. But it doesn't last. Next day he hands me the bottle and says, 'Eva, take this home and put in cocktail cabinet. Then go to Booze Brothers and get me cheap bottle of whisky. Here's twenty dollars. We must not waste good whisky. We must save it!'

'What do you mean we must save it?' I explode. 'You're in a hospice, for Christ's sake! No one knows how long you have to live, but it may not be long. If you are ever going to enjoy a good whisky, now is the time.' I pour him a little nip. He acquiesces and meekly sips.

The doctors say Dad is weak and has started to complain of pain in his liver for the first time—caused by the cancer growth stretching his organs. He was given morphine but it made him disorientated and strange.

'T'was terrible. I didn't knaow who I was. I'm quite happy with just pain-killers, tank you very much. Whatever happens, I want to be fully awake.'

Dad loves the hospice and feels like he is in a five star hotel. He has three attractive women doctors whom he adores. At a consultation around his bed, one of them comments on the Kübler-Ross book, saying she read it in medical school. 'Yes,' Dad tells them in his posh voice, 'I t'ought it time I read it and I am enjoyink it very much.'

I take him out for a few drives and offer to take him back to his house to see the cat. Funnily enough he refuses, and shows no interest in the home that he has loved for over twenty-five years. He does consent to visit Katherina Weiss and we go there for lunch. Katherina makes a big effort and cooks some delicious things and Dad enjoys himself, although he tires easily. At the end he and Katherina give each other a warm hug; Austrian Gentile and Odessan Jew. Some of the old prejudices and animosities have finally come to rest.

Each day I bring him the *Advertiser* and wheel him out to the magnificent garden where we while away the time, chatting. He tells me stories about the time we first came to Adelaide. We talk a lot about the Kübler-Ross book and Dad, resonating with what she is saying, says, 'As you knaow I have never been a religious person, but I have always believed that there is a purpose to this life and that when we die someting else will happen. I feel very content with my life and am ready to move on.'

We have many profound discussions. He agrees with me that each one of us is given a unique dollop of material to face in our life and it is up to us how we deal with it. I am delighted with this as it seems that Dad has come to terms with all the bitternesses and hatreds that have twisted his guts for so much of his life. I am struck by the change in his face. It seems that unburdening his past has lifted a huge weight.

I get a phone call from Greg saying Alexandra has significantly deteriorated since Christmas and has been diagnosed with brain damage. When I tell Dad he looks straight at me and says, 'Eva, please make sure that what happened to Olga not happen to Alexandra. Will you do that for me?'

I realise what an awesome task this is, but promise that I will watch over her and do the best I can.

It seems to me that Dad is preparing for death. He has handed over responsibility for the house, cat and bills. He regards visiting his house as a step backward. He is taking the Kübler-Ross message on board, that death is another stage in the journey and that life is a preparation for it. In fact, a few nights later Dad thinks he is dying. He keeps making big sighs and holds my hand tightly.

'Remember, Eva, my parents were very good people. You tell the world.'

'Don't worry, Dad. I will.'

Then Dad does something very beautiful. He starts to stroke my hair lovingly and puts his hand on my shoulder and murmurs something. I strain to hear. As he strokes me, he looks into my eyes and says more clearly now, 'Eva dorahaya, Eva dorahaya.' This means 'Eva darling' in Russian, and it is the first time he has stroked me and spoken Russian to me since I was a child. I drink in this unusual outpouring of affection like a being who didn't know she was so thirsty. The Russian words of love are like manna dew to my soul, and they are so beautiful that I cry.

I stroke him back and say, 'You know, Dad, I remember the day we first met on the ship and for me it was love at first sight.'

'For me too.'

So we just sit and love each other. What else is there to do? We both relish the magic, and it is as if we are transported somewhere else. It feels that the love has always been there between us despite the thirty-three year estrangement. It is a relief to feel the purity of it. I feel deeply cleansed and healed.

Thoughts about my mother come up. The human beings we were just couldn't handle her collapse into schizophrenia. The anguish of that came like a huge black cloud between us. As if picking up my thought waves, my father says, 'And your mahder, she love you very much too.'

'I know,' I say in a small voice.

'But sometimes her love came out crook.'

I know exactly what he means by the word 'crook', and to me those few simple words are so powerful and mean so much.

We are quiet for a long time, both of us expecting that Dad will slip away to the next stage of his journey. He does, but it is to the blissful land of sleep.

Next day he is perkier than ever. Walking about, laughing and joking with the other patients, drinking nips of whisky.

'What's going on?' I ask the doctor. 'He was at death's door last night!'

'Yes, we know, but it's you being here,' she answers. 'You should hear what he says about you. You are doing him a lot of good.'

He is so well, in fact, that he insists on going for a drive to the beach. He even expresses a wish to go to a Chinese restaurant that Lee has taken him to once before. The next Sunday sees Dad tucking into chicken wings with great relish. Lee and I sit grinning at him. He has always been a sloppy eater and now he is up to his elbows in Chinese sauce. For a guy who was always so paranoid about Chinese restaurants, he is doing really well.

'It's that Quan Yin pendant you gave him, I tell Lee. 'You know, he won't even let the nurses take it off when they shower him. Quan Yin is now looking over him and telling him he is at last allowed to have a good time.'

'No, it's you,' Lee says. 'I find it hard to believe that just a year-and-a-half ago he was cursing the ground you walked on!'

I am present at the consultation next day between Dad and the three female doctors. 'You are in really good shape, Mr Levkowicz,' one of them explains. 'In such good shape that we can't justify keeping you here any longer because this is a hospice for dying people.'

Anyone else in the whole world would be pleased by this news, but not my father. 'What you mean I'm not dyink? Look at me!' He points to the catheter attached to his leg, the colostomy bag sitting on his stomach and his thin legs with bunged-up veins. 'Nuttin' works any more. Kaput! What else needs to happen for me to qualify to be dyink? What more is dyink?'

This would be highly amusing—a little beak-nosed man pleading with three women doctors in white jackets and defying medical opinion—but for the fact that he is deadly serious and getting highly annoyed.

I am quite surprised by what the doctor is saying too. 'Look, Mr Levkowicz,' she continues, 'it is highly likely you could live for another three to six months, so we can't keep you here much longer. I'll have a social worker talk to you about your options.'

After the consultation, which has left my father very dissatisfied, I have a word with the doctors, exploring the possibility of me looking after him at home. They chuckle, 'It's not every day we have a patient saying we are wrong and insisting that he *is* dying!'

It is possible I can look after him at home. I need to get a proper hospital-type bed installed and nurses to visit him every day to do the necessary tasks. I go back to talk to Dad about this but his face is as black as thunder. The social worker has unfortunately mentioned the dreaded phrase 'nursing home'.

'What's the matter with these people? Is my money not good enough? I pay the highest rate of tax and they woan' let me stay here!' he rants. 'You knaow how much these nursink homes cost? Five hundred dollars a week! Five hundred dollars!' He is shouting now.

'Calm down,' I say. 'Don't worry, you're not going into any nursing home. I am arranging things so that I can look after you at home.'

But Dad's dander is up. 'What do they mean I'm not dyink? I *am* dyink! And anyway, who pays so much money to go into a nursink home? Those crowded dirty places. Disgustink! Who would pay to be there?' He is incredulous.

'Their families pay,' I venture, knowing any explanation is useless.

'But why do the old people go?' It seems totally senseless to Dad that any old person would voluntarily enter a nursing home.

'It's largely because their families can't or won't look after them,' I say.

'Ah, s'terrible, terrible! They should all refuse to go. Yay-yay-yay!'

I chuckle inwardly, imagining my father leading a demonstration of militant old people in wheelchairs down King William Street in Adelaide, waving walking sticks and refusing to go into nursing homes.

'Look, Dad, I have arranged for you to stay here for a couple more weeks and then I will take you home and look after you. Then if at any time your health gets worse, the doctors say you can come straight back here.'

Dad likes this idea, especially the fact that he can stay here (free) another couple of weeks. 'But what about Jake? What about your family?'

An idea has been hatching in my mind. 'Well, I think I'll go back in a couple of days' time, sort some stuff out at home and then return and take you to your house and look after you for as long as it takes. Jake will come later too and we will look after you together.'

Dad has finally calmed down, although every now and then there is a fresh outburst about nursing homes, about them being 'concentration camps' for the old and how 'they cost a fortune!'

I can't get hold of Jake as he is in Sardinia. Then I have a brainwave. I could fly to Sardinia, spend the last week of the holiday with him, then go to England, sort out some things and return to look after Dad. I reason that it would be good to take a small holiday, especially if I could be in for a six-month stint of caring for Dad.

I discuss this with him and he concurs, even offering to pay for some of the fare. Things are really looking up.

The last thing he says to me before I go is, 'I am very happy you are doink this for me and want to look after me, but please, give Jake my apologies for comink between you.'

I leave strict instructions with the doctors to email me if anything goes wrong with Dad. I then relax. Lying on a beach in Sardinia certainly beats freezing to death in my father's cold house. Jake is delighted to see me. We discuss looking after Dad. He says he is looking forward to getting to know Dad more.

On the last day of the holiday I become violently ill, and as I haven't heard from Australia, Jake and I get on a plane back to England, making sure I sit right next to the loo as whatever has afflicted me is still doing its worst. When we get back to our house we discover the phone lines are down due to a storm. This panics me as I am now cut off from all communication. I prepare to get things ready to return to Australia because the two weeks' grace Dad has at the hospice is nearly up.

Next day we get a phone call from Val. Somehow she badgered British Telecom to fix the lines so she could get an urgent message through to me.

'Eva, Dad died early this morning. I've been trying to get through to you for hours.'

I am totally devastated and bereft. I just can't bear it that I wasn't there with him at the end. I start berating myself severely for having gone to Sardinia, especially when I discover that the last words he said to Luda, who visited him the day before he died, were, 'Doan' go!' That breaks my heart. I feel I deserted him. He died on July 29, 2001 at 7.15 am, in his sleep. I work out that, with all the time differences, the last twelve hours of his life coincided exactly with me being violently ill. Was I suffering with him?

'I soooo wanted to be there,' I moan over and over again.

I stay up half the night, saying prayers for Dad's passage into the afterlife. I can't bear the fact that he died alone. Then I think of my poor mother and how she died alone in that dreadful mental hospital and feel doubly terrible. The only cleansing thing is when I succumb to waves of pure grief. I welcome them when they come. It is like a giant internal washing machine that cuts through all the grime. I feel humbled by my father's humility and dignity in the face of death and wish I had listened to him and not to his doctors. He knew he was dying, and he was ready to go.

❧

Next night I am on a flight to Australia. Jake has insisted I go Business Class and I'm pleased I have done so. I have two seats to myself at the front of the cabin—a private little space (with horizontal bed!) so that I can continue my grieving alone.

The previous morning I had phoned Val to talk about funeral arrangements, and found myself spontaneously saying, 'I love you.'

'I love you too,' she said straight away.

I find that a great comfort. Things have been so difficult between us for so long.

I start to have a chat to Dad, telling him how wonderful it is to travel in Business Class and that I understand how hard it was for him to spend money. I share it—it's a feeling not many people seem to understand. Spending money is like draining away your resources, shedding life blood, throwing away power. Getting a bargain is like a drug. You feel like you are cheating destiny, shoring up the defences without losing any men. It feels very deep, and I don't know if its genetic or acquired.

'I feel I picked this up from you, Dad. I can't even buy anything if it's not a bargain. It feels like I am throwing away security. So you can see, Dad, that flying Business Class really goes against the grain for me. But God, it's nice!'

I feel Dad is with me as I fly and I continue the chat.

'I'm sorry I wasn't there with you at the end. I missed out. I missed out on more contact with you. I'd give anything to have just held your hand as you died.'

Bliss. I manage to sleep for six or seven hours. I am already feeling better about Dad, but a real tightness closes my chest and heart when I think of his poor, hacked-up body.

'Dad, you and I played a fierce dance together. We both played for high stakes and it was often brutal, but we won through in the end with the profound love that underwrote everything. Holding your hand when you died would have been the icing on the cake. But, Dad, I'm the kind of girl who wants it all! I just hope I do you proud at your funeral.'

When I reach Adelaide I put a funeral notice in the *Advertiser*, the paper he received every day for fifty years.

'Alexander Levkowicz, born Odessa, died Adelaide. One-time refugee. Proud Australian.

'You met death with humility and dignity and blessed me with your love. I will always miss you. Your daughter, Eva Maria.'

35 / **Funeral**

'My eyes, my eyes, I'm blind. Take me to a doctor. Quick!' I've just picked up Alexandra from the airport and she is already driving me mad with her delusions.

'You know, Eva, Russian women go blind with grief, especially with the death of a father. I can feel a film spreading over my eyes. I'm going blind. Take me to a doctor now!'

'She's been like this all the way from Melbourne,' says the long-suffering Greg, 'and it seems to make no difference how many times I say, "You're not going blind, Alex." '

I try a different tack. I give her a big hug and say, 'I'm really sad Dad has died. You must be too.'

'Daddy, my daddy,' she cries, and clings to me.

'Would you like to see Dad's body?'

'Ooh yes please,' she says, her mind taken off being a blind Russian woman, for the time being anyway.

So far I am a model of patience but I wonder how I will fare being with her for a whole week.

At the funeral parlour, the funeral director looks a little warily at Alex, who makes a pass at him as she always does with any male that she sees. 'You're very handsome. Are you married?'

I hurry her into the viewing room and explain to the funeral director that we will be quite a while and that he might hear some wailing and crying but shouldn't worry. Looking decidedly worried, he ushers us in and hovers uncertainly before closing the door.

Wailing and crying! That is an understatement. Alex starts howling immediately and sends out the most heartrending shrieks at the sight of Dad in his coffin.

'Oh Daddy, Daddy, Daddy. My beautiful Daddy!'

Even though it is slightly amusing and embarrassing to start with, I am profoundly moved by her grief. She hugs his cold body and pours her tears all over him. She then proceeds to remember out loud all the wonderful times they had together, telling him what a happy childhood he gave her and how she was blessed to have such a father. Then she sings to him in a terribly unmelodious and shrieky voice. I wonder how the funeral director is faring on the other side of the door.

Other times she just prostrates herself over his body, letting out heart-wrenching sobs. This gives me permission to let go my grief too, and we sob together. It is very beautiful and I am determined to let her have all the space she needs to express her grief. I have unsuccessfully been trying to get counselling for her for months but have been told by her psychiatrists, 'Schizophrenics don't need counselling.'

After an hour or so she seems to run out of steam. I take some photos and we say goodbye and leave. As I am about to speak to the funeral director, Alex suddenly announces that she must go back in. He looks most discomfited as we both traipse back into the funeral parlour.

This time Alex surprises me. She launches an angry attack at Dad, and now remembers all the bad times—times when he suppressed her, belittled her and abandoned her. I am impressed how quickly she seems to be moving through the classic stages of grief. After about another hour she finally says, 'I'm done.'

I'm not quite done myself, so I go and sit with Dad and silently say a prayer. I hold his cold hand and quietly say goodbye. It is not as good as holding a warm hand, but it feels more of a completion.

Outside the evening sky is a blaze of red. Alex looks up. 'Look, Eva!' she says. 'The angels have come to take Dad up to heaven.' She is smiling and peaceful.

Quietly we make our way home.

*

Next day at the funeral, I assign Elizabeth Bruce to be Alex's special minder. She has a good relationship with Alex and is pleased to do the job. She also forged a close bond with Dad in his final few months. This caused her great surprise as Dad had been 'the evil one' for so long—the one who was 'so horrible to poor Eva'. She visited him in the hospice several times and brought him special green walnuts soaked in syrup. She would feed him these walnuts and he would just beam back at her with love. These exquisite concoctions have a taste to die for, and it was one of the last tastes Dad enjoyed. I had been pleased to discover that Elizabeth and her mother, Lilian, had visited Dad on the day before he died. Lilian saw that he was fading and asked, 'Has anyone let Eva know?' Apparently at the word 'Eva' my father perked right up and looked around expectantly, thinking I might be there. That makes me feel even worse about abandoning him. I can't get it out of my head that if I had stayed he would have gone on living because he had something to live for. One of the last things Elizabeth did was to feed him one of the delicious green walnuts. She says that he looked deeply and lovingly into her eyes and simply said, 'Elizabet'.'

At the funeral and in subsequent days, I am to discover that many people went to visit Dad in his last few days. This comforts me, but also makes me think that it must have been a little like Piccadilly Circus in Dad's room. He was an intensely private man and didn't like socialising. In the hospice he complained to me that though he loved it there, he was sick of smiling and saying hello to people all the time. I begin to wonder if he had decided to die because he was fed up with so many visitors!

If that was the case he would have been horrified at the funeral. It is packed. All sorts of people are there, even Dad's oncologist, who has found time in his busy schedule to attend.

Denis, Val's husband, introduces Gabriel to his cousin Barney. Gabriel, looking really cute in a bow tie and white shirt and the spitting image of his grandfather, enjoys the fuss everyone makes of him and lights up the funeral parlour with his smile.

I have an emotional reunion with Vlada, whom I haven't seen for over thirty years and had lost touch with. I managed to find her address through the Bulgarian Club. She wears black and is walking with a stick, and says that I have just missed Kirov, who died the previous year of a stroke, aged eighty-two. I am very sad about that. These are the people that enveloped me between their warm bodies when I was a freezing two-year-old. Vlada begs me to visit her soon as she has a secret to tell me.

The funeral director has organised the funeral according to a pre-planned schedule of his own and informs us that we only have five minutes in which to speak. He annoys Val when he takes exception to her choice of song to be played during the committal of the ashes. The three of us decide it is our funeral; we will take as long as we like to speak and the song will be played.

Val reads a poem and then it is my turn. I am very nervous with the big crowd but also feel very supported. The Bruce family are all there plus many other friends, including Katherina, whom I acknowledge publicly as the person present who had known Dad the longest. I tell the truth about Dad, what a difficult, irascible old man he was, and relate several amusing stories which soon have the audience laughing. I start to really enjoy myself and studiously ignore the funeral director, who keeps looking meaningfully at his watch.

The thing I want to get across most is the transformation that happened to Dad in the last few weeks of his life. 'Despite being such a tough nut, and despite all the darkness he witnessed in his life, the sun that shone out of him towards the end was truly amazing. Many people here will know what I mean. He would just smile and be so open that it zapped you right in the heart. I saw the innocent young child in him who, despite being born into a terrible time and into a terrible world, came right out and shone brilliantly with such love. His purity took my breath away.'

I end the eulogy with: 'One of the things Dad had terrible difficulty with all his life was his Jewish faith. He had to hide it most of the time, and I know that only a handful of people here even know he was a Jew. But I want to acknowledge how important it was to him and say a short Jewish farewell. Lehitraot and Shalom.'

Denis follows on and gives the most wonderful eulogy, complementing mine perfectly. He describes how Dad came to Australia with very little, how hard it was for him as a migrant to make it in Adelaide society and how he succeeded beyond expectation. He ends with a Shakespearian quote about King Lear, 'another king who had three daughters'.

During the fifteen-minute speech, the funeral director sidles up to me and complains, 'I'm afraid we can't to do the serenity blessing we had prepared as we are running out of time.'

I say, 'That's fine. Just play Val and Denis's song while we pay our last respects to Dad and that will be sufficient.'

And that is just what happens, though not without a lot of tut-tutting.

As we file past the coffin, Alex, who has been a model of good behaviour, starts bawling loudly and calling, 'Daddy, Daddy!' Val comes up to me, saying, 'Oh gawd, here we go!'

'Don't worry; everyone understands. And believe me, she would have been a lot worse if I hadn't taken her to see Dad's body yesterday.'

The coffin has some photos of Dad on it, including his wedding photo. When Vlada goes up, she ignores the coffin and kisses the image of Olga profusely, crying and moaning, 'Oi oi, Boszhe moi, oi.' She drops to her knees in grief. I am curious to find out what this is all about and wonder if it has anything to do with her 'secret'.

While drinking coffee afterwards an elderly man in rumpled clothes comes up and introduces himself as Colin. 'I helped your father with his car and odd jobs for the last thirty years,' he says. 'You know all that stuff you were saying about his love pouring out? Well, that happened to me too. I went and saw him a couple of days before he died, and the way he looked at me, I felt something happen inside me—as if everything that was bad inside got healed.'

I am inundated with positive feedback and feel pleased with myself that I took the risk and talked about love and truth. I often hold back on this as I feel it's not cool to talk about such things. The only person not entirely happy is the funeral director, but he takes himself off quickly, no doubt to perform a 'proper' funeral.

When I arrive at the crematorium to pick up my father's ashes a few days later, I receive a shock. I am told, slightly bizarrely, that they can't release Mr Levkowicz's ashes as he owes money for his wife Olga's ashes! For twenty-five years her ashes have sat in the peaceful Hibiscus Garden in a backwater of the crematorium in Adelaide. It was here that I had scattered the Ukrainian earth given me by Marya in Tarasivka. Now I am informed that the twenty-five year lease is up and that another $750 is owing.

'So that's why the bugger died when he did,' I quip. 'Good timing, Dad.'

I decide to collect Olga's ashes as well. I have a very good idea what to do with them.

On the way out of the crematorium, I back my father's car into a tree, putting a large ugly dent in the boot. 'Sorry, Dad,' I mumble hastily to the ashes sitting reproachfully beside me.

A few days later I see Colin, Dad's friend, in the street. He looks at the back of the car and says, 'I hope you did that after he died, because if you didn't, that certainly would have finished him off!'

*

Walking down the streets of Adelaide with Alex is challenging. Every now and then she suddenly stops in the middle of the busy pavement and makes some loud announcement, like 'Where's the toilet?' or 'I want a cigarette' or, more embarrassingly, 'Dad said Mum used to menstruate all over the shop' or 'Let's hug.' I subject myself to a big hug with lots of sloppy kisses and Alex enthusing loudly, 'Eva, I love you, you are my favourite sister.' And if she sees anyone looking at us, she says even more loudly, 'She's my favourite sister!' Due to the drugs, she slurs these words and spits on the s's.

I have been waging a long, unsuccessful battle with her psychiatrists to cut the dosage of the drugs she is on. I am worried about the injurious side effects. I researched the drug olanzapine and discovered that the slurring and bad motor coordination I have noticed in Alex are known side effects and that the dose she is on is at the high end. Weighing heavily on my mind is Dad's wish: 'Eva, don't let her go the same way as Olga.'

I am discovering that psychiatry doesn't seem to have progressed much since the 1960s when Olga was a patient. After a spate of experimental alternative therapies in the '70s and '80s, the current treatment consists largely of third-generation psychotropics, which, while purporting to be more accurate and less lethal than before, still seem pretty crude to me. I certainly haven't seen my sister improving on them—she is, in fact, deteriorating very fast. At least lobotomies have been discredited, although electroconvulsive therapy is again on the rise.

While the conventional psychiatric route is mostly drug-oriented, I discover an opposing camp which is against the use of drugs at all. This interests me. I ring up a proponent, but he sounds so dogmatic that I am put off. He regards drug-based psychiatry as Nazi-like suppression of schizophrenics. While I am definitely unhappy with the massive amounts of drugs that were given to Olga and now Alexandra, I believe that psychiatrists are doing their best with such a difficult disease, even though it is from the confines of a narrow mechanistic paradigm.

I find a recovering schizophrenic, who has been on a conventional route for years, who gives me a ray of hope. She says what saved her was a new drug called chlozapine in conjunction with narrative therapy. Narrative therapy encourages schizophrenics to write and present their story. This combination attracts me and I set out to find out more.

*

I take Alex to Glenelg Beach, her favourite place in Adelaide, and over a cup of coffee we talk about her brain damage, the knowledge of which has been upsetting her. I explain to her that this may not be due to the olanzapine but to the massive overdose of drugs she took at the time of her attempted joint suicide with John.

As Dad has left her a substantial trust fund (to be transferred to Gabriel after her death), she feels more optimistic. We discuss things she could do with the money, like trying alternative therapies and being pampered with manicures and massages. I give her information on how she could be more positive about herself and take charge of her life. I hear her good intentions but can't help thinking it is too late. She has a real 'patient' mentality that makes her very self-centred, expecting things to be done for her. I don't know how this deeply entrenched attitude can ever be turned around, especially if she also has brain damage. I have visions of taking her to England and putting her into a therapeutic community-type setting where she would have to learn to take responsibility for herself. As anyone who has lived with a schizophrenic knows, it is really hard work. I don't think I have the capacity to do it, but I would dearly love my sister to get better.

*

At my father's house I do a lot of sorting out. I donate Dad's favourite painting, a self-portrait of the famous South Australian artist George Whinnen, to the South Australian Art Gallery, in memory of Alexander Levkowicz. I also arrange for a brick to be engraved at South Australia's Migrant Museum, a wonderful place that charts all the migrants who have come to Australia since 1770. It has a substantial section devoted to the massive post-World War Two migration of which our family was a part. I brought Dad here before he died and he was moved. He felt acknowledged by the effort expended to record that time. On the brick, which is laid in the courtyard, is written, 'Alexander, Olga and Eva Levkowicz 1950.'

The most exciting find in my father's house is more letters and photographs. A few letters are in German and addressed to Olga Levkowicz with dates in the 1950s. The name on the back is Hoffmann. I am determined to get them translated and find out more of what happened after she disappeared in the cattle truck. Did Dr Hoffmann keep his promise to find her in Magdeburg?

I decide to spread some of Dad's ashes in the sea around Adelaide, before taking the rest back to the Black Sea as promised. Opening the box to divide the ashes is no easy matter, and I drop quite a few on the floor in the process. Feeling terribly irreverent, and apologising to Dad profusely, I sweep some of him up into his own dustpan. My first stop is Port Adelaide where Dad used to come to buy fish. It was here he bought me a miniature oil painting of the Australian outback (haggling down the price, of course), which I treasure. I venture nonchalantly to the edge of the water, thinking of a prayer as I open the box. Just then, a gust of wind whips up and blows the ashes the wrong way. 'Sorry again, Dad,' I mutter, frantically trying to brush him off my clothes and into the water. I am more successful at Grange Beach where we often ate fish and chips and watched the sunset.

The rest of the ashes have a date with Odessa and the Black Sea.

Destiny

When I die, bury me
In the land of Ukraine,
My dear Mother country,
Wide Steppe, wide plain

Taras Schevchenko

Prologue / Ukrainian–Polish Border, 1942

A human can be a slave by fate, but not a slave by nature.
Vasily Grossman

Olga huddles miserably in the corner of the cattle truck. Her throat is terribly parched. It seems years since she drank that vile-tasting bilge that passed as water. The train has been stuck here for hours. Every now and then it gives a violent lurch. Movement at last, she hopes. But it is just another truck being added or taken off. She misses Mama terribly; treasures the last glimpse of that darling strong face; has savoured the last taste of her vareniki, so lovingly prepared; cherishes the last caress on her cheek as Mama kissed her goodbye and murmured, 'Olychka dorohaya.'

She wants to get away from this place. She had been so frightened earlier that day when some girls had been taken from her truck. They were being transported to some village called Belzec. She didn't want to go there—to be stuck in some remote place on the edge of Poland. Dr Hoffmann had promised to get her sent to Magdeburg from where he would pull strings to get her out. She comforts herself with the image of his kindly face and the anguish in his eyes when he informed her she must leave her family.

Oh, some jolting and jerking! Is the train finally starting? She is hit by the sharp metallic smell of the wheels as they start to grind into motion and the black sulphur of the smoke as the engine coughs and splutters into life. They are moving at long last.

36 / **Vlada's Secret**

'I remember when you used to drink eggs raw!' I say to Vlada's daughter Jane. I haven't seen her or her older sister, Lisabet, for over thirty years. When I first met the two girls after Mum's amazing reunion with Kirov at Henley Beach, they were both covered in flies and sleeping in tomato boxes in a shed a few fields away. Vlada is now relatively wealthy as she inherited the entire tomato farm after the owner died.

Vlada envelops me in her comforting, doughy arms just as she always has. I love sinking into the warmth of her flesh, my being still relishing the memory of that icy cold night in southern Czechoslovakia over half a century ago.

She cries as she hugs me. She cries because she is still in official mourning for her husband, but mostly she cries because of Olga. She desperately wants to talk to me about Olga and wants Lisabet to be present so that I can fully understand what she has to tell me (her English is poor and is interspersed with a lot of Bulgarian words.) Lisabet is a short, pleasant, fair-haired woman who doesn't look much different to when we played together as children on the back porch.

'Oh, Evitchka, Sasha never tell me dhat Olya dead until long after. I so upset and can never forgive him for dhat. Never, never!' She thumps the table. This explains why Vlada ignored the coffin and kissed the image of my mother at my father's funeral.

'Oh, Boszhe moi! Evitchka—'She clutches her heart and starts sobbing again. 'Your mahder—she such beautiful lady and, Evitchka, you must knaow it was destiny dhat she come to me. Dhat night when Kirov and I saw her first time wid little you in her arms, and blue with cold, I knaow God send her to me and it my duty to look after her. I love the munts you bot' spend wid us. And she suddenly

313

disappear wid you. Where? We look everywhere! 'Twas terrible. And Ludvig, your fahder, come many times to see if you come back.'

'What? My father came back again to look for me?' This is new. I feel so sorry for this man who is my real father.

'Yeah, he cry and looka sad, sayin' he so sorry. I couldna help him. I didna knaow where you go.' Vlada looks at me beseechingly.

'I tinkin' why God send Olya to me and dhen she disappear? I tear my hair and cry for more dhan year. Dhen we have good luck, Kirov and me; we escape over border. Get away from communists. Kirov, he wanna to go to France. He drive me crazy with dhis! I doan' wanna go to France. All I knaow is I wanna go to Avstralia. I dunno why, but I have strong feelink I must go dhere. We big argue. But I bossy and we not go to France, but Avstralia.'

Vlada thumps the table again.

'I happy we go to Avstralia. Very long way. I sick. When we at Bonegilla I glad. Kirov, he wanna live in Melbourne. But I wanna live in Adelaide. Again I dunno why. All I knaow is I wanna go to Adelaide. We argue. I boss again. We in Adelaide and s'terrible. So hard. We live in tin shed. Lisabet she born, then little Jana. No money yay-yay-yay. Kirov work, work, work like slave. Why we live like dhis? We once rich proud people in Sofia. And dhen suddenly one day, miracle! Kirov see Olya and Evitchka in Henley Beach. You and mahder come back to my life and I say, "Slava Bogho (thank God). Olya has come back to me. I knaow now why I did come to Adelaide." Very happy day. Ah, maya Olychka!' Vlada's large worried face is wreathed in smiles as she remembers. 'Ah, Evitchka, I see Olya in your face.' She grabs my cheeks and shakes them affectionately as she did when I was a child.

'She and you come visit here very much. She always bring much present. Nice tings for children and nice tings for me. We talk much and she tell me about Praha (Prague) and how she so sad. She cry and cry. Her heart, 'tis broken. She so young. So missink her own mahder and family.'

Vlada wrings her hands, trying to fathom why such an angel was so badly treated in Prague.

'And dhen she run away from Praha and come to me and Kirov. But when she go away from us to Avstralia, she no like it. And dhat Sasha, he so terrible! Work, work, work—always work. Olya she cry, she cry and cry. Evitchka, I doan' knaow what to do. She even come to me with you and say, "I left Sasha." And I say, "Good, you stay here wid us. We look after you." '

I remember those times with great fondness. By that time Vlada, Kirov and their children had moved out of the tomato shed into the house we are sitting in now, a modest bungalow on Tapleys Hill Road. Kirov would put me on his knee and I loved sitting there, having nips of his vodka and watching him crunch on raw chilli. Later I would be put to bed in the lounge, falling asleep to the hum of adult voices, enjoying the smoke from Kirov's pipe and feeling warm and safe.

'But after two days she always go back,' Vlada goes on, shaking her large head sorrowfully. 'Dhen she get sick. Terrible. She in hospital for few munts. Dhen she come visit again. I doan' knaow what to do or what to say. You knaow what she like. She look so sad, lost. So terrible. Before she always laughin' and tellin' jokes. Such funny jokin'. So full of life. Always very funny, my Olya. And now she just sit in chair and look out window.

'I shake her and I say, "Olya, you must leave Sasha. You must come here. You must live your life."

'She shake her head sadly and say, "I'm too old, Vlada. I'm fat. Who will want me now?"

' "Olya, doan' be silly! You are young—you are only t'irty-six years old. You have your whole life in front of you. Stop dhis!"

'But it was no good, Evitchka. T'was terrible to see her losink will to live.' Vlada sighs and all her face crumples into a mass of brown folds.

'Dhen I hear she in mental hospital. I go dhere once. S'terrible. I couldna sleep for munts after—I keep seeink all the faces—so bad. And worst of all her poor face. I want to take her out, but I canna.' Vlada wrings her hands and starts to shake.

'And dhen many years go by and I go see Sasha few times. He invite me and Kirov to his big house in Unley Park. Very nice rich house. But he look so lonely. He say Olya in hospital all time. No good. He give me and Kirov some old furniture. T'was rubbish.' Vlada furrows her brow in anger. 'I say, "Sasha, keep your dirty old furniture. Me and Kirov, we do okay."

'Then my Lisabet, she go hospital to have first baby. Lisabet, you tell Evitchka what happen.' I notice that Vlada is still shaking and the blood is draining from her face.

What is it that she wants me to know? I am bursting with curiosity.

'Well,' continues Lisabet, 'I was sharing a room with another woman who was also having her first baby. This woman was a nurse by occupation. Mum would come and visit me every day with her friend. One day when they were about to go, Mum's friend said, "Come on then, Vlada," and they left. The woman sharing my room turned to me with a funny expression on her face and asked, "Are there many women in the Bulgarian community called Vlada?" '

'I said, "No, it's a very unusual name. Why do you ask?" '

'And she answered "Well, where I work in Glenside Hospital there's a woman who keeps calling for Vlada. Every day it is 'I want Vlada. Please can someone find Vlada. Vlada, she Bulgarian. She only person that can help me.' " '

Lisabet shudders as she tells the story. I shudder too, goose bumps rising on the back of my neck. Vlada starts to wring her hands.

'I asked her this woman's name, even though in my bones I knew.

' "Olga," she answered, "Olga." '

'So I told Mum the story next time I saw her.'

I glance at Vlada, who is looking stricken into the distance. She slowly turns to me, anguish etching deeper into her face.

'Evitchka, I didna go. Olya she need me. She callink for me. Ah, Boszhe moi!' Vlada thumps her chest. 'God send nurse to share same room with my daughter to send me message and I didna go. I couldna go. I shoulda gone. Kirov, he even say, "Vlada go!" But I didna. I couldna. I keep tinkin' I will go. But I 'fraid. I doan' like dhat hospital.' Vlada looks at me with such abject misery. Her voice drops to a strangled croak. 'And then Olya die and 'tis too late.' Large tears roll down her flat cheeks and drop on to the folds of her arms.

Doing some quick mental arithmetic, I work out that Vlada received this message just a year before Olga died, in 1975. This means that Olga could speak after the lobotomy but had chosen not to, perhaps in some sort of defiance. Then, when her agony became too unbearable, she called out for her old friend Vlada. I can't bear it and cry too. I cry for the utter loneliness and sadness of my poor mother calling for Vlada. I also cry for Vlada. I hold her as she sobs with grief for Olga.

I give Vlada some items that belonged to Olga and lots of photographs, but I know that none of these things can bring an ounce of solace to her for having failed to heed my mother's call. I tell Vlada that it is precious to me to know how much she loved Olga. I also tell her I will be taking Olga's ashes back to the village of her birth. That brings a wan smile to her sad face.

37 / **Fire Horses**

Chaos hovers like smoke
Its dark paw at my throat
Ludmyla Taran

'Don't you dare bloody ring the ambulance again, do you hear? If
you do they'll lock you up in a mental hospital, pump you full of
drugs and you'll end up just like Mum!'

I am screaming at Alex full blast. So much for my resolve to be
kind and patient.

I am in Melbourne on a mission to make things better for Alex.
She has been exhibiting more 'positive symptoms', the psychiatric
jargon for delusions, since returning from the funeral. Why they're
called 'positive' beats me as they are usually decidedly negative in
nature. Alex smells smoke, thinks she's on fire and feels compelled
to call the emergency services. After the first time she rings an
ambulance in the middle of the night, I speak to her very patiently
at length about it all. She explains that voices in her head tell her
to ring the emergency services. I try to help her distinguish
between the real her and what I call 'her illness', or her voices.

'You must try to ignore what your "illness" is saying to you. This
is important because every time you listen to it and ring an ambulance or fire brigade, the doctors prescribe more olanzapine. And
you do want to get off that, don't you?'

She nods and I think she understands. I am a hopeful fifteen-
year-old again, explaining to Olga that there are no persecutory
lights. Poor, deluded me. I have to learn again that rational argument does not work when dealing with psychotic delusions.

Earlier in the day I asked her health care team to consider Alex
for bereavement counselling. She is now grieving Dad's death as

318

well as that of John, her boyfriend who succeeded in their suicide pact.

'Useless on schizophrenics,' they answered.

I observed to the medical team that she had markedly deteriorated in the last year since the olanzapine dosage had been increased, and asked if there could be any link. I also asked if that or the overdose of epilepsy pills in the joint suicide pact could have caused her brain damage. They told me they believed the brain damage and side effects she is exhibiting are a result of her illness and not the drugs. (How can they be so sure?) They said they must balance the side effects against her 'positive symptoms', so if her 'positive symptoms' increase then up goes the dose. I suggested that perhaps the recent dramatic surge in 'positive symptoms' was a reaction to her father's death and that bereavement counselling, not more olanzapine, could get to the root of her acting-out behaviour. They were dubious, but after much discussion and debate they at least agreed to cut down her tranquillisers and consider a switch to chlozapine.

When I hear that Alex phoned the ambulance again in the middle of the night, I feel that my hard work in convincing the psychiatrists to cut down on the drugs is jeopardised and lose my temper. I feel bad yelling at her. She bursts into tears and says she understands what I'm saying and will do her best.

The place where Alex is living has become unsuitable as it is set up for people to be reintegrated back into the community. Alex has now deteriorated too far for this and is not able to look after herself. I discover that other homes more suitable for her are few and far between, and all have long waiting lists. The only option may be a nursing home that is full of geriatrics.

'But she is only thirty-seven!' I exclaim, ghastly memories of Ward C and seeing Alex disappearing down the same vortex flashing through my mind.

Spurred on by my father's last wish not to let Alex go the same way as Olga, I grab her, put her in the car and announce, 'We're going to find you a nice new home.' She is pleased as she is unhappy where she is.

We visit three different establishments. The first one is very plush with beautiful furniture and gardens, but an atmosphere so stifling that anyone would get the screaming heeby-jeebies within twenty-four hours. The second is not much better. Alex hates both of them. The third is called Grandel and Alex is keen on this one because she has met residents at a weekly social club and they have spoken highly of it. It is also popular, with a long waiting list.

Grandel is a rambling Edwardian mansion with a ramshackle garden in a pleasant, central part of Melbourne. Both Alex and I love it the moment we step into the grounds. I love it even more when I meet Lyn Pendergast, the owner. She and I click immediately. She is a warm, giving person and seems to genuinely love all of her thirty-five children (as she calls them). I observe the way she is with the residents and I'm impressed. A woman goes past with a crown and a long green cape, and Lyn greets her, 'Hello, Queen Guinevere, how are you?' The woman beams and giggles and twirls her cape proudly. Another bloke comes up and starts rattling on to us nineteen to the dozen. 'Oh, meet Arthur—talks the back legs off a donkey, but he's got a heart of gold.' She gives him an affectionate pat.

A dishevelled man with wild hair comes up to Alex and they are overjoyed to see each other. 'Give me some skin, sister.'

'Yeah, Rodney, some skin,' enthuses Alex as they perform an elaborate handshake.

'You comin' to live here, sister?'

'I hope so,' says Alex, looking excited and flushed.

Lyn shows me around and introduces me to the cook, a plump Italian woman.

'Mina here makes fabulous food. You should taste her desserts. I figure these poor people have so little in their lives that the least we can give them is good grub. Mina has been with us for ten years and is just like part of the family. Aren't you, Mina?'

The woman smiles jovially as she throws some pizza dough. Lyn also introduces me to other staff, who have all been there for years too. This bodes well as I know what difficult places these are to work in and how hard they find it to keep staff. Lyn is obviously doing something right.

Lyn is keen on Alex straight away, partly because she wants to attract more young people to her home. 'It's not that I don't like some of the old dears who are here. It's just that I want to take on a few more young ones.'

'But when will you have a place?'

'Well, it's amazing you should walk in today because unexpect-edly I have just had a place become available. The trouble is, it is the most expensive room in the building as it is a single with an ensuite bathroom. Most of the people here share rooms.'

'Perfect,' I say before even seeing it. 'We'll take it.' I know Alexandra's trust fund will easily pay for it.

We look at the room and, though a little on the small side, it is comfortable and homely.

'I love it,' pronounces Alex.

Alex will be showered and dressed every day, her meals will be cooked for her and entertainment and outings laid on. A hair-dresser and chiropodist visit every week.

While Alex chats to Rodney and other residents, I tell Lyn a little about Alex and some of her delusions—like believing she is on fire.

'Oh, don't worry about that, love. Our staff are used to all kinds of things here and know how to handle them. Just last week we had someone who kept going around kicking people. That took some sorting out, I tell you. And when you return to England you can contact me any time.'

To my huge relief Alex is able to move into Grandel immedi-ately. The transition goes smoothly and Alex is happy.

'I'm also near my old stamping ground, Carlton, where I used to live. I can just walk up the road and have a coffee, or a massage. And guess what?' she burbles excitedly. 'I'm in love! Yeah, I'm in love with Rodney. We're going steady. And we go dancing together.'

One of the huge side benefits of Alex moving to Grandel is that she is under a different health authority and therefore acquires a new health team. They are much more flexible than her previous team and immediately provide her with weekly bereavement coun-selling. When I meet them they are so sympathetic and kind that I burst into tears with relief.

Alex enjoys the bereavement counselling but the prognosis is not good. She can't walk well any more and is unable to do simple things like light a match for her cigarettes. The psychiatrist is con-cerned about the rapid deterioration in her motor abilities, and doesn't rule out that it could be due to side effects of the drugs she has been on or the suicide attempt. After all, Alex did take a massive overdose and was in a coma for a short while. The psychiatrist has observed that for some reason Alex reacts more strongly to her medication than other patients do. I am relieved that someone is finally listening to what I have been saying for the last two years. I feel that the psychiatrist cares about Alex and takes into consideration the individual circumstances of her case, rather than sticking to psychiatric theories. The olanzapine has now been changed to a minimum dose of chlozapine.

Alex continues to be plagued by her fire delusions. I wrack my brains how to help her cope with this. As I have had to painfully learn again, reasoning doesn't work. Yelling at her doesn't work. I wonder whether modern psychiatry is right—perhaps drugs aimed at suppressing the delusion are the only way out. Delusions seem so deeply embedded. I think of the narrative therapy I had heard about. In this treatment people are encouraged to write down their story. Unfortunately, Alex can no longer write. Undeterred, I buy her canvases and paints, hoping to harness her artistic abilities. Sadly her motor skills have deteriorated too far and she is unable to express herself this way either.

Inspired by a central tenet of narrative therapy that honours the view of the world that the schizophrenic holds, I put aside my rational mind and enter with Alex the scary world of being on fire. I feel how frightening and distressing it is. She feels she has no control over fire and that she could burst into flames at any minute. She is on constant alert for the smell of smoke or sparks that could come from anywhere and burn her to death. Putting myself in her shoes, I feel an overwhelming need for protection.

That is when I think of fire horses. These are legendary mythical creatures that protect people from fire. We festoon the walls in her room with images of magnificent fire horses. I tell Alex that every time she is worried about fire, she should look at these images and know they will protect her. I also tell her about her grandfather Shika and his love of horses; how his knowledge of them saved Sasha and his family from probable death by fire in Odessa. I tell Alex that Shika's spirit will watch over her too. She loves looking at the fire horses and it all seems to help her a little. I fervently hope so.

I am puzzled why Alex is so bothered by fire as she has never experienced it directly. Both our parents had horrific experiences,

Olga narrowly escaping the firestorms in Magdeburg, and Sasha the wholesale burning of Jews in Odessa. No one was there to protect those thousands of people who were burnt alive in ghastly circumstances. Is Alex picking up on this horror in some strange way? Or carrying the suppressed dread lurking in the vaults of the family psyche? I am convinced that all that pain, helplessness and terror have to be worked through somehow.

I remember a recent conversation I had with my childhood friend Luda. She was complaining about the rudeness of her nineteen-year-old son. 'He drives me nuts. He's always answering back. He's so bad I swear I feel like splitting his head open with an axe.' I am stunned that she is oblivious to the significance of what she is saying; it was she who, as a seven-year-old, watched her father raise an axe to her mother's head. What were the odds that her father saw someone's head split open with an axe during the dreadful dark time of that blood-soaked war he was trapped in? Very high indeed.

Alex goes out with her boyfriend to a monthly dance, organised for people with disabilities. I am touched when informed that Alex and Rodney help each other out with their delusions. Rodney is convinced the Mafia is out to liquidate him, so Alex first checks out the taxi that is to take them to the dance. She then makes sure they are not being followed. When they arrive at the dance she goes in first and gives Rodney the all-clear. In return, Rodney brushes the imaginary sparks off Alex's back and is alert for the smell of smoke. Despite lurking Mafia and incipient conflagration, Alex and Rodney manage to snatch a few dances and have some fun.

I am hugely relieved that Alex's quality of life has improved and that she seems to be handling her fire delusions better. It makes it easier for me to leave her again since I still have one final important task to perform for Sasha and Olga—to return their ashes to the country of their birth.

38 / **The Crimea**

'Eva, it's your turn now!'

With some trepidation I lie down naked on the pine boards. Lena is wielding a besom of oak and birch leaves which she rhythmically swishes up and down my body. I am having a true Russian experience—visiting the local banya, a sauna with a wood fire and cold plunge pool. Lena's friends have hired the whole banya as they do every week. The men bring along their beer and the women their beauty products. The besom experience is surprisingly pleasant. Lena alternates between quivering the besoms over my skin, swirling the hot air around my body and then lightly thrashing. When she has finished, I am tingling from head to foot and covered in fragrant oak and birch leaves. I take my pink wood-maiden body and plunge it into a freezing pool and come out feeling fantastic. Lena then massages me and rubs in scented oils. I can't think of a nicer way of spending a Sunday afternoon.

Lena has kindly consented to help me with laying my parents' remains to rest in their beloved native land. But first we are off to the Crimea to join members of my grandmother's family. Over the last year I have acquired even more cousins, nieces and nephews. In fact, three vanloads of relatives await me at the home of Leonty's daughter Zina in Simferopol, the capital of the Crimea. My cousins Nikolai and Shura have arranged a large family gathering there, and want to take me on a tour of the beauty spots of this region. Leonty stays at home in Nizhnygorsk as he is too frail to travel. Nikolai's son Vladimir, who says his boss has just been invited to Buckingham Palace to meet the Queen, is very earnest when he says, 'I have told all my friends that I am going to the Crimea to meet our very own queen, Eva Chapman from England.'

I also discover that as well as Shura's daughter being named after Olga, Zina's daughter is named after me. I feel comforted by the knowledge that even though my mother and I were on the other side of the world, we were still very much included in the thoughts and rituals of our Ukrainian family.

I get a stark warning from Sergei, Lena's husband, that counteracts my euphoria about discovering more relatives. 'I bet if you were a long-lost cousin who had been living in Siberia for the last fifty years, you would not be getting this kind of welcome. You be careful. They may only be interested because they regard you as a rich Westerner.'

This has, of course, occurred to me. I recently read about some Chinese Americans returning to China only to be met by two thousand people, all claiming to be relatives and all clamouring for goodies from the West. 'Don't worry,' I reassure Sergei. 'If I sense anyone wanting something from me it turns me right off. At the same time, if I want to give anything to these people I will. I am a lot better off than they are materially. Jake and I loved helping my niece Vika get to university and know what a huge difference that has made.'

It isn't long before I have an opportunity to help again. The tour around the Crimea is quite an expedition as our party of seventeen explores the coastline in three large vans. We stop at various places and walk and swim or just sit and admire the spectacular views. I notice that Nikolai sits a lot and will not walk very far. It seems he has something wrong with his legs. I am reminded of when I first met him and he seemed unsteady on his feet, prompting Lena to think he was drunk. I charge Lena to find out from Vladimir what the problem is.

The Crimea has a dramatic and beautiful coastline and is a traditional and popular holiday destination for the people of the former Soviet Union. Sevastopol and Yalta are particularly splendid, but I can't help musing on the dreadful things that happened there during World War Two. Sevastopol, where my grandfather was injured and captured, nestles on a group of hills overlooking a pretty harbour. It was subjected to a dreadful siege in 1942 before falling to the Nazis and most of its elegant buildings destroyed. Yalta, another attractive harbour town, was where Stalin negotiated that forcible repatriation of two million Soviet citizens, a secret pact which profoundly affected the destinies of Sasha and Olga.

'Vladimir tells me there is something seriously wrong with Nikolai's legs but he doesn't have the money to go to the doctor,' Lena reports. I send her back to tell Vladimir that I insist on paying for his father to visit the doctor.

'Oh, he will never accept in a hundred years—he is very proud,' replies Vladimir.

When we regroup back at Zina's flat, I ask Lena to broach the subject with Nikolai during one of their many 'smoking on the balcony' breaks. For the next hour I hear a lot of shouting coming from the balcony. Lena finally appears looking a bit worse for wear.

'I think there has been a breakthrough. He refused point-blank for ages to accept help, but when I told him, "Eva has only just found you and would like you to be around a bit longer," he began to soften. But I think you must come now. He has some questions.'

I go to the balcony. Nikolai looks very fraught and starts grilling me about the fact that he doesn't want me to jeopardise the well-being of my family while doling out money to him.

'It's not a problem, Nikolai—not even for a moment,' I reassure him. 'I really want you to go and see the doctor about your legs.'

At that point Nikolai bursts into tears. I rush to hold him and he bawls his eyes out on my shoulder—huge, tearing sobs punctuated by splutters of apologies. I know that each sob costs him dearly as he fervently believes that grown men should not cry. He has already apologised to me about his brother Vasily's tears when we first met. To him it is a sign of weakness. But I love the fact that he is allowing himself to cry. It feels long overdue. When he can finally speak, he thanks me profusely and then bursts into fresh tears. For me it is a beautiful moment.

Next day Vladimir reports that his father is transformed. Nikolai is profoundly moved that I care about him and his welfare. Vladimir informs us that Nikolai's oldest son is an alcoholic and that this fact, coupled with the deterioration in his legs, had sent his father into a downward spiral of drinking and smoking too much and just wanting his life to end. Now he is determined to cut down on abusing his body and will use my money to go to the doctor to see about his legs. I feel privileged to be in the position to help.

We continue exploring the stunning coastline of the Crimea. I am ensconced in the back of a van with my cousins Zina, Shura and Nikolai, and my trusty translator and soul sister Lena. It is my turn to be the raconteur. My cousins are aching to know what happened to Olga after she disappeared into the Nazi cattle truck. Fortunately I have been able to piece together my mother's movements during the war years beyond what she told me herself, as I have had the letters I found from the Hoffmann family translated. These, in addition to discussions with Vlada and Katherina, mean I can tell the story of what transpired when a young girl of seventeen was torn from the bosom of her family and thrown to the wolves.

39 / **Ostarbeiter**

They call us survivors but not one of us survived.
We merely stayed alive.
Surviving Ostarbeiter

The monotonous sound of the wheels etched itself into Olga's brain as she drifted in and out of fitful sleep. Gnawing pains of hunger mingled with longing for her family as each rattle took her further and further away from her loved ones. It felt like she had been inside this cattle truck for months. She had cried bitterly as the freight train had out of Seitler, glimpsing for the last time the round face of her mother through the iron bars in the side of the car. Many other girls, all about the same age, some even younger, were also crying for their mothers. They had hardly any room in the box car even to sit. Fortunately most of the girls had brought food wrapped up in their bundles. Olga shared her potatoes with a very thin girl crammed in the corner with her. Marina had no bundle of food. Her mother had died of typhus the previous winter and her father had been killed defending Seitler.

The train trundled on through the first night. 'I want to pee!' became a familiar cry. Nadia, a forceful older girl who had taken charge of the truck, had found a crack in the floor, and with a lot of shuffling and grumbling, girls made their way to that part of the truck and relieved themselves.

Next morning the train lurched to a halt. Nadia, who had stationed herself at the small barred window, peered out. The station had been bombed, but Cyrillic letters on a tattered sign prompted her to announce, 'We're still in Ukraine'. The doors abruptly opened. Ah, fresh air! Voices barked at them to get out. They were ushered to pits at the side of the road serving as makeshift latrines. The stench was disgusting, but Olga was glad to stretch her legs.

She saw they were in a railway siding and that extra box cars were being added to the train. More people carrying their belongings were being shoved in. It seemed that half of Ukraine was being transported to Germany! What was the world coming to, she thought as she lined up for what looked like bread and soup. But her spirits rose as she drank down the cabbage-like bilge, thinking perhaps this whole adventure would not be too bad.

After the small meal they were herded back into their car. Hours passed as they waited. The train jolted every now and again. Hope— it might get going. But then stillness. The car got unbearably hot. No movement. Thirst. Nadia started banging on the doors. 'Water, we want water!' Olga and Marina clung to each other in fear.

Nothing. Just silence and the beating of hearts.

Darkness drew in. The doors clanged open again. Orders! Out they got, relieved to be moving stiff limbs. The stench of the latrines! This time just water, slightly brackish and warm, but at least wet. Packed into the car again. Now they heard the welcome sound of the steam engines starting and the slow grinding of the wheels working faster and faster until they settled into a monotonous beat.

This is how it went on for what seemed like months but was probably several days. There were further interminable waits at various borders. Relief at disgusting latrines. Brackish water. Mouldy black bread. Nadia informed them that they were at the Polish border. Here they were taken out and lined up. Ten of the girls were marched off, destination Belzec. Olga was petrified and hung on to Marina. She was relieved when they were shoved back in the truck. Little did she or the others know that Belzec was one of the first concentration camps with gas ovens to be built by their new masters, and that their hapless companions were to be assigned to the dreadful job of processing and marshalling Jews and gypsies to their fate. Of the 600,000 Jews transported to Belzec to be gassed, there was only a single known survivor. All helpers and slaves were liquidated when the camp was disbanded a year later.

They were now slowly chugging through Poland. Some girls cried for home as the train took them inexorably further and further west. Olga was past caring. She hated the hours sitting in freight sidings and just wanted to reach her destination. Crossing

Poland seemed interminable. Any chance she got to look out of the window showed a wasted, bombed and burnt landscape. All the stations, if not bombed, were strafed with bullet holes.

Every now and then she saw bands of people with yellow stars, fixing the tracks. She felt relieved she was not a Jew. She hadn't had much to do with Jewish people—there hadn't been any in her village and very few in Poti, just the local pawnbroker. Her family made disparaging jokes about the Jews, about how miserable and mean they were. But when she saw their lifeless faces staring at the train as it went past, she felt sorry for them and wished this terrible nightmare was not happening around her. It was Dr Hoffmann's kindly face that would come to her in these darkest moments and restore her faith in human beings. She knew that he was not a 'Nemetskiy chort' (German devil), the name Nadia would hiss every time the door was clanged shut by one of the German soldiers. Every now and then Nadia would start singing a patriotic song to keep spirits up. Not many joined in, fearing retaliation. She would scoff and call them a bunch of ninnies.

Germany at last! But the journey was not yet over. Another day and night passed and only then did they halt. Get out. Was this another latrine stop? No. This time they were herded towards some long low huts.

There seemed to be thousands of girls here. Olga gripped Marina's hand as they were ordered to line up. They filed towards a desk where their details were entered in a large book. Each girl was handed a sign reading 'Ost', which she had to fix to her clothing. Olga was now an Ostarbeiter, a worker from the east. After some more thin gruel and mouldy bread, they were pushed towards the dormitories, which consisted of sets of slatted boards onto which six girls were crammed. Nadia objected loudly to being shoved by the female camp commandant. Olga froze in horror as she watched the proud girl felled to her knees by a devastating blow to her face. An ominous silence descended on those who had shared the same cattle truck and had admired Nadia for her courage. Now the girl, blood dripping from her nose, lay cowed on the floor. Any attempt to move towards her to help was repulsed by the guard, who screamed at them to do as ordered or they would get worse.

Olga scrambled miserably on to her bed. Hugging Marina, she fell asleep from exhaustion. At least she could stretch out her legs.

Next day Olga was given a booklet with 'Arbeitsbuch' stamped on the cover. This was her employment identification document. She had learnt that they were in a huge transit camp just outside Magdeburg, waiting to be transported to various work assignments around the country. Her heart leapt at the sound of Magdeburg. At least she was near Dr Hoffmann's family. She asked shyly where she would be sent but had her head bitten off quick smart. Nadia came behind her and whispered dejectedly through swollen lips that some women had been here for months and were still waiting. Olga began to see the true meaning of the word 'Untermenschen'. She and her companions were definitely being treated like sub-humans.

Life in the camp was tedious and humdrum. Olga was assigned to latrine duty. This consisted of digging long shallow ditches, two shovels wide and about half a metre deep. Olga found this work murder as she didn't follow in her sister Anyuta's footsteps when it came to hard physical labour. But the thought of sturdy, strong Anyuta, who could wield a scythe better than any man, kept her going as she dug. When each trench was filled with excrement, she had to cover it with earth and then chlorinated lime. The camp guards were very particular about this. 'We can't have you all dying of dysentery. Germany needs you Ostarbeiters to keep making guns and serve our country as the slaves you are! Schnell!'

Meals were scant. There was one portable stove assigned to Olga's barrack. On this a large pot of soup—if you could call it that—was heated up for the midday meal. At night it was a piece of black bread, often mouldy. Olga would fall exhausted on to her slats. The gnawing stomach pain was familiar and reminded her of the 'hungry years'.

There were many things at the camp that disturbed her. While on latrine duty, she noticed a hut which housed women wearing yellow stars. One of these women fell and was kicked by the camp commandant over and over until she lay like an inert lump. Olga, her face pale with shock, was sure the poor woman was dead, and turned to Nadia, who was shovelling lime. Olga was even more shocked by the hatred she saw in the older girl's face. 'Jew scumbags!' Nadia muttered. 'They deserve everything they get.' Nadia, severely humiliated a few days earlier, had already turned her hatred and humiliation onto someone lower in the pecking order of the camp.

'Masha Zvereva, Olga Nesterenko, Marina Grigioreva, pack your things and come with me.' Bleary-eyed, Olga and Marina hastily got off the slats and packed their few belongings. They and several other girls from various parts of the barracks were to be transported to the Krupp factory. Olga said a tearful farewell to Nadia and the other girls, grabbed her case and Marina's hand, and left the motley crew behind.

Bumping their way to Magdeburg on the back of a truck, Olga was relieved that the strenuous digging of latrines was over. She was delighted that the plan was working so far. She was getting closer to Magdeburg and to Dr Hoffmann, who had assumed the face of a saint in her mind's eye. Clutching her 'Arbeitsbuch', she wondered what lay in store for her.

Olga was in awe of the city as they were driven through the streets to their barracks. The biggest town Olga had ever seen was Poltava, but Magdeburg, with over 300,000 people, had once been the capital of Saxony and was now a thriving, bustling metropolis. Graceful baroque buildings lined the wide majestic streets. The barracks were on the edge of a huge industrial complex. The beds here were a little better than at the transit camp in that each girl had one to herself, but they were only a few inches away from each other. She managed to grab a bed by the wall and shoved Marina into the one next to hers. There was room under the bed for her small cardboard case and a hook above to hang her coat.

She, Marina and ten other girls were marched next morning to the factory. It wasn't very far—past a few more barracks, a derelict yard which contained a few chickens, some brick buildings and then the factory gates. It was a munitions plant on the edge of the main Krupp factory, which made tanks. One of Olga's jobs was to sort out bullets. While she was grateful that she didn't have work that involved hard physical labour, she hated what she had to do. It felt like a betrayal of her countrymen. She couldn't help thinking that each bullet might get lodged in the heart of some Russian or Ukrainian boy—a boy like Leonty, her beloved brother. Thinking of him upset her; there had still been no sign of him when she left. She thought longingly of her mother, Katya and baby Lydia as she worked.

The work was tedious and she was forced to stand for hours on end, arranging bullets on trays. The shifts were twelve hours long and she hadn't even had breakfast. Half way through the day she was given a plate of swede soup. At night the girls were marched back to the barracks where a piece of black bread was doled out. Occasionally they were given a mug of black German coffee. Sundays they had off, but they were expected to clean the barracks from top to bottom.

After a few days Olga was exhausted and starving. Frequently someone would collapse and be dragged out. Once she heard a terrible commotion at the other end of the factory. There had been an accident and a young man whose arm had been mangled in a machine was screaming horribly as he was taken out. The Ostarbeiters were blamed and told that laxness was not permitted in this factory. There was a doctor on duty but he was a rather unpleasant man—not like Dr Hoffmann—and Olga felt he was unapproachable. His job seemed to be to make sure no one slacked. Even people with severe colds were sent back to work.

'We have quotas to meet,' barked the guard. 'While our fine young men are being murdered by your scum Bolshevik brothers, we need to keep them armed. Schnell!'

Olga hated that word and would sometimes dare to mimic it behind the guard's back. Marina and the other girls smothered giggles, and very soon she became the factory clown.

But despite these diversions she could feel her strength slipping away. She didn't know how long she could hold out. Her legs were killing her and she just longed to lie down. She noticed that her periods, which had started less than a year before, seemed to have disappeared. She was glad of this as they had been quite heavy and had given her severe cramps. She also noticed that the other girls used disgusting looking rags, which they had to wash and dry on Sundays.

One evening when they were trudging back, Olga noticed that the door to the chicken yard was not locked. So that night she slipped out and crept into the yard. She knew all about chickens and how to move among them without startling them. She was overjoyed to find a couple of warm eggs. She slipped back to the barracks where she and Marina made a little hole in the top and drank the eggs raw. She couldn't believe how wonderful that egg tasted and could feel goodness being restored to her bones.

Olga soon discovered that life for her and these ten girls was much better than that of most other Ostarbeiters in Magdeburg. Some poor sods had to carry bricks all day long and were guarded by men with Alsatian dogs. Any slackening of pace was a signal to let loose the dogs. Countless Ostarbeiters died, and it seemed countless more were trucked in to take their place.

Olga became thinner and thinner and wondered what had happened to Dr Hoffmann. His saint-like face began to fade from her beleaguered brain.

'Why are all the fences painted green?' I ask as we whiz down to Yalta on the Crimean coast.

'Oh, that was due to Khrushchev and one of his many enlightened orders,' Nikolai answers dryly. He proceeds to inform me of the many shenanigans Khrushchev performed to improve his holidays to the Black Sea. One positive measure was that he commanded that the old tortuous road to Yalta be replaced with the straight one that we are speeding along now. But then Khrushchev decided that the journey would be easier on the eye if all the fences on the one hundred kilometre stretch were painted green. What really galled Nikolai was that Khrushchev then refused to provide funding for the paint job, so each impoverished community along the route had to stump up the cash.

'But the worse thing that befell our mighty leader was that on one of his holidays, poor Khrushchev found the sea too cold at the beach at Yalta. So you know what happened? A section of sea was cordoned off and warmed, at vast expense, so slobber chops could dip his fat arse into it. Can you believe it?' Nikolai is still incensed.

'Animal farm was pretty accurate then,' I observe. 'Everything was equal on the farm except for the pigs and their privileges.'

Three tedious, very long months rolled by as Olga went through the monotonous routine in the Krupp factory. She had just about given up being rescued by Dr Hoffmann when the camp guard came up to her one morning as she dragged her weary body out of bed. 'Olga Nesterenko, get your things,' the guard snapped. 'There is a woman here to see you.'

Puzzled, she packed her case and went outside. A slight woman with lovely fair hair came up to her and enquired, 'Fraulein Olga Nesterenko?'

Olga nearly burst into tears—it was such a long time since anyone had treated her as a fraulein, let alone called her one. 'Yes,' she said uncertainly.

'I am Frau Hoffmann. My husband—'

Olga fell on her and did burst into tears. Frau Hoffmann stroked her hair and gave her a handkerchief. 'My husband has arranged that you come and help me with my two children. It is because you speak good German and were such a big help to him in the Crimea. He has managed to pull a few strings.'

'Is he here now?'

'No, he is not. He is near Moscow.' A shadow fell across her face. 'But come, let us go to my house and you can meet the children. It is only a few blocks away.'

Olga couldn't believe her luck. She felt desperately sorry for Marina and the other girls she was leaving behind, but she promised to come and visit. Marina forlornly waved goodbye.

The Hoffmann house was beautiful and Olga's eyes were wide with wonder at all the fine furniture. An exquisite grandfather clock stood in the hall near a graceful grand piano. Paintings adorned the walls. She had never dreamed that there could be such luxury. The children were delightful, a girl and a boy, and Olga fell happily into her new routine. She noticed that there were other Ostarbeiters working in neighbouring houses doing cooking, cleaning and housework, but she liked to think that she had the best employers in the world. Frau Hoffmann even apologised that she could not pay her. Neither Olga nor any of her friends had ever been paid anything, and she didn't expect it.

'Oh, you should have been paid a little. The Krupp factory has paid the SS for you Ostarbeiten, but the SS pocket all the money for themselves. I was also expected to pay the SS for you, but my husband is a much respected man and, well …' Her voice trailed away. It was obvious that the SS, who had a centre in Magdeburg, were not Frau Hoffmann's favourite people. 'But I will give you a nice room and plenty of food.'

Olga again couldn't believe her luck when she saw her pretty little bedroom with its duck-down quilt. There was only one blot on the horizon: she was forbidden to write to her family. 'I'm sorry,' said Frau Hoffmann, 'but it's impossible. No Ostarbeiter is allowed any communication with family.'

The family hoped that Dr Hoffmann would come home for Christmas in 1942 but unfortunately he wasn't able to. All Frau Hoffmann knew was that he was working in a field hospital near Moscow, and the rumours were that German soldiers were dying in their thousands because of the intense cold and renewed vigour of the Russian armies encircling them. She worried terribly that she would never see her husband again.

While Sasha was helping Leiba and her family in Iasi, life at the Hoffmanns was good for Olga. She was treated as one of the family. She even went on outings and journeys with them, one being to Dresden to visit the children's grandmother. She was awestruck by the beauty of Dresden and its wonderful architecture. The best thing about this trip was that Frau Hoffmann told her to take off her 'Ost' sign. She felt like a liberated young fraulein for a whole day.

Like Dr Hoffmann, his wife was secretly against Hitler. She and Olga had many interesting talks into the night and listened to illegal radio broadcasts. It certainly made a change from the manic ravings of Goebbels, exhorting the German people to rise to the challenge of their new destiny and be the leaders of a wonderful new National Socialist world. To Olga this didn't sound dissimilar to the Soviet rhetoric that had battered her ears in her home country.

Then in 1943 a new menace started: the Allied bombing raids. Magdeburg had a big oil refinery where the Germans manufactured synthetic oil from benzene. This made the city a prime target. The Hoffmann house had a cellar, and Olga helped make it comfortable with rugs, cushions, plenty of candles and stashes of food so that the family could go there and be safe at any time. The first of the raids was in April 1943 and very soon they were a common occurrence. Olga soon got used to the whining of the air raid sirens and to the routine of carrying the sleepy children down to the cellar.

Olga was true to her word and went and visited her friends back at the barracks on Sundays. She would always take food, which Marina would devour hungrily. She liked visiting as she could

336

gabble away in her own language and tell her friends the latest news from the clandestine radio broadcasts. The girls were delighted to know that the Allies were pounding away at Hitler in the West, whooped with joy that the Russians had had a major victory at Stalingrad and were thrilled that the Germans were being repulsed outside Moscow. Olga thought about Dr Hoffmann and prayed that he was still alive.

Just before Christmas 1943, to the joy of the household, Dr Hoffmann came home. Despite another raid during the night of December 29, when they all hastily descended to the cellar, the visit was a warm happy one. Olga was shocked by how grey and tired and aged Dr Hoffmann had become. He said that the war was crazy and it was killing him to watch so many young men die. He told of horrendous battles around Moscow and how Stalin and Hitler were mad. 'These two madmen are playing a deadly game and so many millions are suffering terribly because of it. When will it all end?' He was tired, bone tired, and wished for this end with every fibre of his being.

Some evenings other doctor friends would visit. One of them had recently been assigned to the Krupp tank factory. He bemoaned the terrible conditions there and described his battle with the authorities to try and improve the lot of the forced labourers. Several million Ostarbeiters now worked for the Reich. As Hitler's manpower was stretched over so many fronts and the Reich occupied large swathes of Europe and the USSR, the Nazis brought in even more slave labourers from all over, two million from the Ukraine alone.

'I see the most awful accidents every day—fingers, hands mangled or cut off. The factory is unheated and those poor sods are dropping dead in droves from cold, exhaustion and malnutrition. I've talked to the Krupp directorate about the conditions but they do nothing. In fact, one of them said something along the lines of, "Oh, there's plenty more workers out there—just replace the tired, worn-out ones." I can't bear it and don't know what to do. I smuggle food in for them and try to get as many days off as possible for the sick ones. But if I do too much I will be arrested, and the poor bastards will get somebody a lot worse.'

Olga thought of the doctor she had seen at her factory. She started to worry about Marina, whom she hadn't visited for some weeks, and resolved to see her the next Sunday. But when she arrived, Marina was gone. 'Dead!' said the female commandant. 'Too weak and puny, that one!'

Olga was devastated and cried for the poor orphan girl who had become another small drop in the ocean of hundreds of thousands of deaths that befell the Ostarbeiters.

40 / **Bombing**

A huge chunk of glass flew through the air, narrowly missing Olga's neck. She dived to the ground, cutting her knees on broken shards. She heard a dreadful screaming from somewhere behind her but did not dare look around. This was a daylight raid and the building she was running past to reach an air raid shelter had been hit, blowing out all its windows. The sirens wailed continuously and bombs thudded relentlessly around her.

She had been on an errand for Frau Hoffmann and was several blocks away from home when the bombers flew in. According to the Hoffmann's clandestine radio, British bombers had struck by night and now American bombers were striking by day. Even though she had been secretly pleased that the Allies were with the Soviet Union against Hitler, she was now terrified and aghast at what was happening around her.

She struggled up and ran for the nearest air raid shelter. She pulled off her 'Ost' sign, knowing that Ostarbeiters were not supposed to mix with Germans and were forbidden to use public shelters. Being blonde with a good command of German, she could easily pass as Germanic. But despite all, the shelter was overcrowded and she was shoved away. The bombs kept falling. She joined a small group of fleeing people. The next shelter was also crowded but she pushed her way forward—anything to escape from the cacophony of destruction. Arms pulled her in but immediately shut the trapdoor against the others she was running with.

Suddenly a huge explosion deafened them and part of the shelter collapsed. People screamed. They heard scattered rumblings in the distance. Everyone held their breath. In fact, there wasn't much air to breathe. The shelter was holding far more people than it should. Olga was feeling in danger of asphyxiation when mercifully the sirens stopped their ominous wailing. The trapdoor was opened and in fell three shattered, bleeding bodies—the people Olga had been running with.

Shaking and trembling, she stumbled over the corpses and made her way home. What a narrow escape! Why had she been saved?

Fortunately the Hoffmann residence was still intact, with only the top floor windows shattered. The church across the road had disappeared. Olga helped Frau Hoffmann clear up the mess and life went on.

As 1943 wore on and the Third Reich was battered from all sides, existence for all the inhabitants of German cities became harder and harder. With constant bombardment and the destruction of transport links, supplies of normal goods shrank and food became scarce. Germany was under siege and, like all of the big cities, Magdeburg felt the pinch. Sadly, Frau Hoffmann asked Olga to kill the children's pet rabbit when they were at school, and together they concocted a story that the rabbit had to be moved to the country. Fortunately the children did not connect the move with the rather delicious meat stew they ate the next night. In Berlin people ate crocodiles that were roasted alive when firebombs destroyed the zoo.

The hell from the skies continued. It wasn't just a few planes that flew over but hundreds of them, and they began to unleash new and more ravaging killer devices—blockbusters and phosphorous bombs that emitted an eerie green glow as they shot along streets engulfing hapless human beings with their fiery tongues. Thousands were burned, mutilated and suffocated.

Refugees, their belongings piled on top of horses and carts, began to pour into the city as the Soviet army marched through Poland into East Prussia. Frau Hoffmann took in a family whose house had been totally destroyed. Now there were more mouths to feed, and Olga would cycle to the edge of town and forage in the fields for any potatoes or beets that might still be left in the hard ground. Often she would find a few beets, cut them up really small, cook and stir them into a syrup to substitute for sugar, which was fast running out. Frau Hoffmann was impressed by Olga's resourcefulness, and Olga would tell her stories of the 'hungry years' in Ukraine when her mother became quite adept at making different things out of cherry leaves.

What Frau Hoffmann loved most about Olga was her irrepressible good humour. During nights down in the cellar, when hundreds of Allied planes whined overhead and it seemed that this
interminable nightmare would never cease, her life was immeasurably lightened by Olga's endless supply of funny stories and silly
jokes. The children adored Olga and she entertained them with
shadow plays in which she created interesting shapes with her
hands, throwing up a variety of shadows behind the lights of the
flickering candles. She adopted funny accents and different voices
for all her characters.

Nineteen forty-four wore on. A woman down the street pickled
her dead husband into jars and kept herself alive by eating him
slowly. An assassination attempt on Hitler's life caused a huge
flurry. Goebbels' increasingly hysterical rants assaulted the ears
over the air waves. On her cycle rides about town Olga noticed
more bands of forced labourers being prodded along by guards.
Some wore yellow stars, and by the language she recognised them
as Hungarian. They were being worked to death at the huge synthetic oil plant, Brabag, where coal was turned into benzene. She
heard about their appalling conditions from Frau Hoffmann's
doctor friend. A sixteen-year-old boy had been brought to him
after being savaged by an Alsatian dog for harbouring an illicit
potato in his pocket. The boy died. One day Olga saw a group of
women prisoners being marched along by some guards, one of
whom looked familiar. She was shocked to the core when she saw
that the guard was Nadia. She quickly looked away, not wanting to
witness the level of degradation in the girl's eyes.

But then came the terrible night of January 16, 1945 when
Magdeburg was all but destroyed. At about ten o'clock the alarms
started wailing. Olga and Frau Hoffmann carried the children
downstairs as usual, joining up with the other family camped on
the ground floor. The radio announcer sounded panicky and said
it was a bigger raid than usual and warned all people to get to shelters immediately. Inevitably the bombers came, dropping their
murderous loads. The pounding continued mercilessly for hour
after hour after hour. The whole world felt like it was shaking. The
fear in the air was palpable, and the children started crying as dust
fell down on their heads and the candles threatened to go out.
Explosion after explosion rained down upon them. 'What are they

doing to us?' wailed one of the women from the other family. 'We will all be killed!'

The occupants of the Hoffmann cellar were lucky. Countless other cellars and shelters did not withstand the onslaught. As they crumbled and filled with fire and smoke, thousands of people were forced out onto the burning streets, dodging the green tongues of phosphorous bombs and desperately seeking a safe shelter. The streets were filled with injured men, women and children, Nazis, non-Nazis, Ostarbeiters, refugees, horses, all screaming and howling at the horror around them. Next morning, as the fires still raged, the cost was counted. Ninety per cent of the beautiful old mediaeval town was totally destroyed and sixty per cent of the new town. Hundreds of planes. Five hundred tons of ordinary bombs. Over one thousand fire bombs. Six million cubic metres of rubble. Thousands dead and countless thousands injured, burned and traumatised. The Hoffmann household counted itself extremely lucky that only the top floor of their house had been blown off.

A log entry by Bertie Lewis, flight sergeant with the RAF's 102 squadron, reads:

> January 16, 1945—There was some groaning when we were told at Briefing we were to fly over Holland and Germany heading straight for Berlin and then fool the Germans by turning about 80 miles short of the Big City to bomb Magdeburg. It was felt that the enemy would not believe we were headed for Berlin. We'd be in for a bad night. Unexpectedly when we got over Magdeburg there was little enemy night fighter activity. We could hardly believe our good luck; the trick worked.

But the horror did not stop; the 'bad night' continued. February 3—362 US planes, 400 tons of bombs. February 6—385 US planes, 600 tons of bombs. February 9—418 US planes, 727 tons of bombs.

'What is there left to bomb?' Frau Hoffmann cried in anguish.

But then came the even more terrible time of February 13, 14 and 15, when Dresden, Chemnitz and Magdeburg were the main targets for devastating blows by the RAF at night and the US Air Force by day. Altogether 3600 planes took part. Frau Hoffmann was beside herself worrying about her mother in Dresden. Her own house, though decapitated, was still standing.

And still it went on. From diaries of the 446th Bombing Group:

March 2, 1945 Magdeburg—The group initially decided not to bomb the primary target, the synthetic oil plant, due to the heavy cloud cover, but the lead plane found a hole in the clouds. They got it. Flak was intense.

March 3, 1945 Magdeburg—The final mission to Magdeburg ended successfully as excellent results on the synthetic oil plant were reported.

All Olga could think about were the poor Ostarbeiters who lived around the Brabag plant. All dead. She had also heard that the SS had murdered hundreds of prisoners fleeing in panic from the bombed munitions factory where she had worked. 'Why am I being saved?' she asked herself for the hundredth time.

And still it was not over. There were another two raids in early April. Hitler, a gibbering madman in his Berlin bunker, thought Roosevelt's death on April 12 would save him and bring Germany deliverance from certain defeat. Goebbels ecstatically told Hitler on Friday, April 13, 'It is the turning point!' Next day Hitler announced to the army, 'At the moment when Fate has removed the greatest war criminal of all time [Roosevelt] from this earth, the turn of events in this war will be decisive!' But this was empty rhetoric from a megalomaniac on death row. In the greatest concentration of fire power ever, the Red Army, with its 2.5 million men, forty-one thousand guns, six thousand tanks and four air armies, was massed on the banks of the Oder ready to bear down on Berlin. German officers confiscated white handkerchiefs from terrified young German soldiers so they could not use them to surrender.

People in Magdeburg knew the war was nearly over but now lived in dread of the arrival of Soviet troops. The Americans were coming from the west and the Russians from the east. Most people were praying that it would be the Americans who reached Magdeburg first. Stories of brutal gang rapes, indiscriminate murders and wholesale pillage abounded as Germans learnt of the frenzied revenge of the Red Army on East Prussia.

In the middle of April, a US army reconnaissance battalion

dubbed 'Hell on Wheels' crossed the Elbe and entered Magdeburg. The soldiers occupied a small portion of the city but met such strong German resistance they could not advance any further. The commanding officer sent a message to the German general saying that if they did not surrender, the US troops would withdraw and Magdeburg 'would be bombed off the map'. The Germans refused. In went the planes again. Twelve hours of continuous bombing. After the terrible destruction, 'Hell on Wheels' entered the smouldering city again on the morning of April 17. Now they met little or no resistance. Magdeburg had not only been bombed off the map, but into oblivion.

Magdeburg, after Dresden and Cologne, took third place as the most devastated German city. In 1939 it had a population of 330,000 people. By April 1945 there were only ninety thousand people left. Olga Nesterenko was one of them. She was twenty years old, and as she sifted her way through unrecognisable streets and mountains of rubble, she thought of Marina who was dead at sixteen and wondered again, 'Why me?'

In one way the Magdeburgians were lucky. Their city was one of the last stops in the advance of the American army eastwards. Eisenhower, stepping into Roosevelt's shoes, ordered the US not to advance any further towards Berlin and stand fast on the Elbe. For a variety of reasons they were leaving Berlin to the Russians. So Magdeburg on the Elbe was where the Americans stopped. After a period of coolness, the people of the city tolerated the Americans because they weren't Russians. The Americans also brought in much needed food supplies. Olga was impressed by the American soldiers, and they in turn did not fail to notice the pretty blonde with the heart-shaped face.

While Berlin's gardens and allotments burst into blossom, a huge and dreadful battle raged. Hitler buried himself further in his bunker, still hoping for a miracle. He married Eva Braun and on April 30, when his hoped for deliverance had not materialised, he committed suicide rather than endure the humiliation of capture by the jubilant Russians.

On May 5 the Third Reich was no more and the war in Europe was over.

'See that spot there?' says Nikolai triumphantly. 'That marks the official end of the Soviet Union.'

We are sitting on a bench above a spectacular piece of the Crimean coast. Down below is the village in which Gorbachev was incarcerated at the end of the USSR.

He was holidaying in his Crimean dacha in August 1991 when members of his Party staged a coup and put him under house arrest. The coup failed, but Gorbachev's days in power were numbered. Within a short time the Soviet Union was disbanded.

I ponder its demise and that of the Third Reich and find it incomprehensible that so many crimes were committed in both their names.

'We were only children when the war was over, but why didn't Olga come home?' Nikolai asks. 'She wrote to Ivan Leontivich saying she was on her way.'

Olga had indeed decided to go home and was thrilled that she could write a letter at long last to her family. She was to accompany Frau Hoffmann to Dresden, which was on the way to the Polish border, then continue through Poland on the thousand kilometre trek back to her homeland.

Dresden was shocking, its former glory pulverised to dust. Magdeburg had been bad enough, but Dresden had been bombed even more heavily. Frau Hoffmann's mother had survived the devastating firebombs of February when it seemed that God had abandoned everything that stood for beauty, love and grace. People with hardened, grey faces were going about their daily ritual of trying to find enough food and water. They hated seeing what was happening to them and their lives. It seemed the world had forgotten them. They were now at the mercy of the Russians, who were pillaging the ruined city and taking anything that was left back to Russia.

Olga hugged Frau Hoffmann and said she would never forget her, and indeed never did. She and the Hoffmanns corresponded right up to her incarceration in the mental hospital. These letters are testament to a wonderful relationship wrought during a very dark time—a relationship that refused to be defined by the master-slave imprint foisted upon it.

Transport was in chaos, and the bomb craters that were once roads were littered with abandoned tanks, trucks and the carcasses of rotting animals. This area of Germany had seen grim fighting between the Russians and Germans in the last months of the war, and even the fresh green of early summer was not enough to lift the grey pallor of so much human suffering and death. Olga met up with several other Ostarbeiters on their weary trudge home. All were returning to the countries from which they had been wrenched many years earlier when most were barely out of childhood: Ukraine, Byelorussia, Czechoslovakia, Hungary and Romania. All had terrible stories of survival and counted themselves among the lucky few who had lived to tell the tale.

As they neared the Polish border they were surprised to meet Ukrainian Ostarbeiters coming the other way. 'Turn back,' they advised Olga. 'We have met people who say terrible things are happening to Ostarbeiters returning to the Soviet Union from the West. They are being carted off to the gulags in Siberia.'

'But how can that be?' exclaimed Tanya, a girl from Kiev. Olga was fascinated by her because even though she was in her early twenties, her hair had gone completely grey. 'We were prisoners of the Nazis and taken by force!'

'Ah' was the reply. 'We are all regarded as contaminated because we have been corrupted by foreign values. We are not to be trusted.'

Olga was devastated by this news. She couldn't wait to get back and see her mother, her sisters, Leonty and her nephews and nieces. Her days were filled with fantasies of emotional reunions as she, the heroine-survivor Olychka, was welcomed back into the fold. At a camp by the roadside, the bunch of Ostarbeiters discussed their predicament while eating stale bread dunked in bark tea. Options were few. One group decided to go to a Displaced Persons camp near Dresden. Others, including Tanya, decided to press on through Poland regardless. Olga was not sure. She had become friendly with two Czechs, Jiri and Viktor, who were on their way to Prague. 'Come with us, Olga. You can stay in Prague for a while until things are a bit clearer.' The advantages of this strategy made sense. The Czech border was close and Prague was less than one hundred kilometres away. It didn't feel too much out of her way. She could just delay her homeward journey a little.

Unbeknown to this group of Ostarbeiters, things were even

worse than they had heard. The secret pact made at Yalta in 1945 meant that all Soviet prisoners of war were to be forcibly repatriated to the Soviet Union. 'Operation Keelhaul', as it was named, meant that former Soviet citizens were trapped like rabbits in a net and thrown into gulag camps on charges of high treason. Olga was to find out soon enough that she had to hide her identity and where she came from in order to stay out of Stalin's grim mincing machine, which a decade before had spirited away her brother Ivan to Baku and wrecked the life of her sister Anyuta when she was imprisoned for stealing food for her children.

At the very next checkpoint on their way toward Czechoslovakia, Olga saw that Ukrainians ahead of her were taken off to waiting trucks. Jiri and Viktor ushered Olga away. She looked despairingly at her identification papers.

Olga Nesterenko
Born 2/10/24
Poltava Region, USSR
Parents: Ivan and Alexandra Nesterenko

A dead giveaway!

'We'll have to get you false papers,' said Jiri, who had been working against the Nazis in a well-organised underground group in Dresden. He left Viktor and Olga in another roadside camp and disappeared. Fortunately it was summer and the nights were warm. Viktor was fond of Olga but she did not feel the same for him.

Days later Jiri returned triumphantly with the false papers.

Olga Prosikova
Born 2/10/24
Lvov, Poland
Parents: Josef Prosik and Anna Muraskinova

They all got through the next checkpoint. Olga cast a guilty glance at some of her people who were being led away.

❧

Nikolai and Shura, who have been listening enthralled to my story, begin what sounds like a huge shouting match. 'Why are they so angry?' I ask Lena.

She replies that they are not angry. This is how my countrymen

347

converse. It is true that Nikolai has told Shura to shut up a couple of times because he thinks she is talking bullshit, but that is apparently normal. They are discussing the ins and outs of what happened to my mother after she left her homeland and why they think she became mentally ill.

'It's shocking that poor Olga had to deny the country of her birth and lie about her very own name,' shouts Nikolai. 'A young girl thrown to the wolves like that! No wonder she became mentally ill. It's a disgrace!'

'And to be far away from the people she loved,' continues Shura. 'Oh Eva, my mother was waiting for her to come home for so long! You know, even on her deathbed she was calling for Olga!'

'And you know what, Eva? I can tell you categorically that there has not been any mental illness in this family, except perhaps Shura.' Nikolai digs his cousin in the ribs. 'Your mother and sister got ill because they didn't have anybody—they didn't have us.' He thumps his heart.

I think Nikolai is right; I can see it in the way he deals with Shura, who is a prickly customer and always putting her foot in it. But all the family humour her, and even though Nikolai puts her back in her box when she steps too far out of line, they adore each other. I can see that if Shura had migrated to the other side of the world into an alien culture where nobody understood her, she could very well have become mentally ill too. I myself feel very supported by my family. As we have been travelling about a lot, I keep doing my usual thing in life, which is to lose things and leave things behind. Very quickly I become 'Masha Rastirasha', an affectionate form of 'Molly the Scatterbrain'. All the family become vigilant on my behalf, making sure that I always have my bag or my cardigan. When my world fell apart as Mum descended into madness, I started to lose control over my environment. From being a very tidy child I became a scattered, extremely untidy teenager and adult. My particular quirkiness is totally accepted by the family and accommodated.

My cousins want to know about me and my life and what happened to Olga in Australia. I describe my mother's journey into mental illness, what has befallen Alex and how my sister Val fares. I am grilled by Shura about why Alexandra is in a home. This sort of thing is unheard of in Ukraine. Sick people are always looked after by other family members. I describe the place in which Alex is staying and explain that I think she is being well looked after. However, I feel ashamed that I fall short of their wholehearted attitude towards frail relatives, and think over my efforts to fulfil my promise to my father on his deathbed that I would do my best for Alex. Have I done my best? I think of the last few times I saw her and, despite my best intentions, always ended up losing my temper.

Nikolai urges that I bring Alex over. 'We will look after her,' he insists.

'It's not easy,' I say, ashamed of my own impatience with her, 'she is very ill and difficult.'

'Bring her. It will be fine.'

If it wasn't for the language difficulty and Gabriel, I think it would be a good option.

My female cousins Lydia, Zina and Shura are intrigued by the notion of postnatal depression. They have never heard of it. I can see why such a phenomenon is unknown here. The women are very supportive of each other, and grandmothers have a central role in bringing up their grandchildren. New mothers are rarely isolated and alone as they are in Western culture—as both my sisters were in Melbourne and my poor mother in Prague.

It is the final day of my visit to the Crimea. But there is one last piece of the story to tell, the most mysterious of all: what happened to my mother in Prague. This is the sketchiest part of the whole saga as to this date I have found no one in Prague to shed more light on it. However, I can put together what my mother told me, information I gleaned from Vlada, and a recent memory fragment that rose up from the hidden corridors of my unconscious after a powerful dream.

41 / **Prague**

I am in a beautiful garden. It is late summer and the hot sun beats down on my head of sparse hair. I look up at the huge, tall sunflowers that tower like giants against the fence. My father is playing with me and my grandmother comes towards me smiling to lift me up. I feel very loved and this feels like an idyllic place. I adore being cuddled by my grandmother and I love the new toy that she has just given me—a very soft, brown, velvet clown with beautiful white curls. But where is my mother? I haven't seen her for a long time. I'm beginning to forget what her face looks like. And deep down I know something is terribly wrong. My grandmother hates my mother. This is a deep inescapable truth that sits like a dense cold pebble within my heart. Why can't all these people that I adore love each other? But the painful truth is that my grandmother hates my mother and there's nothing I can do about it.

Olga, Viktor and Jiri arrived in Prague in the summer of 1945. Olga locked away her native identity deep inside and took on being a Pole, born in Lvov. Fortunately Lvov at that time was just across the border from Ukraine, so she could pass herself off legitimately with her Ukrainian-sounding tongue. She loved Prague and picked up the Czech language very fast. She was enchanted with the beautiful fairytale city with its cobbled streets and ancient palaces, enjoying the novelty of being in a metropolis that had escaped being bombed to smithereens. Once a royal capital, Prague shone in its mediaeval splendour.

Olga found a live-in job in the centre of old Prague, cooking and cleaning for a well-off family in their substantial apartment on Vitkova Street. She threw herself into her new surroundings with gusto, making do with the twists in fate that had brought her here. She just hoped that things might change in the future so she could return home safely. She did not dare write to her relatives in case someone discovered that she was a Soviet citizen and would then deport her to a gulag on the spot! She just worked hard and bided her time.

Having become used to the kindness of Frau Hoffmann in Magdeburg, she was shocked at how differently she was treated here—much more like a servant, with a room next to the kitchen where she had to eat her meals separately. Olga missed the Hoffmanns and felt lonely and outcast. The mistress of the house, Marie Krikavova, was a cultured woman whose husband owned a furniture factory. They were wealthy, and the apartment was full of elegant furniture and works of art, reminiscent of a previously opulent Prague. The couple also owned a country house where their only child was staying for the summer. Ludvig, their pride and joy, was being groomed to take over the family business.

As he was returning to Prague soon, Olga had to prepare his room and wondered in anticipation what he would be like. The minute she saw the fair-haired, handsome young man, she was smitten. Her twenty-first birthday was just a few weeks away and she was madly in love. Life quickly became a feverish blur in which she would count time in terms of how many glimpses she had of the object of her desire. She had never felt like this before. It was cataclysmic. Everything else that had ever been important to her receded into oblivion. Her waking moments were weighted with a dangerous balance of anxiety, excitement and anticipation as she tried to do her chores in the apartment. Her attractive looks were not lost on the young Ludvig, and he appreciated any glimpse that was afforded him during her daily routine. He began to come into the kitchen more and more, watch her make knedliky (Czech dumplings) and chat to her.

The fairytale city became even more fairytale that winter. The snow made Prague stunning, small piles of it adorning the majestic statues that graced Charles Bridge. Olga loved this bridge and the walk up the hill to Hradcany Castle and St Vitus Cathedral, which overlooked Prague. There she would enjoy the view across the Vltava River and its magnificent bridges. On one of her days off, she was delighted and terrified to bump into Ludvig in one of the graceful arched walkways below the castle. He invited her to have a hot drink in a coffee house. This was seventh heaven.

It was under a fifteenth-century arch that Ludvig first kissed her.

Mrs Krikavova watched this unfolding romance with horror and warned her son to back off. 'This is just a Polish peasant girl. You watch it!' She had dreams of Ludvig marrying a much better class of Czech girl.

At their next meeting in the coffee house, Ludvig told Olga that his mother had warned him against her. Olga was uncomfortable with this fact, but she was so madly in love she didn't care. She continued with her household tasks and tried to hide her feelings for her employer's son. This passion was to blossom to its full potential shortly afterwards. Ludvig's parents went for a fortnight's break to their country house at the end of March 1946. It was to be the most blissful time of Olga's life. She and Ludvig fell upon each other with great hunger. With youthful tempestuousness they spoke of running away together. All thoughts of returning to her family had been superseded by this grand passion. All she wanted to do was marry Ludvig and be with him forever.

But reality returned with the master and mistress of the house. Reluctantly Olga trudged to her own drab room at the back of the apartment and became a servant again. For one ecstatic fortnight she had been the mistress, sleeping in the young master's bed. Ludvig and Olga continued their relationship clandestinely and grabbed what moments of passion they could.

In June, after a great deal of nausea, Olga discovered she was pregnant. She told Ludvig during one of their meetings in the coffee house. His mischievous face became deathly pale. 'My parents will kill me and you!' He saw her dear, sad face and told her not to worry; he would stand by her. They kept their secret and it wasn't until Olga was six months pregnant that Mrs Krikavova found out. She was livid with rage. Ludvig begged his parents to allow him to marry Olga, but they told him in unambiguous terms that this option was out of the question. He faced a stark choice: Olga or them. He chose his parents. The only thing that stopped Mrs Krikavova from throwing Olga out was that she was carrying her adored son's child.

The months wore on to Christmas and the New Year. On January 5, 1947, in the coldest winter for one hundred years, I was born. But it was not just to the eaves of the Apollinaire Hospital that freezing icicles clung; they also encased the entrails in my tender gut—the misery and uncertainty of my mother, seeping into the depths of my being. My mother never failed to tell me later what a sickly baby I was, always pouring from both ends. The situation was hopeless. She dearly loved my father, but he was too young and weak to claim her and give her the support she desperately needed. Not only was she in an alien country; she was an alien in the house in which she lived. She also felt deeply ashamed to have a child out of wedlock, so even the avenue of her homeland was now shut to her. She could never bear the shame she would bring on her family if she were to return.

I was christened Eva Maria on the ninth of January. My father was listed as unknown but my godmother was listed as Marie Krikavova. A plan was hatching inside my grandmother's head. She wanted to keep me and to have my mother leave.

My mother tried to cope with me, the sickly baby, in the poisoned atmosphere of the apartment on Vitkova Street. But at some point when I was a few months old, she collapsed and had to go into hospital. The reasons are shadowy but I now suspect postnatal depression, which seemed an apt response to the horrible situation she had landed herself in. My grandmother carried me off to her country house to where my father had escaped, and from the look of baby photos of the time, I thrived. One day my grandmother was holding me at the front gate when I saw this strange yet ever so familiar woman walk towards me. She was smiling at me with tears running down her face. My grandmother handed me over reluctantly. I felt drawn and repelled at the same time. Who was this person, so strange yet so unbearably familiar? Olga had been in hospital for months and had come back to claim me. Though he loved me, Ludvig could neither bear the conflict nor bear to see Olga, so he disappeared. Olga continued to be heartbroken.

My grandmother wouldn't let me go so we all moved back to Prague and lived on uncomfortably in the strained household. I became vomity and diarrhoeic again, reflecting the icy tension. My mother and I ate together in the back kitchen after the master and mistress had been served in the dining room. To escape, Olga would often take me through the cobbled streets of Prague up to St Vitus Cathedral, and I would be mesmerised by the patterns made by the sun shining through the magnificent stained glass. Mrs Krikavova was now putting pressure on Olga to leave, to go back to where she came from and to leave me behind. My mother wouldn't have any of it. Stalemate, with me in the middle. As much as I would have liked it all to be different, the unpalatable truth was that I was not born into a loving family unit but one that was torn apart, with me an innocent pawn in an unpleasant game.

Additional pressure came from outside. The political situation in Prague was deteriorating rapidly. Whatever deal had been made at Yalta was now affecting Czechoslovakia too. The most terrible war ever, waged because the freedom of Poland and Czechoslovakia had been usurped by a tyrant, now seemed pointless as these two countries were served up on a platter to be devoured by another tyrant. Stalin saw Czechoslovakia as a useful buffer against the West and also had his greedy eye on her uranium deposits. In early 1948 the fledgling democracy in Czechoslovakia was stealthily overtaken by the Communist Party and the country was swallowed up by the Soviet empire.

Draconian laws, including curfews, suppression of the press and curtailment of freedom of movement and travel, swept the shocked country. My grandparents were devastated—their world collapsed around them. Over the next few months their factory was taken over by the state, Ludvig's father was forced into manual labour and his mother was compelled to join long, grey queues just to buy scarce basic commodities. The large, spacious bourgeois apartments gracing the River Vltava were crudely partitioned into three or four sections to house workers of the revolution. It was only a matter of time before the beady-eyed new communist dictatorship would order the same fate for the Vitkova apartment.

Mrs Krikavova said more firmly that Olga had to go and leave me behind. Olga was in a quandary. She didn't want to stay. She was appalled that the regime that had destroyed the life of her own family was now stalking her here. She wanted to go, but she was determined she would not leave without me. In early 1949, during another freezing winter, she gathered her few belongings in the dead of night, wrapped me up as warmly as she could, and walked in the only direction she felt was safe—south.

*

It is with great reverence that I approach the last stage of my journey in Ukraine. I clutch the bag containing the ashes of Olga and Sasha as I check in at Simferopol Airport. Lena and I are meeting Jake in Kiev, from where we will go first to Tarasivka and then on to Odessa. Twenty members of my family have come to see me off. It is an emotional farewell.

As I put my luggage through, there is confusion about my papers and I accidentally leave my passport behind at the desk. There is a commotion as I'm called back to retrieve it. This affords me a last glimpse of the clan, who, having witnessed the passport fiasco, all wave frantically at me. They call out in unison so that the whole airport can hear:

'Dasvidanya (goodbye), Masha Rastirasha!'

42 / **Let Her Be a Queen in Heaven**

The Sula River that flows peacefully through Tarasivka is where I expect to throw my mother's ashes, in view of the ancient archaeological mounds where she used to play as a child. But when we arrive in Tarasivka, my mother's cousins, Ivan and Marya, have a different idea. Unbeknown to me, they have arranged a full-blown Russian Orthodox funeral at the cemetery. I am a bit taken aback by this, as I wanted the ceremony to be more private and personal. The priest is unfortunately the spitting image of Lena's husband Sergei, so we are convinced we will get the giggles. I feel easier when I see the stunning rural setting of the cemetery, on the edge of the village surrounded by haystacks, cherry blossom and families of ducks and geese. We stand before a freshly dug hole, which I am informed is the very last plot available before the cemetery is closed to further inmates. My grandfather's family, including Marya wearing a black scarf dotted with pink roses and her brother, Ivan Leontivich, looking spruce in a brand new suit, are there. The priest is flanked by a small choir consisting of a trio of women holding sheets of music. I feel slightly ridiculous standing at the edge of the grave swathed in my black scarf supported by Lena, cousin Luda and Jake.

I am in the middle of wondering whether this likely farce will turn out to be an endurance test and not at all what I want when I see them. The old ladies. There are about a dozen of them, dressed in a variety of headscarves and shabby floral dresses. At first I thought they were passers-by, but Luda informs me in a whisper that they are friends of Aunt Marya and some knew Olga as a little girl. They have come specially to support me and the family, standing humbly in their wrinkled socks and stockings, holding lit candles, tears rolling down their equally wrinkled faces. I am so overwhelmed by their simplicity that all doubts that this might be a farcical undertaking are drowned by a sea of tears that well up from inside me. I am also unprepared for the pure voices of the choir, and as their melody drifts over the cemetery, these tears are in danger of becoming huge racking sobs. Interspersed with the priest's prayers the trio sing an achingly beautiful refrain, over and over again:

Let her be a Queen in Heaven;
Let her be swathed by the softest of white feathers.

This is particularly poignant for me. My mother, who once thought she was Queen of Australia, can now have her wish to be a Queen, in heaven.

At the head of the grave stand the gravediggers, simple peasants, again very shabbily dressed. One, who is my aunt's neighbour, holds the pot of ashes while the other holds a loaf of bread freshly baked by Luda. Any vestiges of being a sophisticated, civilised Westerner disappear totally as I break down and just openly grieve my mother. Even after twenty-seven years the tears run like rivers. I am supported by Jake's endless supply of tissues, Lena's murmuring translation in my ear and, most of all, by the profound love that flows from these simple, unpretentious folk. I feel *I* am in heaven as the pure sounds intermingle with the cherry blossoms that drift down like soft feathers. The priest absolves my mother of any sins and expresses gratitude that she has returned to her humble place of birth after having been so far away, on the other side of the world. After the ashes are put in the ground we each throw in three handfuls of rich black earth. The choir continues to sing a beautiful dirge. I turn to Ivan Leontivich who hugs me between tears and says, 'I have always dreamed of this moment.'

We are then shown where my grandfather's parents lie. I notice that almost half of the headstones adorned by photos of the dead are dedicated to the name Nesterenko. My mother has truly come home and is now enveloped in the 'chernaya zemlya', the black soil, of her birth.

As we walk around the village down to the river, I refresh myself with the sights and sounds that would have assailed the girl Olga in the May springtime. It is stunning. Because the weather pattern is six months of snow and six months of sun, all the fruit blossoms burst out simultaneously in a symphony of mottled white—apricot, cherry, plum, apple and pear. The words to the famous Russian song 'Katyusha', which Olga loved to sing, come back to me:

Rastvetayli, yabloni i grushi
Poplili tumani nad rekoi
Vihodiyla na vereg Katyusha
Na visokiy na vereg krutoi

Pust on spomnit kak ana lubila
Pust on spomnit kak ana payot
Pust on spomnit ktorova lubila
Ot Katushu piridai privet.

Apple and pear trees burst into blossom
like misty clouds by the river bank
Where you once walked, Katyusha
By the steep river's edge.

Let people remember how she once loved
Let people remember how she once sang
Let people remember how she was loved
Give Katyusha all our love.

I can see Olga running down to the river through mists of falling blossoms, the spring breeze flicking wisps of hair into her face; laughing, singing, her heart brimming over with hope and love for a future that the wonder of spring promises.

I look at the mounds where ancient Slavs once toiled, and try to pat a baby goat that runs startled to its mother. Ah, the mother bond is so strong, and I cry afresh for the lovely young woman who bore me and loved me the best way she could, which was, in the words of my father, sometimes 'crook'.

Now I face the last step in the process of healing my family, scattering Sasha's ashes in the Black Sea. Had this process only begun in earnest three years earlier? It seemed like a lifetime ago when I set out to mend the relationships between me and my family, and now look where I am.

43 / **The Black Sea**

*Don't ever let hate, in whatever form, overpower
your soul—nothing good has ever come of it.*
David van Hessen, Dutch Jewish victim of the Nazis,
in his last letter to his family, 1944

'Don't these guys know that the Cold War is over?' I am incredulous. 'We just want to scatter my father's ashes, not plant a nuclear device in Odessa harbour, for Christ's sake!'

Lena is dryly matter of fact. 'It's like this in Ukraine everywhere. Stalin, suspicion and subterfuge live on in people's minds.'

We have no option but to wait while harbour officials prepare for an impending nuclear strike, just because a trio of people have requested to enter the harbour area. It's not like Odessa is even a major port any more. Those days are long gone. An occasional cruise ship idles in every now and then, and a few dilapidated hulks of what used to be warships rust away by the quays. Clutching our weapons of mass destruction—namely the ashes, flowers and candles for Sasha's ceremony—we negotiate with B-grade movie security police (who have us on the cameras, they tell us) to get clearance to go into the port.

We manage to get through at last, and find a man with a sailing boat who is willing to take us out to sea. Oleg is a journalist moonlighting as a fisherman, and he is very enthusiastic about what we have hired him to do. We watch in trepidation as he hangs like a monkey trying to unfurl the sail, which is stuck at the top of the mast. Lena waits with the patience of a long-suffering queue professional who is prepared to stand for days for a loaf of bread. While we sit I think of the memorial I visited the day before in Prokhorovsky Square. Entitled 'Road to Death', two black slabs of

360

granite mark the gateway through which Hana and Shika and thousands of others made their final journey in the winter of 1941–42. I think of the death camps, Vapniarca, Berezovka and Domanevka, where thousands of Odessan Jews died horribly. I say a prayer for Hana and Shika, those 'good people'.

Finally we board the *Unona* and are underway, wafting out to sea on a gentle breeze. Oleg says he is taking us to a special place in the harbour where many war heroes have been buried. *Oh, Dad will have good company,* I think.

It takes about an hour to sail to this spot. As we move gently through the water I look over at Odessa bobbing on the horizon. I see a handsome, dark-haired woman walking on a grassy hill with two little boys, pointing out the ships to their excited faces; I see a smiling young lad running laughing along the cliff tops with his brother and cousins; I see a lone boy with hopeful eyes, keeping a frisky bullock in line on a star-studded night; I see two brothers running terrified, dodging Stuka bullets, tomatoes dropping in splodges from their hands; I see dreadful crimes that were perpetrated there, things no human being should ever see; and I weep with shame. I've reached a stage of life where I can't just pass the buck any more and blame the Nazis, or the Romanians, or the Ukrainians. Every time I yell at Alex or am unkind to others, I am contributing to the negativity and hatred that just happened to spill over megafold sixty years ago in this world we all share.

We finally arrive at the special spot in front of a promontory to the south of Odessa harbour. We light the candles. The vast sky is full of black clouds as the boat rocks gently in the inky sea; it is not called Cherno More (Black Sea) for nothing. We all say a prayer and voice any thoughts that we have about Sasha. I throw in the ashes, interspersed with red, white and pink carnations.

Just at this point a ghostly Russian male choir starts to sing a dirge that seems to emanate from the dark heavens. Goose bumps form on the back of my neck. Is this a movie? Or am I imagining things? But no, Lena and Jake are just as startled as I am. Oleg explains it is indeed a recorded Russian choir that sings from a loud speaker at Alexandrovskiy Park on the promontory, every hour on the hour, for all the heroes buried at sea. We just happened to start our ceremony dead on one o'clock (or did Oleg engineer it that way?). The beautiful music is very moving and befitting to our very own hero, whom we commit to the water. A sea bird dives down among the ashes and flowers. This excites Lena and Oleg, who tell us that the significance of this in Russian tradition is that if a bird swoops into the ashes before they sink, the soul of that person will pass into the bird. As if the music and the bird soaring away aren't enough, rays of light pierce through the black clouds and sparkle like gems among the floating flowers and sinking ashes. If Alexandra were here, she would be convinced that angels are trumpeting our father to his final resting place.

The ashes have sunk into the inky depths, the flowers are floating away and the candles are blown out. Lena and Oleg are at the other end of the boat, leaving Jake and me with our thoughts and tears. Jake regrets he didn't have the opportunity to care for Sasha at home, as he would have liked to have got to know him better. I am struck by the magnitude of the relationship I had with this extraordinary man.

What a dance we had! We loved each other right from the start, when I sat on his knee on the *Skaugum* while Olga ran about flirting with sailors. He wanted to leave Olga on many occasions, but stayed for me. When I left at twenty he was distraught. Why couldn't I sacrifice for him as he had for me? A painful thirty-three year rift ensued. And then in the last year-and-a-half the profound love came flooding back and we were both healed.

We sail quietly back to the harbour.

44 / **Looking Back**

They banished me from my country
like a sparrow is banished from its nest.
The Dead Sea Scrolls

'I want Vlada!' The words break my heart as I fly away from Ukraine and think of poor Olga, calling out through the fog of drugs, lobotomy and ECT for her friend. What good could Vlada have done if she had gone to see her in 1975, or her sister Maria the year before? Who knows? Just to see their loving faces would have given Olga some solace. I feel warm and held by my Ukrainian family and only wish that my dear, sweet mother had experienced the same luxury.

I feel a sense of completion that I have taken Olga and Sasha back to where they came from—Olga to her Black Earth and Sasha to his Black Sea.

When I made the wish that I wanted to heal my family, not in my wildest dreams did I imagine that it was me that needed to be healed. My father's words on his deathbed, 'Eva dorahaya', always make me cry with joy. Thank God that the thirty-three year rift was healed before it was too late.

It has helped me enormously to have found such love in my home country and to know that it was always there, pouring out towards us from the other side of the world.

I see the faces of all the people in Ukraine who have immeasurably enriched my life. Just calling me 'Masha Rastirasha', for example. When my mother made her ugly descent into psychosis, I literally couldn't face the outside world. My facial twitch and my scatteredness are my 'mental illness', my failure to cope, my cry for help, my 'positive symptoms'. As 'Masha Rastirasha' I am accepted and loved just as I am.

When I look back over my parents' lives I am grateful to all the people who helped them, especially when times were hard and the solace of their own families was denied to them. The kindnesses of the Rabbi of Bindermichl, Dr and Frau Hoffmann, Dora Clinger, Vlada and Kirov, the gypsies, shine like jewels in the dark.

I have a vision of two birds, both with damaged wings—both thrown from the nest too early, barely surviving the avalanche of predators and the cold of the stony ground. They experienced some of the most terrible tragedies of the twentieth century: ideological repression, starvation, genocide, holocausts and the most destructive of all wars, which tore the guts out of Europe, Russia and the Ukraine. Both Olga and Sasha were subjected to particularly virulent forms of prejudice—she as 'vermin kulak', 'Untermenschen' and disgraced slave; he as 'vermin Jew'—at the hands of Ukrainians, Nazis and the communist state. Olga and Sasha limped away from all this to Australia, but though they survived when millions didn't, they paid a terrible price. For one it was madness and early death, for the other a hard, bitter loneliness. I am a child of that cauldron. We all suffered, my sisters and I; in our kitchen, in our bedroom, in the hallway; in the everyday stuffing of our lives. At the mercy of two people deranged by inhumanity, treachery, cruelty and unimaginable horrors.

By the grace of God I have survived intact, a bit fluttery around the edges, but intact nevertheless, and because of this I can tell our story. I hold both birds, Sasha and Olga, in my hands, quivering, fragile, bewildered. I look back, not wanting to shirk the pain, humiliation and soul-searching that involves. And most of all, not wanting to shirk a love most profound that beats in every quiver of a broken wing. A love that changes everything.

I am humbled to have had two such parents, Olga and Sasha, who emerged, scarred and beaten, from the bowels of the twentieth century and managed to give me enough strength to climb into the twenty-first century, whole and free. Slava Bogho.

364

Sasha and Olga's naturalisation ceremony

Eva with her father, Sasha, 2001